# INNOVATION

# LEADERS

# INNOVATION
# LEADERS

## How Senior Executives Stimulate, Steer and Sustain Innovation

## Jean-Philippe Deschamps

JOSSEY-BASS
A Wiley Imprint
www.josseybass.com

*Other Wiley Editorial Offices*

John Wiley & Sons Inc., 111 River Street, Hoboken, NJ 07030, USA

Jossey-Bass, 989 Market Street, San Francisco, CA 94103-1741, USA

Wiley-VCH Verlag GmbH, Boschstr. 12, D-69469 Weinheim, Germany

John Wiley & Sons Australia Ltd, 42 McDougall Street, Milton, Queensland 4064, Australia

John Wiley & Sons (Asia) Pte Ltd, 2 Clementi Loop #02-01, Jin Xing Distripark, Singapore
129809

John Wiley & Sons Canada Ltd, 6045 Freemont Blvd. Mississauga, Ontario, L5R 4J3 Canada

Wiley also publishes its books in a variety of electronic formats. Some content that appears
in print may not be available in electronic books.

*Library of Congress Cataloging-in-Publication Data*
Deschamps, Jean Philippe.
    Innovation leaders : how senior executives stimulate, steer, and sustain innovation/
Jean-Philippe Deschamps.
      P.   cm.
    Includes bibliographical references and index.
    ISBN 978-0-470-51524-2 (cloth)
  1. Creative ability in business—Management.    2. Technological innovations—
Management.    3. Organizational change.    4. Leadership.    I. Title.
   HD53.D47    2008
   658.4′092—dc22

                                                        2008007635

*British Library Cataloguing in Publication Data*
A catalogue record for this book is available from the British Library

ISBN 978-0-470-51524-2 (HB)

Typeset in 11.5/13.5pt Bembo by SNP Best-set Typesetter Ltd., Hong Kong
Printed and bound in Great Britain by TJ International Ltd, Padstow, Cornwall, UK

# CONTENTS

# LIST OF FIGURES

# LIST OF TABLES

# PREFACE
# MAPPING THE INNOVATION
# LEADERSHIP TERRITORY

This book is built around one main idea: The belief that *innovation requires a specific form of leadership, distinct from other mainstream types of leadership*. This conviction, rooted in years of empirical research with companies at different stages of their innovation learning curve, is expanded and supported in three ways:

First, by characterizing 'innovation leaders,' those senior executives who relentlessly stimulate, steer and sustain innovation in their companies. We will propose a number of common behavioral traits or attitudes of these leaders, depending on whether they focus on the front end or back end of innovation. We will also highlight what they actually do to promote the innovation agenda in their company, bottom up or top down.

Second, by suggesting that different innovation strategies require different styles of leadership. This assumes that senior managers should explicitly define the content of their innovation strategy and understand the various leadership imperatives of each of their strategic choices.

Third, by opening a few preliminary paths toward understanding what conditions stimulate the development of an innovation leadership environment. We will also underline some of the basic requirements for attracting, developing and retaining innovation leaders.

Let's briefly review this proposition and its implications.

## Is There a Special Form of Leadership for Innovation?

The fact that innovation requires a special form of leadership will probably seem obvious to most innovation practitioners. As the evidence suggests, not all leaders can claim to be innovation leaders!

Leadership qualities are not universally applicable – most organizational leaders tend to be good at and attracted by certain types of strategies. Many feel more comfortable operating in a given range of contextual, i.e. environmental, or company situations. For example, corporate leaders who are talented at extracting the best performance from existing operations may not be naturally inclined to pursue risky innovation strategies. Similarly, executives with unique skills at detecting acquisition opportunities and going aggressively after them may not be good at spotting and targeting unmet market needs. Financial wizards may not feel comfortable steering innovative new product development programs and being first to market with a totally new product category, and so on.

By following this line of thought, and comparing executives in innovative companies with their counterparts in more traditional firms, we might make a first hypothesis, i.e. *that innovation probably requires a special form of leadership.*

To support this initial proposition, we need to ascertain that innovation leaders do, indeed, show a combination of characteristic behavioral traits that are seldom found, at least to the same extent, in other more traditional management leaders. Characterizing the specific attributes of these champions allows us to draw a first generic profile of innovation leaders.

## Are There Different Types of Innovation Leaders?

If we accept that innovation proceeds in two very different modes – bottom up and top down – then we may also assume that not all leaders will be able to handle both modes equally effectively. And this brings us to our second hypothesis, namely that *there is not a 'one-size-fits-all' approach to innovation leadership!* There are probably several different types of innovation leaders and it may be interesting to characterize them, if only for senior management to know how to attract, develop and deploy them.

Besides classifying and describing them on the basis of their preferred mode of operation – bottom up or top down – it is worth noting the different roles and behaviors of leaders in the two broad stages of innovation, i.e. the 'fuzzy front end' and the 'speedy back end.' We know from practice that it takes a very different personality and leadership style to preside over the front end of innovation from idea to concept, where creativity and risk taking are vital, compared with steering the back end from concept to launch, which requires discipline and speed in execution. Real-life innovation leaders often have a natural or 'default' mode of operation, and this is why it is useful to recognize that different types of leaders may be needed at different stages of innovation.

## What Do Innovation Leaders Really Do?

Describing the common traits of innovation leaders and their preference for a stage of innovation is only a first step. If they exist as a distinct category among corporate executives, then it should be possible to determine the specific nature and focus of their efforts. What do they do to promote, steer and sustain innovation that other leaders would not necessarily consider as their first priority?

This emphasis on what innovation leaders *really do* has to take account of the two distinct modes of innovation. How can leaders promote bottom up innovation, which occurs through the spontaneous mobilization of entrepreneurial innovators and champions, without much direct intervention from management? And what do they do to focus and steer the action of their staff top down? We need to address these important questions regarding the role of innovation leaders in each of these modes:

(1) What are the drivers of bottom-up innovation and how can leaders influence them? What do leaders do to encourage, promote and support bottom-up innovation? And conversely,

(2) What are the drivers of top-down innovation? I.e. What do innovation leaders do when they see it as their duty to stimulate and steer innovation proactively, without waiting for a spontaneous initiative?

Since both modes are complementary, we may make a third hypothesis, i.e. *that real innovation leaders focus on both modes of innovation, bottom up and top down.*

## Should We Match Leaders with Strategies?

Our discussion so far might lead the reader to assume that innovation is a plain, uniform process, whether it occurs bottom up or top down. This is obviously a gross simplification because, as we all sense from experience, there are very different types of innovations. If this is the case, then arguably, not all leaders will be equally talented at handling all types and variants. This brings us to a fourth hypothesis, namely that *different leadership skills and styles may be required for different types of innovation strategies.*

Innovation can indeed be characterized differently depending on its objective (business reinforcement vs. new business creation); its scope (new product/service vs. new system/business model); its intensity (radical vs. incremental); and its boundaries (internal vs. open/external innovation). These various dimensions determine at least four generic innovation strategies. Each innovation strategy will usually require a different management focus in terms of process, organizational mechanism, culture and people. Each innovation strategy may also, in turn, call for a particular leadership style on the part of senior leaders.

We can therefore postulate that a certain style of leadership corresponds to each of these generic innovation strategies, and that it is important for management to ensure that the company entrusts its chosen innovation strategy to the right kind of leader.

## Can We Build an Environment Favorable to Innovation Leadership?

Many CEOs and their top management teams wonder how they can make a quantum leap in innovation performance and – even more importantly – how they can sustain it over time. We believe – and this will be our last hypothesis – that *innovation will be sustained only if the company succeeds in building a favorable environment for innovation leadership*. This means understanding what it takes to turn a cadre of solid managers into dedicated innovation activists.

Describing an innovation leadership environment is not easy because it can take several forms and many culture and process elements need to be brought together in a mutually reinforcing 'system.' Logitech, the computer and mobile accessory specialist, features many of the components and drivers of an innovation leadership environment. By adopting innovation enhancing values and attitudes, and addressing both culture and process, top management should be able to attract, develop, deploy, motivate and keep a cadre of innovation leaders who, in turn, will sustain innovation.

In summary, this book aims to provide a *first map* of the hitherto underexplored territory of innovation leadership. It does so by highlighting the different types and stages of innovation – bottom up/top down; front end/back end – and the different characteristics and styles of innovation leaders. It also provides some guidelines to help you direct your company along the right path toward stimulating, steering and sustaining innovation.

# ACKNOWLEDGMENTS

This book is the result of almost 30 years of hands-on immersion in the fascinating and evolving topic of innovation management. It started in the early 1980s at Arthur D. Little (ADL), a truly innovative consulting company, when, together with colleagues from Europe and the US, I interviewed a sample of innovative companies to discover innovation's key drivers and obstacles. This initial group included, among others, Frederik van Oene, Bob Tomasko, Kamal Saad and Tom Sommerlatte, who have since become friends and discussion partners. Together, we held innumerable and passionate exchanges on the essence of innovation, its culture and process, and we developed our first conceptual tools to map and measure it. I thank them all for sharing their insights with me and for their continuous support.

My research continued in the 1990s with another ADL colleague, Ranganath Nayak – co-author of the best-selling book *Breakthroughs* – who inspired me and became my sparring partner. Together, we co-authored the book *Product Juggernauts: How Companies Generate a Stream of Market Winners* (Harvard Business School Press, 1995). The time I spent with Ranganath was immensely stimulating and I thank him for his prolific ideas on innovation management and his enduring friendship.

Many other colleagues from ADL and its high-technology affiliate, Cambridge Consultants in the UK, contributed to expanding my knowledge of innovation management. Even though I could not cite them all here, my special thanks go to them.

Of course, most of what we learned came from the first-hand experience of our clients, some of them impressive, others struggling to master this elusive capability called innovation performance. Whatever their success, they all deserve my profound respect and gratitude.

My move into the world of management development and academia was organized by Derek Abell, former dean of IMEDE; Peter Lorange, IMD's president; and Jim Ellert, dean of the faculty. By accepting me as a member of this prestigious school, they manifested not only their trust in me but also their belief in the importance of innovation as a top management topic. I owe them a deep debt of gratitude.

In the past 11 years, many IMD faculty colleagues have stimulated and supported me. I am particularly grateful to three organizational behavior faculty members – Preston Bottger, Dan Denison and Robert Hooijberg – who shared some of their leadership insights with me and encouraged me to write this book. My thanks also go to the faculty colleagues who invited me to contribute to the collective books they initiated and led, including Don Marchand (*Competing with Information*, Wiley, 2000), Paul Strebel (*Focused Energy: Mastering Bottom-up Organization*, Wiley, 2000) and Preston Bottger (*Leading in the Top Team*, Cambridge University Press, 2008).

A number of IMD open-enrollment program directors opened their sessions to me and my innovation topic, showing both their trust and support over the years. I would particularly like to thank Nirmalya Kumar and Dominique Turpin for welcoming me on their *Program for Executive Development*; Georges Haour, my partner in the program *Managing the Innovation Process*; Ralf Boscheck on *Managing Corporate Resources*; Paul Strebel and Peter Killing on *Breakthrough Program for Senior Executives*; Bill Fischer on *Driving Strategic Innovation*, offered in partnership with MIT; and Ralf Seifert on *Mastering the Technology Enterprise*, offered in partnership with the two Swiss Federal Polytechnic universities. I also wish to thank Jan Kubes and Benoît Leleux for offering me the opportunity to coach teams of MBA students on their *International Consulting Projects* and *Start-up Coaching Projects*. They all helped me learn and gave me a unique testing ground for my ideas.

At IMD, I learned a lot from the companies that attended our programs. A special thank is due to Tetra Pak, which became my prime client and led me to develop a special interest in innovation leadership. Tetra Pak's CEOs – Gunnar Brock, Nick Shreiber and, more recently, Dennis Jönsson – opened their doors to me. Members of the Group Leadership Team, notably Bo Wirsén, Nils Björkman and Göran Harrysson, encouraged me, as did Ralph Hägg, head of the Tetra Pak Academy, and many others. Faculty colleague Mark Vandenbosch, with whom I taught many of the Tetra Pak programs, inspired me with his outstanding teaching skills and deep marketing insights. My thanks also go to Logitech, and particularly to Yves Karcher, who generously shared his experience with me.

When I started focusing my research specifically on innovation leadership, I was lucky enough to interview four prestigious senior innovation leaders, whose quotes are prominently featured in this book: Bill George, former CEO and chairman of Medtronic and successful author himself; Daniel Borel, the cofounder and former chairman of Logitech; Pekka Ala-Pietilä, former president of Nokia; and Ad Huijser, former CEO of Philips Research and member of the company's board of management. Their in-depth interviews provided me with invaluable insights on the essence of innovation leadership. Their thoughts constitute a kind of red thread throughout this book.

I used the result of these seminal interviews in a chapter on innovation leadership that was published in the *International Handbook on Innovation* (Elsevier Sciences, 2003), edited by Larisa Shavinina of Université du Quebec. Larisa was the very first person to encourage me to translate my ideas and experience into a practitioners' book. I am very grateful to her for having encouraged me so warmly.

In 2005, the two leaders of the International Association of Product Development (IAPD) in the US, Kemp Dwenger and Beebe Nelson – two talented innovation evangelists – gave me the opportunity to present my ideas to a group of managers from large, innovative US companies. It is their interest and encouragement that made me decide to go ahead and write this book.

I am also deeply grateful to the senior executives who provided many of the details of the stories in this book – particularly Bill George on Medtronic; Stefan Andersson, Nils Björkman and Bo Wirsén on Tetra Pak, Mike Ramsay, the charismatic founder of TiVo; Guerrino De Luca, the new chairman of Logitech; and Paul Bromberg on Philips DAP.

Of course, this book would not have been possible without the strong support of my publisher, Wiley, and its US partner, Jossey-Bass. Francesca Warren, Jo Golesworthy, Michaela Frey, Nick Mannion and their editorial colleagues believed in my project and wholeheartedly accepted the book. Their trust and encouragement proved an invaluable source of motivation.

Turning lots of insights into a book is no mean task and I was helped by extremely talented and effective research colleagues at IMD. Atul Pahwa researched and wrote two of the cases in this book and co-authored the third one. Michèle Barnett Berg conducted insightful interviews for me in Silicon Valley and helped review my chapters.

IMD editor, Lindsay McTeague, was immensely helpful in turning my text into readable English with considerable patience, talent and tact. Persita Egeli-Farmanfarma advised me very effectively on permissions and copyright issues. And my assistant Valérie Baeriswyl helped me throughout. My deep appreciation and gratitude go to them all.

Last but not least, I am immensely indebted to my wife, Danièle, herself an author of several books, for her unwavering encouragement and support over a year of hard work.

# PART I

# DEFINING AND CHARACTERIZING INNOVATION LEADERS

# CHAPTER 1

# A SPECIAL FORM OF LEADERSHIP FOR INNOVATION?

*Innovation leadership? It is passion; it is learning; it is humility in front of mistakes and errors – understanding that they are necessary elements to learn faster than the others – and it is the target setting . . . yes, stretched targets!*

Pekka Ala-Pietilä
Former President of Nokia[1]

Many companies claim that innovation is one of their critical values and priorities. Stakeholders are reassured that management is vibrantly committed to innovation as a source of customer value, organic growth and job protection. However, the reality is often less bullish than the intent. R&D may be busier than ever developing new products, but how many can be called truly innovative? Projects are proliferating in most companies, for sure, but which ones will reinvent their category or take the company into a brand new market? Why don't product managers dare to go beyond renewing current products or providing line extensions? Which management teams have successfully crafted an innovation vision and built an effective innovation culture and process within their organizations?

If the innovation testimonials contained in so many annual reports were accurate, we would have thousands of examples of truly innovative companies, and the mystique of who does it well would be of little interest. Yet when we look beyond the message for the marks of an archetypically innovative company, only a dozen or so really stand out. These iconic companies, often cited by innovation pundits and the media as first in class, become fallible and begin to lose their 'magic innovation touch' when changes occur within the leadership ranks. Some examples:

- 3M struggled to integrate the Six Sigma credo of its former CEO, James McNerney, into its traditional innovation culture.
- Apple experienced a performance roller-coaster before the return of Steve Jobs as CEO.
- Intel struggled to diversify its product line fast enough to face the growing market of mobile devices.
- Procter & Gamble had sluggish organic growth before the appointment of A.G. Lafley as CEO.
- Corning witnessed each of its blockbuster markets flounder and is constantly trying to reinvent itself.
- Dell had to kick-start its growth again after its highly praised direct business model reached a plateau.
- Others like Sony, Pfizer, Nokia and Airbus were put on a pedestal for their innovativeness, and yet have gone through turbulent times in the past few years.

Why does this happen?

## THE LEADERSHIP FACTOR

Some companies surprise the market with one brilliant innovative move – like Pilkington with its float-glass technology – and then fall back into an innovation dormancy. Others may have an innovative surge but are unable to sustain it in the long term. These innovative spells, when not triggered by pure serendipity, generally reflect a high degree of faith and determination on the part of the current executive team: faith in the competitive power of innovation; determination to turn it into a core capability. But CEOs and management teams change, as do market and competitive conditions. New leaders often bring with them new management and change priorities. Newly arrived CEOs may introduce management philosophies and processes that boost innovation, as A.G. Lafley did at P&G with the 'connect and develop' approach. Sometimes they launch new policies and tools to improve business performance that restrict their staff's traditional innovation freedom, as exemplified by McNerney's controversial introduction of a systematic Six Sigma process at 3M.[2] Unless innovation is deeply ingrained in the genes of the company, in both culture and process, it is liable to become a second-level priority when leadership changes.

## Many Try . . . Few Keep at It!

At some stage, most companies will launch a company- or division-wide innovation improvement campaign. Some zealous management teams attack the problem with a top-down approach, launching a massive innovation change program throughout the company. The Centurion program initiated by Royal Philips Electronics' CEO Jan Timmer in the 1990s fits in this category. These efforts focus on restructuring the company's innovation process and organization. Some companies may gain benefits from a streamlined process, but it is paramount for the company culture to change, or behaviors will remain the same and innovative results will flounder.

By contrast, the majority of management teams approach innovation in a low-key, pragmatic way. They do not engage in a big public change program, but instead look for low-hanging fruits, fixing the deficient parts of their innovation process as they find them, step by step. This may improve performance initially, but without an overall innovation vision and model, company culture and behavior generally do not change, which prevents the full benefit of their efforts being realized.

Fewer companies manage the process well. One that has succeeded is the packaging giant Tetra Pak. The leadership team not only overhauled the company's innovation capabilities, which has improved and streamlined processes, but is also working hard at mobilizing staff. Using its company-wide leadership development and culture change programs, Tetra Pak continuously promotes the adoption of innovation initiatives. The company has also put in place innovation steering mechanisms that should promote innovation in the long term and safeguard against changes in top management.

Most management teams today do a reasonably good job of streamlining and formalizing their innovation process and adapting it to the imperatives of their industry. The determining factor for *sustained* innovation performance – or lack of it – seems to be the level and consistency of commitment to innovation at the top. Management attitudes to innovation create the 'collective innovation leadership' and this is generally ingrained in the company culture. This is why we propose that there is a *specific and distinctive form of leadership for innovation*, which not all leaders possess and which this book will illustrate.

## Innovation Leadership

There is no shortage of books and articles describing the core characteristics of innovative organizations. Jones and Austin, for example, have compiled a list of five core characteristics of 'innovation leaders':[3]

- in-depth customer insight;
- leading-edge technical awareness;
- inspirational leadership;
- motivational organizational rewards;
- sharing knowledge.

But these 'differentiators of enhanced innovation performance,' as they call them, relate more to the collective management of innovative companies than to specific individuals. To date, there has been no formal attempt to paint a comprehensive portrait of 'innovation leaders' as defined in this book.

Based on empirical research, this book will analyze the profiles and attributes of various innovation leaders. The portrait will be impressionistic to include a great diversity of characters. Each brush stroke will add a dimension to our description of the special forms of leadership that foster innovation.

## Defining Leadership

Professor Preston Bottger, who teaches organizational behavior at IMD business school in Lausanne, has coined a simple definition that conveys the full dimension of leadership:

> Leaders do or cause to be done all that must be done and is now not being done to achieve what we say is important! They provide a sense of purpose, direction and focus. They build alignment and get commitment![4]

When it is applied to innovation, this definition has several merits.

First, true leaders are action-oriented change agents; they don't just think and talk, they *'do or cause to be done . . .'* Most companies state that innovation is important, but what do they really do other than invest money in R&D?

Second, this definition highlights three types of fundamental questions raised by most innovation drives:

(1) Leaders provide a *'sense of purpose,'* i.e. Why are we doing it? What are the benefits of a change in innovation? What are the penalties if we don't do it?
(2) They propose a *'sense of direction,'* i.e. Which way should we go? What innovation model should we adopt?
(3) They introduce a *'sense of focus,'* i.e. What are our priorities? Where should we concentrate our efforts?

Third, this definition stresses that if innovation is to become a corporate capability, it cannot be confined to a specialist function or a small group, for example to new business development or R&D. It has to permeate the entire organization, become a priority and then an expectation – with this kind of commitment the motivation will be there to make it happen.

## Is There a Special Form of Leadership for Innovation?

I like to ask this question to executives who participate in my innovation courses, forcing them – unfairly, I admit – to give a simple yes or no answer. The answers are usually split. Those who come from R&D and register specifically for a course dedicated to innovation, tend to vote overwhelmingly 'yes.' Coming from the innovation functions of their business, they may not be able to articulate what innovation leadership entails, but they understand it instinctively. By contrast, executives attending a single session on innovation as part of a general management course seem to be more split in their responses, even though the 'yeses' usually prevail.

Those who answer 'no' typically argue that purpose, direction and focus are needed in all business endeavors, including innovation. Consequently, a true leader should be able to become an innovation leader if and when conditions require it. Executives who do not believe in a special form of leadership for innovation tend to refer intuitively to mental models of what leaders actually *do*. Some of the most popular leadership models support their claim that leadership is a universal trait that embraces innovation (refer to Appendix A for a reference to such models).

By contrast, managers who believe that innovation requires a special form of leadership maintain that if this weren't so, then most business leaders would excel at innovation if they paid attention to it. But as the evidence shows, this is not the case in many companies. Furthermore, few of the leadership icons celebrated by the media for their achievements in shareholder value creation, like Jack Welch at GE, could claim that innovation is their forte. Most would not qualify as innovation leaders and the opposite also seems to be true, i.e. not all innovation leaders are fully fledged business leaders. These arguments convince many managers that since innovation is different from most other business endeavors, it probably requires different attitudes and behaviors.

## FACING THE INNOVATION IMPERATIVES

Before trying to characterize the unique traits of innovation leaders, let's look at some of the essential aspects of innovation, and reflect on the challenge they raise for business leaders. We shall focus on six of these innovation imperatives:

- the urge to do 'new things';
- an obsession with redefining customer value;
- the courage to take risks;
- an ability to manage risk;
- speed in spotting opportunities and in project execution;
- a shift in focus and mindset from business optimization to business creation.

## Innovation Requires an Insatiable Urge to Try New Things

It goes without saying that innovation is about challenging the status quo and introducing new and, one hopes, better products, processes, services or management approaches. Innovation requires curiosity, experimentation and openness to change. Innovation leaders are those who constantly challenge the present state of affairs, encourage wild ideas and instigate trying new things in their companies.

Despite frequent management denials, many companies adopt an 'if-it-ain't-broke-don't-fix-it' stance. Therefore, innovation leaders must have the courage to foster a climate of experimentation and permanent change in their organizations.

It's no surprise that few mavericks and innovation champions exist in most top management teams. Career progression often favors managers who deliver results without making waves, not the revolutionaries. The creators of the 'organized chaos' so dear to innovation scholars[5] often meet obstacles and resistance on their way to the top. To stimulate innovation, however, companies must promote 'challengers,' not just 'fixers.'

## Innovation Requires an Obsession with Redefining Customer Value

Innovation has to do with adding value, and the way to add value is through leadership, argues Nick Shreiber, former CEO of Tetra Pak:

One can add value in many ways. The most important, perhaps, is through leadership – a very elusive concept! Just like good judgment, good leadership is hard to define, but you know it when you see it! Leadership can inspire an organization to reach goals it had never dreamed of, and will encourage each employee to reach his or her full potential in pursuit of their objectives. Inspired leadership will encourage new ideas through innovation and entrepreneurship and will provide the resources to implement them.[6]

In hindsight, highly successful innovators have generally established new standards of value in their industries. For a long time, value creation came primarily from leading-edge technology-based products or processes. Michelin redefined the notion of value in tires – as expressed in mileage life – with its radial tire technology, and Sony did something similar with its PlayStation game consoles. Nowadays, value creation can come from introducing radically new business models or management methods. It is no longer necessary to be a great technical innovator to qualify as an innovation leader. By radically changing the economics of the PC industry, not the product itself, Michael Dell can arguably be called an innovation leader:

People look at Dell and they see the customer-facing aspects of the direct-business model, the one-to-one relationships. What is not really understood is that behind these relationships lies the entire value chain: invention, development, design, manufacturing, logistics, service, delivery, and sales. The value created for our customers is a function of integrating all those things.[7]

Kim and Mauborgne suggest that redefining value starts with questioning current industry assumptions by asking four probing questions:

- Which of the factors that our industry takes for granted should be eliminated?
- Which factors should be reduced to well below the industry standard?
- Which factors should be raised well above the industry standard?
- Which factors that the industry has never offered should be created?[8]

Consciously or instinctively, innovation leaders challenge industry assumptions in order to unearth opportunities for a quantum jump in customer value. A strong customer orientation often fuels this urge to redefine value. Value creators, typically, have an insatiable curiosity about their customers' needs, empathy with their conscious or subconscious frustrations, and an instinct for what they might need or want in the future. As Akio Morita[9] stressed in his story of Sony's legendary Walkman®, this type of curiosity is not synonymous with a thirst for traditional market information. No market research, he argued, would have indicated a need for the Walkman®. Morita is referring, rather, to the kind of customer intimacy that comes from a deeply ingrained, instinctive curiosity. Sony's past advertising slogan – 'You dreamt it! Sony made it' – reflects the company's view of its innovation mission: To redefine value constantly by correctly guessing the customer's unarticulated desires, and applying its technological expertise to satisfy them.

The challenge for innovation leaders is to encourage this constant reappraisal of value factors despite the fact that, at times, such an attitude may prove highly destabilizing. Challenging the current ways of delivering value in your industry is very difficult when you are an established player and even more so when you are the market leader. As Harvard Business School professor Clayton Christensen convincingly demonstrated, introducing disruptive technologies and defying the status quo is much more natural for new entrants looking for ways to challenge incumbents.[10] This is why many innovations have originated with outsiders who forced their way into the market with radically new concepts.

The highly successful story of the no-frills, low-cost airlines – first pioneered by Southwest Airlines in the US, then by Ryanair and easyJet in Europe[11] – provides a good illustration of this rule. Their founders challenged every single prevailing assumption in the traditional airline industry[12] to come up with a revolutionary business model. This gave them unbeatably low costs and allowed them to redefine the notion of value for budget-conscious air travelers. Arguably, it would have been very difficult for any traditional airline to introduce such radical changes internally.

## Innovation Requires the Courage to Take Risks

One of the most widely recognized drivers of innovation is management's willingness to take risks. It is hotly debated because risk taking is subject to all kinds of interpretations. In its classical definition, *risk taking for innovation* is related to the concept of entrepreneurship – being ready to bet one's resources on a new, and often untested, business proposition.

The challenge for innovation leaders is to live by this principle on a day-to-day basis and make the rest of the organization comply with it as well.[13] Although many companies describe risk taking as one of their core values, they often fail to change their performance review and reward systems accordingly. Managers are rarely penalized for not taking risks, especially if they are meeting their targets. The right to fail comes up invariably in most innovation speeches, but it is not necessarily carried into practice.

Andy Grove,[14] Intel's legendary former CEO, adds two very interesting dimensions to the risk taking imperative. First, he claims that innovation leaders must have the courage to focus, which means identifying unambiguously either the things they will *not* do or the things they will stop doing. Second, Grove believes that innovation leaders must have the courage to 'self-cannibalize,' i.e. to make their own business obsolete before others force obsolescence on them. As we know, it takes courage to kill one's own products before their full potential has been exploited and to replace them with higher-performance – but unproven – ones, as a venture capital partner suggests:

> You have to decide you're going to eat your own business yourself, as opposed to having eToys or Amazon or somebody else doing it for you. This is a very different mindset from most companies that are trying to protect what they've got, as opposed to cannibalizing.[15]

It is this policy, coupled with management's belief in the now famous Moore's 'law'[16] that enabled Intel to stay at the top of its industry for so long. Whereas the willingness to take entrepreneurial risk applies to all managerial echelons, Grove's observations apply only to the highest level of innovation leaders, the CEO and his/her key executives.

## Innovation Requires an Ability to Manage Risk

The debate about acceptable levels of risk in an innovation project often pits risk takers (usually the project champions) against those who shrink from taking risks (typically senior managers). Innovators often complain that the controlling attitude of their top managers hides a fundamental aversion to risk, while the more conservative proponents of risk management accuse risk takers of being irresponsible. This debate is fruitless because both arguments are right. Innovation is as much about good risk management as it is about risk taking.

The challenge for innovation leaders, therefore, is to strike a balance between single-minded, enterprising risk taking and pragmatic, cautious risk management. The first attitude is necessary for pushing ahead and brushing away objections. In a sense, frontline innovation champions should be so determined and persistent that they could be accused of being both blind and stubborn. Innovation leaders, by contrast, carry the burden of ensuring that all the known risk factors have been identified at each stage and properly managed – a precarious balance, as this needs to be done without discouraging innovators and entrepreneurs.

A dilemma arises whenever the CEO or business unit head is simultaneously the champion of a particular project *and* the leader who is supposedly responsible for containing risk. No one will dare oppose his/her hierarchical head by spotlighting dangerous risk factors on the boss's favorite project. The story of Philips' ill-fated CDi[17] illustrates that danger. It was well known within Philips that its determined CEO, Jan Timmer, had adopted the CDi as his pet project, as he had successfully championed the CD-Audio years earlier. Many in the company argue today that the CDi concept had inherent flaws and that its proponents blindly underestimated the competing PC-based technology, CD-ROM. Very few dared to openly challenge the notoriously tough CEO, and finally, after a few years and huge losses, Philips abandoned the project.

A similar story can be told about the energetic pursuit of the market for genetically modified organisms (GMOs) at Monsanto. Its CEO, Robert Shapiro, was consumed by the vision of

Monsanto becoming a life sciences powerhouse on the strength of its genetic engineering technology. And he was convinced that realizing his vision meant betting the company's future on GMOs and promoting them aggressively worldwide. But experts are likely to point out that, after the controversy over the company's commitment to GMOs erupted in the media, Monsanto's top management failed to grasp the power of the arguments of GMOs' detractors. It is hard to be a visionary, risk taking innovation champion, while at the same time being a cautious risk analyzer and container. This balance is the challenge of innovation leaders.

## Innovation Requires Speed in Spotting Opportunities and in Project Execution

Silicon Valley innovators and entrepreneurs have known for a long time that the best idea or the best technology does not necessarily win – the winner is the one that is implemented first.[18] Whoever comes first learns fastest. Success with new products comes from launching first, then learning fast to correct mistakes before others have prepared their response, and relaunching a superior product as competitors start coming in. In the words of Matt Hobart, a 28-year-old Silicon Valley entrepreneur:

> If you have an idea, it's safe to assume that four or five people have the same idea. But it's not the person with the best idea who wins. It's the person who can execute quickly. [19]

That kind of speed requires three unique skills:

(1) the ability to search continuously for opportunities;
(2) management decisiveness at all stages in the process; and
(3) speed in execution, typically achieved through a pragmatic reliance on external and internal resources, and, of course, highly effective teams.[20]

Innovation leaders instinctively create an environment that values the search for opportunities and the generation of ideas to exploit them. They typically encourage people to flag opportunities early and make their ideas bubble freely upward for discussion. The challenge lies in the decision process. On what grounds should the project go ahead? What criteria should be met at each stage? When and on what basis should the plug be pulled? As the champions of risk taking entrepreneurs, innovation leaders are bound to allow their staff both a fair amount of freedom to experiment and the necessary resources. Finding an acceptable balance is a challenge, and so is the need to decide fast, whatever the decision. In Silicon Valley, innovators usually get the same advice from venture capitalists: If you are going to fail, at least fail fast and fail better!

## Innovation Requires a Shift in Focus and Mindset: From Optimizing Business to Creating Business

Business unit heads are generally responsible for new product development in their fields and innovation is generally pursued to protect and grow the current business, seldom to create new businesses. This is why most companies struggle to exceed the growth rate of their industry. How can Unilever or Nestlé grow in the mature food industry except by creating entirely new, and hence faster-growing, product categories? Now that the second-generation mobile phone market is nearing saturation, the same question applies to Nokia and Motorola. Creating new businesses is completely different from tweaking product lines to introduce extensions.

So, innovation leaders face a double challenge. The first is to strike the right balance between running the current business and growing new businesses, or as Professor Derek Abell puts it, between mastering the present and preempting the future.[21] The sudden shift in what financial markets demand in the way of share performance – from growth potential yesterday to profitability today – makes finding the right balance a tough task. The challenge is for companies to avoid the tyranny of success and learn to 'organize both incremental and disruptive innovative activities.'[22]

The second challenge for innovation leaders is sensing untapped market needs and choosing promising areas to pursue. Here, innovation leaders must have the ability to shape a vision that will guide them toward new business opportunities.

We have so far talked about innovation and its imperatives in generalities, as if innovation was a uniform process without any 'subspecies.' The reality is more complex and, as we have all observed, there are many different types of innovations. As a consequence, it is legitimate to ask whether different styles of leadership are required to handle the different types of innovation. This is what this book is about. But before attempting to define and characterize various types of innovation leaders, we will first establish a broad typology of innovations.

## DEFINING AND CHARACTERIZING INNOVATION

Even though everyone talks about innovation, there is still confusion as to what the word really means and entails in the business world. 3M distinguishes between research – transformation of money into knowledge – and innovation – transformation of knowledge into money. The Organization for Economic Cooperation and Development (OECD) proposed the following general definition of innovation:

> . . . an iterative process initiated by the perception of a new market and/or new service opportunity for a technology-based invention which leads to development, production and marketing tasks striving for the commercial success of the invention.[23]

Although this definition is slanted toward technology- and product-based inventions – by no means the only types of innovation – it has the merit of considering innovation as a wide-ranging business undertaking.

### Defining the Processes in Innovation

Another way to define innovation is to refer to its processes, grouped around easy-to-remember 'i' words. The following series can help define what innovation covers: *Innovation is the combination of two processes – invention and implementation.*

*Invention* is itself the result of *immersion* in the market to identify unmet needs, or immersion in the problem at hand. This is followed by a phase of *imagination* to envision the potential benefits of addressing that opportunity, *ideation* to develop and select attractive new concepts to meet the identified need, and *initiation* of a concrete project or venture.

*Implementation*, in turn, consists of an *incubation* phase to develop and test the new product or service, followed by an *industrialization* process to make it and deliver it in large quantities. This is followed by an *introduction* phase with an initial launch, followed by roll-out and full deployment, complemented at each customer site by a phase of *installation* and *integration* to ensure that the new product or service is adopted and integrated into the customer's organization and processes. This simplified typology will lead us to explore different types and styles of innovation leaders.

Innovation observers and scholars have long pointed to the existence of two very different patterns of innovation generation and diffusion within a company: 'bottom up' and 'top down' (see Figure 1.1). This distinction has a direct bearing on our topic because, as we see in the following chapters, each mode requires a different type of focus on the part of innovation leaders.

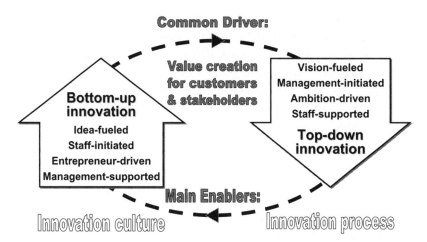

**Figure 1.1** The two modes of innovation

In the *bottom-up* mode, innovative ideas originate spontaneously from people at the operational level, whatever their function. These ideas get developed out in the open and the resulting projects flow upward for management funding and support. This type of innovation is driven by the commitment and dedication of internal entrepreneurs who feel encouraged and empowered by management. The main driver of bottom-up innovation is the entrepreneurial culture of the organization, which encourages individual initiatives, experimentation and risk taking.

*Top-down* innovation, by contrast, is initiated by management in response to an ambition or the vision of an attractive business opportunity. The big idea that generally results from that vision flows downward to the teams that are then mobilized for its implementation. The main driver of top-down innovation is the organized process by which an innovation vision is made 'actionable' by management and ultimately implemented.

In truly innovative companies, both modes can coexist because they are complementary. The most promising ideas from those generated in a bottom-up mode may be appropriated higher up by management and turned into top-down projects with strong management involvement and guidance. Similarly, a top-down initiative may be launched by management, but handed over to the staff with the mandate to generate creative ways to implement it bottom up.

Nevertheless, some companies are known for using one of the two modes as their 'default' innovation pattern. For example, 3M was long qualified as an archetypical bottom-up innovator, at least until the arrival in 2001 of its CEO James McNerney who tried to rebalance its focus toward more top-down innovation. In contrast, Japanese technology companies like Canon are said to be more inclined to innovate in a top-down mode with strong management involvement.

Professor Eric Mankin from Babson College highlights that the two innovation modes differ on at least three criteria:

(1) the number of initiatives;
(2) the way results are generated; and
(3) the level of iteration.

**Table 1.1** Best Buy vs. GE

| Criteria | Bottom up<br>Best Buy | Top down<br>GE |
|---|---|---|
| **Number of initiatives** | Many small bets | A few big bets |
| **Generates results via** | Many successes, building employee commitment | Big successes, building new markets and businesses |
| **Level of iteration** | High, built on experimentation | Low, emphasis on picking the right target |

Reproduced with permission from Eric Mankin, 2005.

Table 1.1 highlights how Mankin contrasts the approaches of retailer Best Buy (a declared bottom-up innovator) and GE (a proponent of top-down innovation) on these three criteria.[24]

But these two innovation modes differ also in their leadership focus and requirements. By nature, bottom-up innovation occurs spontaneously – i.e. without direct management intervention – in the right kind of culture or climate. The main role of leaders in encouraging bottom-up innovation is to proactively develop a highly supportive culture.

Top-down innovation, by contrast, is steered by management. Making the vision a reality is what top-down innovation leaders excel at doing.

## INNOVATION LEADERS: A DIFFERENT BREED?

### Defining Innovation Leaders

In summary, innovation leaders can be defined as those *senior* executives who promote an *innovation agenda* in their company. Whatever their function or position, they instigate, sponsor and steer innovation in their organization. Through personal conviction or competitive necessity, they are obsessed with providing superior new value to customers. Even in the face of resistance from their top management colleagues, these executives stand up for innovators and challengers of the status quo. They know how to mobilize their staff behind concrete initiatives and they do not hesitate to personally coach innovation project teams.

Many times in innovation literature, they are named 'champions,' 'sponsors' or 'promotors.'[25] Whatever they are called, true innovation leaders tend to share the same determination and are not afraid to risk their credibility with top management in case of failure. Lewis Lehr, the highly charismatic former CEO of 3M, described the behavior of an innovation leader very convincingly when he said, 'We learned to follow the fellows who follow a dream!'[26]

The ideal place for an innovation leader is, obviously, at the head of the company or one of its businesses. The archetype is the CEO of the company he/she has helped create. Famous names spring to mind: Edwin Land at Polaroid, Robert Noyce at Intel, Steve Jobs at Apple and Bill Gates at Microsoft and, more recently, John Chambers at Cisco, Jeff Bezos at Amazon or Larry Page and Sergey Brin at Google. But charismatic entrepreneurs are not the *only* innovation leaders worth considering. Innovation leaders can be found at various management levels in different types of companies. They also come from different parts or functions of the organization, with a particular emphasis on marketing and R&D.[27] With or without top management blessing, they are committed to keeping alive the company's innovation legacy – if it exists – or, more often, restoring it. Depending on their personal orientation, they see themselves as the linchpins of their company's *innovation process* and/or the evangelists of an *innovation and entrepreneurship culture*.

Innovation leaders use a variety of levers to improve their company's innovation process and forge a strong innovation culture. They seem generally to share a number of *distinctive leadership characteristics*, particularly when compared with other excellent but more traditional business leaders.

## The Need for a Network of Innovation Leaders

Marvin Bower, McKinsey's legendary managing partner and leadership guru, maintains that '. . . a business should be run by a network of leaders positioned right through the organization.'[28] This belief probably applies even more to innovation leaders than to any other types. Indeed, innovation is never the result of a single person's efforts, either at the project level or at the sponsoring level. As the well-known saying goes, 'It takes only one "no" coming after nine "yeses" to kill a project.' Innovation is in danger if it lies in the hands of an isolated leader in the top management team, whatever his/her charisma. The first role of an innovation leader is, therefore, to breed or attract others to take on leadership roles, propagate innovation values and support concrete projects.

It is relatively easy for a lone innovation leader to build a team of subordinates sharing similar values and behaviors for two reasons. First, people tend to be attracted to like-minded people. And second, unless they are authoritarian, innovation leaders usually exude a high level of openness and communicate enthusiasm, to say nothing of passion. Working for them is exciting!

The situation is more complex at the top management level. Lone innovation leaders, unless they occupy the top job themselves, may be unable to influence the profile and behavior of their top management colleagues. They need to muster CEO support to be effective. If they show growth and results, they can hope to propagate their values through sheer emulation. When they have established a reputed stable of talent in their organizations, they transfer some of their best and most motivated staff into other divisions, in the hope of initiating a bottom-up movement of contagion.

# MAPPING OUR JOURNEY

## Defining and Characterizing Innovation Leaders

As we have established that there is a special form of leadership needed for innovation, Chapter 2 will further paint the portrait of innovation leaders by characterizing what differentiates this subset from other types of leaders – behavior, common personality traits, instincts and actions. As there is a broad universe of innovation leaders, Chapter 2 will classify innovation leaders according to their focus on a particular aspect of the innovation process, i.e. the *front end* vs. *the back end* and show that they naturally tend to adopt a preferred mode of innovation, i.e. *bottom up* or *top down*.

Bottom-up innovation and what leaders can do to encourage and sustain it will be the main theme of Chapter 3. Bottom-up innovation is the embodiment of the company's innovation culture, which often reflects the history of the organization and the legacy of its founders or charismatic leaders. This does not mean that bottom-up innovation is limited to companies that have kept their historic innovation heritage intact. In fact, through their attitudes, policies and processes, leaders can exert a strong influence on at least four direct enablers of innovation, i.e. the company's *organizational creativity*; the systematic deployment of *teams of complementary champions*; the encouragement of *customer intimacy practices*; and the promotion of a *'can-do' climate*.

Chapter 4 will explore the characteristics of top-down innovation and highlight how leaders reinvent their business, introduce disruptive technologies or steer their company into new market space. Top-down innovation usually stems from management's realization that changes in the market environment or technology offer big opportunities to disrupt an established industry. Innovation leaders mobilize their organization to seize that opportunity. They make sure that the big initial idea is turned into an *actionable vision*, i.e. one that leads to concrete implementation roadmaps and a *seamless process*.

Chapter 5 will focus on one of the role models for innovation leadership in companies, i.e. the chief technology officer (CTO) or chief research officer (CRO), sometimes called chief innovation officer (CIO). It will also examine the extent to which the role of these technical executives is changing, in terms of *visibility* within the senior management group, and it will highlight the CTO/CIO's new leadership challenges:

(1) instilling a vision and sense of purpose for the role of science and technology;
(2) providing a sense of direction for investments in science and technology;
(3) enforcing a sense of focus on the technologies to be developed vs. those to be outsourced; and
(4) becoming corporate entrepreneurs to turn technology into new businesses.

## The Leadership Imperative of Innovation Strategies

The first part of the book is based, implicitly, on the assumption that innovation is a generic process that proceeds in a fairly similar fashion, whatever the circumstances and the company. Innovation leaders, it implies, display common characteristics and the differences among them pertain mainly to their natural emphasis – on the front end vs. the back end – and their preferred mode of intervention – top down vs. bottom up. The reality is arguably more complex and we all know that innovation takes on the most varied forms. It is therefore safe to assume that different innovation leadership styles may be needed for different types of innovation.

Chapter 6 will outline four different innovation thrusts, based on the development of:

(1) *new/improved products, processes or service offerings*;
(2) *totally new product categories or service offerings*;
(3) *totally new business systems or models*; and
(4) *new/improved customer solutions*.

These four thrusts share one common trait, i.e. an almost obsessive quest for a unique customer value proposition. However, each requires a distinct emphasis in terms of *process, structure, culture and people*. CEOs ought to map whether and how their senior officers meet some of the innovation leadership traits required by their innovation strategy. The following four chapters will illustrate each of these aspects with an example and characterize their specific leadership imperatives.

The incremental development of new/improved products or services is the most prevalent type of innovation axiom, probably accounting for the bulk of R&D expenditures in most companies. The leadership imperatives of this type of thrust will be illustrated in Chapter 7 by the transformation of Medtronic from a renowned but weakening competitor in the industry it created – cardiac pacemakers – to a 'born-again' innovator and market leader. This story features a strong leader willing to confront a lenient but complacent culture and introduce a sense of urgency and a high degree of process discipline. This example also highlights the role of top management in supporting the new culture and its courageous and sometimes unpopular champion.

One can compare the leaders who focus on the incremental development of new/improved products to *tough sports coaches*, very demanding with their team but able to motivate them to give their best to win. Their emphasis is on *challenging, setting goals and measuring*.

The creation of a totally new product category through radical innovation is a less frequently adopted strategy. Few senior management teams feel comfortable taking a very long-term payback perspective and tolerating the uncertainty of moving into a completely new market space. This is nevertheless what Tetra Pak did when it decided to develop a retortable carton alternative to the ubiquitous metal can used for more than a century by the food industry. This example will be outlined in Chapter 8. It highlights the importance of management's initial vision; its persistence through the unavoidable ups and downs of a risky project; its dogged determination to remain faithful to its initial value proposition; and its willingness to steer and run such projects with a strong business focus.

Innovation leaders who concentrate on the development of totally new product categories or service offerings have many of the leadership characteristics of *no-nonsense sponsors*. They tend to be very supportive of their teams, but if they are visionaries, they also know how to keep their feet on the ground. They know how to make their teams confront and systematically address each obstacle in their way, in order to reduce risk. Their emphasis is on *nurturing, challenging and empowering*.

The generally long time frame of these innovation projects and their multi-functional emphasis often make it difficult for a single senior manager to steer such projects from beginning to end. Collective leadership by a team of senior managers is a key requirement. This means that various types of leaders will have to step in and out during the life of the project, while maintaining as much continuity as possible in what can be called an *uninterrupted chain of leadership*.

The creation of a totally new business system, together with selected internal or external partners, will be covered in Chapter 9. Most often it is accompanied by the introduction of a radically new business model, capable of deeply transforming an existing industry or creating a totally new one. TiVo, the iconic US proponent of view-on-demand TV, presents a good example of a 'business system' with its various components: hardware, software and service. The TiVo story highlights the critical importance of specific leadership skills for handling this type of innovation.

The leaders capable of pulling off such system businesses or, more generally, business model innovations, have skills similar to those of *pragmatic architects*. They are capable of devising complex constructions and leading teams of different organizations to implement them, down to the finest details. Their emphasis is on *visioning, partnering and master-planning*.

Chapter 10 will focus on the development of incrementally new products that aim to offer customers a richer experience, because they provide a more comprehensive solution to their problems or needs than traditional products. These new 'solution-products' often consist of different elements, for example a product and the consumables that go with it, or a product and its customized delivery device. They may be provided by complementary partners, working together under different types of arrangements. We will illustrate this phenomenon by looking at what is happening in the home coffee business with the introduction of single-serve systems, notably by Sara Lee and its partner Philips (Senseo).

Leading such developments requires a deep understanding of what makes a good customer experience and the willingness to reach out to complementary partners that will share the same objective and deliver that experience in a repeatable fashion. This type of innovation thrust shares some of the characteristics of system business innovations, but is a lot less complex to orchestrate. To pull it off, however, leaders must have skills similar to those of *orchestra conductors* with their emphasis on *interpreting, orchestrating and integrating* the necessary input.

## Developing a Cadre of Innovation Leaders

The concept of a 'chain of leadership,' introduced in Chapter 8, stresses the importance of having a number of innovation leaders willing to play complementary roles in the course of an innovation project. As Chapter 11 points out, this will happen only when the company has developed an innovation leadership culture, i.e. a set of management values and behaviors that foster the emergence and empowerment of a cadre of innovation leaders. Few large companies exhibit a visibly strong innovation leadership culture, at least such as the one prevailing in Logitech, the American and Swiss digital accessories company. Logitech has managed to grow profitably while maintaining the innovation spirit of its start-up era. Logitech's culture has developed through the combination of five critical elements:

(1) A strong innovation legacy, rooted in the company's creation history and shaped by its defining moments, innovation achievements and threats.
(2) A deeply competitive industrial and market environment, highlighting the critical importance of innovation as a survival process.
(3) The visibility and influence of its major innovation role models, notably its founder and the CEO he chose to replace him.
(4) The company's embedded values and its current management attitudes, policies and processes.
(5) A great degree of attention to managing innovation as a process mixing creativity and discipline.

To conclude, Chapter 12 will address some of the key concerns of senior managers wishing to build a cadre of innovation leaders.

It will avoid discussing whether leadership is an innate or developed talent, and whether you hire on attitudes and train for skills or the reverse because the answer to the two questions is, obviously: Both. Instead, we shall focus on what leaders of innovative companies do to: (1) assess; (2) attract, select and hire; (3) develop and deploy; and (4) retain talented individuals to lead their innovation efforts.

## ENDNOTES

1. Ala-Pietilä, P. (2001). 'Leadership and Innovation.' Videotaped interview by J.-P. Deschamps, IMD, Lausanne, reproduced with permission. After stepping down as Nokia's president, Pekka Ala-Pietilä co-founded Blyk.com, a new mobile network for 16- to 24-year-olds that is funded by advertising.
2. Byrne, John and Hindo, Brian (2007). '3M's Innovation Crisis: How Six-Sigma Almost Smothered its Idea Culture.' *Business Week* Cover Stories podcast, June 11.
3. Jones, T. and Austin, S. (2002). *Innovation Leadership*. London, Datamonitor Plc.
4. Bottger, P. (2008). 'The Leadership Imperative.' *Leading in the Top Team: The CXO Challenge*. Ed. Preston Bottger. Cambridge, Cambridge University Press.
5. Peters, T. (1987). *Thriving on Chaos*. New York, Alfred A. Knopf.
   Quinn, J.B. (1985). 'Managing Innovation: Controlled Chaos.' *Harvard Business Review*, May–June: 73–83.
6. Shreiber, N. (2002). 2001 MBA graduation speech. Published in IMD's Webletter@imd.ch, January.
7. Technology Review (2001). 'Direct from Dell: At 19, he revolutionized the selling of PCs. AT 36 he's ready to take on HP, Sun, EMC and Cisco.' Q&A with Michael Dell. MIT Enterprise, July. http://www.technologyreview.com/articles/qa0701.asp.
8. Kim, W.C. and Mauborgne, R. (1997). 'Value Innovation: The Strategic Logic of High Growth.' *Harvard Business Review*, January–February: 103–112.
9. Morita, A. (1987). *Made in Japan*. London, William Collins, pp. 79–83.
10. Christensen, C.M. (1997). *The Innovator's Dilemma*. Boston, Harvard Business School Press.
11. Kumar, N. and Rogers, B. (2000). 'easyJet: The Web's Favorite Airline.' IMD Case No. IMD-3-0873.
12. They introduced point-to-point connections using low-cost airports, with no possibility of adding connecting flights; direct sales (90% via the internet), bypassing travel agents; sales staff paid on commission; no fixed prices for flights (extensive use of 'yield management methods'); no tickets; one type of aircraft; no business class; no meals; etc. – but high punctuality levels and unbeatable prices.

13. Perel, M. (2002). 'Corporate Courage: Breaking the Barrier to Innovation.' *Industrial Research Institute*, May–June, pp. 9–17.
14. Grove, A.S. (1996). *Only the Paranoid Survive*. New York, Bantam Doubleday.
15. Dunlevie, B. Benchmark Capital Management Co. Quoted in Stross, R.E. (2000). *eBoys: The First Inside Account of Venture Capitalists at Work*. New York, Crown Publishing Group.
16. Gordon Moore, one of Intel's founders, predicted in 1965 that the number of transistors inserted on a silicon chip would double every 18 to 24 months. As Intel tried to follow that 'law,' it became a kind of self-fulfilling prophecy.
17. CDi: Compact Disk interactive, a precursor of CD-ROMs and DVDs, introduced by Philips toward the end of the 1980s and abandoned in the early 1990s owing to the growing success of CD-ROMs.
18. Rogers, E.M. and Larsen, J.K. (1984). *Silicon Valley Fever: Growth of High Technology Culture*. New York, Basic Books.
19. Ratnesar, R. and Stein, J. (1999). 'This Week's Model.' *Time*, 19 September.
20. Cooper, R.G. (2003). 'Profitable Product Innovation: The Critical Success Factors.' *International Handbook on Innovation*. Ed. L.V. Shavinina. Amsterdam, Elsevier Science, pp. 139–157.
21. Abell, D.F. (1993). *Managing with Dual Strategies: Mastering the Present, Preempting the Future*. New York, Free Press.
22. Katz, R. (2003). 'Managing Technological Innovation in Business Organizations.' *International Handbook on Innovation*. Ed. L.V. Shavinina. Amsterdam, Elsevier Science, pp. 775–789.
23. Garcia, R. and Calantone, R. (2002). 'A Critical Look at Technological Innovation Typology and Innovativeness Terminology: A Literature Review.' *The Journal of Product Innovation Management* **19**(2): 110–132.
24. Mankin, E. (2005). 'Top-down Innovation at GE.' *Babson Insight*. http://www. babsoninsight.com/contentmger/showdetails.php/id/847 accessed 23 November 2007.
25. Hauschildt, J. (2003). 'Promotors and Champions in Innovations: Development of a Research Paradigm.' *International Handbook on Innovation*. Ed. L.V. Shavinina. Amsterdam, Elsevier Science. In his chapter, Hauschildt distinguishes between three types of promoters – 'promotors by expertise,' 'power promotors' and 'process promotors' – who need to work as a 'troika' to stimulate and support innovation.
26. Lehr, L.W. (1979). 'Stimulating Technological Innovation: The Role of Top Management.' *Research Management*, November: 23–25.
27. Although entrepreneurial CEOs of start-ups and large company founders like Steve Jobs and Jeff Bezos undoubtedly qualify as innovation leaders – more instinctively than consciously for the former – they will not be the only subjects of this book. I will focus also on members of the top management team and senior executives of large established companies.
28. Bower, M. (1997). 'Developing Leaders in a Business.' *The McKinsey Quarterly* **4**: 4–17.

# CHAPTER 2

# WHAT'S SPECIAL ABOUT INNOVATION LEADERS?

*Innovation leaders are those unique people who possess or are able to mobilize the full set of qualities needed to deliver an innovative product.*

*Daniel Borel*
*Cofounder and former Chairman of the Board of Logitech*[1]

If there was any doubt about the existence of a special form of leadership for innovation, it quickly evaporates when one hears senior executives of iconic innovative companies talking about leadership. Steve Jobs at Apple, for example, exhorted the 2005 Stanford graduating class to 'Stay hungry. Stay foolish.'[2] His insistence that 'you've got to find what you love,' is his way of saying that innovation rhymes with passion which, as we shall see later, is one of the key attributes of innovation leaders.

## INNOVATION LEADERS SHARE SIX ATTRIBUTES

In the absence of specific in-depth studies characterizing the way innovation leaders think, behave and act, it is instructive to hear what a few top executives from innovative companies have to say on the subject. Interestingly, leaders from four global companies – Logitech, Medtronic, Philips and Nokia – independently come up with a very similar list of innovation leadership traits.

From their comments and those of other senior executives with a view on the topic, we suggest that innovation leaders generally share six attributes. Some of these characteristics are specific, almost innate *behavioral traits*; others can be called instinctive *action biases*:

- A 'mix of emotion and realism,' as Logitech's cofounder and former chairman calls it, or an unusual combination of creativity and process discipline.
- The acceptance of uncertainty, risks and failures, coupled with an urge to make their staff learn from them.
- A high degree of passion for their mission and for innovation, as well as the burning desire to share this passion with their staff.
- The willingness to proactively search for external technologies and ideas and then to experiment with them.
- The courage to stop projects, not just to start them, and the flair to decide when to persist vs. when to pull the plug.
- A talent for building and steering winning teams and a knack for attracting and retaining innovators.

This chapter will review these six innovation leadership traits, recognizing that not all leaders share every single characteristic.

## A Mix of 'Emotion and Realism' . . . An Unusual Combination of Creativity and Process Discipline

If we define innovation as the process by which an invention is successfully brought to market, there are clearly different broad phases in this process. At its front end, innovation deals with spotting opportunities, generating ideas and developing concepts. These tasks require all kinds of qualities which could be summed up in the term 'organizational creativity.' But innovation leaders are not purely creative, as Ad Huijser, a former member of Philips' Group management and CEO of Philips Research observes:

> You always need creativity in innovation, so . . . innovation lead-
> ers . . . are creative, but in a balanced way. They are not creative
> every day with a new idea because you cannot lead an organization
> towards innovation if you change the direction every day.[3]

Indeed, as implementation proceeds, the process focuses on developing products (or services), then industrializing and commercializing them. In this execution phase, functional and team process
discipline takes precedence over pure creativity. This duality of
requirements in the same process – creativity and discipline – is
what makes innovation so difficult to lead from beginning to end.
Daniel Borel, cofounder and former board chairman of Logitech
– the digital accessories specialist – defines this dual capability as
'a mix of emotion and realism':

> Innovation leaders are those unique people who possess or are able
> to mobilize the full set of qualities needed to deliver an innovative
> product, understanding and mastering all the aspects that will even-
> tually lead to introducing a viable product in the marketplace. . . .
>   Emotion and passion are key drivers of innovation. Execution
> may be key, but it is down to earth and does not make people
> dream.
>   The real leader is the one who can put everything in a frame-
> work, who can find the right mix between emotion and realism![4]

We shall see later in this chapter that truly 'balanced' innovation
leaders, i.e. those with an equal focus on creativity and discipline,
are rare. People tend to have a preferred 'default' position when
it comes to innovation management. Some focus instinctively on
the creative front end of innovation, while others concentrate
more naturally on the back end, the execution phase.

## The Acceptance of Uncertainty, Risks and Failures . . . Coupled with an Urge to Make their Staff Learn from Them

Chapter 1 stressed that innovation, by its very nature, requires the
courage to do new things, and hence take risks, and the ability to
manage uncertainty in order to contain those risks. Indeed, most
executives list the acceptance of risk and its companion quality,

tolerance of failure, among the top attributes of innovation leaders. In the words of Ad Huijser from Philips:

> Innovation is about doing new things and in every new thing, in principle, there is some risk. So, taking risk is one of the characteristics of innovation leaders, and so is balancing risk with the size of the opportunity and the portfolio of risks you take – because innovation is not about one single attempt; it is, in sequence or in parallel, a number of risks you take. And in that sense, innovation leaders dare to take risks, but at the same time, they balance it with defensive actions and they take sensible risks . . . They know what kind of risk they take, and for what reason![5]

According to Nokia's former president, Pekka Ala-Pietilä, risk taking is not something that can be mandated; it has to be deeply rooted in the company culture:

> The culture ought to have certain elements which . . . [enable] risk taking. So, I feel it is a bit difficult to encourage people to take risks by bluntly saying . . . 'I am encouraging you to take risks'. It should start so that it is a self-motivating, self-evident, obvious way of acting in a given situation.[6]

Risk taking cannot be dissociated from a real acceptance and tolerance of failure, as long as people learn from their mistakes. As Daniel Borel at Logitech puts it:

> Tolerate mistakes! Accept failure . . . otherwise you'll kill innovation. [There] is a fine line between success and failure. Sometimes, it's just luck. But the good news is that you learn more from failures than successes! Experience makes the difference and, as people say, 'Good judgment comes from experience,' but they forget to say that experience comes from bad judgment!
>
> In our business, you would rather be right six times out of ten, than two out of two to make sure you do not miss out on opportunities. But as an innovative leader, you must accept that failure is part of the game, the goal being to learn and make less mistakes than others.[7]

The right to fail and the close link between failure and learning is, of course, widely recognized by venture capital firms, notably in Silicon Valley where failure is seen as a normal phenomenon. As *The Economist* once remarked: 'In Silicon Valley, bankruptcy is treated like a dueling scar in a Prussian officers' mess.'[8] But a number of qualifiers must be underlined that restrict this right to fail, as illustrated by the well-known one-liners below:

> No matter. Try again. Fail again. Fail better!
>
> Samuel Beckett

> Fail often to succeed sooner!
>
> IDEO motto[9]

> If you're going to fail in the future, please have the courtesy to do so in some new and interesting way!
>
> Geoffrey Moore[10]

> Why do the same mistake twice when there are so many mistakes to choose from!
>
> Oscar Wilde

All these wise sayings highlight the learning aspect of failures. Geoffrey Moore, quoted above, is recorded as having said that the difference between losing and failing is that a loser is a company or a person that never learns from mistakes, while a failure is someone who has made a bad decision but can be trusted not to make the same mistake again. Indeed, even though it may be painful for the management team and their financial sponsors, failure is one of the best ways to gain experience. The whole point of the 'first mover' advantage, so cherished by venture capitalists, is the opportunity to gain a 'first learner' advantage.

This recognition of the learning value of failure is better understood and accepted in the world of science and technology than in the world of business. In the words of Bill George, former CEO and board chairman of Medtronic, the medical technology company:

> There is in [every] creative innovation leader a high tolerance for failure. In fact, he or she realizes, as I do, that most of the great breakthroughs come through failure, through an experiment that does not go as you thought it would. The experiments that go as you think they would, all they do is confirm previous knowledge. The experiment that doesn't go that way leads you to say, 'Oh! What can I learn from that?' and then you apply that to making it better. I think there is a lot of learning in failure. And yet, a lot of high performance-oriented people can't tolerate failure. But the innovation leader has a high tolerance for failure.[11]

But such tolerance of failure and the willingness to learn from it will not develop unless management promotes an attitude of humility in the company.

## A High Degree of Passion for their Mission and for Innovation . . . As Well as the Burning Desire to Share this Passion with Their Staff

Passion probably comes immediately after risk taking and tolerance of failure in the list of attributes managers seem to expect from innovation leaders. We will not debate whether passion is an inherent characteristic of leadership in general or an exclusive and distinctive trait of innovation leaders – opinions are split on the question. One thing is sure, though – passion seems to be a common trait of all innovators and innovation leaders, whatever the company. Indeed, if leaders in general tend to demonstrate a high level of emotional involvement in the mission they assign themselves, this is particularly true with innovation leaders. Whether they are of the creative type and work at the front-end of innovation, or whether they belong to the disciplined, execution-oriented group, all innovation leaders have one thing in common – a high level of energy and an almost innate ability to communicate it to their staff.

For entrepreneurial-type innovation leaders – those who create their own companies in Silicon Valley, for example – passion is generally a direct byproduct of their desire to 'strike it big,' i.e. to build the next phenomenal-growth company and reap the rewards. As Apple's Steve Jobs candidly explained:

> A lot of people ask me, 'I want to start a company. What should I do?' My first question is always: 'What is your passion? What is it you want to do in your company?' . . . Almost every company I know of got started because nobody else believed in the idea and the last resort was to start the company. . . . Starting a company is so hard that if you're not passionate about it, you will give up.[12]

Venture capitalists expect passion and energy as a prerequisite when selecting their candidates for funding, as the quotes below show:[13]

I never invest in someone who says they're going to do something;
I invest in people who say they're already doing something and just
want the funding to drive it forward. Passion counts for more than
experience.

Steve Jurvetson, Silicon Valley venture capitalist

Starting a company is like going to war. You have to be insanely,
passionately, nothing-can-stop-me committed.

Audrey MacLean, Silicon Valley entrepreneur and business angel

In established companies, different motivators can spark the passion
that innovators share with their leaders. Managers may be passionate about their customers, about their 'bet-the-company' projects, or simply about winning in the market. For example, at
Logitech, this type of winning passion is fueled by intense competition with Microsoft in introducing new technology. Each
'first' is celebrated with enthusiasm and 'second place' is deplored.
At Nokia, winning means maintaining global leadership of the
wireless telecommunications business. In fact, Nokia and Logitech
are so convinced of the importance of passion that they select their
new staff according to their level of passion. Pekka Ala-Pietilä
at Nokia expresses this conviction unambiguously:

> Whatever you do, if you don't have a passion, then you have lost
> the biggest source of energy. If you have teams and individuals who
> don't have the passion – the passion to change the world, the
> passion to make things better, the passion to always strive for better
> results and always excel – then you will end up with mediocre
> results.[14]

In some companies, particularly but not exclusively in the healthcare sector, passion is directly derived from all managers' strong
belief in the company's mission and vision and a commitment to
live by it. Johnson & Johnson and Medtronic are typical examples
of companies with intense attachments to their corporate mission.
At Medtronic, Bill George reckons, everyone is emotionally committed to live out the company's mission, i.e. to alleviate pain,
restore health and extend life:

> People who had no passion for the patients, the doctors, the actual
> process of the company, did not fare very well in the Medtronic
> culture. . . . The execution-oriented innovation leaders share the

same passion as the creative types, but it is a different way of looking at the world. In a way, they say, 'What good is your idea if it is in a lab and never helps a patient? I want to drive it and get it to market to help patients, because, you know, these people are out there, dying every day.'[15]

## The Willingness to Proactively Search for External Technologies and Ideas . . . and then to Experiment with Them

The rapid proliferation of new technologies that has characterized the past decade has triggered a profound change in the way many companies manage innovation. Business and technology leaders are increasingly aware of the need to tap all possible sources of technologies and ideas, both internally and externally. Open-source innovation[16] – the external sourcing of technology, molecules, product concepts, design or product development services – has become a necessity in many industries. This is particularly true in pharmaceuticals, with promising developments in biotechnology and the proliferation of specialized start-ups. Today, analysts reckon that 25% to 30% of the large R&D budgets of pharmaceutical companies is spent on externally sourced technologies or purchased 'leads' (new chemical entities), as well as in research partnerships with universities or contract research firms. The same phenomenon can be observed, albeit to a lesser extent, in so-called high-tech sectors like information technology or digital electronics. However, it is only starting in more traditional, mature industries, such as fast-moving consumer goods and materials. Companies in these industries have generally built their in-house competencies over decades and still rely on their internal resources for the bulk of their development activities.

US consumer goods giant Procter & Gamble is a notable exception, exemplifying perfectly this trend toward the externalization of sources of innovation. Unlike many of its competitors, P&G has embarked on a systematic process to search for and exploit external technologies in its product concepts.

Most business and technology leaders know how tricky it is to convince a group of R&D staff to go out and buy technology or development work from external sources, even in industries that have led the way in this type of open innovation. Scientists and engineers tend instinctively to resist outsourcing tasks they believe they could handle if only they were given the chance. The famous not-invented-here (NIH) syndrome is real in the R&D departments of most companies. As a senior Philips business manager once remarked publicly at an innovation seminar:

> No self-respecting Philips technical guy would dream of taking somebody else's technology when he could develop it himself . . . and do it much better . . . and take much longer![17]

As most managers have probably experienced, it takes a lot of determination and plenty of explaining, cajoling or even threatening – and hence strong leadership – to fight NIH, and not just in R&D. If most companies rely occasionally, or even frequently, on technology outsourcing, only a few have made it part of their company values. TiVo, whose story will be covered in Chapter 9, is one of them. Mike Ramsay, TiVo's cofounder and former CEO and chairman, inserted two fundamental principles in the company's initial charter:

(1) Not to reinvent the wheel and to do things internally only if it adds real value; and
(2) To partner and cooperate openly with the best partners available.

More than a decade later, the company remains faithful to its values.

Logitech has adopted the same pragmatic philosophy, as Daniel Borel notes:

> An innovation leader has to be open-minded in a way that goes much beyond just accepting new ideas from within. . . . Our company was started by engineers and, as you can imagine, we used to value in-house engineered products. Yet, over the years, we have hired people whose specific job is to bring in outsourced technology. . . .

And that has been something extremely important for us – the ability to take input from inside, from outside, and provide a product or solution that is the best of both worlds. At the end of the day, what truly matters for the end user is to have a cool Logitech product that offers the best technology at an affordable price. . . . This is why you must be ready to benchmark, to challenge your own expertise, and if there is something better outside, get it from outside.[18]

## The Courage to Stop Projects, Not Just to Start Them . . . And the Flair to Decide When to Persist vs. When to Pull the Plug

Whereas innovative entrepreneurs focus their energy mostly on starting things, innovation leaders have oversight responsibility for the effective use of the company's resources, so they occasionally need to act as project 'hatchet people.' Killing projects, particularly when there is no obvious technical reason to do so – only market or economic uncertainties – is generally one of the most difficult and less understood parts of a leader's job. All chief technology officers (CTOs) and R&D managers know it well! Ad Huijser, former research tsar at Philips, sums up the feelings of his R&D peers in the comments below:

I fully agree with those people who say, 'Leadership is pulling the plug.' This is, of course, only one part of leadership; The other one is starting things! But starting is easier than stopping in a research environment. Stopping is what really asks for making choices, and that means taking risk because you may be stopping something of value. Therefore, stopping projects asks for more leadership than starting projects. So, the real leaders dare to make choices and to say no to things they don't believe will have added value for the company. . . .

A creative environment, for me, is an atmosphere in which creativity can flourish, but at the same time it is constrained by budgets, by manpower, etc. So, if you want to create new things, you have to stop other things. . . . It stimulates people to do both and to be very critical of their own ideas – not at the start, but during the course of the action.[19]

As a member of Philips' top management, Huijser recognizes that it is easier to kill projects at the research level, when cumulative investments are still limited. At a later stage, when a project has become a tentative business undertaking, killing it becomes much more difficult. The traditional 'sunk costs' syndrome reinforces entrepreneurs in their belief that success might well be just around the corner!

Management therefore needs the ability to decide when to persist and when to pull the plug. In case of doubt, conservative managers will generally push to stop a risky venture, knowing that no one can ever be proved wrong for having killed a project. Innovation leaders, by contrast, will accept the risk if they intuitively sense that despite all uncertainties there is market potential. Many breakthrough innovation success stories tend to lend credence to the power of 'adaptive persistence,'[20] i.e. innovation leaders' ability to keep supporting a project, in spite of discouraging early results, while endlessly exploring ways to help the team crack the market.

Innovation leaders may keep supporting an uncertain project and resist their colleagues' exhortations to pull the plug if they are deeply convinced of the superior advantages of their new product. This conviction may stem simply from 'gut feel,' as happened with Nespresso™, Nestlé's espresso system.[21] A number of senior managers supported this new premium system within Nestlé while the team tried selling it in the institutional office market, then to the HORECA[22] sector initially without much success. Nespresso finally became successful, but only much later in the consumer market through an internet-based consumer-club concept. The business broke even about 16 years after the company bought the patent! It is worth pointing out that one of the Nespresso champions within Nestlé's top management was Camillo Pagano, whose father – so the story goes – was a 'barrista'[23] in a coffee bar in Rome. Upon tasting Nespresso against his familiar Italian benchmarks, Pagano knew intuitively that the system would be a winner. This probably helped him convince his German and Austrian colleagues in the executive committee, CEO Helmut Maucher and executive vice president Rupert Gasser. These managers were possibly less intuitive than Pagano but equally confident of the product's potential (and probably also of Pagano's instinct.)

Risky innovation projects may also be allowed to continue, despite their uncertainty, if management senses strong interest from its customers. Tetra Recart, Tetra Pak's innovative 'carton food can' project featured in Chapter 8, could easily have been killed by management when its sponsoring organization, a branch of the Group, was dismantled. But the serious interest of potential customers in pursuing product tests reassured the packaging company's innovation leaders that their project had a future.[24] Several of Tetra Pak's other high-risk innovation projects[25] did not have that advantage and were terminated by the same innovation leaders that kept Tetra Recart alive. Bo Wirsén, a member of Tetra Pak's Group Leadership Team (GLT), comments:

> Nils [Bo's colleague on the GLT] and I actually came on board two big projects together when we set up the 'pace plus' projects, both of which we decided to discontinue. And that was something new for Tetra Pak. The company was quite good at starting projects and then, when we saw problems with commercialization, we tended to deviate, to look for other angles than to face up to reality and say, 'Guys, we've had enough. Let's close it down!' . . . This was quite a shock, I think, to the technical community, because they had not seen a decision on that sort of level taken before.[26]

In Chapter 8 we will discuss the importance of allocating responsibility for these high-risk, high-impact projects to a team of senior managers working together as part of an empowered steering group, as opposed to entrusting them to a single individual. Teams tend to make better judgments when it comes to discerning when to persist with a risky project vs. when to pull the plug.

## A Talent for Building and Steering Winning Teams . . . And a Knack for Attracting and Retaining Innovators

The team is at the heart of most, if not all innovations, and leaders play a critical role in assembling teams, as Ad Huijser at Philips notes:

> Innovation leaders quite often express the vision behind which the troops align, but at the same time, they are very much team players because they cannot do it themselves. Innovation is absolutely a team effort, and innovation leaders know how to make and build teams, because you need a number of capabilities at the same time to make it happen. And balancing that team is a capability that you quite often see as the strong point of an innovation leader.[27]

Few advocates of innovation teams are more vocal than the folks at IDEO, America's leading design studio and innovation culture evangelists.[28] A commonly heard saying at IDEO is: 'Enlightened [team] trial and error succeeds over the efforts of the lone genius.' To reflect the sense of passion that animates design teams as they work on an innovation project, IDEO calls them 'hot groups.'

As the firm's ultimate innovation leader, David Kelley – IDEO's founder and former CEO – devoted considerable attention to the process through which teams are assembled and formed. Because he believes that teams perform better when they are made up of volunteers, IDEO has instituted a very original approach to forming teams. The company is organized around 'hot studios,' a Hollywood-like system for quickly building teams around projects and disciplines. Under this approach, studio heads – IDEO's second-level innovation leaders – do not pick the teams they need. They describe the project for which they are responsible and the location they will be using. Designers are then allowed to select the projects they want to work on . . . and their leader. IDEO managers are also keenly aware of the fact that it takes a lot of positive reinforcement to turn a group of inspired individuals into a 'hot team,' even if it consists of volunteers. This is why they devote so much time and effort to thinking about how to make their managerial and physical environment friendlier for teams.

Traditional companies rightly argue that IDEO is a maverick organization. But while the management style at IDEO may be unorthodox, when it comes to the attention its leaders pay to composing their teams, it is certainly not an isolated case. The experience of large Japanese technology-based companies shows a similar pattern. In firms like Canon and Toshiba, the highest-ranking innovation leaders – usually CTOs or chief engineers – are usually not hierarchically responsible for R&D departments, which often report to divisional or plant management. Nevertheless, they consider it one of their key tasks to advise on the leadership and composition of important new product development teams. Japanese innovation leaders make up their own 'hot teams' with the same devotion and care as a barman mixing an exotic cocktail. They look for balance in age, seniority, experience, skills, personality and even mindset. This contrasts sharply with many of their Western counterparts, who sometimes assemble teams rather rapidly on the basis of staff availability.

For many decades, common sense dictated that innovation leaders would try to assemble teams with 'compatible' people. Management would select people to work on their innovation projects on the basis of their competence, of course, but almost equally important, on their attitudes. 'Select people on attitudes and train for skills' was the common wisdom. The propensity to work in teams and collaborative spirits were sought; strong egos and prima donnas were avoided.

That type of common sense has been recently challenged in a new book, *Virtuoso Teams*,[29] which advocates that exceptional projects should be run by exceptional people. Using compelling examples drawn from breakthrough teams in all kinds of areas – performing arts, science, sport and exploration – authors Bill Fischer and Andy Boynton dare to go against the accepted common sense on teamwork. They recommend combining exceptionally talented people in the same team, even if it can lead to ego clashes. Hiring for talent and training for attitudes becomes the recommended norm. Virtuoso team leaders, the authors suggest, follow seven rules. They:

- drive the culture, vision and action within the team context;
- recruit the very best talent and never settle for what is available;
- double-stretch the customer and the team to achieve ambitious goals;
- spotlight the individual 'I' within the team, and not the conventional 'we';
- cultivate a marketplace for talent within the organization to facilitate the creation of virtuoso teams;

- actively span boundaries and act as powerful conduits of ideas;
- stimulate idea flow by managing space, processes and time.

Nokia's Pekka Ala-Pietilä extends the team building scope of innovation leaders beyond the boundaries of his company. In the mobile telecommunications business, different players for hardware, software, services and content need to come together and understand how to contribute in the best possible way to expand the market:

> We have to make sure that there are companies which can come together and win together. We feel that this is not a 'win-win' world! It is a 'win-win-win-win' world, because there are so many partners.[30]

## INNOVATION LEADERS TEND TO FOCUS ON A STAGE OF INNOVATION

The ability to lead is not an absolute and uniform skill. Different kinds of leadership may be required for different types of objectives. The common denominator in leadership is the ability to mobilize, motivate and direct a group of people toward a worthwhile goal. But as the nature of the goal changes, various types of leadership, or at least different leadership styles and attitudes, are necessary. And this also applies to innovation.

As briefly mentioned earlier, if we define innovation as the process by which an invention is successfully brought to market, it consists of two broad phases: A creative front end, where ideas and technologies are generated and turned into validated concepts; and a disciplined back end, where the focus is on turning a concept into a finished product or service and going with it to market.

Both ends involve complex cross-functional processes, but these processes are very different in nature and require very different and complementary talents, attitudes and styles of leadership. Indeed, some observers suggest that the front end of innovation calls for 'question asking' leaders, while the back end requires 'problem solving' ones. This is why it may be useful to distinguish between front-end and back-end innovation leaders. Since few executives combine these two sets of qualities at once, one of the key tasks of top management is: (1) to ensure that there is an adequate cadre of front- and back-end leaders in the company; and (2) to make them work well together. Charles O'Reilly III and Michael Tushman, business school professors at Stanford and Harvard respectively, use the word 'ambidextrous' to describe the leaders who manage to make such a duality of different talents coexist.[31]

Managing innovation as an integrated and seamless process thus requires good high-level team integrators with a deep understanding of what it takes to steer the different phases in the process and an ability to mobilize the two complementary types of leaders. These senior innovation leaders must be able to draw out the best from a diverse team, as Logitech's Daniel Borel explains:

> If you look into companies, it is very hard to find someone who is great in execution and at the same time is great at the purely creative part of innovation. Thus, the great innovation leader is the one who is able to build a mixed team that brings together people with different psyches, and get them to work together and share the same language for the sake of the company.[32]

Medtronic's Bill George uses a sports metaphor to underscore the need for a plurality of talents that the innovation leader must attract and deploy:

> You might think of it like a [football] team. You need somebody who is going to score. You need someone who can defend. You need somebody who is disciplined, someone who can make the brilliant move! It is almost like two cultures operating in one, if you can think about that, because it is not easy to pull off.[33]

Let's explore the leadership profile required to manage each of these two sides of innovation.

## Leading the Creative Front End of Innovation

The front end of innovation is all about sensing new market needs, exploring new opportunities, experimenting with new technologies and generating new ideas about the right customer problems. It is also about seeding and developing new concepts for products and services, as well as nurturing new ventures throughout their early stages. It involves a non-linear, even divergent, process that requires a great deal of *organizational creativity*.

Innovation leaders who focus on the front end tend to possess a range of unique qualities:

- extreme openness to new ideas;
- insatiable curiosity about the outside world;
- acute sense of observation;
- acceptance of 'out-of-the-box' thinking;
- predisposition to networking;
- urge for exploration;
- ability to detect patterns in weak signals;
- willingness to experiment and learn;
- acceptance of uncertainty and readiness to pursue risky avenues; and
- tolerance of failures.

These leaders have a relatively well-known profile because it is the one most often described in the innovation literature.

On the people-management side, they tend to be perceived as inspiring visionaries, great motivators and good coaches. They are generally effective at attracting and retaining creative people – they often act as magnets for innovators and entrepreneurs – because they tend to create a climate of adventure and challenge. At Medtronic, according to Bill George, a role model for this creative type of innovation leadership was Glen Nelson, his vice chairman and de facto chief innovation officer:

> He was always open to new ideas. He was always going to try something. He was always willing to put some money aside to fund a new venture that came along, having no idea whether it was going to work or not.[34]

George considers that the main qualities of this purely creative, front-end innovation leader are curiosity and tolerance:

> He is really intrigued by the technology; he is very hands-on; he very much knows the products. He can take an idea and has a

vision that, maybe, this is a kernel of an idea. It is like a needle in a haystack, but he is always looking for that needle and says, 'How can you make this work?' and not, 'Oh, that'll never work!' Sometimes, the business leader may say, 'That'll never work! Look at all the flaws in it.' and he will say, 'No, look, there is potential in there!' It's like taking a diamond in the rough and polishing it up to make it into something.[35]

## Leading the Disciplined Back End of Innovation

Innovation, obviously, does not stop with the generation of good market-oriented ideas for new products or services. Concepts need to be fleshed out and turned into business propositions and products or services that can be developed, engineered and produced efficiently in terms of both time and cost. These processes, which constitute the critical back end of innovation, are convergent and geared to a single objective: Get to market fast to reap the rewards. Whereas the front end deals with exploring and inventing, requiring a good deal of *organizational creativity*, the back end is about planning superbly and then – and only then – 'running like hell.' It demands strong *organizational discipline* in planning and execution. Creativity is not absent from the back end, but its focus is on finding solutions to the many problems that are bound to occur.

Surprisingly, the innovation literature pays less attention to the leadership traits required for steering these critical back-end activities. Are such leaders merely good 'executors'? In fact, experience shows that back-end innovation leaders exhibit a completely different palette of qualities to their front-end counterparts:

- rigor in analysis;
- implementation focus;
- operational knowledge;
- ability to coordinate multiple functions;
- speed in decision making and action;
- clarity in objectives;
- willingness to dedicate resources;
- pragmatism in managing risk;

- skills in problem solving; and
- sense of urgency created by a strong desire to go to market!

On the people-management side, back-end innovation leaders display an infectious ability to lead their troops from within and engage with them in product battles. They are demanding, particularly in terms of time-to-market, but they also tend to be available, accessible and emotionally committed. They may share the same level of passion as the front-end innovation leaders, but their passion is of a different nature. They consider their job finished when they see their new products or services reach the market successfully.

Medtronic's Bill George stresses back-end leaders' pressing urge to go to market:

> It is the disciplined person that is going to ensure you get the new products to market, because he or she knows that it is only when you get to market that the rubber meets the road, so to speak, and creates the innovation that generates the revenues for the next round of innovation. . . . He or she would take a little bit less of a product, accept a less perfect product knowing that, well, we can improve it the next time around! This person is driven to get it to market.[36]

The second characteristic of these leaders, again according to George, is a strong sense of discipline and speed:

> The business- and execution-oriented innovation leader also knows what it takes to go through the regulatory process, the quality insurance process and the production, i.e. gearing up a production line so you are not producing only a hundred, you are producing a hundred thousand.[37]

In conclusion, any CEO eager to boost innovation needs to ensure that the management team includes both front- and back-end innovation leaders. But this distinction, although useful, does not go far enough because it assumes that innovation comes in only one variety, i.e. that it is a generic process applicable to all types of innovation endeavors. In reality, as we all intuitively know, there are many different types of innovations and this is why Chapters 6 to 10 will characterize the leadership imperatives of different innovation strategies.

## INNOVATION LEADERS WORK ON PROCESS AND CULTURE

At their inception, most companies were innovative. They were born from the vision and ambition of their owners, for sure, but this vision usually focused on a market opportunity and an innovative idea for exploiting it. In their early stages, innovative companies typically benefit from a strong, almost instinctive entrepreneurial culture. Most probably, few spend much time building and formalizing what we would today call an innovation process, i.e. a systematic and repeatable approach to generating innovations (see Figure 2.1).

Over time, as they grow in size and complexity, and as new management replaces the founding team, many of these early innovators lose some of their natural entrepreneurial spirit. Instead, they tend to develop more formal methods, procedures and mechanisms for managing innovation. Such processes are certainly helpful and at times indispensable, but they do not completely substitute for culture. Nevertheless, since it is generally easier to build a process than to change a culture, streamlining the innovation process generally conveys the positive message throughout the organization that management cares about innovation and is determined to enhance it. This, by itself, often helps improve the

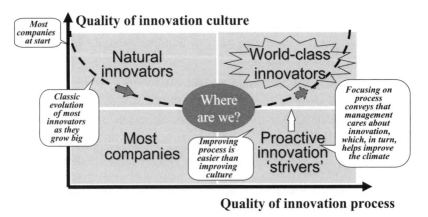

**Figure 2.1**   A focus on culture and process

innovation culture in the company, thus creating a virtuous circle.

Lewis Lehr, former CEO of 3M, sums up how this combination of culture and process creates a challenge for management:

> Innovation can be a disorderly process, but it needs to be carried out in an orderly way. The truly good manager finds the means to manage a disorderly innovative program in an orderly way without inhibiting disorderly effectiveness.[38]

Before concluding this chapter, it may be useful to summarize some of the innovation parameters that we have introduced so far (see Figure 2.2).

Bottom-up innovation is the spontaneous mode of innovation. It is not mandated or organized by management. It happens whenever operational managers and staff generate innovative ideas to meet market needs or improve performance, and implement them, generally but not always through local or divisional projects. Bottom-up innovation will flourish if the company encourages the development of organizational creativity at all levels, a key element of any innovation culture. Senior innovation leaders who, by nature, are intrigued by new technologies and ideas – the front-

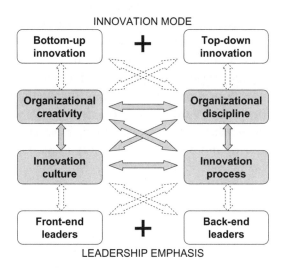

**Figure 2.2** Innovation parameters

end innovation leaders – will typically manage to support and fund these local initiatives. Through their personal bias, behavior and influence, they will naturally focus their attention on developing, over time, a favorable innovation culture, a culture of exploration, experimentation and entrepreneurship.

Top-down innovation, by contrast, is initiated by senior management, generally to implement its vision of an attractive market or competitive opportunity. It is implemented by the organization, often through a highly visible corporate project. It requires a great deal of organizational discipline, typically through a focus on process. Implementation-oriented senior innovation leaders – the back-end innovation leaders – will be involved in these and other projects. Through their personal bias, behavior and influence, they will naturally focus their attention on developing, over time, an efficient innovation process from vision to market reality.

World-class innovative companies, obviously, do not rely only on bottom-up or top-down innovation. They *want both* and focus their efforts on *creativity and discipline*, working simultaneously on both their *culture and process*. They also know that there is a disciplined *process to enhance creativity* and they apply its rules to generate winning market- and customer-oriented ideas. Similarly, they realize that there is a way to build and promote a *culture of discipline* in their organization. So they work on both dimensions with the help of a cadre of *front-end and back-end innovation leaders*.

Individual innovation leaders, although they share some of the generic traits mentioned in this chapter and recognize the two complementary dimensions, naturally tend to adopt a preferred mode of innovation, i.e. either bottom up, with a focus on culture, or top down, with a focus on process. We shall see in Chapters 3 and 4 what it means to build an innovation culture to enhance bottom-up innovation and establish an innovation process to go, top down, from vision to reality.

## ENDNOTES

1. Borel, D. (2001). 'Leadership and Innovation.' Videotaped interview by J.-P. Deschamps, IMD, Lausanne, updated and edited by Daniel Borel in November 2007, reproduced with permission.

2. Commencement address to the Stanford graduating class of 2005 by Steve Jobs, CEO of Apple Computer and Pixar Animation Studios, delivered on 12 June 2005. Stanford report: http://news-service.stanford.edu/news/2005/june15/grad-061505.html.

3. Huijser, A. (2001). 'Leadership and Innovation.' Videotaped interview by J.-P. Deschamps, IMD, Lausanne.

4. Borel, D. (2001). 'Leadership and Innovation.' Videotaped interview by J.-P. Deschamps, IMD, Lausanne, updated and edited by Daniel Borel in November 2007, reproduced with permission.

5. Huijser, A. (2001). 'Leadership and Innovation.' Videotaped interview by J.-P. Deschamps, IMD, Lausanne, reproduced with permission.

6. Ala-Pietilä, P. (2001). 'Leadership and Innovation.' Videotaped interview by J.-P. Deschamps, IMD, Lausanne, reproduced with permission.

7. Borel, Daniel (2001). 'Leadership and Innovation.' Videotaped interview by J.-P. Deschamps, IMD, Lausanne, updated and edited by Daniel Borel in November 2007, reproduced with permission.

8. 'Vital Intangibles: What it Takes to Come Top in Technology.' *The Economist*, March 1997.

9. IDEO is a highly regarded design house and contract development consultant in Silicon Valley, California. IDEO's innovation management philosophy is explained by the brother of IDEO's founder Dave Kelley and a senior partner in the firm: Kelley, T. (2001). *The Art of Innovation: Lessons in Creativity from IDEO, America's Leading Design Firm.* London, HarperCollinsBusiness.

10. Moore, G. (1999). *The Red Herring*, October. Well-known innovation marketing author of *Crossing the Chasm* (1991. New York, Harper Collins Publishers) and *Inside the Tornado* (1995) New York, Harper Collins Publishers.

11. George, B. (2001). 'Leadership and Innovation.' Videotaped interview by J.-P. Deschamps, IMD, Lausanne, reproduced with permission.

12. Jager, R.D. and Ortiz, R. (1997). *In the Company of Giants: Candid Conversations with the Visionaries of the Digital World.* Chapter 1 'Steve Jobs: Apple Computer, NeXT Software, and Pixar.' p. 21. New York, McGraw-Hill.

13. Quotes collected by James Pulcrano, member of the EMBA faculty team at IMD in Lausanne, as part of his study trips with EMBA participants in Silicon Valley.

14. Ala-Pietilä, P. (2001). 'Leadership and Innovation.' Videotaped interview by J.-P. Deschamps, IMD, Lausanne, reproduced with permission.

15. George, B. (2001). 'Leadership and Innovation.' Videotaped interview by J.-P. Deschamps, IMD, Lausanne, reproduced with permission.

16. Chesbrough, Henry (2003). *Open Innovation.* Boston, Harvard Business School Press.

17. The Philips business manager was Jack Seery, former managing director of the Overseas business unit of Philips' Consumer Electronics division. The context of his comment is featured in the author's previous book, *Product Juggernauts* (1995). Boston, Harvard Business School Press, pp. 327–338.

18. Borel, D. (2001). 'Leadership and Innovation.' Videotaped interview by J.-P. Deschamps, IMD, Lausanne, updated and edited by Daniel Borel in November 2007, reproduced with permission.

19. Huijser, A. (2001). 'Leadership and Innovation.' Videotaped interview by J.-P. Deschamps, IMD, Lausanne, reproduced with permission.
20. In a paper entitled 'Can We Teach Adaptive Persistence?' presented at the Ninth Annual Business/Economics Teaching Conference in Chicago in April 1999, Lilly, Redington and Tiemann note that adaptive persistence is 'being able to overcome miscalculation and mistakes and take advantage of serendipitous events outside of one's field of vision.' People who possess adaptive persistence are:

    - open-minded (willing to look at the problem from different viewpoints);
    - curious (questioning, seeking answers);
    - intellectually honest and brave (confident to take a stand when the evidence is present or change a position when the evidence is not);
    - independent;
    - dogged.

    Source: http://org.elon.edu/econ/pages/thesis2003.doc.
    The role of adaptive persistence in business strategy was widely discussed following the publication of Richard Tanner Pascale's seminal article on the 'Honda Effect' in the Spring 1984 issue of the *California Management Review*.
21. Kashani, K. and Miller, J. (2000). 'Innovation and Renovation: The Nespresso Story.' IMD Case No. IMD-5-0543.
22 HORECA is a common acronym used in Europe to characterize a segment of the commercial catering market. It stands for HOtels, REstaurants, CAfés.
23 A preparer/server in a coffee bar (Webster's *New Millennium Dictionary of English*).
24. Deschamps, J.-P. and Pahwa, A. (2004). 'New Business Creation at Tetra Pak: Reinventing the Food Can.' IMD Case No. IMD-3-1448.
25. Tetra Pak borrowed the concept of 'pace plus' projects from 3M. At 3M, each division was supposed to select one pace plus project in its project pipeline. Pace plus projects received a lot of attention from their sponsors, got top management visibility and gave rise to a certain level of competition among divisions (the best pace plus projects were given awards). Tetra Pak's group management added two important elements to this concept: Pace plus projects, even highly technical ones, had a senior business manager as project leader and a member of the Group Leadership Team was asked to act as Steering Group Chairman.
26. Author's videotaped interview with Nils Björkman and Bo Wirsén from the Group Leadership team of Tetra Pak (2005).
27. Huijser, A. (2001). 'Leadership and Innovation.' Videotaped interview by J.-P. Deschamps, IMD, Lausanne, reproduced with permission.
28. Kelley, T. (2001). *The Art of Innovation: Lessons in Creativity from IDEO, America's Leading Design Firm*. London, HarperCollinsBusiness.
29. Boynton, A. and Fischer, B. (2005). *Virtuoso Teams: Lessons from Great Teams that Changed Their World*. Harlow, FT Prentice Hall.
30. Ala-Pietilä, P. (2001). 'Leadership and Innovation.' Videotaped interview by J.-P. Deschamps, IMD, Lausanne, reproduced with permission.
31. O'Reilly, Charles A. and Tushman, Michael L. (2004) 'The Ambidextrous Organization.' *Harvard Business Review* **82**(4): 74.

32. Borel, D. (2001). 'Leadership and Innovation.' Videotaped interview by J.-P. Deschamps, IMD, Lausanne, updated and edited by Daniel Borel in November 2007, reproduced with permission.
33. George, B. (2001). 'Leadership and Innovation.' Videotaped interview by J.-P. Deschamps, IMD, Lausanne, reproduced with permission.
34. George, B. (2001). 'Leadership and Innovation.' Videotaped interview by J.-P. Deschamps, IMD, Lausanne, reproduced with permission.
35. George, B. (2001). 'Leadership and Innovation.' Videotaped interview by J.-P. Deschamps, IMD, Lausanne, reproduced with permission.
36. George, B. (2001). 'Leadership and Innovation.' Videotaped interview by J.-P. Deschamps, IMD, Lausanne, reproduced with permission.
37. George, B. (2001). 'Leadership and Innovation.' Videotaped interview by J.-P. Deschamps, IMD, Lausanne, reproduced with permission.
38. Lehr, L.W. (1979). 'Stimulating Technological Innovation: The Role of Top Management.' *Research Management*, November: 23–25.

# CHAPTER 3

# STIMULATING BOTTOM-UP INNOVATION

*[Google] sees its employees as the fount of innovation; they're expected to generate ideas and then compete to move those into the product pipeline. In theory, the fittest − those that solve a user need − survive!*

The 360 Techblog[1]

Companies that manage to tap and exploit the creativity of all their staff enjoy a powerful competitive advantage over highly regimented ones, in which people are supposed to do only what they are told to do. Auto industry observers have frequently identified one of Toyota Corporation's secret weapons against its Western competitors: its in-house suggestion scheme. Toyota's version of the classic and often disregarded idea box system is said to generate over 2 million ideas a year, with over 95% of the workforce contributing suggestions, which represents over 30 suggestions per worker per year. The company is proud to announce that over 90% of the suggestions it receives are implemented. This validates the belief of a number of innovation observers that if you want to uncover great ideas, generate a large quantity of them.[2]

Bottom-up innovation implies that employees not only take the initiative to generate ideas but are also empowered to implement at least some of them. An archetypical example of bottom-up innovation is the well-known story of 3M's Post-It pads. Champions Spence Silver – the inventor of microsphere adhesive, a strange non-sticking glue – and Art Fry – the relentless application hunter – did not merely submit their idea to management; they developed it underground with the blessing of some of their supervisors, like Geoff Nicholson, until it became a product. And then the team did not stop pushing until management agreed to market it, thus achieving one of 3M's greatest commercial successes.[3]

True bottom-up innovators have that elusive entrepreneurial characteristic oft sought by management. It is therefore interesting to reflect on what innovation leaders can do to create the conditions under which such types of innovations will flourish.[4]

## ENCOURAGING BOTTOM-UP INNOVATION: CLASSIC APPROACHES

Optimistic managers believe that every employee has an innate creative capability that can be mobilized. This means that unless they are prevented from doing so by their hierarchy, most people will aspire to make their mark on their company by coming up with creative ideas to improve things or create new businesses. If this is so, management's main task in promoting bottom-up innovation is to remove obstacles and facilitate the collection of ideas.

Obstacles are often linked to management attitudes, including:

• lack of interest in ideas that do not fit with existing priorities;
• lack of patience when facing poorly developed ideas; and
• not-invented-here syndrome.

But most managers also know that bottom-up innovation needs to be stimulated and promoted, and they use a variety of means to do so.[5]

### Set Ambitious Managerial Objectives for Innovation

A well-known hands-off approach for management consists in setting an ambitious overall innovation target for a business unit, expressed as a given percentage of sales to come from products introduced in the past two, three, four or five years. This stimulates bottom-up innovation because the target, if stretched enough, cannot generally be met through ordinary means – it requires a considerable and sustained innovation effort. Of course, the success of the approach depends on how serious management is in judging performance against this target, as opposed to traditional measures such as meeting or exceeding sales and profit objectives.

Well-known proponents of this method include extensive users of key performance indicators (KPIs), such as 3M, Hewlett-Packard and Medtronic. The medical device maker's former CEO and chairman, Bill George, illustrates this graphically in the following statement:

> We have a policy at Medtronic that 70% of our revenues would come from products introduced in the last 24 months. That puts enormous pressure on the organization to develop new products. I think two of the great innovative companies of the United States are 3M and HP, and they had a policy of ... 25% to 30% of the revenues to come from products introduced in the last four years—so we really upped the game![6]

Beyond its sheer simplicity, the advantages of this lever are twofold:

(1) By measuring the percentage of sales from new products, management puts the emphasis on successful introductions, not just the number of new products launched.
(2) Once the target has been reached, it can simply be raised again, as the management of 3M and HP have done regularly. It becomes a moving target.

However, the approach is not universally usable or easy to deploy. Its main disadvantages are also twofold:

(1) It cannot be used in a wide range of traditional sectors, for example in the process or materials industries, which do not compete on the basis of new products per se.
(2) It requires a rigorous definition of what constitutes a 'new product' to prevent managers from playing games and proliferating small product variants to meet their target.

## Allow Staff to Pursue their Own Ideas in Company Time

Innovative ideas seldom emerge when staff are hurriedly dealing with day-to-day tasks or fire-fighting incoming crises. Innovation requires time:

- time to observe;
- time to dream, think and imagine;
- time to speculate with others; and
- time to experiment.

This aspect is of course particularly important in the R&D area.

In the past, when corporate-funded central research labs were the norm, scientists, generally shielded from excessive business pressures, had that kind of time. But in the search for increased R&D productivity and business orientation, many of these central labs have been split, and the bulk of their staff brought under the responsibility of business unit managers. The remaining corporate research organizations, when they exist, have generally seen their funding significantly modified. A large share of their budget is now being passed on to business units, which therefore gain a claim on their output.

This transformation has generally achieved the desired objective, i.e. making R&D much more business-oriented, as decentralized labs become solely dedicated to serving and supporting their business colleagues. The negative consequence of this funding change, however, has been a reduction in the time horizon of scientists, researchers and engineers, who now mostly focus on the short to medium term. Senior research managers in companies such as ABB, Siemens, Philips and DuPont – four historic innovation giants – have expressed their fear that the 'short termism' of some of their business management colleagues is threatening the innovation capacity of their companies.

3M claims to have solved the problem with its now famous 15% rule: Every researcher or engineer within 3M is officially free to devote 15% of his/her work time to the pursuit of personal research interests, without supervisory approval. Other companies like Google have emulated the rule, also for R&D, in the hope of giving their staff some breathing space for bottom-up innovation. Google engineers are encouraged to spend 20% of their working time on personal projects that do not necessarily have any broad utility.[7]

3M R&D insiders reckon that this system works well because the company has a strong internal networking culture. Since most innovations at 3M are traditionally team based, the time spent by initial idea generators as part of their 15% allotment can indeed be leveraged as colleagues help develop the concept, within the limit of their own free time allotment.

3M was also famous for promoting a culture that encouraged exploration and experimentation, conveying in a tangible way management's strong interest in innovation. The benefit of this institutionalized freedom is more psychological − 3M insiders confess − than real because, in practice, researchers are subject to strong business pressures and often have to take their 15% time out of their personal free time.

The limit of this approach, however, is that it is not easily transferable to functions other than R&D. Unlike their technical colleagues, operational managers, for example in marketing and sales, do not generally track the time they spend on specific projects, hence could not benefit from a similar 15% rule. They are not measured on their allocation of time, but on their results.

Nevertheless, the spirit of this principle remains valid and this is why many businesses apply it by setting up functions dedicated to developing new ideas and technologies, for example new business development departments or incubators.

## Establish a Process to Collect Ideas and Reward Idea Generators

As the Toyota example at the beginning of the chapter shows, the most natural way for leaders to stimulate bottom-up innovation is to set up a process and mechanism to tap the brains of their staff and to do so systematically. Although the good old physical 'suggestion box' has not entirely disappeared, particularly for blue- and white-collar workers in plants and administrative offices, it is increasingly being replaced by 'virtual idea boxes' on the corporate intranet.

Some companies have gone further and appointed 'idea advocates' or 'idea sponsors' in various parts of the organization. These senior managers, typically chosen for their open-mindedness and strong corporate influence, are supposed to be the direct receivers and defenders of people's ideas. Their main objective is to give contributing staff an alternative and safe conduit for submitting their ideas. This recognizes the fact that immediate supervisors may not be open to ideas that have little to do with the daily tasks they have assigned to their staff. These special 'idea defenders' have multiple roles, including:

* identifying the kernels of opportunities behind the raw ideas they receive;
* helping the originator of the idea to defend it;
* assisting in 'packaging' the idea to present to management;
* defending it against hasty negative judgments in management discussions; and
* coaching the idea submitter during the initial idea validation phase until the next review.

Other companies – such as Tetra Pak, the liquid food packaging giant – have appointed 'idea matchmakers,' i.e. managers with a wide network of contacts and rich company experience, capable of connecting idea submitters with potential internal users or implementers. Tetra Pak's intranet-based idea management system offers two entry points to its staff: An 'I have an idea!' button and a corresponding 'I need an idea!' button. This system, and the associated matchmakers' network, creates a sort of internal market and clearing house for ideas.

But not all companies that have implemented formal idea collection methods have succeeded in keeping their system working productively over long periods. Failures are often caused by the non-observance of a few essential rules that govern this type of undertaking and which are summarized below:

(1) It is essential that the organizers rapidly acknowledge every single idea deposited in the system, irrespective of its actual value, with a follow-up promise. The lack of a timely response soon triggers a 'so what, why bother' attitude on the part of idea submitters and a steep decline in the number of suggestions.

(2) There must be transparency regarding both the process followed for evaluating ideas and deciding on their selection, rejection or postponement and the composition of the bodies responsible for doing so. Follow-up messages, if negative, must clearly explain the reasons for the decision and encourage the submitter to keep contributing.

(3) Ideas selected and implemented must trigger some sort of reward or benefit for the submitter. These do not have to be financial − recognition is a great motivator − but when they are of a monetary nature, for example a bonus or premium for savings achieved, they can be modest. It is the reward element itself that is important.

(4) In order to keep a high level of motivation, and thus momentum, management needs to keep track of, measure and publicize the results of its idea collection drive. This can include, for example, the number of ideas received; the percentage of ideas selected; the number of ideas implemented; and the new business or new savings generated.

(5) Leaders must also be aware that idea collection drives will naturally plateau and decline over time unless staff interest is regularly stimulated by new campaigns. Changes and novelties can be introduced in the type or categories of ideas sought − for example for a major cost-reduction drive − or in the rewards offered.

An impressive example of idea management that seems to work enduringly is provided by Solvay, the $9.6 billion Belgian chemicals, plastics and drugs company. Interestingly, Solvay's innovation drive and system originated and grew in its base chemicals division − a business focusing on a number of fairly traditional commodities, like sodium carbonate − before extending to the entire company.

Working closely with the 'Group Innovation Champion,' Jacques van Rijckvorsel, a number of senior managers drive Solvay's innovation efforts. One of them, Olivier Monfort, a member of Solvay's top management team in charge of both Solvay France and a new business department of the chemicals division, participates actively in the orchestration of the firm's bottom-up innovation process, referred to internally as 'participative innovation (kaizen).' He also shares in a parallel effort to generate and steer what he calls 'disruptive innovation.'

Van Rijckvorsel, Monfort and some of their colleagues, including Brigitte Laurent, Solvay's dedicated 'innovation champion,' are perfect examples of the innovation leaders that this book aims to depict. Some of their colleagues in this highly respectable *grande dame* of the chemicals industry (the company is over 140 years old) would probably call them 'innovation activists' because they are determined to use all possible means to promote innovation in their company. For example, the company ensures that all Solvay Group managers, whatever their function, have a significant innovation factor embedded in their personal scorecard. Innovation involvement, they claim, is taken into account in performance appraisals and influences compensation and career progression.

Solvay applies the five rules above systematically. Ideas submitted by the staff are first evaluated and further developed by a number of identified facilitators, who act as 'relayers' in the organization, pretty much along the lines of Tetra Pak's 'idea matchmakers.' Retained ideas are then sent to a number of 'experts,' whose judgment is indisputable. They will validate the ideas and dispatch the ones selected to the most appropriate units for implementation.

Solvay's 'participative innovation' management system is complemented by a network of 'innov'actors,' champions whose task is to help line managers launch innovation initiatives in their department and implement them. Interestingly, this very concept has been adopted by a number of French companies who have developed their own 'innov'actors,' thus creating a network of innovation champions eager to exchange experience across companies.

Solvay has established and supports an elaborate system of innovation trophies to acknowledge and reward the best contributors to Solvay's 'participative innovation' campaign. Trophies reward the best ideas selected in six different and complementary categories:

- new business;
- customer-focused projects;
- performance improvements;
- management improvements;
- sustainable development and corporate social responsibility; and
- transposable innovations (i.e. ideas 'stolen with pride' from external or internal sources and transferred within the company).

In the spirit of maintaining the momentum, Solvay has upped its ambitious innovation goals for its managers for the period 2007 to 2009:

- 100% involved: All executives have their innovation objective and every employee has at least one innovative idea per year.
- 50% of innovative projects undertaken with external partners through a structured cooperation agreement.
- 30% of new sales coming from products or activities introduced in the past five years.

Management also presents its various innovation initiatives as part of overall campaigns marketed internally under a particular umbrella theme. These themes are relaunched every few years with a light twist in focus but maximum continuity – e.g. 1997: 'Innovation for Growth'; 2001: 'Innovation and Competitiveness'; 2005: 'Growth and Competitiveness through Innovation.'

## Encourage People to Move Ideas Forward

Encouraging all your staff to spontaneously contribute ideas that management can then evaluate and have implemented is a good thing, indeed. But going one step further and asking people to work in teams, not only to generate ideas but also to develop them into validated concepts is even better. Teams are much more creative and productive than individuals, and ideas generated as the result of a rigorous customer-oriented team process go much further than spontaneous, often half-baked, individual ideas.

Companies that are keenly looking for growth opportunities through innovation – be it for new products, services or activities – should therefore not hesitate to entrust this responsibility to one or more '*venture teams.*' Their mission should be to explore opportunities, to generate, evaluate and validate ideas, and then to develop them into new concepts or solutions ready for inclusion in the corporate development pipeline and portfolio decisions. Ideally, venture teams should be composed of young 'high-potential' managers, because this is a good testing ground for entrepreneurial leadership. Team members should be chosen on the basis of their openness and enthusiasm, not just their skills. Venture teams obviously need to be coached by senior innovation leaders as they fulfill their mission.

The process of how to go from customer problem to opportunity and from ideas to concept is convincingly illustrated in a video developed by ABC's *Nightline* with IDEO, the famous Californian design house.[8] This video is one of the most popular teaching tools on innovation used for executive development at IMD in Lausanne, Switzerland. It shows how a team of IDEO designers was able to reinvent a traditional product – the supermarket shopping cart – in one week, ending up at the end of the exercise with a very innovative concept. The video demonstrates the power of a structured idea management process,[9] which goes way beyond traditional brainstorming exercises. It also illustrates the importance of entrusting the venture to a dedicated team with an open-minded attitude and a broad mix of skills. (We shall come back to the importance of team diversity later in this chapter.) The strength of the IDEO video is that it conveys, in 20 minutes, pretty much all you need to know in order to do the same thing in your company. A short manual to help management introduce the method, including the 15 steps in the process, is shown in Appendix B.

Companies like Logitech and Philips' Domestic Appliances division are avid users of the approach in their technical departments, and they have trained a number of their staff to facilitate the process, a must to make it operational. But a structured idea management process, along the lines of the one described in the IDEO video, can be used for many more applications than reinventing an existing product. It can be applied directly to:

- create a radically new product or service concept;
- develop ideas for totally new business opportunities;
- generate concrete ideas in support of a company objective, e.g. cost reduction;
- invent ways to improve functional or organizational effectiveness;
- solve technical or operational problems; and
- get out of a crisis.

## Build a Mechanism to Decide on and Invest in New Ideas

Innovation leaders, particularly front-end ones, are by nature and interest 'spotters' and 'backers' of good ideas, but their role does not stop there. They should be given the power to decide what to do with them and the means to invest in their implementation. As noted earlier, innovation calls for a delicate balance between risk taking and risk containment. Innovation leaders are constantly confronted with this difficult challenge, since they are usually the ones who are in contact with and manage front-line innovators. Consequently, they tend to get involved very early on in evaluating new product, process, service or business ideas. They must decide, alone or as part of a group, which ideas they should bet on, which they should shelve for a while and which they should diplomatically turn down.

Obviously, it is critical for the innovation leader to take the right decision. Flair is needed to ensure that interesting opportunities are not passed over and business resources are not squandered on useless pursuits. The difficulty comes from the fact that creative ideas cannot be evaluated with the same methods and certainty as other types of management decisions.[10] They cannot be assessed in the same way that most companies analyze investment opportunities, e.g. with a detailed justification analysis leading to a single 'go/no go' decision point. They need to go through a process of progressive refinement and risk reduction, with funding in phases and in proportion to the removal of major uncertainty factors. This always involves a high degree of management ambiguity that innovation leaders need to accept and explain to their management colleagues.

To keep their creative staff motivated, and hence maintain a positive innovation climate in the future, innovation leaders must ensure that decisions on new ideas are discussed, taken, justified and communicated through a transparent process. Increasingly, innovative companies are entrusting this important screening and backing of ideas to a collective body, which some call an '*Innovation Council*,' Whatever its name, this innovation management mechanism bears the important responsibility of selecting the best opportunities for funding, either by the corporation or by one or several business units.

There are many advantages in delegating this important task to a management group, instead of a single manager:

- broader and more formal review of the ideas' merits and risks;
- more objective assessment through multiple perspectives;
- more credible justification for decisions (positive or negative);
- a pool of resources for coaching initial projects; and
- more visibility and transparency in evaluating and selecting ideas.

But the key advantage is the possibility for top management to bring innovation leaders together − traditional and conservative managers should be kept out of such a body − to give them a chance to influence the flow of new corporate projects.

Generally, this kind of body will operate within strict management guidelines and budgetary supervision; in other words, they are not fully empowered to go ahead and invest on their own.

There are exceptions to this rule, though, as exemplified by Shell's highly innovative GameChanger concept, started in response to falling oil prices in the 1980s. GameChanger is a small organization responsible for devising and managing a process whereby ideas are stimulated, captured, nurtured and matured, until they are ready to be taken up by the business and pursued through existing mainstream business and technology development processes. The purpose of GameChanger is to extend the pool of ideas and accelerate the passage of good ones, as Royal Dutch Shell's CEO, Jeroen van der Veer, describes:

> In this new century, the type of organization needed for innovation will be different from that of the past. Rather than a hierarchical pyramid, I see a world-spanning network. We have built networks for the creation and cultivation of ideas – and their implementation – using a program called GameChanger. Initially developed to foster internal entrepreneurial spirit, Shell's GameChanger scope has broadened to look externally for game-changing ideas. It began with the Exploration and Production division with a small eclectic group of GameChangers and has expanded across the organization to include GameChanger groups both at the corporate level and in business units.[11]

The GameChanger concept fits with what Mark Rice calls 'radical innovation hubs,'[12] which he defines as 'vehicles through which leaders can efficiently and effectively engage in making innovation happen!' Compared with Shell's turnover, the GameChanger investment budget ($20 million for the Exploration and Production division in 2004, or 10% of its R&D budget) may seem modest. What is unique, however, is the fact that GameChangers are free to allocate the money as they see fit without having to justify this to senior management. The leverage factor created by this idea funding and nurturing system has been significant, generating substantial additional earnings and creating a number of new activities and joint ventures. Examples of successful GameChanger projects include:

- the creation of global communications and visualization systems;
- the development of 4D seismic technology;
- the conception and realization of 'expandable tubulars' (to drill deeper/faster); and
- the creation of 'Well Dynamics' (a joint venture with Halliburton).

A former Leader GameChanger at Shell International Exploration and Production, the late Jack Hirsch, considered that the role of the innovation leader is akin to that of a 'cheerleader!' He/she should be supportive and always positive, an enthusiast, a motivator, a cajoler. But that does not exclude some rigor. He explained that the success of the GameChanger approach lay in a number of basic principles:[13]

- Cater to passionate proponents of radical innovation ideas that break the rules of existing businesses, wherever they come from, as long as these managers are ready to participate in their implementation.
- Accept ideas only if they are innovative, appropriate for Shell and wouldn't be funded by the organization (GameChangers see themselves as 'angel investors' sponsoring good ideas).
- Validate ideas through a small panel of experts (i.e. by peers, not by the hierarchy) and do it fast (good ideas can be approved and resourced within a week of submission).
- Have the experts submit their evaluation independently but not make the funding decision. It is the GameChanger organization that makes all investment decisions without having to justify them.
- Ensure discipline in the management of ideas as they go through a funneling process (from a portfolio of ideas to a portfolio of experiments; a portfolio of ventures and eventually a portfolio of businesses).
- Increase the level of funding progressively as projects pass through various toll-gates and become full-scale R&D projects ready for transfer to existing units (for profit improving ideas) or for commercialization (for new businesses).

In summary, as Tim Warren, former director of Research & Technical Services for Shell International Exploration and Production and now chairman of Shell companies in Australia, notes, you can encourage innovation if you make sure four things happen:

(1) Everyone who aspires to innovate finds it easy to do so, i.e. the system is transparent, quick and well resourced.
(2) Each idea gets a chance to grow before it faces a firing squad.

(3) You have the right people cossetting and nurturing ideas in the early growth stage. That means things like peer review of initial ideas, rather than submission to distant panels of superiors.

(4) Everyone in the organization is aware that innovation is succeeding. Encouraging innovation makes sound business sense![14]

## BUILDING AN INNOVATION CULTURE: FOUR DRIVERS

In the long term, the most effective way to stimulate bottom-up innovation is to make the company culture more conducive to creativity and entrepreneurship. Managers often feel uncomfortable about exhortations to change their company culture, an element over which they feel they have no practical hold. It is a commonly accepted wisdom in many companies that the culture is inherited from previous generations. It has been shaped by numerous historical events and economic factors and is almost impossible to change deeply, at least in the short term. Exceptions are rare and limited to deep crises followed by the arrival of a radical new CEO, like Carlos Ghosn at Nissan.

We cannot fundamentally challenge that viewpoint and claim that every company should try to re-create the culture of a 3M, Apple or IDEO. However, within any given corporate culture, there are specific elements that condition and encourage innovation, some of which can be strongly influenced by practical measures that managers can take.

Gary Hamel is a proponent of this proactive philosophy, advocating that companies should be 'Bringing Silicon Valley Inside.'[15] His argument is that, in Silicon Valley, ideas, capital and talent circulate freely, gathering into whatever combinations are most likely to generate innovation and wealth. He calls this phenomenon 'resource attraction' and maintains that it is at the root of innovation in 'the Valley.' His recommendation: Set up similar markets within your company:

(1) A market for capital – let the best projects, wherever they come from, compete for company resources;

(2) A market for ideas – tap the brains of all your staff and external sources and make sure the best ideas will be pursued, irrespective of where they come from; and

(3) A market for talent – staff your best projects with your very best people, whatever their business unit affiliation.

These measures are all related to policy decisions that management can easily take on its own. Yet, the resulting philosophy is likely to profoundly change the company's innovation culture.

Experience shows that management has a number of levers at its disposal to stimulate bottom-up innovation without having to embark on a traumatic company-wide culture change process. These levers deal with:

• boosting organizational creativity;
• mobilizing teams of champions;
• promoting a customer-centric attitude; and
• encouraging a 'can-do' climate.

The rest of this chapter will review these levers and highlight their implications for management, in terms of decisions and actions.

## Boosting Organizational Creativity

The word 'creativity' often conjures up the image of an individual suddenly hit by a brilliant idea under the shower! This is because, in our individualistic Western culture, we think more often of individual creativity than of a collective or organizational phenomenon. Yet, it is the latter that stimulates and enables innovation. As noted in Chapter 2, innovation is a team process and innovation leaders focus on building and steering winning teams, as is commonly done in Japan.

In most Western companies – think of pharmaceutical firms, for example – there are probably ample amounts of individual creativity, particularly in R&D. But the ability to deploy that creativity in effective and efficient teams is probably less impressive. It is ironic that in Japan the tendency is exactly the opposite: Organizational creativity is perceived to be the norm and a number of companies are now looking for ways to enhance individual creativity. Although traditionally discouraged by the Japanese educational system, individual creativity, if amplified and leveraged by a team process, is now perceived as an essential element to foster the kind of out-of-the-box thinking that is so important for radical innovation.

Management can do at least four things to enhance a company's organizational creativity:

(1) promote staff diversity;
(2) hire, tolerate and deploy constructive mavericks;
(3) look for and promote 'broad bandwidth' managers; and
(4) encourage external contacts systematically.

### Promote Staff Diversity

When talking about corporate culture, management gurus sometimes refer to 'corporate DNA' to reflect the fact that a corporation's fundamental values are often embedded in its history and make-up. The metaphor is appropriate for a discussion on organizational creativity, which is always enhanced by a rich diversity in the company's genes, i.e. in the background, profile and viewpoints of its people.

Diversity is desirable for innovation because creativity feeds on the confrontation of complementary or even opposing perspectives and ideas, and this does not happen when everyone in the organization comes from the same mold. Companies that always recruit the same kind of people – banks tend to recruit financially trained managers; insurance companies, actuaries and lawyers; chemical companies, chemists and chemical engineers, etc. – are depriving themselves of rich sources of organizational creativity.

Diversity is needed on several dimensions:

• *Diversity in gender*. Numerous studies have shown that, compared with men, women have different ways of connecting their rational left brain with their more intuitive right brain. In addition, as we have all noticed, women do change the dynamics of teams to which they belong or which they lead because of their very different way of interacting with people. Yet, women still remain a minority on many innovation teams, particularly at the senior management level. Organizational creativity is definitely enhanced when gender parity is achieved.

• *Diversity in age.* Young people are expected to come up with bolder solutions to problems, simply because they are not hindered by past experience; more senior staff are supposed to have good judgment because of their experience. This is why it is always beneficial to build innovation teams with a broad mix of ages. To benefit from this duality, some companies have even structured their innovation projects by having two competing teams – a 'junior team' and a 'senior team' – working in parallel on the same project and then taking the best of both outputs at the end.

• *Diversity in origin and culture.* Truly global companies, in terms of cultural diversity within their staff, are rare. Most corporations, and not just in Japan and Europe, tend to fill their management ranks with nationals who, because of their origin and upbringing, will tend to react to events in a similar way, thus reducing opportunities for out-of-the-box thinking. To increase their chances of integration and promotion, nationals from other cultures also feel the pressure to smooth out their cultural differences and adopt the style of their employer's home country, thus losing their unique insights – to the detriment of creativity.

• *Diversity in educational background.* Companies are generally inclined to hire the majority of their staff from a few well-defined 'hard' disciplines they know and trust: lawyers, accountants, marketers, business graduates, engineers and the like. 'Softer' social sciences tend to be neglected, although they are useful – even in high-tech industries – for understanding complex psychological customer or employee reactions. A lack of people with a background in such disciplines – psychologists, anthropologists, ethnologists, sociologists – usually goes hand in hand with a deficit in gender parity, since many of these professions are preferred and embraced by women.

In conclusion, organizational creativity can be effectively enhanced through a systematic staff diversity policy, both at the hiring stage and in career progression moves and management appointments. This is usually the responsibility of the company's human resources officer, who therefore should always be a full member of all the innovation steering bodies or mechanisms.

## Hire, Tolerate and Deploy Constructive Mavericks

The biggest killer of organizational creativity is 'groupthink,' i.e. quick consensus achieved by people who think conventionally along parallel and always appropriate ways. IDEO's exhortation to 'encourage wild ideas'[16] for innovative idea generation cannot be dissociated from the recommendation to hire and tolerate constructive mavericks.[17] Mavericks are those individuals who never follow the crowd, preferring to pursue their own ideas and challenge the status quo. They are the ones who always question 'the way we do things here' and come up with radical alternatives, sometimes totally unrealistic but at times brilliant.

Mavericks can often be found in R&D, less so in business management and quite rarely in senior management positions because they tend to be, at best, 'unpolitical' in their dealings with management. There are notable exceptions, of course, even in CEO positions. For example, Apple's Steve Jobs would probably not mind being called a 'maverick CEO'; nor would Niels Jacobsen, the Danish CEO of Oticon – one of the world's hearing aids leaders and recipient of the 2003 European Company of the Year award – who managed the implementation of what was then called a 'spaghetti organization.'[18]

Mavericks are commonly found in creative industries like advertising or the media. They also tend to join companies that have a reputation for innovation, but usually shun very rigid, autocratic or regimented organizations where people are supposed to follow the 'party line.' They will suffocate in such kinds of companies and could turn destructive after being constructive. To survive and thrive, they need some elbowroom and above all freedom of speech and, to a large extent, a license to act on their ideas and change things.

Of course mavericks, if given a totally free hand, can become like unguided missiles, creating a lot of excitement through the speed with which they obtain early results, but also capable of inflicting heavy damage in the longer term. This is exactly what happened in the case of the young trader Nick Leeson at Barings Bank.[19] For a while, he generated huge profits for Barings Bank, but finally brought the financial institution down through his creative yet totally uncontrollable deals and the smoke screens he lay over them. This story should not be interpreted as a sign that banks and financial institutions, which are highly sensitive to compliance issues, should not hire mavericks. It simply means that mavericks must be given free rein but only with some management supervision.

The presence of a number of mavericks – not just an isolated one – and the way they are listened to and deployed is therefore one of the important indicators of a creative organization. Companies that cannot identify their mavericks – they are usually easy to notice because they tend to be vocal—should worry about their bottom-up innovation culture. Note, though, that the issue for management is not to keep its mavericks over a long period – these personalities tend to grow weary of staying in the same organization for too long. The challenge is to build a 'can-do' climate (as explained later in this chapter) that is 'maverick-friendly' so as to attract them on a regular basis and to deploy them productively for as long as they deign to stay, then hire new ones.

### Look for and Promote 'Broad-Bandwidth' Managers

A Japanese participant in an innovation seminar – he held a senior position at NEC – defined the profile of the innovative managers his company was trying to attract by coming to the blackboard and drawing three vegetables: An oblong potato, a thin carrot and a mushroom with a large head and deep stem! He then explained his drawing as follows:

We don't want to hire 'potatoes,' i.e. people who have a lot of breadth in terms of their functional or discipline coverage but no depth! These are shallow generalists who end up knowing nothing or very little about everything. We don't favor 'carrots' either, those specialists or experts who build a lot of depth in their chosen field but have no breadth, because they choose to remain in their narrow area. They will end up knowing everything there is to know on nothing or very little. What we are looking for are mushrooms, i.e. individuals who combine a breadth of interests and knowledge with some depth in a number of areas. These are the kinds of managers to whom we entrust our critical innovation projects.

Without using the term, this Japanese manager described exactly what is meant by 'broad-bandwidth managers,' a phrase used by a number of high-tech firms including Microsoft.

Breadth is needed in three areas:

- breadth of interest, because it is akin to curiosity, a critical requirement for innovators and their leaders;
- breadth of thinking, because it reflects an ability to detect weak signals and recognize patterns, an important characteristic for innovation; and
- breadth of experience, because it reflects a person's accumulated learning and wisdom, so essential in evaluating risk factors, backing projects and coaching teams.

But depth is also needed, at least in some areas, because it is essential to be credible and lead people, and thus be respected.

Innovation leaders should therefore try to recruit managers with a 'mushroom-profile,' rather than 'carrots' or 'potatoes.' More importantly, they need to promote managers with this kind of broad bandwidth, despite the fact that management often prefers to entrust responsibility to highly focused people, simply because they equate this with a high degree of results-orientation. Once again, the burden is put on the HR function to define, find evaluation measures for and track the elusive bandwidth characteristic in aspiring candidates and promotable managers.

### Encourage External Contacts Systematically

The preceding paragraphs argued that organizational creativity can be enhanced through the purposeful build-up and management of human resources – i.e. by hiring and deploying staff with diverse and complementary profiles, including mavericks, and promoting broad-bandwidth managers. But organizational creativity cannot flourish only through a purely inbred approach. It needs to be fed continuously with external input, i.e. deep market, customer or competitor insights, new product or service ideas, emerging knowledge on technology trends, and the like. External contacts are an essential stimulant and amplifier of internal creativity.

Innovation leaders should therefore encourage their staff to get out of the office and into the outside world, and they should make sure people learn from these external contacts and share their learning with colleagues. In short, they need to encourage a proactive and broad exploration of market information and knowledge sources.

For example, IDEO's innovation process always starts with immersion of the whole project team in 'the market,' defined very broadly. You cannot creatively redesign a product – IDEO managers argue – without first capturing and understanding the experience of those who will build, sell, use and repair that product. And there is no shortcut for getting such insights: You need to get out of your office and talk to people, live. IDEO's maverick CEO, Dave Kelley, the initiator of this practice, comments:

> The trick is to find these real experts, so that you can learn much more quickly than you could by just kind of doing it in the normal way and trying to learn about it yourself . . .
>
> In corporate America, many bosses . . . measure . . . who're the good people. Are the people who are performing the ones whom they see at their desk all the time? They couldn't be further from the truth! The people who are really getting the information are out there talking to the buzzes of the world, going to meet other experts . . . Much more useful than sitting at your desk![20]

We shall see later in this chapter how innovation leaders can galvanize their staff to build a customer-centric attitude, a prerequisite for ensuring such kinds of fruitful market contacts.

But organizational creativity is not spurred only by a multitude of market contacts. It is also enhanced by tapping external providers of knowledge and technologies. This goes beyond the outright purchase or licensing of technology, often called 'technology outsourcing.' Networking with existing or emerging technology sources and creating linkages with them, for example through cooperative development, contributes a lot to stimulating internal learning and innovative thinking. This kind of networking has already become standard practice with many innovative companies. It is particularly developed in the pharmaceutical sector, where large traditional drug firms have woven a complex web of research and technology development relationships with small innovative biotech firms. It is also common in the so-called high-tech sector of the electronics industry – think of HP, Nokia, Medtronic, Logitech, Canon and Sony. It is only starting in other sectors such as consumer goods.

The contribution of external technology networking to organizational creativity, thus innovative thinking, is becoming so powerful that a number of advanced companies are now managing their *know-who* activities as proactively as their *know-how* building efforts.[21] They generally do so through a combination of well-known mechanisms:

- Appointing 'technology gatekeepers' for each main family of technology. Technology gatekeepers are generally chosen from among the company's most advanced R&D experts. They are supposed to keep abreast of the latest technology developments in their allocated area through networking, i.e. meeting external experts; tracking web-based communications; establishing contacts with universities; attending scientific conventions and the like.
- Creating a 'scientific or technology advisory council' to guide senior technical management. These councils typically gather prominent external experts, often chosen from among well-respected members of the scientific academic community. Their mission is to track and signal to the company all kinds of early developments in technologies of relevance to the company.

- Setting up a dedicated 'technology scouting function' within the R&D organization. This kind of function, which exists in companies like HP or Intel, acts as the permanent 'eyes and ears' of the company on new technologies and ideas. It locates sources of new technologies and puts company scientists and engineers in contact with these potential knowledge providers and partners.

## Mobilizing Teams of Champions

Bottom-up innovation occurs when people within an organization take the initiative, i.e. when they come up with an innovative idea and run with the ball, alone or with colleagues, to implement it, ideally with the blessing and support of their hierarchy. Bottom-up innovation is one of the many forms of corporate entrepreneurship; it is driven by the enthusiasm of a few 'champions' – innovators and managers who are ready to take a career risk to push ahead with their ideas. Innovation leaders eager to promote bottom-up innovation need to pay particular attention to these precious entrepreneurial individuals. They need to identify, cultivate, empower, support – i.e. shield and coach – and reward these champions.

It is useful to distinguish between three types of champions, according to their focus: (1) technical champions, (2) business champions, and (3) executive champions.

- *Technical champions* are often found in R&D or engineering departments. They may be at the origin of an intriguing technical discovery worth sharing with their colleagues, even if they cannot think of an immediate business application. If the technology seems promising enough, they will not rest until they have enlisted colleagues for its exploitation. Alternatively, technical champions may not be the initiators of an innovative product idea but they will work with the idea originator to make it technically feasible.
- *Business champions* are those members of the business organization – from marketing, product management and similar functions – who are able to sense a potential market opportunity,

in itself or behind an innovative technical discovery. Business champions will generally know how to sell their idea to management in order to get funding and support, and they will often volunteer personally to bring their idea forward together with their technical colleague.

- *Executive champions* – true innovation leader archetypes – are those members of senior management who are ready to hear the stories of their technical and business champions and decide to take the risk of backing their project ideas. They will first act as advocates for innovation champion teams vis-à-vis top management, helping them secure resources and get started. They will also devote plenty of their own time and effort to coaching their teams until their projects are either discontinued or implemented.

Successful bottom-up innovation requires the combined presence and intervention of these three types of champions. In their executive championing role, innovation leaders therefore need to ensure that no project is allowed to go beyond a certain exploratory phase without the simultaneous enrollment and balanced cooperation of a technical and business champion. A number of large R&D organizations have adopted this rule, arguing that if scientists or engineers cannot convince their business colleagues of the merits of their discovery, then they will have a hard time convincing customers to adopt it. In reverse, if marketers cannot convince their technical colleagues of the value of their product idea, then it might signal that the proposed ideas have little technical merit. The Tetra Pak story described in Chapter 8 will provide a compelling illustration of the power of 'champion teams.' It also highlights the fact that important and long cycle development projects will typically mobilize a number of technical, business and executive champions over time, in what I call a 'chain of leadership.'

## Promoting a Customer-Centric Attitude

Companies that are good at bottom-up innovation generally share an innate or acquired customer orientation. It starts with a deep-rooted conviction that most innovation efforts aim to create new customer value. This conviction translates into a quasi-obsessive search for new opportunities to add this extra value. It is not unusual in these companies to find innovation leaders who will instinctively lead by example, by engaging personally in customer contacts and encouraging their staff to search for unarticulated customer needs or wants. Note that the term 'customer' should be interpreted broadly; it encompasses all those who distribute, purchase and use the new product or service.

A lot has been written in the strategic marketing literature on customer value creation and it is not the purpose of this book to summarize it. Nevertheless, since it is the responsibility of innovation leaders to promote a strong customer orientation, it may help to outline the three main schools of thought regarding customer value creation – play the same game but better; play the same game but with different rules; and play a new game with new rules – and reflect on their common implications. The three strategies are not mutually exclusive; truly innovative companies, like Toyota, use them all depending on the circumstances.

### Play the Same Game but Better!

Advocates of this first type of strategy, for example the authors of the book *Simply Better*[22] argue that many companies have gone too far in trying to differentiate their offering and in cramming their products with features few customers really need or want. How many people use the many washing programs in their dishwasher or the endless and often redundant features of Microsoft Office programs? Playing the same game but better means going back to the basics of the business and finding out the *key* attributes that really matter to customers. It also implies doggedly trying to outperform competitors on these important values in order to exceed customers' expectations.

Michelin was one of the well-known pioneers of this strategy, focusing its R&D efforts for many years on a single critical tire attribute – durability/longevity – a category it dominated thanks to its 'radial' technology. Toyota also excels at this strategy, which it has adopted for its mass volume cars. The company has realized that what car buyers care for above all is trouble-free operations, and has thus spent a lot of effort on becoming and remaining the reference in terms of car quality and reliability.

## Play the Same Game but with Different Rules!

Proponents of this second type of strategy, for example promoters of the 'value innovation' concept,[23] recommend changing the rules of the game by redesigning the perceived 'value curve' of their products. This, they suggest, implies rejecting their competitors' commonly accepted assumptions regarding the way to do business and considering established hierarchies of attributes as irrelevant.[24] Value innovators do not hesitate to 'underdeliver' on certain attributes in order to 'overdeliver' on others. More importantly, they will find and emphasize new attributes that may have been totally neglected by competitors, despite being very appealing to large segments of the market.

As mentioned earlier, the emergence of low-cost airlines like Southwest Airlines or Ryanair is a typical illustration of value innovation principles, with many traditional operating assumptions and service attributes being jettisoned by the new players in favor of a single critical customer benefit – lowest possible air ticket prices.

Many observers believe that Toyota has established a position in the US luxury car segment by adopting a variant of this strategy. As a new entrant in a segment dominated by established US and German manufacturers, Lexus had to change the rules of the game to build its image, and that meant improving customer service by an order of magnitude. Of course, Lexus had to fare well on other product attributes favored by its competitors, like quality, design or car performance, but these alone would not have given it a competitive advantage given its lack of image. Pioneering a new standard of service and pampering customers gave it the missing edge.

## Play a New Game with New Rules!

Champions of this third type of strategy maintain that companies will never create anything really new unless they move from a

'market-driven' to a 'market-driving' mode.[25] The former emphasizes listening intently to customers' wishes to satisfy them as fully
as possible; the latter means relying on one's vision to invent
totally new products that will ultimately meet customers' unarticulated, latent needs, thus creating new industries or business
models.

Amazon, IKEA and Starbucks are often cited as good examples
of 'market driving' innovators as they deliver products and services
that the market had never thought it would want before they
became available. With its Prius hybrid cars, Toyota has obviously
followed this strategy quite boldly. No customer ever asked for a
hybrid engine before it was made available, yet many people were
concerned about environmental issues and fuel costs. Toyota was
not willing simply to satisfy articulated customer needs extremely
well. It chose to drive demand toward a new type of environ-
mentally friendly car, a latent need with some of its most socially
aware customers, thus creating a brand new industry segment
which it now dominates.

## Common Imperatives of these Value Creation Strategies

At the heart of these three approaches lies a common company
characteristic, i.e. a deep company-wide interest in the customer
as well as a talent and process for second-guessing the market,
which some authors call 'customer sensing.' Bottom-up innovation companies often feature both a *customer-centric process*, to detect
opportunities for value creation, and a *customer-centric culture*, to
ensure that the voice of the customer is heard throughout. Innovation leaders can do a lot to develop both aspects.

### A customer-centric process

The process for detecting opportunities for value creation, irrespective of the strategy followed, goes much further than what
marketers generally label 'market research.' In its traditional form,
market research focuses on data – observations of market facts and
their extrapolation into trends – and turns this data into informa-

tion by adding meaning, i.e. judgments on the significance and implications of these facts and trends. This type of research is important, but mostly to support current operations.

To innovate, companies need to go a lot deeper in their customer exploration activities and develop an uncanny ability to:

(1) Understand why customers do what they do or buy what they do. This requires a process for detecting subtle yet significant signals of changes in the market and in customer or consumer behavior – those *insights* so actively sought by consumer goods companies; and

(2) Sense what customers would buy if it was offered. This is akin to predicting likely future behavior – that elusive customer or consumer *foresight* that Akio Morita advocated when he declared that no market research would have identified a consumer need for Sony's Walkman®.

This type of capability is generally found in companies that have developed a customer-centric process, something that does not appear spontaneously, but needs to be strongly encouraged by management. In a customer-centric process, people look for insights that go beyond the traditional but narrow research emphasis on customer likes/dislikes. Intuitively or methodically, they try to put themselves in the customers' shoes. This means understanding the context in which customers experience the product or service, including on the emotional side. They derive from it a list of desired outcomes and translate these outcomes into a set of prioritized customer needs, both tangible *and* intangible, expressive or emotional, and ultimately into product concepts and design choices. Figure 3.1 illustrates this type of process.

## A customer-centric culture

To be effective, a customer-centric process needs to take place in an environment where employees value customers, hear their voice and do their utmost to surprise and satisfy them. This type of environment – I call it a customer-centric culture – is rare in large companies. It is the role of innovation leaders to create it and, most importantly, to sustain it over time.

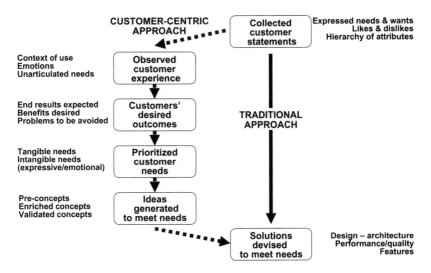

**Figure 3.1**  Customer intelligence process

Bottom-up innovation will have a greater chance of occurring if a customer-centric culture pervades the whole company and particularly R&D and engineering, not just marketing and sales. This will happen only when senior management, including innovation leaders, show the way in words – constantly reminding people that their salaries are paid by customers – and in deeds – visiting customers systematically themselves and building customer-centered intelligence processes. They need to convince all departments, even those that are not in direct contact with customers, that they have a role to play in sensing the market and ultimately in satisfying customers.

Intuit, the successful Silicon Valley supplier of personal finance software, and its neighbor Logitech are two examples of companies where top management is determined to build a customer-centric culture pervading all functions. Scott Cook, Intuit's former CEO, was known to want to turn *every* person in his company who interfaces with customers into a 'customer listening post.' He also spurred the creation of a new function within Intuit – the 'customer insight manager' – whose role is to steer the process by which Intuit staff visit customers at home in order to watch them and note their experience and feelings as they use the company's software packages. Cook's philosophy comes across very convincingly in a now famous videotaped interview which is sprinkled with observations such as the ones below:

> There are thousands of opportunities per day for learning . . .
> Capture the voice of customers . . . Listen to their lives!
> Be excited and energized answering questions . . .
> Create opportunities for listening . . .
> Win loyalty through listening . . .
> Engineers need and want customer feedback . . .
> Spend time with customers . . . Adopt a customer!
> We want people to feel great as they use the product . . .
> Get first-hand contact with a customer while he is working . . .
> Make customers feel good about interfacing with the company . . .
> Success comes when customers are successful! You owe them success![26]

Daniel Borel, Logitech's cofounder and former board chairman, expresses a similar customer-centric philosophy in his interviews:

> With more than 50 industry 'firsts' to its name, Logitech is dedicated to innovation. But more importantly, the company does not innovate for innovation's sake. We create new products that people want to buy and love to use . . . because they add value, they provide innovative solutions to make their computing experience easier, richer or more fun. If people say, 'Intel is inside,' then I would say, 'Logitech is outside.' Outside meaning it is the visible part of the iceberg. . . . The products we make are products you hold. They are products which must carry emotion – like your watch, which is your own, your keyboard, your mouse, you touch it, you feel it. . . . This vision captures the minds of people working for us, and continuously stimulates them: 'How can we bridge the gap between the technology itself and the end user?[27]

Yves Karcher, engineering director of Logitech's Retail Pointing Device unit and a typical innovation leader for his staff, lives by these principles and has even surprised his marketing colleagues by catching the customer research bug! He is known to take pictures of the desktop scene or laptop bags of the people he visits to communicate computer mouse usage patterns and customer problems to his staff as vividly as possible. Recently, he undertook, mostly by himself, a series of in-depth interviews with potential customers or users of a new cordless device that he planned to develop to run PowerPoint presentations. He wanted to understand, first hand, how customers managed their presentations and their feelings while doing so. This enabled him to build deep user insights that led to original design ideas which he then had to sell to his commercial colleagues, thus becoming a more proactive partner for marketing. Karcher now strongly encourages his senior project leaders to adopt this research practice themselves.[28]

In summary, bottom-up innovation can be stimulated if leaders actively promote a customer-centric culture, i.e. an environment in which people share at least four beliefs and accept their implications in terms of attitudes and required activities:

- Belief No. 1: Customers/consumers are everywhere and they are all different.
  This calls for an attitude of *curiosity* and an emphasis on *watching*.
- Belief No. 2: Customers/consumers have frustrations! They also experience delight.
  This calls for an attitude of *empathy* and an emphasis on *sensing*.
- Belief No. 3: Customers/consumers compare; they use products and learn.
  This calls for an attitude of *rigor* and an emphasis on *researching*.
- Belief No. 4: Customers/consumers give clues; they know better.
  This calls for an attitude of *humility* and an emphasis on *listening and hearing*.

## Encouraging a 'Can-do' Climate

In a bottom-up innovation mode, employees should feel authorized and encouraged to implement the ideas they have generated, once they have passed the validation stage and been selected. This will happen only if the company has built an entrepreneurial culture and employees feel they work in a 'can-do' climate. In most cases, this kind of culture will not emerge spontaneously. Innovation leaders need to work hard to create and sustain a spirit of adventure, challenge and self-fulfillment that will stimulate innovation initiatives.

The innovation climate of a company is directly influenced, positively or negatively, by a number of specific management *attitudes*, *policies* and *processes*. Research conducted across a wide spectrum of companies[29] led to the identification of specific innovation-enabling or hindering factors in each of these three categories. The most influential ones are listed in Appendix C and the ones typically found most deficient in companies are highlighted in Figure 3.2.

Management teams wishing to improve their innovation climate would be well advised to conduct surveys at regular intervals – for example every two or three years – to identify:

(1) Which of the climate factors listed in Appendix C does their staff perceive as having a critical impact on innovation in the company. Research indeed shows that certain factors that are viewed as particularly important in some companies, or even industries, may be perceived as neutral in others. Responses to climate factors strongly reflect established company cultures.

| Management Attitudes | Management Policies | Management Processes |
|---|---|---|
| Lack of concrete signs of management's deep commitment to innovation | Lack of specific rewards for innovators and recognition of their contribution | Lack of an explicit process to formulate an innovation vision, strategy and priorities |
| Low risk taking attitude by management and low tolerance of failure | Lack of systematic tracking of innovation efforts, progress and results | Numbers-driven planning process with insufficient attention to opportunities |
| Excessively short payback horizon for management's investment decisions | Reluctance to fully empower innovation teams and free them from bureaucratic rules | Lack of process to expose management and staff to the field and customers |
| Little effort to draw lessons from past failures and disseminate the learning | Limited resources allocated to innovation and/or resources subject to financial results | Arcane, slow and non-transparent decision-making process |

**Figure 3.2** Innovation climate factors found deficient in many companies
Source: Author's research and consulting experience.

(2) Which of these factors are found particularly deficient in the company, compared with the respondents' perception of what constitutes an 'ideal' condition. It is interesting to contrast responses across different organizational layers and functions of the company, as they may point to specific issues that need to be addressed in parts of the organization.

Innovation climate surveys cover many of the factors that are, or should be, addressed by traditional employee satisfaction surveys. A positive innovation climate will indeed generally correlate with a high degree of employee satisfaction and management motivation. So the two surveys can easily be combined and conducted simultaneously by the human resources function. Management should of course widely communicate the results of the survey, acknowledging and discussing the identified obstacles and the corresponding improvement priorities.

In summary, innovation leaders can do a lot to create favorable conditions for bottom-up innovation to occur spontaneously in their organization. Chapter 4 will show what they need to do if they want to launch a proactive innovation process top-down.

## ENDNOTES

1. http://360techblog.com/google-bottom-up-innovation/2006/10/25.
2. Sloane, P. (2004). 'Innovation Strategy: To Uncover Great Ideas, Generate a Large Quantity of Them.' *Innovation Tools* website, September 3. http://www.innovationtools.com (under Articles/Enterprise Innovation) accessed 27 November 2007.
3. Nayak, P.R. and Ketteringham, J.M. (1994). '3M's Little Yellow Note Pads: Never Mind I'll Do It Myself.' *Breakthroughs!* Rev. ed. San Diego, Pfeiffer and Company, Chapter 3, pp. 50–73.
4. De Jong, J.J. (2004). 'How Can Leaders Trigger Bottom-Up Innovation: An Empirical Research into Knowledge-Intensive Services.' Zoetermeer, SCALES – Scientific Analysis of Entrepreneurship and SMEs. In a previous article: 'Leadership as a Determinant of Innovative Behavior: A Conceptual Framework' (2003, Zoetermeer, EIM Business & Policy Research), written together with research colleague D.N. Den Hartog, the authors listed 13 leadership behaviors that could affect the innovative behavior of employees:

- 'Innovative role modelling: A leader may enhance innovation by providing an example of innovative behavior . . .'
- 'Intellectual stimulation: . . . Involves increasing employees' awareness of problems and stimulating them to rethink old ways of doing things . . .'
- 'Stimulating knowledge diffusion: . . . Whenever one hears about others' problems in current work he/she may come up with suggestions or ideas for solutions how to solve these problems . . .'
- 'Providing vision: . . . could enhance subordinate innovative behaviour because it may provide a frame of reference that indicates what kind of ideas will be appreciated . . .'
- 'Consulting: Participation in decision-making can be another trigger for subordinate innovative behavior . . .'
- 'Delegating: . . . occurs when a leader gives a subordinate the responsibility and autonomy to determine independently how to do a job or a certain task . . .'
- 'Support for innovation: . . . Experiencing support may help employees to feel free to act creatively and generate ideas . . .'
- 'Organizing feedback: Concepts . . . could be improved considerably by making sure that those who are developing or implementing them receive feedback on an initial version . . .'
- 'Recognizing: . . . includes giving praise (compliments), awards (certificates of achievement, private budget, increased autonomy) and ceremonies (public speeches and celebrations) . . .'
- 'Rewarding: . . . positive contribution of concrete tangible rewards on employees' motivation to innovate . . .'
- 'Providing resources: . . . even exempting employees from their usual task to help them concentrate all their efforts on the development and implementation of their idea . . .'
- 'Monitoring: . . . could impede subordinate innovative behaviour because it makes them feel insecure and unsafe at work – their jobs may be threatened if they make mistakes . . .'
- 'Task assignment: . . . Assigning employees with challenging tasks may have a positive impact, since intrinsically motivating tasks serve as a trigger for creativity and innovation . . .'

The research results with a number of knowledge-intensive service firms, published in his research report, verified their hypothesis fully on five factors:

- consulting;
- delegating;
- recognizing;
- giving challenging task assignments, and
- limiting monitoring.

Positive impact was found, but to a lesser extent on two more factors:

- support for innovation, and
- providing resources.

However, surprisingly, no positive correlation was found on four factors:

- intellectual stimulation;
- stimulating knowledge diffusion;
- providing vision; and
- rewarding employees with financial incentives.

And a negative correlation was found on two factors:

- innovative role-modelling; and
- organizing feedback.

5. Adair J. (2007). *Leadership for Innovation: How to Organize Team Creativity and Harvest Ideas.* London and Philadelphia, Kogan Page.
6. George, B. (2001). 'Leadership and Innovation.' Videotaped interview by J.-P. Deschamps, IMD, Lausanne, reproduced with permission.
7. Refer to: http://360techblog.com/google-bottom-up-innovation/2006/10/25.
8. Available at http://www.abcnewsstore.com.
9. Rowbotham, L. and Bohlin, N. (1996). 'Structured Idea Management as a Value-Adding Process.' *Prism*, Arthur D. Little, 2nd quarter 1996: 79–93.
10. Mannarelli, T. (2001). 'Unlocking the Secrets of Business Innovation.' Mastering People Management/Managing Creativity. *Financial Times*, 29 October, pp. 10–11.
11. Quote from: http://www.klinegroup.com/intelligentInsights/109.pdf.
12. Rice, M.P. (2004). 'Leading Innovation: Creating the Future.' *Babson Insight*, 21 July.

   'In the book: *Radical Innovation: How Mature Companies Can Outsmart Upstarts* my coauthors and I defined the concept of a "radical innovation hub" – the firm's system (collection of structures, processes, knowledge and talent) for supporting radical innovation. The hub is the organizational mechanism for capturing learning from individual projects and from the portfolio of projects, and for applying that learning to improving the performance of the portfolio of radical innovation initiatives. Firms that sustain a commitment to innovation and that accumulate learning develop a mature competency. In turn, this competency allows the firm to impose a measure of managerial discipline on an activity that is fundamentally chaotic – with high levels of technical, market, organizational and resource uncertainties. Hubs perform a variety of functions in helping firms systematize the innovation process.'
13. Unpublished speech delivered at a workshop on 'Leading Innovation,' organized on 7–9 June 2005 by the International Association for Product Development (IAPD), the Learning Center, Marlboro (MA). Summary available on http://www.iapdonline.com/es44.htm.
14. Warren, T. (2000). 'Technology Solutions for a Global Business.' Presentation available at http://ons2000.ons.no/papers/twarren.pdf.
15. Hamel, G. (1999). 'Bringing Silicon Valley Inside.' *Harvard Business Review*, September/October: 71–84.
16. Kelley, T. (2001). *The Art of Innovation: Lessons in Creativity from IDEO, America's Leading Design Firm.* London, HarperCollinsBusiness.

17. Taylor, W.C. and LaBarre, P. (2006). *Mavericks at Work*. London, HarperCollins.

18. Gould, M., Stanford, M. and Blackmon, K. (1994, revised in 2002). 'Revolution at Oticon A/S: The Spaghetti Organization.' IMD Case No. IMD-4-0235.

19. Refer to http://www.bbc.co.uk/crime/caseclosed/nickleeson.shtml.

20. Quote from ABC's *Nightline* TV program series: 'The Deep Dive' dedicated to IDEO's innovation approach. Video obtainable from: http://www.abcnews.com.

21. Harryson, S.J. (2000/2002). *Managing Know-Who Based Companies*. Northampton, Edward Elgar.

22. Barwise, P. and Meehan, S. (2004). *Simply Better: Winning and Keeping Customers by Delivering What Matters Most*. Boston, Harvard Business School Press.

23. Kim, C.W. and Mauborgne, R. (1997). 'Value Innovation: The Strategic Logic of High Growth.' *Harvard Business Review*, January–February: 103–112.

24. Kim, C.W. and Mauborgne, R. (2006). *Blue Ocean Strategy: How to Create Uncontested Market Space and Make the Competition Irrelevant*. Boston, Harvard Business School Press.

25. Kumar, N. (2004). *Marketing as a Strategy*. Boston, Harvard Business School Press, pp. 177–210.

26. Heskett, J.L., Sasser Jr., E.W., Schlesinger, L.A. (1994). 'People, Service, Success: Listening to Customers.' Harvard Business School video, Boston. Video obtainable from: http://harvardbusinessonline.hbsp.harvard.edu.

27. Deschamps, J.-P. and Pahwa, A. (2003). 'Innovation Leadership at Logitech.' IMD Case No. IMD-3-1337, updated and edited by Daniel Borel in November 2007, reproduced with permission.

28. Deschamps, J.-P. and Barnett-Berg, M. (2005). 'Logitech: Learning from Customers to Design New Products.' IMD Case No. IMD-5-0679.

29. Research conducted by the author in the 1980s and 1990s, together with a number of colleagues at consulting firm Arthur D. Little, led to the creation of a proprietary diagnostic tool and approach – the 'innovation climate index.'

# CHAPTER 4

# STEERING INNOVATION TOP DOWN

*[Traditional] professional management isn't going to give you the kind of growth you need in a slow-growth world . . . Our challenge is to take nanotechnology into the future. We've got to do personalized medicine. We've got to do renewable energy!*

*Jeff Immelt*[1]
*CEO of General Electric*

Chapter 3 highlighted how innovation leaders can actively encourage spontaneous, unplanned bottom-up innovation. Most recognize that breakthroughs, at times, occur through a combination of serendipity and entrepreneurship. But all-round innovation leaders do not want to rely only on these hard-to-manage factors. They are not resigned to seeing their role restricted to a kind of benign laissez-faire, i.e. to hiring creative people, giving them the freedom to experiment and launch projects, and hoping that somehow innovation will emerge! Well-rounded innovation leaders can be deterministic and will not hesitate to get involved personally in several ways:

• First, they believe that innovation benefits from proactive management. If innovation begins to disappear off the company's radar screen, they will quickly get it back on management's agenda – for them innovation is a competitive necessity.

- Second, they see innovation as a cross-functional process that only happens when specific responsibilities are allocated and progress tracked. They set up a process, a governance system and organizational mechanisms to make it happen, top down.
- Third, they recognize that innovation is not just the responsibility of a few specialized functions, like Marketing or R&D. It is a company-wide effort that must be continuously encouraged and developed with innovation-enhancing campaigns.
- Finally, they see innovation as the best way to grow and seize emerging market opportunities. They get personally involved with high impact innovation projects: visioning, launching, steering and coaching these efforts. They get personally involved in innovation searches and projects.

## SEEING INNOVATION AS A COMPETITIVE NECESSITY

Many companies that are thriving today began by coming up with an innovative product or service. Innovation was their founding process and probably ranked high among their early managers' preoccupations. Over time, however, as companies grow and structure themselves, their initial innovation instinct and attention tends to weaken. Innovation gradually becomes only one of the company's supporting activities, no longer its raison d'être. It is confined to specific functional departments – usually R&D and Marketing or New Business Development.

Occasionally, a number of threatening external events or internal issues can induce senior managers to bring innovation once again to the top of the corporate agenda. Such revivals are often fueled by a pressing vision – a competitive necessity. This often occurs when someone new arrives – a dynamic new CTO or CEO with a strong belief that innovation is the best organic growth engine. Some of the big innovation drives that have made the headlines were tied to the arrival of a new CEO. Think of Steve Jobs returning to Apple, Jeffrey Immelt's rise to the top spot at GE as well as A.G. Lafley at P&G.

Such cycles in the perceived importance of innovation – sometimes 'on,' other times 'off' – are rare in technology-intensive companies that operate in a hyper-competitive market environment. These companies cannot afford to lose track of their innovation imperative. Their challenge is to keep innovation constantly at the top of their management agenda and to keep improving even after the company has reached a leadership position, just to stay in the race.

## Bringing/Keeping Innovation on the Top Management Agenda

When growth rates flatten or competition gets tough, most CEOs look to energize their organizations and ramp up the pursuit of new innovation pathways, both internally and externally. Senior executives view innovation as an acute strategic imperative and understand fortifying efforts in this area guards against external market threats and can improve performance internally.

Through observation, analysis or intuition, good corporate leaders are normally able to sense all kinds of threatening market or competitive developments early on and to react to them. Innovation leaders generally go further and propose an innovation response to these situations.

### Deploying Innovation in Response to External Threats

Severe threats to future profits or growth are powerful management incentives to reassess a company's innovation strategy and process. Four types of threats typically trigger such revivals:

#### Threat 1: Disruptive technology

The most dramatic threat is the challenge of a disruptive technology being brought to market by a competitor or a new industry entrant. When the survival of a company is at risk, management must come up with a strong innovation response. Often, the challenge appears at the industry level and calls for a rapid and drastic reappraisal of past strategies, technological investments and traditional approaches. A good illustration of this threat is the rapid displacement of silver halide photography by digital cameras and web-based photo diffusion. At Kodak and Fuji, it triggered a dramatic increase in the attention and focus given to innovation, and a complete mobilization of these organizations behind a new digital vision.

## Threat 2: Performance erosion

Less traumatic but equally worrisome for management is a gradual but steady erosion of market share and profitability, often owing to the arrival of more innovation-effective competitors. This type of threat is severely affecting US and European volume car manufacturers today. All are struggling to meet the uncanny market acumen and product development effectiveness of Japanese and Korean competitors. The current crisis experienced by GM and Ford in the US is further amplified since their main competitor, Toyota, is also the originator of a disruptive technology with its hybrid engines. Only a major innovation drive coupled with a change in strategy will revive the fortunes of these struggling giants. Medtronic's innovation revival journey, featured in Chapter 7, started from the same realization: The company was losing ground to new competitors in an industry it had invented – cardiac pacemakers – and it needed to boost its innovation effectiveness by a quantum leap.

## Threat 3: Commoditization

The third type of threat is the gradual commoditization of products or services. It pervades many industries, even in growth sectors, when novelty factors wear off and intense competition leads to drastic price-cutting campaigns. The situation is aggravated when investments in production capacity only come in large chunky bits like the current PDP and LCD technologies in the flat-screen display industry.[2] Former Japanese leaders, such as Sharp and Matsushita/Panasonic are being forced to launch yet another innovation drive just to stay in the race with their Korean and Taiwanese competitors, who in turn are not remaining idle as they see mainland Chinese competitors tooling up. All are intensifying their R&D efforts and directing their process innovation endeavors toward cost reduction and yield optimization.

### Threat 4: Stock market pressure

While this last type of threat may be subtle, it still puts the spotlight on a company's innovation performance. Depressed share prices are indeed a strong reminder to management that stock markets are merciless in cases of lack of growth – think of the punishment taken by pharmaceutical share prices when companies miss a Federal Drug Administration (FDA) approval deadline. This type of pressure remains constant in traditional industries like foods and beverages, particularly as the acquisition route shows limits in terms of potential returns. Coca-Cola felt this type of stress after analysts perceived that it had lost its growth momentum and botched its European entry into bottled water with Dasani. Unilever is under a similar pressure and has yet to launch a major innovation drive to support its 'path for growth' agenda.

## Considering Innovation as an Internal Necessity

Innovation will get back on top of the corporate agenda without any particular external threat if management believes (with conviction) that it will bring the company significant market, competitive and internal benefits. In such cases, management ambitions are the trigger for an innovation drive.

### Ambition 1: Changing the rules of the game

By instinct, innovation leaders constantly look for opportunities to gain competitive advantage through innovation. They intuitively search for better ways to win in their industry. This kind of attitude is probably what induced A.G. Lafley at P&G to introduce his new 'connect & develop' innovation program. His innovation vision combined two complementary thrusts that were radically new to most other players in the fast-moving consumer goods industry:

(1) Introduce products that bring new and real value by focusing on the attributes wanted by consumers and not met by competitors. For example new product packages for household cleaning products that deliver a measured amount to the exact spot, thus increasing consumer friendliness.
(2) Increase the number of innovative concepts deployed by the company and shorten their time to market by exposing R&D and Marketing to various external technologies and ideas.

### Ambition 2: Reaching organizational excellence

Innovation leaders may also embark on a renewed innovation initiative simply out of a desire to increase their organizational effectiveness. Senior managers are often shocked to see innovation functioning suboptimally in their organization. As a result, they will search for ways to improve the processes used to develop new products and increase the time/cost effectiveness of their R&D investments and efforts. They will be motivated to reach the same level of effectiveness in their innovation process as they have achieved in other areas of the organization.

Tetra Pak provides a good example of this kind of inclination. It initiated a company-wide innovation campaign with a single overarching objective: Achieve excellence in a process judged critical for the company's future. Senior Tetra Pak leaders were not directly reacting to any specific and direct competitive threat. However, they knew that increasing competition in their core market – packaging for ambient milk and juice – would erode their margins over time unless they found new, attractive and cost-efficient packaging solutions for their customers. The company had a strong R&D culture from its innovative past, but management was aware that the resources being spent on new products were not always productive. Tetra Pak's extensive corporate innovation effort aimed to put the company among the 'best-in-class' innovators in its industry and safeguard against competitive market threats to its future.

## Ambition 3: Motivating and mobilizing people

Most innovation leaders instinctively know that mobilizing people on an innovation agenda generally has a motivational effect on their internal staff. Putting the emphasis on innovation sends a positive message. It galvanizes people by authorizing them to question the status quo and encouraging them to contribute. It motivates everyone to meet an exciting goal and challenge. Finally, it may help recruiting efforts, especially in industries that compete for talent, by reinforcing the company's image as a cutting-edge employer.

## Seeing Innovation as the Only Sustainable Strategy

As we have discussed, some companies embark on innovation in response to particular threatening situations; others adopt innovation as their core strategy and process. The latter have gone beyond the stage of having to mobilize their staff on a formal innovation-boosting exercise, simply because their management is constantly in search of more effective ways to manage innovation. Their leaders are day-to-day innovation practitioners and behave like 'innovation activists.' They don't have to put innovation on top of the corporate agenda − it is there permanently! In such companies, innovation is everyone's No. 1 priority.

There are multiple drivers of this type of obsession. Two, however, are prevalent: The speed of competitive and technological developments, on the one hand, and the amplitude of industry and technology cycles or waves, on the other hand.

## Rapid technological change

Companies in consumer electronics, information technology, telecommunications, medical technology and ethical pharmaceuticals, among others, are all driven by a frantic pace of technology and product development and an intense degree of competition. In these sectors, you win or lose by your ability to:

(1) stay ahead of and implement each new technology wave;
(2) constantly update a promising product development pipeline.

These efforts keep innovation at the top of management's concerns. Companies in these industries are under permanent pressure to reassess their innovation process in order to improve the quality and increase the speed of their new product introductions.

Logitech, featured in Chapter 11, provides a good example of a company condemned to innovate as fast as its large (Microsoft) and nimble (American or Asian) competitors. Logitech's senior executives never bother to regulate in detail how the company should go about developing innovative new products. A few fundamental behavioral and process rules have been established regarding the adoption of external technology or the structuring of project pathways. Engineering and marketing managers have been given an incredible amount of freedom to invent new ways to be more efficient and stay ahead of the competition. Innovation has always permeated the Logitech culture!

## Long and powerful technology waves

Innovation has become, by necessity, a core process in another group of industries – those that may not be as fast paced but still experience significant technology waves. Semiconductors, medical imaging and high-tech materials are examples of this category. Participants in these industries face the permanent challenge of detecting and investing in the next technology waves early enough to build the necessary capabilities and be seen as first movers in the new marketplace.

In summary, whatever the triggering factor – external threat, internal ambition or way of life in their industry – many companies embrace innovation as a core process. Their management feels the same pressing obligation to achieve a quantum leap in R&D and innovation effectiveness to keep their lead, or regain it if it has been lost. When innovation spirit and momentum have been lost, innovation leaders need to mobilize the organization top down and launch an innovation-enhancing campaign.

## Formulating an Innovation Vision and Strategy

Preston Bottger, cited in Chapter 1, suggested that senior executives play their leadership role to the full when they provide their staff with a clear:

- Sense of purpose – why do we need to do certain things?
- Sense of direction – which way should we go? And
- Sense of focus – what should and will be our priorities?

These three elements are fundamental for innovation leaders wishing to start a top-down innovation drive.

Presenting innovation as a competitive necessity – irrespective of whether it is triggered by threats or opportunities – and listing all good reasons to engage in a new (or revived) innovation drive, is the way for many innovation leaders to give their staff a *sense of purpose*. When it is directly tied to market battles – a connection that is relatively easy to achieve – innovation ceases to be a vague goal and becomes a condition for survival on which everyone can be mobilized.

Providing both a *sense of direction and focus* for innovation is a much more complex task for innovation leaders, because it means formulating a compelling innovation vision and strategy. Few management teams seem to have taken that step convincingly. Those who have, like A.G. Lafley at P&G, Steve Jobs at Apple, or Larry Page and Sergey Brin at Google, have been celebrated like exceptional visionaries. A clear sense of direction and focus is essential for top-down innovation, for sure. But it is also useful for bottom-up innovation because it channels the organization's creative energy toward desired areas, removing the risks of 'random,' and hence irrelevant or low priority, innovation.

This aspect is so important that it deserves a chapter to itself. Chapter 6 – 'Recognizing the Leadership Imperatives of Your Innovation Strategy' – will propose a high level framework to classify generic innovation thrusts and understand what leaders have to do to implement their chosen innovation strategy.

## SETTING UP A PROCESS, GOVERNANCE SYSTEM AND ORGANIZATIONAL MECHANISMS

One of the first tasks of the senior leadership team is to ensure that the company manages innovation proactively as a process. Although this theme was amply covered in a previous book,[3] it may be useful to remind the reader of what it really means in practice. Concretely, it implies adopting the classic guidelines of good process management and adapting them to innovation. This requires the establishment of dedicated process management guidelines and mechanisms.

### Process Management Guidelines

Innovation, like all corporate processes, should be managed formally, and this implies respecting five broad imperatives, summarized below:

### *Imperative 1: Unbundle and Map the Process*

The problem with innovation – as with many other complex, cross-functional processes – is that few managers are able to see and understand the entire process picture, which weakens their ability to plan and contribute in a broad context. Typically, most managers only see their part of the process. Managing innovation requires helping everyone in the organization take a high level view of the process to understand:

- The overall process architecture;
- The various process steps or phases;
- The input and output of each step; and
- The way the various steps are interconnected.

This requires the adoption of a common company-wide process model, template and terminology, while accepting specific imple-

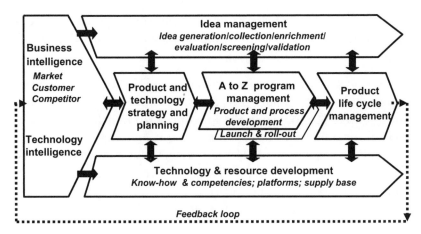

**Figure 4.1**  Innovation process model

mentation variants reflecting differences across business units. The universal model that I advocate (refer to Figure 4.1) is simple and comprehensive as it extends beyond the traditional new product development (NPD) process, both upstream and downstream. It shows innovation as a set of ongoing, interlocking and dynamic sub-processes.

## Imperative 2: Allocate Clear Process Management Responsibilities

Companies that have adopted a process management philosophy know that processes, like functions, need to be explicitly managed. This applies of course to the innovation process and its sub-elements. Senior management needs to ask three kinds of questions:

- Who should be in charge of each sub-process within the overall innovation framework? Have we appointed appropriate 'process owners'?
- Who should empower, supervise and advise the process owners, once appointed? Have we identified committed process coaches or sponsors?

- Who should orchestrate it all and integrate all the sub-processes? How and to whom should we entrust the overall management of innovation?

Process owners will typically be distinct and dedicated individuals, responsible for developing the process (if it does not already exist), documenting it, mobilizing the line organization behind its implementation, supporting it and improving it continuously.

Process coaches are expected to empower process owners, i.e. give them the necessary authority to intervene in areas beyond their own organizational boundaries. They should audit the process, supervise and support improvement initiatives. Process coaching tasks can be allocated either to individuals or cross-functional 'bodies,' which then become collectively accountable for the process. For example, the chief technology officer (CTO) will often coach most, if not all, of the technology-related process owners. By contrast, it might be difficult to entrust supervision of the idea management process to a single individual. A cross-functional 'Innovation Council' may be a better alternative. A classic allocation of process management responsibilities is briefly outlined in Figure 4.2.

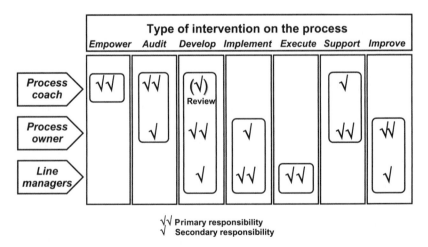

**Figure 4.2** Process management responsibilities

| Indicators | Stage 1 Missing | Stage 2 Chaotic | Stage 3 Described | Stage 4 Controlled | Stage 5 Managed | Stage 6 Optimized |
|---|---|---|---|---|---|---|
| • Process awareness widely shared | NO | YES | YES | YES | YES | YES |
| • Process mapped and understood | NO | PARTLY | YES | YES | YES | YES |
| • Process owner and coach in place | NO | PARTLY | YES | YES | YES | YES |
| • Resources (people, funds) available | NO | PARTLY | PARTLY | YES | YES | YES |
| • Competencies and tools available | NO | NO | PARTLY | YES | YES | YES |
| • Process performance measured | NO | NO | PARTLY | PARTLY | YES | YES |
| • Problem anticipation and solving in place | NO | NO | NO | NO | PARTLY | YES |
| • Problem prevention in place | NO | NO | NO | NO | NO | YES |

Freely adapted from Watts Humphrey's
Capability Maturity Model

**Figure 4.3**   Process maturity stages

## Imperative 3: Assess and Improve Each Sub-Process

Once the innovation process has been defined in terms of content and boundaries and management responsibilities have been allocated, senior executives should ask process owners and coaches to launch an audit of their process. It is indeed useful to start a process improvement drive with a realistic understanding of the maturity stage of each process.

There are different ways to judge the level of development or maturity of a process. A convenient scale can be created by adapting to the innovation process the famous Capability Maturity Model (CMM) developed by the Software Engineering Institute.[4] Figure 4.3 summarizes the criteria that could be used for that purpose and it defines six different maturity stages. Essentially, each process management team should be ready to answer the following questions: Is the particular innovation sub-process for which I am responsible:

- Missing altogether?
- Existing but chaotic?
- Defined and described?

- Controlled and measured?
- Managed?
- Optimized?

Concretely, the evaluation of each innovation sub-process should cover:

- The adequacy of the input to the process: Do we have the right resources to conduct the process effectively, in terms of people involved, information sources and budget?
- The efficacy of the process itself: How well are we handling the process in terms of sequencing of the various tasks, the value and timeliness of our activities and of our internal communications?
- The quality of the deliverables of the process: How well does our process deliver what is expected from it, in terms of output quality, timeliness and cost efficiency?

Once an assessment has been made and validated by their coach, process owners will need to prepare an improvement plan for their process. They will mobilize teams of line managers to invent – if it does not already exist – redesign or even rethink their process. It is, of course, a good habit to start the improvement drive with an external benchmarking exercise to identify best practices.

### Imperative 4: Use Cross-Functional Teams Throughout

If there is one fundamental imperative in innovation, it is the fact that the process and all its elements must be managed by cross-functional teams. In fact, hardly a single sub-process highlighted in Figure 4.1 is purely functional. This principle is now well accepted for program and project management, but it is valid for some of the front-end processes as well, which, on paper, could be perceived as belonging to either Marketing or R&D.

- The business intelligence process, for example, should not be the sole preserve of marketing. This is true even though marketing research specialists play a key role in providing tools, training staff from other functions in interviewing techniques, organizing well run focus groups and helping to analyze findings. Business intelligence is a process that should involve *everyone* in the organization.

- Technology intelligence will naturally be dominated by scientists and engineers from R&D who will act as 'technology gatekeepers' in their discipline areas. But it should also involve manufacturing-engineering for process technologies as well as information systems specialists for information technologies.
- The technology resource development process, likewise, should not be left entirely in the hands of technology specialists. Whether or not to invest in particular technologies, outsource a given technology or to develop in-house are choices of considerable strategic importance and business managers should stay involved.
- Idea management is also a cross-functional process, as it is now well proven that a diversity of perspectives enriches the quality of ideas generated and the rigor with which they are evaluated and ultimately retained. Since R&D tends to be more advanced than marketing in creativity techniques, often the idea management process owner comes from R&D.
- Finally, product and technology strategy and planning are, by their very nature, cross functional processes since the two aspects are interdependent, whether technology is perceived as driving the product strategy or vice versa.

### Imperative 5: Set up and Track Indicators of Process Performance

When innovation is organized top down, management will want to measure progress on a regular basis. Process-oriented organizations know the importance of choosing a few meaningful indicators – not too many – picked out of the four categories of indicators:

- Lagging indicators, which measure the results of past actions. They are generally the most commonly used, often because they are the easiest to measure.

- Leading indicators, which track activities that are assumed to have an impact on future results. They are less frequently used.
- In-process indicators, which characterize compliance with process performance targets. They are frequently measured by process-oriented companies.
- Learning indicators, which reflect the speed with which progress is accomplished in a number of critical areas. Few companies use them systematically.

Figure 4.4 presents some commonly used indicators in each of these four categories.

## Process Management Mechanisms

Innovation leaders know that the classic management mechanisms of their company – think of the various committees and task forces that proliferate in most organizations – have not been conceived to steer and manage innovation. Innovation is, a complex, multi-faceted and cross-functional process combining highly creative elements and disciplined activities. It requires specific management mechanisms.

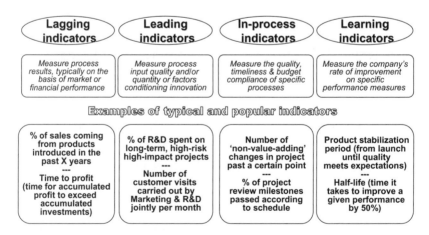

**Figure 4.4**  Indicators of process performance

Appointing dedicated process owners is a first necessary step, but it is not sufficient. Process coaching responsibilities need to be allocated, either to individual senior managers or to collective groups of managers. In addition, other mechanisms may have to be created to handle the execution of specific processes. Finally, as indicated earlier, management needs to decide who is going to orchestrate the entire process. Choosing the right mechanisms – for each individual process and overall to steer innovation top down – is an important task of innovation leaders.

## Different Mechanisms for Different Types of Processes

Processes – and this applies to all the innovation sub-processes – fall into three broad categories with very different characteristics and requirements, and hence distinct management mechanisms:

### Discrete processes

Processes of a set duration, with a clear beginning and end, can be described as discrete. Most of the special assignments entrusted to project teams or innovation task forces follow a discrete process pattern. In the field of innovation, the ubiquitous project, whether set up around a research topic, a product development undertaking or a market exploration mission, is the perfect example of such a process.

The mechanisms traditionally used to handle discrete processes are well known: They comprise the project management organization and cross-functional teams. In fact, there are not many good ways to manage a discrete process other than to set up a project. Project managers or leaders are appointed for the duration of the project, either from a pool of dedicated project handling specialists or from the line organization. They assemble a cross-functional project group and work together as a team toward their objective.

### Recurring processes

Like discrete processes, recurring processes have a beginning and an end, but their activities tend to be repeated over time at different intervals. The archetype of a recurring management process is budgeting – it follows a well-established ritual at a specific period in the year. In innovation, too, there are several recurring processes – and sub-processes. It is through recurring processes that:

- business intelligence specialists condense the key findings of their research at periodic intervals;
- ideas that have accumulated in the company's idea bank get evaluated, screened and programmed;
- product and technology strategies are formulated or revised, then translated into concrete product and R&D roadmaps or plans; and
- projects are reviewed at important scheduled toll gate meetings during which they receive both the go-ahead and the resources they need.

Recurring processes generally need to be entrusted to dedicated cross-functional groups of individuals empowered to handle the process on behalf of management. Many of these ad hoc mechanisms are called committees. For example the product committee determines which new products ought to be introduced when – a key element of the product strategy and planning process.

But the term 'committee' tends to be used loosely. As a result the word does not convey a clear image to its members or to the company at large. Is a committee entrusted with executive authority? An advisory mission? Or a coordination role? This is why I advocate designating the exact role and level of empowerment these mechanisms hold.

- For example, the term 'board' should be used for those highly empowered mechanisms with an executive mission. Calling the group of senior managers in charge of the product and technology strategy and planning process the 'strategy board' gives it immediate recognition as a high level decision making body. A similar sense of authority will be conveyed to the mechanism responsible for reviewing and approving projects at toll gates if it is called the 'program review board.'
- The word 'council' should be used, by contrast, for all the advisory mechanisms that abound around the innovation

process. Unlike boards, councils do not take business decisions; they make recommendations to management. This is why many companies have created technology councils with external advisers to guide senior management on its technology investment decisions. Similarly, marketing councils gather market company representatives to provide guidance on product choices or launch policies. Innovation councils are sometimes created to evaluate and recommend new product ideas to management.

- Finally, 'coordination groups' describes the organizational bodies that management entrusts with coordination missions across functional, operational and business unit or geographic boundary lines.

## Ongoing processes

By definition, ongoing processes are supposed to be permanently activated, not recurring in successive cycles. For example, the collection of business intelligence or the generation of ideas should belong to the ongoing process category. They need to go on permanently. Customer or competitor insights should be generated everyday by almost everyone, as should ideas for innovative new products. Of course there will be regular recurring cycles for the analysis and consolidation of these insights as well as for the evaluation and selection of ideas, but their generation and collection should be ongoing.

Managing ongoing processes is a major challenge as it has to be integrated in the day-to-day mission of managers. New organizational mechanisms need to be put in place to steer these processes, particularly the intelligence process. They often take the form of 'networks' of field resources who volunteer to perform intelligence gathering functions in addition to and as part of their normal job. Intelligence networks need to be facilitated by dedicated 'network animators,' responsible for extracting and analyzing the data, information, insights and foresight generated. Therefore, in addition to current marketing functions, management ought to consider setting up several types of intelligence management mechanisms:

- Networks of 'market sniffers' to detect emerging and unarticulated customer needs and critical market or product issues, as perceived by customers;
- Networks of 'competitor scouts,' responsible for anticipating future competitors' moves, each network focusing on a specific actor;
- Networks of technology gatekeepers, each gatekeeper being assigned to monitor technology trends in a particular scientific or engineering area.[5]

The organization of these mechanisms can be entrusted to a dedicated innovation intelligence support function, sometimes called 'advanced marketing' – advanced because it should think ahead!

To sum up, Figure 4.5 presents various mechanisms that companies have implemented to manage each of their innovation sub-processes. Arguably, no single known company has implemented all of these mechanisms given the fact that few companies manage all these sub-processes formally. The important thing for management is to decide which processes it should focus on and which mechanisms are most adapted to stimulating and steering these processes.

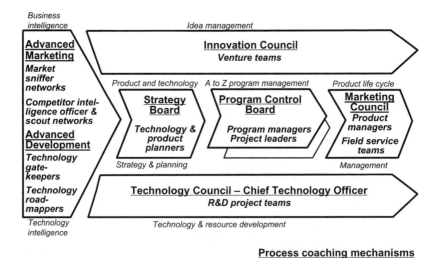

**Figure 4.5** Innovation management mechanisms

## Governance Mechanism to Steer the Innovation Process as a Whole

Setting up effective mechanisms to manage the various innovation sub-processes is critically important, but so is the integration of all these elements into a single seamless and repeatable process. The challenge for top management is to decide who should integrate, orchestrate and conduct the overall innovation effort of the company. This question often remains unanswered or at least incompletely addressed.

A wrong answer – yet one frequently found in large companies – is to consider that innovation has scientific and technical processes, which can be entrusted to the CTO or CRO, and commercial processes, which belong to the Marketing or Business Development functions. This splitting of innovation into two functional camps is dangerous because it can encourage a silo mentality between the business and technical sides of the company. As stated earlier in this chapter, innovation and *all* its processes are fundamentally cross-functional and so cannot be apportioned among functions.

The experience of successful innovative companies indicates that three options can be contemplated for governing and managing the process in an integrated fashion.

### Option 1: Appointment of an independent 'innovation officer' (or manager)

Some companies have implemented this solution with success. Others have tried it and quickly abandoned it when it did not work well. The task of orchestrating the entire process across business units, functions and geographical market areas is highly challenging. It is a daunting task, both in its magnitude – i.e. the breadth of its coverage – and its sometimes sensitive political implications (because the innovation officer will often have to interfere with the line organization.) The risk is also that the rest of the organization sees the appointment of an innovation officer as a way for the top management team to delegate the task to a specialist down the hierarchy and hence to stop being actively involved.

Companies that have made this solution work well internally have succeeded because their appointment of an overall innovation officer met three important conditions. Indeed, based on their experience, the function and its holder will be accepted:

(1) If the company has an established tradition and culture of process orientation from top to bottom. Then managers are likely to understand what it means to manage a process. They will value and respect the role played by a dedicated process owner, even if he/she intervenes in their business and organization.

(2) If the innovation officer is perceived to have strong support from the CEO and the top management team. This status can be reflected in the title, reporting relationship and membership of key management groups, as well as vocal senior management support and actions. Without top management support, it becomes 'mission impossible.'

(3) If the senior manager chosen for the role has an impressive personal track record in innovation; a cross-functional and business-oriented perspective; political sensibilities; and lots of contagious energy. The appointment of a manager with the wrong or a weak profile will discredit the function.

## Option 2: Extension of the job of the CTO

Many Japanese technology-intensive companies have adopted what could be considered a variant of the first option by entrusting the entire process to their CTO (often called chief engineer in Japan). These talented senior individuals definitely meet the three conditions described above, particularly regarding their track-record – they are often chosen from among the notoriously accomplished 'fathers' of the company's biggest and most successful innovation projects. They are also always important members of their top management team.

This option is quite different from the solution that was dismissed earlier in this chapter, i.e. that of appointing two simultaneous owners – a CTO dealing with the technical side of innovation and a business manager addressing the commercial side. Under this solution, the chief technology officer becomes the de facto boss of the *whole process*, including its commercial aspects. This is conceivable only if the CTO in question is totally aware of the commercial and strategic aspects of the business, which is often the case with Japanese chief engineers. Unlike some of their Western counterparts, Japanese CTOs integrate the business and competitive dimensions into their equation. In technologically advanced companies, particularly if the CEO is a sales-oriented person, CTOs feel responsible for charting the innovation route for years to come. They therefore embody and oversee the innovation process, both in terms of methods and content.

## Option 3: Establishment of a collective management body: The 'innovation board'

This solution has been adopted less frequently than the other two, yet it is probably the most natural way to overcome the challenge of entrusting a complex cross-functional process to a single individual. An 'innovation board,' particularly if created at a high level in the organization and it reports to top management, is indeed a vehicle to promote:

- collective leadership and shared accountability for this critical process;
- ongoing, open communications with all stakeholders; and
- continuity in leadership, despite occasional changes in membership.

The innovation board should be responsible for developing, steering and perfecting the process of innovation in the company and overseeing its culture and climate. It should not interfere directly with the content of innovation, i.e. with specific decisions regarding new projects and new businesses, which should remain the preserve of the line organization.

Members of the innovation board should be selected from among the company's recognized champions of innovation, preferably representing its key businesses and functions. Senior human resources and corporate communications officers should be invited to join, given their role in mobilizing managers and ensuring that they embrace and support the innovation agenda.

The decision as to who should chair the innovation board is an important one. At the start, if management is really serious about putting innovation on every manager's agenda, then the CEO would be an ideal choice. His/her presence will naturally realign the rest of the management team behind that priority. Once the board is active, a change is possible and a new chair could be either the most senior technology officer (advisable in technology-intensive companies) or a senior business manager with strong innovation credentials.

## MOBILIZING PEOPLE ON INNOVATION-ENHANCING CAMPAIGNS

Senior managers faced with the need to trigger an innovation-revival movement in their company may feel hesitant about what to do concretely, particularly if the company is starting almost from scratch without any innovation infrastructure or many ingrained habits! Where and how to start? How to rebuild lost momentum top down?

The experience of companies that have successfully revived innovation, after years of benign neglect, points to a number of lessons. In most cases, these companies have followed a pragmatic step-by-step approach to mobilize their staff, starting at the top. Consciously or intuitively, they have applied a systematic process and some of the key principles of change management. Their journey and success factors are summarized below.

### Adopting a Step-by-Step Mobilization Approach

### Step 1: Selecting and Appointing a Small 'Innovation Steering Group'

In companies that are really starting from scratch, or those that want to rethink entirely how they go about innovation, management may rightly assume that innovation is everyone's job, but de facto that means that it is nobody's specific responsibility. This does not make it easy to start an innovation drive. As a consequence, the top management team should first select a small group of high level, strongly motivated and cross-functional executives – the future innovation leadership team – and entrust them with the mission of designing an innovation-boosting program.

This small innovation steering group should have four characteristics:

(1) It should be small, i.e. between three (minimum) and five or six (maximum) people to be able to work together informally;
(2) Its members should be credible and empowered. The chair person – if not all members – should come from the top management team;
(3) Its members should be highly motivated, energetic and total believers in the importance of innovation and determined to make things happen;
(4) It should be cross-functional and include representatives from business units as well as from central functions (like R&D, Marketing and/or HR).

## Step 2: Entrusting Four Preparatory Tasks to the Innovation Steering Group

Going public with the implementation of an innovation-boosting program should only happen when management is ready. So, the initial mission of the innovation steering group should be to work, essentially alone, on the following tasks:

### Task 1: Choose and define an innovation process model and philosophy

The innovation steering group should first agree on what innovation means for the company and define its various constituents, i.e. the sub-processes that it includes and their boundaries. The high level model for innovation proposed in Figure 4.1 can be used as a starting point. It should also ascertain the company-specific drivers of innovation, in terms of both process and culture. This exercise of defining and modeling innovation can be done in two complementary ways:

(1) by sharing personal experiences and ideas in the group, and agreeing on the model that best suits the company's current environment; and

(2) by discovering, and adapting to the organization's needs, what other relevant companies have done – and this means benchmarking.

### Task 2: Conduct a pragmatic innovation diagnostic to identify priorities

Next, the Innovation Steering Group will need to conduct a 'quick and dirty' diagnostic of the current status of innovation in the company, identifying broad deficiencies in process and culture, key obstacles to innovation and obvious change priorities. This preliminary diagnostic is best done through a number of one-to-one interviews with representatives of key functions and business units. Interviews will make it possible to understand not only the root causes of the problems that need to be addressed but also possible change avenues. The end result of this preliminary diagnostic should be a list of improvement priorities, categorized for both the short and long term. Selecting priorities can be done rather quickly by determining:

(1) the culture and process issues that seem to be the most critical for innovation in the company;

(2) the ones that appear to be the most broken or deficient; and

(3) the ones that, intuitively, seem to be the easiest to fix.

Low-hanging fruits will be found at the intersection of these three parameters as shown in Figure 4.6.

### Task 3: Propose specific process management responsibilities

Improvement programs may need to be launched in different areas simultaneously and this means appointing the first process owners and coaches for specific improvement projects. At the start, the number of management responsibilities to be allocated will be limited because only a few processes will emerge as priorities. But the choice of managers to be appointed by the senior management

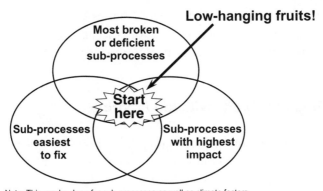

Note: This can be done for sub-processes as well as climate factors

**Figure 4.6**    Selecting innovation improvement priorities

team is critical, as these managers will have to move things forward at a brisk pace without much support. The more senior and energetic they are, the better the chance of their success.

When significant resources to implement specific change programs become necessary, then the mechanisms that have been put in place will need to be beefed up and empowered. The initial innovation steering group may well have to be extended, in terms of functional and geographical membership, to involve a broader range of managers with personal stakes in the improvement projects. The innovation steering group can then be turned into an innovation board. Appointing such a high-powered and visible innovation management mechanism is the surest way to convey two important messages to the organization:

(1) Innovation is such a critical process that it needs to be steered and supported on an ongoing basis and at a high level.
(2) Innovation is a process that pervades all of the company's disciplines, functions and geographical markets.

*Task 4: Suggest a change program to get started with concrete actions*

To be balanced, the program should include a combination of actions with a relatively quick payout – the low-hanging fruits – as well as actions with a longer-term impact. Best practice companies have included in the second category things such as the establishment of an intranet-based innovation management and tracking tool or the launch of mindset-changing management development programs.

### Step 3: Going Public with the Program

Once at least some of the preparatory tasks above have been accomplished, management should be able to mobilize a broader group of managers and initiate specific programs. One of the best ways to go public is to gather a wider group of managers at a corporate conference focused on innovation. Such a conference should bring together managers from the second and third lines of command, those whom top management perceives as the future second wave of innovation champions. These managers should be asked to cascade the message down in their own departments or operating units. Conservatives and skeptics should not be included in such a gathering as its purpose should be to obtain commitments.

### Step 4: Implementing Change Actions

There are many options regarding where to start and what to do in practice. The limit is the level of ambitiousness of the management team and their willingness to dedicate resources to this type of innovation-boosting program. In general, these actions can be classified into three broad categories:

#### Actions focusing on building an innovation process

They deal with the recognition that innovation is one of the company's core processes and thus needs to be managed formally. Typical actions include:

- appointing process owners for each of the main sub-processes within innovation and starting serious process improvement actions;
- agreeing on and implementing a number of innovation-specific indicators, and initiating systematic tracking of these indicators;

- establishing an intranet-based innovation site for sharing project information and supporting specific processes.

### Actions dealing with innovation culture and mindset

They deal with the softer aspects of innovation and the general attitude of the various management layers regarding innovation. Typical actions include:

- creating a specific task force to identify and address softer or cultural obstacles to innovation (in terms of management attitudes, policies or process);
- staging 'mobilization events' (innovation forums, innovation prizes and awards, etc.) to capture people's imaginations and unleash their enthusiastic cooperation;
- organizing seminars on innovation management, gathering managers from different business or organizational units to share experience and ideas.

### Tangible innovation-enhancing projects with, hopefully, a quick payback

They may deal with a variety of concrete benefits linked to specific aspects of the innovation process, such as:

- initiating a 'learning from customers' or 'lead user' program for a specific market application, to identify breakthrough opportunities;
- creating a short idea management training seminar that could be rolled out systematically across various operating units;
- starting a cross-functional lead-time reduction drive (from need identification to market roll-out).

## Respecting the Conditions of Effective Change Management Programs

The practical experience of companies that have successfully carried out an internal growth and innovation drive teaches us a few basic lessons on the key requirements for the success of this type of program. In many ways, these lessons are not unique to innovation drives; they apply equally to all change management efforts.

## Showing Indefatigable Top Management Commitment

The first condition for success is the obvious importance of demonstrating *strong and lasting commitment* to this endeavor from the senior management ranks. The 'killer' for all change initiatives is the perception that this is the latest 'management fad of the month' – unlikely to stick and not worth worrying about! Managers will obviously do, or pretend to do, something to show their loyalty to the initiative, but deep down it will be 'business as usual,' and they will ensure that they meet the traditional performance measures the company has always measured – period!

The only antidote to this type of risk is a true and unwavering commitment from the CEO and his/her top management team that this is *the* way to go. Innovation benefits are never instantaneous. The companies that have been most successful and become innovation powerhouses are those that treated innovation as a core process and tirelessly worked to improving their efforts year after year.

Management's real commitment should be communicated through a series of forceful and consistent messages, repeated again and again. More importantly it should lead to visible measures and steps that will gradually convince operational people that management 'means business.' These concrete measures typically fall into three categories:

- In the 'stick' category: Selecting and enforcing new performance measures and/or bypassing skeptical and lukewarm managers or, even worse, 'resistors'.
- In the 'carrot' category: Implementing a range of rewards (financial and non financial) and career acceleration moves for high performers and role models.
- In the 'support' category: Creating support mechanisms; allocating resources and modifying policies and systems in support of the new drive.

## Maintaining a Clear Focus and Priority

The second condition for success is to ensure that the innovation drive does not become lost or weakened among a series of too many other initiatives, which will also mobilize management's attention and dilute efforts. The clearer the focus and the simpler the message, the better! But this does not mean that it should be the only change initiative. Innovation drives are compatible with ongoing efforts toward operational excellence, provided there is clearly perceived accountability for everyone at the top management level.

## Communicating an Explicit Change Agenda and Process for Innovation

Embarking on a company-wide innovation journey implies that the company and its managers go through a real change process to embrace innovation as a core value. Change has to happen at three levels:

- At the mindset level, since most managers have not paid much attention to it in the past.
- At the organizational level, since people will have to learn to work in cross-functional horizontal teams across organizational units and markets.
- At the process level, since many of the classic processes in innovation (for example idea management and portfolio management) may have to be formalized.

As with any change process, an innovation drive consists of three essential phases:

### Phase 1: Building shared awareness of the need to change the current status quo

First, managers need to be given a chance to understand:

- why the company has to make a drastic efforts in terms of innovation, given the competitive and growth pressures it is facing;

- what benefits are expected (in terms of growth, better margins and, ultimately, share value); and
- what the penalties are for not doing it (stagnation, loss of market share as customers shift to more innovative solutions, etc.).

Second, they have to assess where the company is starting from:

- What achievements have been realized in various corners of the company?
- What resources are available (or not available)?
- What is the status and level of their own innovation process and performance?
- What obstacles need to be overcome to move ahead?

Finally, managers need to know what top management is planning to do, concretely, to help move the company ahead.

### Phase 2: Fostering a shared understanding of the way to manage innovation

Once managers are convinced that it is worth changing things to innovate more and better, they have to agree on the best way to go about it. They need to assimilate the chosen innovation process model; understand what priorities they should start working on; and 'internalize' the kind of innovation leadership attributes they should develop in themselves and in their team to lead and support the effort.

This second phase typically entails two kinds of company-wide activities:

- Process development activities, to establish missing processes and formalize or improve deficient ones.
- Management development activities, for example innovation seminars in which models are proposed, common issues are discussed, and desirable behavior patterns are introduced. These seminars should start at the top of the pyramid before cascading down to lower operational echelons.

The experience of innovative companies in the second phase highlights the importance of starting the management development program as early as possible. This avoids the perception from the field that the work on processes is an isolated corporate effort and has no direct link to the market. The earlier and more involved these managers can be in the process development activities, the more they will feel vested.

### Phase 3: Obtaining shared commitment to action from line management

Even when managers become aware of and understand what needs to be done in the field of innovation, it is still important to ensure that action is taken and efforts are sustained by:

- setting up performance measures or indicators ('you get what you measure'); and
- rewarding (or sanctioning) behavior and performance along the dimensions desired.

Of course, obtaining shared commitment to action does not stop with the establishment of performance metrics and a reward system. It also involves identifying and launching a number of highly visible corporate projects capable of creating excitement and mobilizing people. These projects must be chosen carefully to be realistically feasible.

## GETTING INVOLVED IN INNOVATION SEARCHES AND PROJECTS

Innovation drives are not only launched in response to a threat or to streamline an inefficient process; they can be initiated to tap an unexploited market opportunity.

Even if they are not visionaries, top managers must be able to specify where they expect to see innovation happen in their company. If innovation is to support their business strategy and priorities, instead of allowing it to occur randomly, they must point it in specific directions. Asking questions like:

- In which area do we need to search for innovation and for what purpose?
- Which market or segment do we want to rejuvenate?
- What aspect of our value chain do we want to focus on?

- To what unmet or ill-met customer needs do we want to give priority?

Innovation drives in pursuit of a market opportunity fall into two broad categories:

(1) focused breakthrough projects, designed to implement a specific and totally new product or service idea and create a new market;
(2) broad-based searches for implementable opportunities in a given market space that is considered highly promising.

In both cases, an organized search for innovation reflects strong management ambition to break new ground and a compelling vision as to where opportunities lie.

### Focused Breakthrough Projects

Contrary to what many people believe, breakthrough projects do not have to happen only in a somewhat haphazard or serendipitous fashion. They can be planned and initiated by management, either to exploit an innovative product or service idea and meet a largely unmet market need, or to leverage a highly promising technology. Many Japanese innovation breakthroughs in consumer electronics, office automation, photography and cars have occurred in a top-down fashion, through the vision and determination of top management teams wishing to capture a share of a fast-growing market space. The same can be said of innovations launched by Apple. Innovations like the Macintosh, the iTunes/iPod and, more recently, the iPhone were not random acts but the fruits of a well-thought-through top-down process, under the scrutiny of Steve Jobs. They started by identifying currently unsatisfactory solutions to potentially high market demand.

> The company found digital music players 'big and clunky or small and useless' with user interfaces that were 'unbelievably awful.'[6]

They continued with a structured process involving both internal functions and external partners, all under the direct supervision of innovation leaders.

Chapters later in this book will describe in detail significant break-through innovations implemented by two companies in a top-down fashion:

• Tetra Pak (in Chapter 8): The introduction of a revolutionary carton package to replace the traditional metal food can; and
• TiVo (in Chapter 9): The launch of a totally new TV viewing, programming and recording system.

But not all vision-led innovations have to be equally spectacular. They do not need to be revolutionary in all dimensions to be called breakthroughs. In fact, significant businesses can be created by recognizing a new trend early enough, riding it and building on it. The innovative aspects may come from adding truly unique elements to the offering of competitors, thus carving a significant competitive advantage. This is exactly what ING – the Dutch financial services giant – did with the creation of ING Direct, its web-based discount banking subsidiary, now one of the success stories in this particular sector of the banking industry.

Like most banks in early 1997, ING was fully aware that internet banking would mark the start of the demise of traditional 'bricks and mortar' retail banking branches. But the vision of a few senior ING managers, including its Canadian president and CEO, added an innovative touch to the idea of offering web-banking services. This vision was a straightforward observation of a phenomenon that had been very successful in related sectors, like stock trading, but had not yet reached the retail banking industry, i.e. offering a limited range of quality services at discount prices:

> What's missing in Canadian banking is what we see in other industries: discounters. We see them in telecommunication and we see them in retail. Why don't we see them in banking?
> [The concept of ING Direct was to become a] credible financial institution dedicated to convenient and consistent service, with an array of high-value, simple product offerings, each of which would be attractive to a broad range of age groups.[7]

The business model adopted by ING Direct in Canada, and later in a number of other countries, was rather new for the retail banking industry. It was based on a very limited product range (savings accounts and investment certificates, later extended with mortgages) providing unusually attractive rates and offered on a 24/7 basis by phone or internet. Substantial marketing communications with a clear, easy-to-understand positioning was designed to speed up the customer acquisition process and overheads and margins were cut to the bone to make the economic model work.

By 2003 the concept of ING Direct had expanded in seven countries through a well-established process. Its asset base had reached € 72 billion and the company was reaching over 6 million customers, with 300 000 new customers joining each month. The company had extended its product range and channels somewhat, but it remained loyal to its original value proposition, as the general manager stresses:

> We focus on savings accounts and simple loans. You cannot get any simpler than that. Instead of using a single channel – the branch – to offer many different products, we offer only a few products through multiple channels – the internet, telephone, mail, and ING Direct cafés.[8]

### Broad-based Searches

Management can also launch innovation drives in an open-ended way. The aim, in such cases, is to identify unspecified yet promising opportunities in a new market area that management judges attractive for its growth and innovation potential. The initial vision, albeit often vague at the outset, determines the boundaries of the search area and triggers a focused pursuit of concrete product or service opportunities. When it follows such a vision-led process, innovation is no longer random. Would-be frontline innovators in marketing or R&D receive a mandate to explore the well-defined areas that management has identified and prioritized. Their task is to generate the best ideas, concepts and solutions for implementing the vision.

This kind of exploratory search will generally require a very different approach than the one normally adopted by the company.[9]

It can be entrusted to a new business development group, when it exists, or even to task forces of managers from the current business. Often, these managers will be asked to develop and manage the businesses that have been identified and selected as a result of that search.

With the creation of its Consumer Health and Wellness business unit, Philips, the Dutch giant, provides a good illustration of this type of broad-based innovation search. Gerard Kleisterlee, Philips' CEO, was convinced that his Group needed to find new profitable growth areas to complement its current business portfolio. Philips management wished to leverage the company's research and medical technology expertise and its consumer goods marketing and distribution flair. The company is well known for its outstanding R&D capabilities; it is also among the world's top three medical technology players and is a leader in light bulbs, small domestic appliances and consumer electronics. The sector of consumer healthcare seemed particularly attractive to Philips on two grounds:

(1) The market barely exists today, or at least is very fragmented in terms of companies and product offerings; yet
(2) Market analysts believe significant future growth is promised in most developed markets as an aging population spends more of its income on health and wellness products.

In announcing the creation of the new Consumer Health and Wellness business unit, Kleisterlee was clearly signaling to his organization where he wanted his staff to search for innovation opportunities. All the managers joining the new unit knew that they would have to build a sizable business mostly through innovation, since acquisitions would be made primarily to access the platforms and brands from which innovative new products could be launched.

Large-scale, top-down, focused innovation searches, like the one at Philips, have not been so widespread in the past, even among large companies. The persistent urge to grow in fast-maturing industries and the emergence of new market needs is likely to accelerate the process. The buzz currently surrounding alternative energy sources is generating a lot of interest in this type of approach from oil, utilities, engineering and chemical companies. This is why we can expect a lot more of these top-down initiated, broad-based innovation searches. In most cases, they will require a high degree of innovation leadership.

## The Innovation Leader as 'Vision Roadmapper' and Implementation Planner

Vision alone does not change things. When dreams and ambitions remain vague and without any concrete guidelines, they are unlikely to mobilize people to their cause. Innovation leaders should be personally involved in charting a roadmap toward their vision. Their involvement in implementation will vary according to the nature of the challenge and the management level at which they operate.

When they occupy the top job, innovation leaders are usually keen to choose – or at least influence the choice of – the leaders of their critical corporate innovation projects. They typically see their role as providing strategic direction, empowering, releasing resources, and ensuring that obstacles to implementation are removed. When Jürgen Schremp, DaimlerChrysler's former CEO, formulated the vision of his group being among the first automotive manufacturers to offer fuel-cell powered cars, he clearly left it to others in his management team to plan how to achieve that ambitious objective. Nevertheless, as CEO, he played an important role in assigning the mission to trusted aides and in clearing the way to extend the scope of the company's technology and business alliances to Ballard Power Systems, the Canadian fuel-cell engineering specialist, and Ford Motor Company.

When they sit at the supervisory level, as on the Executive Committee, innovation leaders may in fact get much more involved, for example in supervising innovation teams. Many companies – like Tetra Pak – have adopted the practice of having a member of their top management team personally supervise each major corporate innovation project and coach its project leader. This brings two major benefits. Firstly, it provides the team with a high-level supporter and protector. A senior coach can shield a team from the natural tendency of any corporate hierarchy to encroach on its autonomy, and thus to reduce its level of empowerment. Second, the senior coach is exposed to the day-to-day reality of the project, and shares the team's experience and learning.

Closer to the operational level, the innovation leader may direct the overall project, taking responsibility for charting the project path from vision to implementation. Years ago, when Hiroshi Tanaka, managing director of Canon's Office Products Development Center, became the official champion of the company's ambitious 'family copier' project, his challenging mission could be summed up in a few words: Develop a very small, service-free personal copier to retail under $1000. His first role as innovation leader was to develop a game plan that would meet his CEO's vision. This meant planning the project management organization, the project itself, the way to fence competitors out, and the launch and roll-out. His task was not only to chart a path for a breakthrough mission but also to convince his skeptical team that the job was feasible and, ultimately, to lead them to success.[10]

The first part of this book has built a descriptive portrait of innovation leaders along several of their dimensions. In the first four chapters we discussed who they are, how they behave and what they do, concretely, to promote innovation bottom up and steer it top down. In Chapter 5 we will focus on the functions where innovation leaders abound – that of the chief technology officer (CTO) or chief research officer (CRO), acting as chief innovation officers (CIO).

## ENDNOTES

1. Quotes by Jeff Immelt selected by Innovation & Business Architectures Inc. (http://www.biz-architect.com/top_down_innovation_at_ge.htm) from two interviews:

   • 'Bringing Innovation to the Home of Six Sigma,' by Diane Brady in *Business Week Online,* 1 August 2005. http://www.businessweek.com/ @3Umkb4cQEH7eyAwA/magazine/content/05_31/b3945409.htm

- 'The Fast Company Interview: Jeff Immelt,' by John Byrd in *FastCompany*, July 2005, **96**: 60. http://www.fastcompany.com.

2. PDP stands for plasma display panel; LCD for liquid crystal display.
3. Deschamps, J.-P. and Nayak, P.R. (1995). *Product Juggernauts: How Companies Mobilize to Generate Streams of Market Winners*. Boston, Harvard Business School Press.
4. Carnegie Mellon University: Software Engineering Institute (1995). *The Capability Maturity Model: Guidelines for Improving the Software Process*. Boston, Addison Wesley-Professional.
5. Deschamps, J.-P. (2000). 'From Information and Knowledge to Innovation.' *Competing with Information: A Manager's Guide to Creating Business Value with Information Content*. Ed. Donald A. Marchand. Chichester, John Wiley & Sons, Ltd.
6. Kahney, L. (2006). 'Straight Dope on the iPod's Birth.' *Wired News*, 17 October. http://www.wired.com/gadgets/mac/commentary/cultofmac/2006/10/71956 accessed on 27 November 2007.
7. Ryans, A. (1999). 'ING Bank of Canada (A): Launch of a Direct Bank.' Ivey Case No. 9A99A010.
8. Robertson, D. and Francis, I. (2003). 'ING Direct: Your Other Bank.' IMD Case No. IMD-3-1343.
9. Hamel, G. and Prahalad, C.K. (1991). 'Corporate Imagination and Expeditionary Marketing.' *Harvard Business Review*, July–August: 81–92.
10. Deschamps, J.-P. and Nayak, P.R. (1995). *Product Juggernauts: How Companies Mobilize to Generate Streams of Market Winners*. Chapter Four 'Devising a Bold Game Plan.' Boston, Harvard Business School Press, pp. 113–124.

# CHAPTER 5

# APPOINTING AN INNOVATION CONDUCTOR[1]

*. . . Who is responsible for innovation in your firm? Now, most people will quickly point to the head of R&D if the organization has one. That's probably not a bad first choice, except that it argues that all ideas will come from only one group or business function within your organization. Do you really want to stake everything on just one organization? What if your business partners or customers have suggestions or ideas? Will they naturally funnel to the R&D team?*

*Jeffrey Phillips*
*Blogger – Innovate on Purpose[2]*

The previous chapter proposed three different mechanisms for managing innovation, each corresponding to a different way of assigning overall responsibility for innovation in the company. In one of them – the Innovation Board – top management entrusts the mission to a high-level, cross-functional collective entity. In both of the others, the task is assigned to an innovation-dedicated individual, usually a senior manager. This corporate innovation champion can be either a chief innovation officer (CIO) or a chief technology officer (CTO), sometimes called chief research officer (CRO) in science-based industries. (*For simplicity, this chapter will use the acronym CTO as a generic term for the CTO/CRO function.*)

## CTO OR CIO?

The main differences between these positions relate essentially to the background and functional origin of the person in question, and as a consequence to the main focus of his/her action.

In principle, CIOs could come from any function within the organization and their appointment can be envisaged in all kinds of companies, even those operating in a non-technical environment. CIOs will typically be responsible for overseeing and facilitating all types of innovation – i.e. new product, service, method, business model and process innovations – across all functions. They are supposed to search for and support ideas wherever they originate, internally or externally. They are also expected to work on their company's innovation culture, process and resources. In short, CIOs are empowered to embrace innovation in all its aspects, technical and non-technical.

CTOs, as their name indicates, exist mostly in science- and technology-intensive industries, and they represent the technical community in their companies. With a scientific or engineering background, they typically reach top management after successfully managing projects of increasing importance and leading, first, discipline groups, then entire R&D labs or information technology departments. When they rise above their traditional R&D management responsibilities to take on a corporate role, they tend naturally to focus on new technology-based products, processes and services.

Companies hesitating between entrusting their innovation management responsibility to a CIO or to their CTO – if this role exists – should consider three choice factors.

The first determining factor is the nature of the industrial environment. Companies that compete directly or indirectly on technology will find it natural to entrust responsibility for their innovation process to the highest ranking science or technology officer. Since this type of function does not generally exist in service or low-technology companies, the alternative is to appoint a CIO. In short, CTO or CIO? The answer is generally dictated by the competitive environment.

The second influencing factor is the breadth of experience of their CTO. Many CTOs are broad enough, both in their thinking and interests, to define their innovation mission quite comprehensively. Their technical upbringing, R&D experience and technology focus should not preclude them from considering all facets of innovation. In fact, breadth is precisely what differentiates a CTO from a functional R&D or information technology head. In short, broad-based CTOs should be able to operate equally well when dealing with innovation culture and process as they do on technology development and deployment.

The third guiding factor is linked to the possibility of extending the reach of individual CTOs by teaming them up with senior representatives from other functions. Even in technology-intensive companies, it is always possible to broaden the scope of the CTO's innovation agenda by appointing an Innovation Board of senior business-oriented managers. In such cases, the Innovation Board as a whole would play the role of the CIO, allowing the CTO – who might chair the Innovation Board – to focus fully on technology-based innovation.

Given that many companies have appointed their CTO as their prime 'innovation tsar,' it is worth spending some time on understanding the emerging leadership role of these senior managers.

## THE FIRST MISSION OF CTOS: TECHNOLOGICAL INNOVATION

> . . . My job at Microsoft is to worry about technology in the future. If you want to have a great future you have to start thinking about it in the present, because when the future's here, you won't have the time.
>
> Nathan Myhrvold
> Former CTO of Microsoft[3]

### A Critical, yet Little-known Function

The financial market and management media spotlight on so-called tech-firms has generally focused on the most charismatic chief executive officers (CEOs) of these companies, and in some cases on their chief financial officers (CFOs). Hardly any general articles, however, mention the names of chief technology officers (CTOs). Yet, these senior executives are the ones who, behind their CEO, make or strongly influence the important technology and innovation choices on which these companies bet their future. Indeed, they are generally responsible for recommending the technologies that need to be developed or outsourced, the research programs that are worth supporting and the technical partnerships that will give the company an edge. In this sense, they have a strong influence on decisions that have a 'make or break' impact on the company's destiny.

There are several reasons for the rather low public profile of CTOs, particularly when compared with CEOs and CFOs.

First, because of the very nature of their function, these executives have few opportunities to take a public stand and answer questions from journalists or industry analysts. Many of the things they are working on tend to be obscure to non-specialists and in any case subject to corporate secrecy rules. Generally, these managers who developed their low-key personalities in the tempered world of science and technology do not resent this lack of public exposure.

Second, unlike the CFOs who tend to assume comparable responsibilities across various companies and industries, CTOs do not share the same role or enjoy the same status in all companies. In fact, there are still significant disparities in their level of power and influence. They do not even share the same title, since the term 'CTO,' or its foreign language equivalents, is still relatively unknown in many companies and countries.

Finally, and this will be developed later in this chapter, the outside world has not yet fully appreciated the extent to which the CTO role is evolving. Beyond their traditional mission as the company's most senior science and technology executive and an expert resource on technology issues, CTOs are becoming fully fledged members of the top management team. They are increasingly viewed as the sponsors, architects and champions of their firm's future product and process offering. In the most advanced companies, CTOs are actually positioned as tomorrow's 'new business creators.'

## A Common Origin in the R&D Function

> I am the first person with that title [CTO] in our company. Before
> that, I was heading R&D in one of our four business units and
> most of my time was spent supervising projects for my unit and
> managing our large development staff. Why did we set up this CTO
> function? I guess to build bridges between our R&D units and learn
> to work together on shared technologies. We must not reinvent the
> wheel and, most importantly, we need to look beyond our own
> courtyard to identify and secure those new technologies that will
> change the name of the game in our business for years to come.
> But honestly, my job is still far from being well defined and I still
> have to find out what my priorities should be in the eyes of my
> top management colleagues. I also need to work out how I am
> supposed to interface with my former R&D colleagues who now
> report in dotted lines to me while continuing to receive their
> marching orders from their business unit VPs!
>
> New CTO of a medium-sized high-technology company

The role of CTO has only recently emerged in the executive
team. Previously this function was indistinct from the traditional
role of head of R&D or engineering. The change can be put
down to two factors. One is the growth of large, multi-product,
multi-business and multi-technology corporations in the 1970s.
The second is the realization that technology is a critical asset
that needs to be competitively managed with a long-term
perspective.

The CTO function originated in part from the evolution of
corporate organizations as they moved from a functional hierarchy
to a business unit approach. This trend spread like wildfire in the
1970s. The organizational disruption often led to the dismember-
ment of large integrated R&D centers and the creation of focused
strategic business unit (SBU) labs. By breaking up R&D into
smaller units and making them report to dedicated business leaders,
CEOs hoped for a more business-responsive R&D. However,
they soon realized that decentralization risked fragmenting
resources, a loss of shared creativity and the gradual duplication
of competencies. Many former R&D chiefs suddenly found themselves with neither staff nor labs under their direct supervision. In
many cases, these senior technologists were asked to coordinate

R&D competence across organizational boundaries with a small central staff. Some kept the R&D acronym in their title, becoming vice president R&D or R&D director.

The second driver of the changing CTO function was the burst of new technologies that emerged in the 1980s and 1990s, which revolutionized entire industries and forced companies to broaden their technology portfolio. For example, engineering plastics and digital electronics revolutionized the car industry, and molecular biology and biotechnology changed traditional chemistry-driven drug development. The emergence of these new technologies brought R&D management teams to reassess their technology strategies and induced them to build new competencies. Many traditional R&D labs did not immediately master some of the new technologies, though. This reinforced the need for senior technologists on the top executive team. And thus, the CTO became the guardian of the company's long-term technological competitiveness.

Today, most large technology-intensive companies have appointed a CTO. This trend is also increasing in medium-sized companies. CEOs are assigning a member of their top executive team to represent the company's scientific and technical functions on the board of management. However, their titles and functions vary widely between companies. An experienced CTO and first-hand observer of the function, Roger Smith, acknowledged the prevalence of a wide diversity of CTO characteristics and came up with an interesting typology of CTOs, as shown in Figure 5.1.[4]

## CTO/CRO: A Common Interest Despite Different Titles

Differences between CTOs and CROs stem essentially from the way they define their discipline and choose their process emphasis.

CROs tend to see their world as science-driven. They focus on the research and discovery process. Creating and exploiting knowledge and new science and technology-based businesses commercially fuels their drive. CROs are found in research-intensive

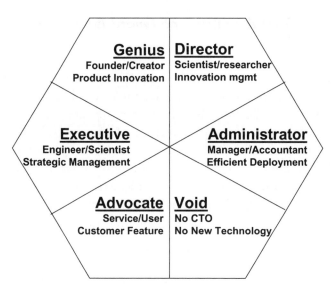

**Figure 5.1**   CTO categories, skills and focus
Source: Reproduced with permission from Roger Smith, Group CTO, Titan Corporation.

industries such as pharmaceuticals, medical technology, advanced electronics and specialized chemicals. They carry a variety of titles, e.g.: vice president science and R&D; scientific director; corporate research officer; research vice president, and so on. Some of them have an even bigger title: CEO – Research.

By contrast, CTOs talk and think more often in terms of technology, i.e. applied science, with a focus on developing new products or manufacturing processes. They traditionally concentrate on technical choices and management processes such as technology forecasting, roadmapping, auditing, development, outsourcing, sharing and deployment. CTOs are typically found in the mechanical, electronics and information technology industries. They are appearing in other industries too, with titles like chief technology officer; senior vice-president technology; and corporate technology director.

Arguably, the boundary between these two titles remains blurred, as many executives straddle the two types of function. Whatever their titles, CTOs are generally expected to fulfill four core responsibilities.

## Supervise R&D Activities and Guard Intellectual Property (IP)

A survey of 30 CTOs of multinational companies, conducted at IMD in 2000, shows how these technology officers defined the scope of their responsibilities. Table 5.1 indicates the percentage of CTOs with direct (i.e. hierarchical) line responsibility over a number of particular functional areas, and the percentage with only dotted line (i.e. overseeing) responsibility over the same areas. It shows that some CTOs were the hierarchical supervisors of all central or corporate R&D labs – this is often the case in the pharmaceutical industry – but that a significant proportion of them

**Table 5.1** Scope of CTOs' responsibilities (line vs. staff)

| What are your job responsibilities today? | Direct Line | Dotted Line |
| --- | --- | --- |
| Innovation process management | 59% | 32% |
| Knowledge management | 41% | 32% |
| New, technology-based, business development/venturing | 36% | 27% |
| Corporate central research organization | 27% | 41% |
| Divisional or SBU R&D organization (CTOs) | 27% | 50% |
| Quality management | 27% | 32% |
| Information technology/informatics | 23% | 45% |
| Intellectual property management | 23% | 55% |
| Technology and operations support management | 18% | 45% |
| Manufacturing process innovation | 18% | 50% |
| Engineering management | 14% | 59% |
| Decentralized corporate competence centers | 9% | 64% |

**Table 5.2** The growing scope of CTOs' responsibilities

| Area of CTO/CRO Responsibility (combination of direct line and dotted line responsibilities) | % listing the item in 1995 | % listing the item in 2000 |
|---|---|---|
| Innovation process management | 55% | 91% |
| Intellectual property management | 36% | 77% |
| Divisional or SBU R&D organization | 45% | 77% |
| Knowledge management | 50% | 73% |
| Decentralized competence centers | 41% | 73% |
| New, technology-based business development | 41% | 64% |

actually had limited direct line responsibilities. Many of them played mostly coordination, alignment and stimulation functions. Their emphasis was on functional integration.

Table 5.2 shows how these responsibilities had evolved five years later. The scope of CTO responsibilities had increased in all areas and could be expected to continue to do so, although significant disparities still remained regarding their coverage.

## Manage the Deployment of Scientific and Technical Staff

The top executive team usually views the corporate CTO as the high-level human resource officer of the scientific and technical staff. Though they may not have a hierarchical relationship with their staff, CTOs are usually responsible for hiring highly qualified staff and overseeing the allocation of senior R&D personnel.

The rotation of scientists and engineers from central labs to business unit labs – and, as often happens in Japan, from labs to plants – is important as it ensures that R&D staff are exposed to the reality of business. It also creates vacancies for new scientists with cutting-edge competencies, as the CTO of a large electronics manufacturer states:

One of my most difficult jobs is to convince some of my most senior research managers that they should leave our corporate R&D organization to join one of our business units. These people, often, have stopped doing R&D work. They just manage others and, at one point in time, it is in their and the company's interest that they should move to the business side so as to leave room for new talent and allow me to maintain a flatter central R&D organization.

## Allocate Corporate Funds to Strategic R&D Programs

CTOs are generally the deciding authorities on high-impact R&D programs designed to pioneer a new technology, catch up with competitors or launch a new technical activity between or across divisions or business units. This role includes monitoring whether funds are used effectively and nurturing projects until they come to fruition. This portfolio role, even for those with limited line responsibilities, is one of the most powerful ways to influence the company's research and technology strategy. CTOs in Japanese technology-intensive companies – often called chief engineers – derive most of their top executive influence from this particular role. So does the CTO of a global engineering company quoted below:

In our company, the bulk of our technology and R&D investments are in the hands of our business units. They decide where and how to spend their R&D resources. As a result, we have tended to favor incremental product line extensions. It is to overcome that risk that I have set up a budget for corporate-funded high-risk/high-impact projects. This allows me to ensure that we are going to work in new areas that our business units would not want to pioneer alone.

## Advise CEOs, Boards and Top Management Colleagues

Educating top management colleagues in scientific and technological issues is a classic role of the CTO. Some companies still use their CTOs primarily in this limited, non-executive function. They are the 'experts' management pulls out and consults on critical technology choices, then sends back to their labs. But, in today's technology-intensive environment, this expert function is often insufficient. Executive management needs people who understand the strategic implications of technology choices, the strategy of the company and the impact of technology on the bottom line.

## THE CHANGING ROLE OF CTOS: FROM MANAGING TO LEADING

For decades, R&D and its senior managers have been shielded from short-term business pressures. That view of the world is changing rapidly. The evolution of global markets and technologies, the growing complexity of companies and the increasing pressure to increase shareholder value are forcing CTOs to consider short-term results. Market and financial expectations for top- and bottom-line numbers are now passed on to technology chiefs. Increasingly, CTOs are being asked to contribute directly to the company's growth and profit. Long-term tracking of R&D projects and their profitability is another challenge CTOs have to master.

These pressures are causing CTOs to shift their emphasis from managing functions, people and assets to leading a transformation. This shift means instilling a sense of purpose, direction and focus in all technical departments. Aligning scientists and engineers with the company's strategic direction helps to build cohesion and increases the company's chances of success.

However, despite this trend toward a more strategic involvement in company affairs, CTOs will always be judged on the company's overall R&D effectiveness. If there are not many new products in the company's pipeline, CTOs will not be credible as full partners at the strategy table. R&D must be seen to be efficient with time and money and effective by introducing competitive new products and features. In short, the credibility of CTOs hinges on R&D's results. To hold a seat at the executive management table, CTOs must earn the respect and trust of their colleagues in their functional area.

## Instilling a Sense of Purpose in the Role of Science and Technology

CTOs have always been expected to develop and optimize technical competencies and R&D funds. Today, they need to raise a new sense of purpose within their staff, reminding them continuously that they are responsible for contributing to the future growth of their company through winning new products and processes.

> In the past, like most of my colleagues – all young scientists out of the university – I joined the company's R&D group as I would have joined a post-graduate research position, attracted by the prospect of working on exciting new technology, traveling to attend scientific conventions and becoming famous through widely published new discoveries.
>
> Well, that is long gone, I am afraid. Today, as CRO, one of my first jobs is to make our staff more market- and business-oriented. We have to justify our existence and the funds the company invests in Research. My business colleagues look to me and to Research as the source of new technologies that will make them win. They also expect us to invent and deliver the new products and businesses that will make us grow as a company. My job is to deliver results and I am evaluated on the perception that my board of management have of whether I am bringing a satisfactory return on R&D investments!
>
> CRO of a global electronics company

Pressures for growth and performance generally trigger a renewed sense of purpose and urgency at all levels. Sitting at the top of their scientific and technical community, CTOs will be expected to get ready for a quantum leap in R&D's contribution to business success. Having climbed the ladder through R&D management, their traditional emphasis was on functional efficiency. As they reach the top team, this aspect of their job declines in importance. But their role as guardians of the company's long-term scientific and technological competitiveness is rapidly expanding.

This substantial change in management agenda and emphasis is clearly highlighted in an opinion survey conducted by IMD among CTOs from leading international companies. These senior

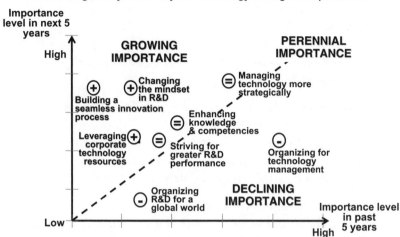

**Figure 5.2** The changing agenda of the CTO/CRO
Source: IMD CTO survey, 2000 (N = 30).

executives were asked to list their priorities in the past five years and the ones that would retain their attention over the next five years. A summary of the survey results is shown graphically in Figure 5.2.

Out of the eight broad challenges proposed, the vast majority of executives indicated declining importance in two traditional aspects of their job:

- Organizing R&D for a global world, i.e. spreading R&D resources to tap scientific brains and operate in all parts of the world.
- Organizing for technology management, i.e. addressing traditional R&D organization issues, technology funding and technology management processes.

In contrast, the survey highlighted a continuing emphasis on three perennial strategic missions:

- Managing technology more strategically, i.e. linking technology and business strategies more effectively, particularly for the long term.

- Enhancing knowledge and competencies, i.e. focusing on creating, using, sharing and protecting knowledge, as well as discarding irrelevant knowledge.[5]
- Striving for greater R&D performance, i.e. improving R&D's contribution to business success, essentially through more strategic project selection.

These important aims call on leadership skills more than on organizational or managerial abilities.

Finally, three priorities appeared with increasing brightness on their radar screen, all relating to the ability of CTOs to transform their organization, which requires strong leadership qualities:

- Changing the mindset in R&D, i.e. introducing a stronger business focus and a more acute sense of urgency among the scientific and technical community.
- Building a seamless innovation process, i.e. communicating and working more effectively with other functions, for example marketing or manufacturing.
- Leveraging corporate technology resources, i.e. paying greater attention to technology insourcing and outsourcing to capitalize on the specific strengths of technology partners.

## Providing a Sense of Direction in Science and Technology

CTOs have always been expected to help their company manage and optimize its technology portfolio. Today their mission is, more than ever, to preempt the future by identifying and investing in critical new technologies that will sustain the businesses of tomorrow. CTOs are becoming their company's 'chief navigators.'

> One of my important missions was to ensure that our company stayed abreast of, and used, all those new technologies that are radically altering the way we develop drugs.
>     For years, I was the advocate and promoter of combinatorial chemistry, high-throughput screening techniques and bioinformatics. When these had been reasonably mastered, we embarked on

boosting our knowledge of genomics and proteomics to be able to benefit fully from our partnerships in those domains. The search for new technologies is an unending quest in the pharma industry.

Former CRO of a large drug company

Perhaps the most challenging part of the job is that CTOs are expected to provide the board and top executive team with clear directions on where and how much to invest in science and technology. Deciding on the appropriate level of R&D spending – generally expressed as a percentage of sales – is one of the most debated top management issues in technology-intensive industries. CTOs are, inevitably at the center of that debate. The R&D budget, whatever the method used to make it look rational, is ultimately the responsibility of CTOs. Investment allocation in R&D will reflect:

- a *vision* of where and how technology will shape the future of the business and create opportunities;
- management's level of *ambition* regarding the risks it is willing to take in introducing new technologies;
- *faith* in the power of science and technology to outperform or out-innovate competitors.

### Formulating a Vision for Technology

CTOs play a decisive role in bringing about management's vision, ambition and faith regarding technology. That process, which can be called 'technology visioning,' is similar to what process management teams use to sharpen, reorient or renew their business vision. Specialists[6] claim that a company vision is composed of two linked facets:

- A picture of an 'envisaged future,' highlighting a desirable future state of the company, and how it wants to be perceived by its stakeholders.
- A 'core ideology,' stating what the company stands for vis-à-vis its stakeholders and the values it promotes.

This is sometimes distilled into a short policy statement that is communicated to the outside world. The same process applies to

**Technology is a means to implementing the business vision**

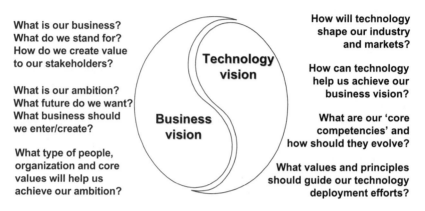

What is our business?
What do we stand for?
How do we create value
to our stakeholders?

What is our ambition?
What future do we want?
What business should
we enter/create?

What type of people,
organization and core
values will help us
achieve our ambition?

**Technology vision**

**Business vision**

How will technology
shape our industry
and markets?

How can technology
help us achieve our
business vision?

What are our 'core
competencies' and
how should they evolve?

What values and principles
should guide our technology
deployment efforts?

**Figure 5.3**  The interdependence of technology and business visions

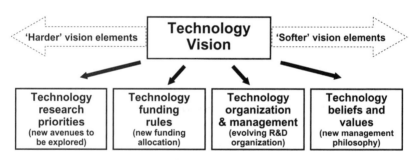

'Harder' vision elements

**Technology Vision**

'Softer' vision elements

| Technology research priorities (new avenues to be explored) | Technology funding rules (new funding allocation) | Technology organization & management (evolving R&D organization) | Technology beliefs and values (new management philosophy) |

**Figure 5.4**  The 'hard' and 'soft' elements of a technology vision

technology, which is a means of implementing the business vision as illustrated in Figure 5.3. Normally, the business vision will drive the technology vision. However, in technology-intensive industries, the reverse often happens.

Through a process of technology visioning, CTOs should provide a sense of direction to the company's R&D efforts. There are generally two sides to it, a 'harder' side and a 'softer' side, as shown in Figure 5.4.

## Envisaging the Future Regarding Technology (The 'Harder' Side)

Envisaging the future entails defining the scope of the company's technology coverage and identifying competencies that are critical for the company to master. It is up to CTOs to recommend which areas of R&D should be investigated, developed and grown (or pruned). CTOs also play a key role, along with CFOs, in recommending and justifying the funding level for future investments.

Envisaging the future also means defining the role of technology in the company strategy. Cisco Systems Inc. provides a good example of the link between business and technology visions. The company's vision – becoming the preferred internet-enabling company and total solution provider on the basis of its product superiority – has rapidly been translated into a clear technology vision and a serial technology acquisition strategy (a strategy that was only viable when the company's stock price was high). The company has learned how to select technology targets carefully, acquire them rapidly and integrate them immediately. Its vision has been translated directly into action.

A company will never be able to maintain a technological lead from only its own resources. CTOs must ensure their organization is open to using the best technologies, regardless of the source. It is often less expensive to license or acquire a new technology rather than developing it in-house. In fact, it is not uncommon for companies today to post technical challenges online and receive bids from other companies to fulfill some of their technological needs, as P&G did with its 'connect & develop' strategy. The strategy was not to get rid of P&G's researchers, but to better leverage them. From about 15% in 2000, the proportion of external innovations has thus risen to more than 35% in 2006, and 45% of the initiatives in the company's product development portfolio have key elements that were discovered externally. This strategy has already led to a dramatic increase in R&D productivity and innovation success rate.[7]

## Developing a Core Ideology Regarding Technology (The 'Softer' Side)

Some CTOs have gone beyond envisaging the future. They have formulated and promoted policies and proposed desirable behaviors, beliefs and values about technology as well as a guiding framework for its deployment and management. For example, at 3M, technical managers know that the technologies deployed belong to the company and not to their business units. Everyone in 3M's technical community is expected to practice the values derived from such a belief: A systematic sharing of technologies across labs and business units – an elusive goal in many corporations.

The softer side of a technology vision deals with changing working behavior and the mindset about technology in the organization. Clarifying this ideology and getting it adopted is one of the key leadership roles of CTOs. This includes:

- Establishing and building a consensus of beliefs and values within the company's scientific and technical community;
- Making these beliefs and values explicit, for example in the form of a 'technology charter,' as illustrated in Table 5.3.
- Getting the technology charter endorsed by management and communicating it widely to R&D's business partners;
- Designing and running a program of change to embed the new behaviors into day-to-day lab reality, as shown in Figure 5.5.

A final aspect brings us to one of the fastest-growing areas of concern captured in the CTO survey: Changing the mindset in R&D. The nature of the new mindset is typically company-specific. In companies with a strong central R&D function, the objective of the change program is often to make the staff more responsive to business demands. R&D is expected to be flexible to business demands, to be cost-conscious and pay close attention to the speed of development. In other companies with a strong growth objective, such as Dow Chemical Co. and Royal Philips Electronics, the efforts may focus more on entrepreneurship and new business creation. In the pharmaceutical industry, CTOs often

**Table 5.3** Outline of the technology charter of a leading chemical company

I.   The fundamental role of technology in business success and the nature of the company's innovation challenge, i.e.
   * *the roles of proprietary vs. non-proprietary/outsourced technologies;*
   * *the relative importance of technology forecasting vs. market sensing;*
   * *the rules concerning technology ownership, usage and accountability;*
   * *the proper time horizon of the company's technology investments.*

II.  The strategic management of technology and the role of chief research or technology officers, i.e.
   * *the level of enforcement of technology synergy across businesses;*
   * *the policy regarding technology outsourcing, partnering or venturing;*
   * *the role of CTOs as business 'supporters' vs. new business 'creators';*
   * *the power and intervention authority of divisional CTOs.*

III. The particular role, function or mission of the central research organization vs. divisional R&D units, i.e.
   * *the contribution of research and appropriate level of R&D decentralization;*
   * *the role of research in developing new competencies and businesses;*
   * *the mission of research in attracting, developing and transferring talent;*
   * *the attitude of research regarding technologies falling outside business priorities.*

IV.  The internal organization of the Research Center, its funding and the evaluation of its output, i.e.
   * *the merits of organizing along 'disciplines' vs. 'technology platforms';*
   * *the relative importance of corporate vs. business unit funding;*
   * *the measurement of research output in terms of value created;*
   * *the policy regarding sub-critical and peripheral research activities.*

V.   The management of human resources in technology (hiring, performance evaluation, career management), i.e.
   * *preferred profile and breadth of skills of incoming scientists and engineers;*
   * *rotation of scientists between research and development centers;*
   * *involvement of R&D leaders in strategic business management issues;*
   * *focus of R&D staff evaluation (R&D output quality vs. business success?)*

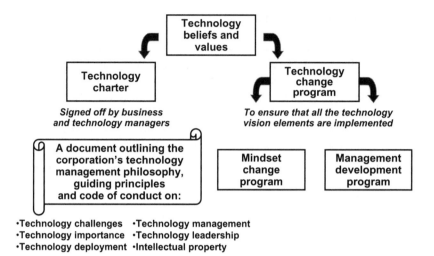

Figure 5.5   Grounding shared technology beliefs and values

promote a more effective collaboration between research centers, both within the company and with external technology partners (for example with smaller associated biotech firms.) Regardless of their focus, these programs tend to require continuous attention from CTOs. Changing the mindset of the people working in R&D is not an easy or short-term task.

## Enforcing a Sense of Focus on Technology

CTOs have always been expected to be the guardians and promoters of their company's competencies. Today, their priority is to ensure that they focus their internal resources on core – i.e. differentiating – technologies while encouraging their staff to be open and to accept and leverage external technologies.

> Our CEO is very much concerned by the fact that many of the technologies and competences that we are deploying are becoming very mature. They are not giving us much competitive advantage anymore. So, I have started investigating opportunities for outsourcing some of our traditional R&D activities, in the same way as we started outsourcing part of our operations and services. The idea is

> to free resources so as to invest more in new competences to support our drive in nutrition.
>
> CRO of a global food company

As future-oriented leaders, CTOs will be expected to guide the company and align the technological focus with the company's strategy. Being accountable for the long-term technological competitiveness of their company, CTOs often have the following formal responsibilities in their job description:

- Identify technologies that have the highest competitive impact on the company's businesses today. Identify technologies that will or might replace existing methods and be disruptive to the entire business or industry.
- Audit the company's competitive technological position in a realistic and objective manner. Analyze opportunities and threats that might result from major technological strengths and weaknesses.
- Contain the risk of technology fragmentation. Ensure that enough resources are devoted to the company's most vital technologies even at the expense of reducing investments in less critical areas.
- Invest in new critical technologies ahead of time (but not too early). Choose investment strategies that reduce risks to an acceptable level while maintaining flexibility.
- Outsource non-essential technologies that waste resources and do not offer any particular competitive advantage. Outsource in a way that guarantees access to key technologies needed to remain competitive.

Each item highlights one of the most fundamental roles of CTOs, and one that requires a lot of courage on their part: *Make choices and focus.*

Intel's Andy Grove recognized that choosing to focus all his company's resources on microprocessors and abandoning memory development and fabrication was perhaps the most difficult decision in his career.[8] Despite the predicted growth in demand for computer memory and Intel's competitive position, Grove realized that he could not grow the memory business in parallel with the promising microprocessor business. There was the real risk that Intel would become a mediocre competitor in two businesses. The company's fabulous growth shows how inspired (or fortunate) this decision was to focus on microprocessors, a domain where Intel claimed a leading technological position. Not all companies have to confront dilemmas of such magnitude. Nevertheless, the need to focus on certain technologies with its corollary – abandoning or outsourcing other technologies – is widespread.

The delicate task of identifying candidates in the two categories – technologies to be acquired and developed and technologies to be abandoned or outsourced – clearly belongs to the CTO. But the task does not stop here. The most critical part of a focused technology strategy is implementation, where three significant challenges need to be addressed:

- How to acquire and deploy new knowledge time- and cost-effectively. To deal with this issue, the CTO will often recommend strategic acquisitions or partnerships. Here, leadership skills will be tested because the new technologies (and often the associated people) have to become established in the 'new' organization. Grafting new knowledge onto a somewhat skeptical R&D organization is not easy.
- How to phase out less critical technologies without losing competitive advantage. This issue is even more delicate. Technologies equate to knowledge and knowledge resides in people. Abandoning a hitherto important area of knowledge often means losing key people. Not all scientists and engineers can be easily re-trained, and sometimes the objective is to reduce headcount and internal costs. CTOs must be acutely aware of the threat of demoralizing staff. Averting that risk without giving up on the company's overall objectives is another strong test of their leadership capabilities, and probably the most difficult task of all.
- How to make scientists and engineers 'unlearn' the technologies that have become irrelevant, lose their traditional perspective and fully adopt the new technologies or work methods. Developing the capacity to 'unlearn' or shed obsolete knowledge is – according to Professor Kazuo Ichijo[9] – a survival

skill for all companies confronted with an accelerating series of technology waves. He claims that Sony's delayed reaction in riding the wave of flat screen panels was, to a large extent, caused by the inability of its engineers to shift gears quickly enough, which meant discarding old cathode-ray-tube knowledge to leave room for the new PDP and LCD technologies.

## THE EMERGING ROLE OF CORPORATE ENTREPRENEUR

Traditionally in our company, corporate R&D was there to develop and master the technologies needed to support our businesses. When we realized that our business units could not bring us the growth our shareholders expect, then we decided to change the focus of our corporate R&D center. It is still to support current business, but it has also the mission to open new territories and generate new business. This is why we have started a program to boost the entrepreneurial spirit of our scientists and we created a special group responsible for following up on promising project ideas with a business creation potential.

CTO of a global chemical company

In a growing number of mature companies, CTOs are expected to leverage the company's R&D resources to create new business. A priority for the top management team in this 'post-re-engineering' period is to build new 'legs' for growth This emphasis on new business creation has led to a variety of innovative management practices.

At Bayer Group, Philips and Mitsubishi Chemical Corp., management demands for new business creation have been translated into new corporate R&D funding policies and criteria. Purely exploratory research is maintained, but at a lower level than in the past.

CTOs are increasingly encouraged to build a corporate development group of their own. There are many variations in this respect. In some companies, CTOs have set up a small strategic group as part of their corporate labs to study and pursue new business creation opportunities. Other companies have set up

R&D-funded new business incubators of their own. These organizations are responsible for pursuing opportunities until they can be transferred to existing business units or spun off as separate ventures. DuPont was an early adopter of this incubator concept with its 'commercial demonstration group,' which reported directly to the CTO.

Philips is a more recent adopter of this incubator concept. Ad Huijser, CEO of Philips Research, turned into a venture capitalist – funding start-ups founded on ideas and concepts originating in the company's central research labs. This 'technology incubator,' as it was called, created a group of enterprises completely independent of the divisions. Huijser organized a 'board' to supervise these activities; he also created a relationship with outside VC firms willing and able to invest third-party money when needed. Huijser claims that his incubator changed his research organization completely; it changed the divisional attitude and also changed the way the Philips board discussed 'innovation.' In the last six months before he stepped down as CEO of Philips Research, Huijser changed his concept, developing a new model with three separate incubators for Technology, Healthcare and Lifestyle, each with its specific area of interest, its own board, its own financial resources and support staff, and independent reporting lines.

Considerable effort and corporate funds are put behind such strategic research initiatives, i.e., innovative projects capable of generating new business streams. Other companies, such as Motorola, have traditionally conducted systematic searches for technology-based business opportunities in their roadmapping process. Business and technology reviews, led by cross-functional teams including CTOs, focus on trends and developments that point to new opportunities. They can trigger requests for corporate funding and new business development initiatives of significant size and risk.

Such emphasis on new business creation is not universally recognized (or successful in creating value) at a time when many companies are under pressure to focus on their core business. Corporate entrepreneurship may not appear prominently on the current job description of CTOs, but this is likely to change, and a new set of responsibilities may soon be added, such as:

- Review and change R&D funding policies and criteria to ensure adequate resources are allocated to strategic initiatives. Lead the development of new businesses, not just the enhancement or protection of existing ones.
- Set up processes, build partnerships and promote attitudes that will lead R&D to systematically evaluate new technology-based business opportunities.
- Participate actively in the creation of a corporate development group to pursue new opportunities.
- Coach infant businesses throughout their early lives. Ensure high-potential projects are quickly entrusted to business-oriented project leaders.
- Build partnerships between the company's business units and R&D to support the new business ventures. Help them set up as independent organizations or integrate into the existing business.

The message is loud and clear – the CTO position is gradually becoming that of the chief innovation officer (CIO). The new mission is to lead the company toward new opportunities for growth. If the dual role of all senior executives is to 'master the present' and 'preempt the future'[10] the CTO has always been expected to favor the second part of the job. Increasingly, however, the CTO is expected to go even further – to create the future. This means fostering an organizational climate for innovation. The CTO must also breed future 'innovation leaders' who will lead projects and build businesses.

## FACING THE CHALLENGE AS PART OF THE TOP EXECUTIVE TEAM

My job as a CTO cannot be defined as easily as that of my senior colleagues from Finance or HR. Since we have decentralized all our R&D resources into our divisions, I am not running a department any more. I am simply influencing other people's decisions. My degree of influence is fundamentally dependent on how my boss – the CEO – and my divisional colleagues look at it and how they trust my judgment. As long as our current CEO and our Divisional VPs are not very 'technical,' they let me have a lot of responsibility and freedom in technology-related decisions, but that could change with a new CEO.

CTO of a medium-sized engineering company

In the top executive team, CTOs often maintain a privileged relationship with the CEO when the company relies heavily on technology and innovation. But the main day-to-day relationship of CTOs is with divisional presidents or business unit heads that they must both support and challenge.

The primary role of CTOs is to support the company's businesses. They manage corporate R&D resources and budgets, build partnerships with external sources and provide strategic guidance on technology. But at the same time, they often find themselves in a challenger role vis-à-vis their top management team colleagues. This situation often happens when their colleagues are tempted to take shortcuts or under-invest in new technologies in their quest for short-term results. Non-technically trained business managers may underestimate the strategic significance of certain technologies.

> Years ago, as digital electronics was emerging, it took me a lot of time and effort to convince my colleagues not to close a small lab we had in that area. That lab was building knowledge in digital signal processing but it was not directly productive because our products were still based on analog technology. My colleagues viewed that little team as an expensive overhead item that they wanted to cut. My reaction was: 'Not over my dead body!' Today, they could not imagine what would have happened had I not protected that lab.
>
> Retired CTO of a large electronics company

## A Change in Roles

One challenge that CTOs face is in helping their executive management colleagues understand (usually with the help of the CEO) that the CTO role has changed in at least four key areas:

- **Change in positioning**: From being a *specialist resource* within the senior management group, CTOs are increasingly becoming *full members of the top executive team*, sharing in key business decisions, not just technology ones. This broadening of horizons is bringing about a dramatic change in perspective. Their loyalty is no longer oriented toward R&D or the scientific community, but toward company stakeholders and management colleagues. This change is putting pressure on CTOs to become credible business partners, sharing the same understanding of business dynamics and the same vocabulary as their management educated colleagues.

- *Change in scope*: From managing a *functional slice* of the corporation – R&D and technology – CTOs are increasingly being asked to steer a number of critical *business processes* involving numerous other functions. Typical examples include the innovation process from idea and technology to market and the new business creation and venturing process. Additionally, because so many technologies come from outside the firm, the partnering or supplier management process can also fall within the CTOs' realm. Another challenge for CTOs to master is to steer cross-functional management teams and negotiate trade-offs between conflicting technological and business objectives.

- *Change in objective*: From developing and optimizing the *use of corporate assets*, both technological competencies and R&D funds, CTOs are increasingly being asked to deliver tangible *output*. Introducing winning new products and processes and sustained growth and value to customers and shareholders is an expectation of the job – not a stretch goal. This change in expectations is again putting pressure on managers, who may have started work in an environment in which management expected R&D to justify its efforts, but not its results.

- *Change in emphasis*: From managing *hard issues* (i.e. technologies), CTOs are increasingly being asked to focus on *softer* ones as well. Managing changes in culture and mindset, teamwork, communications and motivation, not just inside the labs but also across functions, is another new challenge. This change in emphasis is making new demands on the traditional management skills of CTOs. It clearly calls for a greater and broader sense of leadership.

## Unique Leadership Profile

Ultimately, your success is going to be linked to your personal credibility, both vis-à-vis your scientific and technical staff and with your management colleagues. This credibility has to be rooted in your competences, of course, but it goes beyond. You will be credible if you have a vision, make the right choices and walk the talk to make it happen. But for our type of function, success is also linked to your sense of pedagogy and force of persuasion in both directions. You need to be pedagogic and persuasive with your scientific and technical staff, to align them with our long-term business objectives and bring about interdisciplinary and cross-functional collaboration. But you need the same qualities to influence your top management colleagues in the way they think about technology and deploy it for business advantage. Maybe CTOs need a special form of leadership!

CTO of a global telecommunications company

In summary, aspiring CTOs need to exhibit three important characteristics:

First, they must exhibit leadership talents. This chapter has highlighted what it really means for these high-ranking science and technology executives to instill a sense of purpose, direction and focus. Leadership is about aligning their technical community behind the company's vision and objectives and building a commitment to change.

Second, to qualify for the job, they must be credible as senior executives, scientists and technologists to both technical and business colleagues. Their credibility will reflect a successful career in R&D and at the interface between R&D and the business. They also have to be well connected, able to network with external sources. They must demonstrate business acumen and be able to put science and technology into a strategic business context. They must have a track record of 'delivering the goods,' bringing results in a competitive field.

Third, aspiring CTOs need a number of personal qualities. They need a high level of tenacity to fight their classic enemies: Fragmentation of effort across businesses and labs; orthodoxies and the resulting distorted view the company will have of the future; short-sightedness made worse by ignorance; and over-specialization.[11]

They also need passion to inspire and sell projects to their colleagues. They have to be able to teach colleagues how technology affects the business. Finally, CTOs also need a fair amount of diplomacy in dealing with their executive colleagues to ensure that the right decisions are made and supported.

## ENDNOTES

1. This chapter is adapted from my chapter (2008) 'The CTO Chief Technology Officer: Corporate Navigator, Agent of Change and Entrepreneur' in *Leading in the Top Team: The CXO Challenge,* edited by Preston Bottger. Cambridge, Cambridge University Press.
2. Phillips, J. (2007). 'Innovate on Purpose' (Blog): http://innovateonpurpose. blogspot.com.
3. Brockman, J. (not dated). 'Nathan Myhrvold: The Chef.' Digerati website, available on: http://www.edge.org/digerati/myhrvold/myhrvold_p2.html accessed 28 November 2007.
4. Smith, R.D. (2003). 'Maximizing the CTO's Contribution to Innovation and Growth.' *Research Technology Management,* July-August. http://www.ctonet.org/resources/MaximumCTO.pdf accessed 28 November 2007.
5. Ichijo, K. (2004). 'Strategic Leadership for Managing Knowledge-based Competence of a Corporation.' Unpublished paper presented at IMD's Strategic Leadership Conference, August 2004.
6. Collins, J.C. and Porras, J.I. (1996). 'Building Your Company's Vision.' *Harvard Business Review,* September–October, **74**(5): 65–77.
7. Huston, L. and Sakkab, N. (2006). 'Connect and Develop: Inside Procter & Gamble's New Model for Innovation.' *Harvard Business Review* **84**(3): 58.
8. Grove, A.S. (1996). 'Why Not Do It Ourselves: The Memory Business Crisis and How We Dealt With It Is How I Learned the Meaning of a Strategic Inflection Point.' *Only the Paranoid Survive.* New York, Currency Doubleday, pp. 81–97.
9. Ichijo, K. (2004). 'Strategic Leadership for Managing Knowledge-based Competence of a Corporation.' Unpublished paper presented at IMD's Strategic Leadership Conference, August 2004.
10. Abell, D.F. (1993). Managing with Dual Strategies: Mastering the Present, Preempting the Future. New York, Free Press.
11. Doz, Y. (1995). 'The CTO as Entropy Fighter: An Action Agenda.' Unpublished paper presented at the Fourth Conference on Global Issues of Technology and R&D, Management Centre Europe, Brussels, June 1995.

# PART II

# THE LEADERSHIP IMPERATIVES OF INNOVATION STRATEGIES

# CHAPTER 6

# RECOGNIZING THE LEADERSHIP IMPERATIVES OF YOUR INNOVATION STRATEGY

*Strategic Innovation is the creation of growth strategies, new product categories, services or business models that change the game and generate significant new value for customers and the corporation.*

*InnovationPoint*[1]

The first part of this book outlined the profiles of innovation leaders who successfully stimulate bottom-up or steer top-down innovation. The only distinction we have made so far between these two types of leaders was according to their selected focus on either the 'fuzzy front end' or the 'speedy back end' of the process. It is an oversimplification to assume that innovation is a fixed process, as we know it comes in several guises and that different types of innovations require varied innovation strategies.

For example, you might want to develop innovative new products or services in your current markets to grow and beat competitors. But you could also look for opportunities to create totally new product categories and tap new markets through innovation, and this is a very different strategy. Similarly, and sometimes in parallel with the previous moves, you might be tempted to come up with a totally new business model to gain a cost advantage, or introduce an innovative new system and enrich your current offering to offer a more comprehensive solution to your customers.

If these are all different innovation strategies, it is reasonable to assume that each effort will require different profiles and strengths from your management. Therefore, you should ask two questions:

- What innovation strategy do we want to follow? and
- What kind of leadership profile does this choice require?

These questions will be addressed in the following three segments:

The first part will set the stage by recommending that, as a top management team, you should clearly define your company's innovation strategy and its priorities. In other words, you need to determine and communicate the type of innovation that you are proposing to pursue from among four generic innovation thrusts.

The second part will suggest that, to be effective, each innovation thrust that you choose has to be led in a way that satisfies a particular set of conditions. These imperatives relate to four areas:

- enabling processes;
- structure and organizational mechanism;
- cultural traits; and
- staff profile.[2]

The third part will advocate that each innovation thrust requires a different change lever and leadership style, recognizing that all of them may be needed if your company chooses to pursue all four thrusts simultaneously.

Ultimately, as a top management team, you should ask whether your company's senior innovation resources are sufficiently aligned with your strategy; in other words whether your senior officers match up with the leadership requirements of your innovation strategy.

# FORMULATING AN INNOVATION STRATEGY

## Recognizing and Classifying Innovation Thrusts

Senior managers often state that they want more innovation, usually without explaining *why, where, how and with whom* they want to innovate. The following four questions define the main features or 'thrusts' of a company's innovation strategy which determine specific leadership imperatives.

- *Innovation objective* – why innovate?
  Innovations are pursued for two broad objectives: (1) to *energize and expand a current business* in its existing markets, or (2) to *create a totally new business*. Of course, these objectives can be combined.
- *Innovation scope or focus* – where to innovate?
  Innovations can be classified according to their focus. You may want to innovate on *products or services* – introducing a new 'black box' or stand-alone service – or alternatively by developing a *new business model or business system*. This can take the form of an integrated set of products and services from different partners, brought to market as a package and priced in a new way.
- *Innovation intensity level* – how much to innovate?
  You can choose to be *incremental* in the changes you bring to current products, services or processes, or more *radical* leading to completely new product and service concepts, technologies and business models.
- *Innovation boundaries* – with whom to innovate?
  Innovations can be developed and implemented in two ways: *Internally*, using your company's capabilities and resources, or *externally* through deliberate collaboration with partner(s) – suppliers, customers and even competitors.

Innovation intensity and boundaries – if restricted to an either/or option (incremental or radical; internal or external) – are always subject to debate. An innovation that is radical in one company may be characterized as incremental by a competitor. The level of innovation is relative to your own reference models.

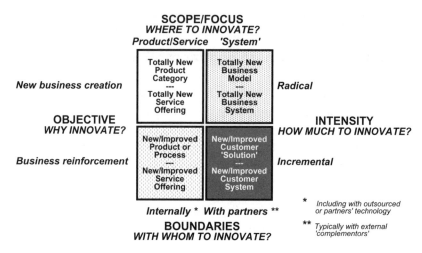

**Figure 6.1**   Typology of innovation by strategic focus

Also, innovations are rarely conducted only internally – external factors like suppliers are usually involved – causing most innovation projects to fall somewhere between the two extremes.

These four dimensions can be combined, as shown in Figure 6.1, into four entirely different innovation thrusts. You should recognize them explicitly, choose the ones that you will pursue as a priority, and use them to characterize and communicate your innovation strategy, which can be a combination of the chosen thrusts. You should then discuss their implications, particularly on leadership.

These four thrusts propose a simple typology of innovation choices:

- The internal development and launch of a *new and/or improved product, process or service offering*, typically to grow and reinforce the current business in an incremental innovation mode.
- The internal development of a *totally new product category or service offering*, typically to grow and create a totally new business, next to the existing ones, in a radical innovation mode.
- The development and launch, together with partners, of a *totally new business model or system*, typically to grow and create a new business in a radical innovation mode.

- The development and launch, together with partners, of a *new and/or improved customer solution or customer system*, typically to grow and reinforce the current business in an incremental innovation mode.

This classification reflects the fact that, from a management point of view, developing a 'black-box' product or service is very different – and carries a different type of risk – than introducing a new business model or business system, or even a complex product solution. Indeed, whereas the development of a new product or service is often the result of an internal process, even though it may involve the use of outsourced technology and suppliers, the development of a radically new business model or system often requires the cooperation of several external partners, outsourcing suppliers or 'complementors.'

These four thrusts are neither mutually exclusive – innovations can be pursued simultaneously across several of these areas – nor the only ones conceivable, of course. For example, you could think of developing a new and innovative business model or a customer solution without involving a partner. This happens when the diversified business units of a corporation, all focusing on the same broad market space – think of IBM's divisions – exploit market synergies across them. At IBM this means combining its hardware, software and consulting services to offer customized solutions to clients.

The four dimensions shown on a two-by-two matrix in Figure 6.1 give a useful framework and lens to look at the complex reality of innovation thrusts. Let's briefly review each of these individually to help determine what distinctive leadership characteristics each requires.

## Introduction of a New/Improved Product, Process or Service Offering

This first broad innovation thrust is definitely the most common. Most innovation efforts aim to gain an incremental product line, process or service advantage in the eyes of the customer – be it in terms of product range, quality, performance, features, delivery or cost. Many times, especially in traditional industries, it is the only innovation thrust that companies know and try. Doing so, mobilizes the bulk of R&D efforts and budgets across the world, and it dominates a high proportion of the business literature on new product development and benchmarking.[3]

This type of innovation generally proceeds in a bottom–up mode, driven by the combined initiatives of marketers, product managers and R&D engineers, all anxious to keep their products competitive. Since innovation is part of their day-to-day responsibilities, they do not have to refer up to get new projects authorized, except of course in exceptional cases requiring major investments. Occasionally, though, this type of thrust can be initiated and mandated top down by management. This happens when a business experiences an alarming loss of market share, caused by the fast-degrading competitiveness of its products or services. In such cases, senior management feels obliged to intervene and mandates a change.

### Introduction of a Totally New Product Category or Service Offering

Often characterized as 'breakthrough' in the press or literature, this type of innovation is what captures the imagination of journalists, innovation scholars and business analysts.[4] The greatest successes lead to blockbuster products or services, sometimes even to 'cult' products like Apple's iPod or iPhone that redefine markets and industries. Remember when the fax, videotape recorders, CDs and DVDs were invented, or the craze when Palm's Pilot created the PDA (personal digital assistant) category and Starbuck's introduced its coffee shop concept. All of these innovations have become part of a global innovation lexicon. However, in the majority of cases, the development of a totally new product or service category by a company is an exceptional phenomenon, not the norm.

Every so often a breakthrough will occur in an unplanned bottom–up way, usually by accident, thanks to the creative dedication of determined entrepreneurs, like the ones behind the creation of 3M's famous Post-It™ pads[5] or Searle's aspartame.[6] In most other cases, breakthroughs result from a top-down process, fueled by management's vision[7] and ambition to bring the company into a completely new market space. It is hard to imagine that the development of the hybrid engine concept, at both Toyota and Honda, could have proceeded entirely in a bottom-up fashion, given the huge resources that such innovations require. The original technical ideas may have seeped from creative engineers upward to the higher management echelons. However, these ideas had ultimately to be picked up, endorsed and funded by management in a top-down process. The same can be said of Apple's iPod players and most other breakthroughs. Why is that so?

Whenever it falls outside the scope of existing business units, the creation of a totally new product or service category is a strategic move requiring the full backing of top management, even if the idea originated in a bottom-up mode. Unless the initiative is part of an explicit branching out strategy – sometimes called growing 'beyond the core'[8] – business unit leaders are unlikely to risk funding innovative ideas that will lead to the creation of new businesses they will not be able to consolidate or manage. As a consequence, this innovation thrust will tend to proceed either in a pure top-down mode, driven by management in the pursuit of a new market space, or in a combined bottom-up/top-down process, but with the full backing of the corporate leadership group. Whether bottom up or top down, breakthroughs will not happen without supportive innovation leaders within top management.

## Introduction of a Totally New Business Model or System

'System innovation' is an abstract concept that can be difficult to comprehend as it encompasses many different forms. Merriam-Webster's dictionary defines a 'system,' in its generic form, as either 'a regularly interacting or interdependent group of items forming a unified whole,' or 'a group of body organs that together perform one or more vital functions.' In this book, we will discuss two types of 'system innovations':

- new business models; and
- new business systems.

A business model defines how a company goes to market, prices its goods or services and – more importantly – plans to make money. Some managers may not see the creative redesign of a business model as an innovation, because they do not see it involving new products or services. Yet, it can be a powerful way to enhance a current business. Look at radical business model innovations, like Dell's direct sales model or the low-cost airlines' operating models, e.g. Southwest Airlines, Ryanair[9] and easyJet.[10] All are built around the smart use of external suppliers/partners to deliver important components of their service. Although many business model innovations have originated from new market entrants, it is a desirable innovation thrust for established players who find themselves caught in a competitive stalemate.

The same is true for innovations that lead to the creation of new integrated 'business systems,' often with partners, who combine discrete products and services in a full system approach. These system innovations require partners to be closely aligned. Each must provide a piece of the overall system or ensure the attractiveness of the combined system to customers.

Bank or credit card payment systems – created by networks of independent partner banks, together with credit card companies and the cooperation of merchant service providers – illustrate a successful new business system concept. Examples abound in other service areas:

- In insurance – various types of 'assistance contracts' were launched for tourists, homes or businesses by insurance companies and independent emergency service providers.
- In telecommunications – telecom operators routinely work with handset suppliers and content providers to offer various mobile service packages, like DoCoMo's revolutionary i-mode.
- In the media – US-based TiVo works in cooperation with the television broadcasting channels to offer record-on-demand TV; and Apple cooperates with music labels to offer its iTunes system on iPods.

New business models or business systems – at least the ones we shall consider here – generally require the involvement of different partners to deliver a common product, service, process or activity, each party providing a piece of the final system or supporting it. For that reason, business model and business system innovations usually result from a top-down process. Forming a partnership network involves complex negotiations and strategic deal-making activities which require the involvement of top management.

## Introduction of a New/Improved Customer Solution

Marketers all over the world have embraced a new mantra: 'Don't sell just a product (or service), provide a solution, and deliver an experience!' The idea is always the same, i.e. create greater value by meeting and satisfying more of the customers' needs. Kim and Mauborgne[11] redefined the notion of customer value and highlighted the difference between 'conventional logic':

> An industry's traditional boundaries determine the products and services a company offers. The goal is to maximize the value of those offerings. . .

and 'value innovation logic':

> A value innovator thinks in terms of the total solution customers seek, even if that takes the company beyond its industry's traditional offerings. . .

Solutions are devised to offer a significant leap in customer value through innovation.

Many companies believe they offer solutions when they make product enhancements for increased customer convenience, offer an extra service or when increased product offerings create a one-stop shopping alternative for their customers. In reality, offering customer solutions, particularly innovative ones, goes beyond tweaking a product line to come up with extended product and service concepts. Moving to solutions and experiences starts with a complete mindset change. Vendors must understand their customers intimately, including how they interact with suppliers and among themselves, say in web-based 'customer communities.'

They must also personally experience the context in which their products will be used, and learn about their customers' expectations and their sources of frustrations and delight.[12]

Innovative solutions are often conceived as integrated systems consisting of several elements. We have already mentioned that IT solution providers like IBM or HP offer consulting services with their main hardware and software products. Consumer goods solutions often sell a system with a dedicated consumable, like the coffee systems offered by Nestlé (Nespresso™), Kraft (Tassimo™), or Sara Lee and Philips (Senseo™) – or a product and its delivery system (many household products from P&G). Equipment goods solutions generally come from bundling a piece of machinery and a package of services, including installation, training, operational assistance, maintenance and the like. In construction materials, they may include the product, for example prefabricated ceiling elements, and the specially designed equipment that contractors use to mount and assemble them on site, cost- and time-effectively.

In diversified companies like IBM or HP, solutions can be engineered by combining the offerings of several complementary business units. But solutions often require the cooperation of different companies, as seen in the recent emergence of new espresso and coffee systems. Coffee manufacturers have cooperated with espresso or coffee machine manufacturers to develop and market integrated systems for the home consumption market. By making sure that the components of these systems are aligned and optimized, the coffee manufacturers can effectively sell not only an *experience* but also a perfect and replicable cup of coffee or espresso.

Developing and marketing new or improved customer solutions through partnering, even when partners come from other business units within the company, adds complexity to the innovation process. This is why such innovation thrust calls for the initial involvement of top management and proceeds predominantly top down, especially as external partnerships or ventures are formalized. Minor innovations that only enhance a business unit's offering and the customer's experience without external input will continue to be initiated bottom up.

In conclusion, these innovation thrusts have a predominant top-down component in three out of the four scenarios. This challenges some of the traditional clichés and beliefs that innovation is a spontaneous process that can neither be mandated nor managed. In reality, management has a very important role to play, hence the importance of understanding the tasks and roles of innovation leaders.

## ALIGNING YOUR MANAGEMENT EFFORTS WITH YOUR STRATEGY

Although the four broad thrusts outlined above differ significantly from each other in terms of strategic objective and content, they share some common innovation-specific characteristics. As a consequence, their instigators and drivers are likely to feature at least some of the six generic behavioral traits of innovation leaders mentioned in Chapter 2. And because innovation generally requires the mobilization of a 'chain of leadership' – further discussed in Chapter 8 – and not just the determined action of a single leader, each thrust will benefit from a combination of what we called 'front-end' and 'back-end' innovation leaders.

Now let's go beyond generic leadership characteristics and explore the specialized responses that these four thrusts require. Does steering the internal development of a totally new product or service category require the same leadership that it takes to rethink a business model or conceive and set up a radically new business system? Can the same leader move effortlessly from coaching a traditional new product development project to imagining and orchestrating a customer solution involving the input of external suppliers?

Advocates of leadership as a universal talent argue that true leaders can sense what is needed for the success of the company and then mobilize their staff behind this vision. However, experience shows that leaders tend to have different skills and are attracted by various types of challenges. So, before discussing which leadership style is best suited to the four innovation thrusts

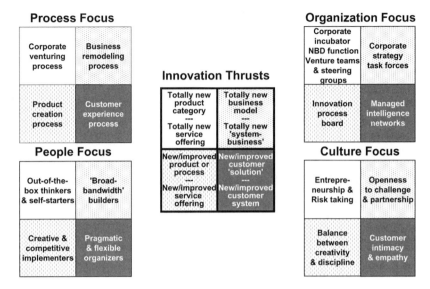

**Figure 6.2** Focus areas under each innovation thrust

described above, let's review the specific leadership challenges and imperatives of each thrust. We will do so using four distinct parameters:

- *Enabling process*: which process will be most instrumental in implementing each thrust?
- *Structure*: what specific organizational mechanism do we need to guide each thrust?
- *Cultural traits*: what type of organizational culture will be most conducive to sustaining each thrust?
- *Staff profile*: what kind of people do we need to drive each thrust?

Figure 6.2 summarizes the enabling processes, organizational mechanisms, cultural traits and staff profiles that are best adapted to each of the four thrusts. These different areas of management focus do not pretend to be all-inclusive, nor are they mutually exclusive. They are just indicative of the priorities that innovation leaders should recognize when they choose any of these four thrusts.

## Developing a New/Improved Product, Process or Service Offering

As noted earlier, most companies focus the bulk of their innovation efforts on incremental product improvement, rejuvenation and extensions, as well as on research activities to support product development. Best practices are usually well known, but not always applied and recognized. A number of key points still deserve top management attention. Let us review briefly what each particular thrust requires in terms of process, organization, culture and people.

### Focus on a Seamless Product Creation Process

Companies competing on producing new/improved products or services within their chosen markets should recognize 'product creation' as a core process and strive to make it seamless. Defining the process as 'product creation,' as opposed to the classic 'new product development' (NPD), prompts managers to look at the complete set of cross-functional activities and strategic decisions that shape the process from idea to market. You should ensure that everyone in the organization understands the process in its totality and knows what he/she can contribute in each of the sub-processes mentioned previously in Figure 4.1.[13]

Making the process truly seamless requires dedication and courage on the part of innovation leaders in order to (1) force open all functional and organizational silos and insist on making every part of the process cross-functional; and (2) empower program/project leaders and their team, sometimes in spite of the reluctance of their operational hierarchies.

### Empower the Innovation Board as a Key Steering Mechanism

Managing a complex cross-functional process like product creation requires setting up an appropriate – i.e. high level and multidisciplinary – steering mechanism. The Innovation Board described in

Chapter 4 is a good example of such a mechanism. Focusing on product creation and improvement, it allocates specific process ownership and responsibilities to dedicated managers, process owners and coaches, and monitors their progress. It also establishes a fully empowered project organization and helps launch initiatives to enhance innovation in the company, including performance metrics and management training and development programs.

### Promote a Culture of Creativity and Discipline

The complementary values of creativity *and* discipline, highlighted in Chapter 2, apply particularly well to the continuous development of new/improved products and services, innovation's backbone. Innovation leaders should be clearly identified as proponents of both qualities. Since the two cultures rarely coexist within the same leadership, product creation requires the combination of front-end leaders who personify a culture of creativity and back-end leaders who act as the guardians of innovation discipline. It will be up to the CEO to defend a balance between the two cultures and their proponents.

### Look for and Deploy Creative, Competitive Implementers

To be effective and sustainable over time – because product battles never end – a product creation thrust requires a combination of talents, particularly from its program managers and project leaders. Their ideal profile should comprise three broad attributes (a realistic combination for one person):

- *Creativity*, to identify and capture all possible differentiation opportunities, even in established and mature products and markets, and find solutions to market and customer problems.
- *Competitive or winning spirit*, to improve products and processes relentlessly, without complacency, and doggedly shorten lead times to beat competitors and win in the market.

- *Implementation focus*, to leverage the full power of innovative ideas through superb execution, both at the operational project level and in the market launch process.

People who combine these qualities tend to be scarce but they *do* exist, and innovation leaders must compose and balance teams that incorporate the desired profile.

## Developing a Totally New Product or Service Category

Creating a totally new product or service category in an unknown market – a radical innovation akin to a breakthrough – presents a completely different set of challenges to managers who are used to developing new/improved products or services. It is a high-risk/high-reward innovation thrust, and the boldest possible move from a product or service development point of view because it leads the company into completely unknown territory in terms of technology and/or market. Choosing this thrust has several implications for management, in terms of action focus.

### Set up a Corporate Venturing or New Business Development Process

The creation of a totally new business through innovation involves high risk and generally originates from a top management decision. It is frequently implemented as part of the corporate venturing or new business development (NBD) process. The resulting projects often need central funding to alleviate the risk for business units that are either interested in or even the initiators of the new venture. Even though projects are set up for such types of innovation, as for more traditional NPD activities, the project management structure and process – including the review mechanism – are different. The uncertainty and risk level of these projects requires a high degree of transparency and personal involvement of corporate leaders who will be involved in key go/no-go decisions.

### Entrust Ventures to a Corporate Incubator or New Business Development Function, and Create Teams Supervised by Project Steering Groups

Disruptive technology developments that give rise to new ventures are usually initially launched and nurtured by corporate or divisional R&D labs. Once projects have matured and received management's go-ahead, they need to be hosted, led and supported by a series of specific organizational mechanisms.

Projects falling outside the scope of existing business units – when the targeted market is entirely new to the organization – may be entrusted to a corporate incubator, if such a structure exists. Often such incubators are located in the R&D organization, at least for technology-intensive projects. Other organizational positioning could be under the supervision of the NBD manager at the corporate or divisional level.

A small venture team, composed of senior managers, is set up to explore each new opportunity, assess its attractiveness and prepare a business plan, if it receives a green light. Once the opportunity is approved, the team evolves to a full venture project team. Management will typically appoint a high-level steering group to coach and supervise the new venture, until it can either be spun off or set up as a distinct new business unit.

### Foster a Culture of Entrepreneurship and Risk Taking

Creating a totally new product or service category requires entrepreneurship and the management skills to encourage responsible risk taking. The first challenge for leaders is to live up to this principle on a day-to-day basis and have their managers comply as well. The second challenge, as stressed in Chapter 1, is how to strike a balance between enterprising risk taking and pragmatic risk management. Management must empower the venture team as it faces obstacles on the project path while maintaining focus on the objectives that will determine success. The second attitude ensures that, at each stage, all known risk factors have been identified, minimized and properly managed.

### Staff the Venture with 'Out-of-the-Box' Thinkers and Self-Starters

The development and successful introduction of a totally new product or service category – in short, the creation of an entirely new business – requires the deployment of people who challenge the status quo and are energized to create something new and run with it. The challenge for management is to create the conditions and climate in which these pioneering entrepreneurs can thrive and be successful and – should the venture prove unsuccessful – to redeploy them without loss of morale.

## Developing a Totally New Business Model or Business System

These two innovation thrusts both rely heavily on a creative process redesign (or rethink) approach. While each has the potential to provide its originators with unbeatable strategic advantages, successful execution is challenging. Also, the necessary involvement of external partners adds to their planning and organizational complexity.

Developing a new business model can create a sustainable strategic advantage, particularly if it leverages the company's unique capabilities and those of its suppliers/partners in areas where competitors have weaknesses.

Developing a new business system can lead to a 'winner-takes-all' market position if the new system enters the market first, is flawlessly implemented and quickly becomes the established standard.

Choosing these thrusts implies another set of priorities for top management, quite different from those previously described.

### Become Adept at the Process of Business Remodeling

Reinventing a *business model* involves a cross-functional analytical process similar to the one used for business process reengineering.

The creative part of the process generally comes (1) when teams systematically challenge, one after the other, hitherto accepted industry assumptions and practices, whether tacit or explicit; and (2) when they question the way the company has so far organized its activities. Of course, the process does not stop with the analytical remodeling part and the documentation of a business case. The most critical aspect is implementation, which relies on the effective management of the transition between the old and the new business model. The difficulty with business model innovations is the need to move from one type of model to another without endangering the company's profitability, alienating customers and disorganizing operations. Some authors have effectively covered this specific challenge.[14] Implementing a completely new business model generally leads to radical changes in business practices and requires major restructuring and reskilling efforts.

Creating a new *business system* is also the result of an analytical modeling exercise, but that process does not center so much on the company and how it relates to its market and customers. It focuses to a larger extent on (1) understanding how various actors along a given value chain can intervene to add value for customers in a particular need area; and (2) detecting opportunities for reconfiguring the way they work together to everyone's benefit, because successful systems are built on 'win-win' proposals.

In short, business system innovations emerge when companies imagine better ways to serve the market, bring partners together and bundle products and/or services to meet customers' existing needs more fully or address their latent needs. Of course, this type of innovation is conditioned by the availability of partners who are able and willing to design, provide and integrate the missing pieces of a given system. They can do it either as part of a traditional, commercial relationship or as a consortium. It also requires a project management process that ensures that each partner (1) aligns its 'deliverables' with the agreed strategy and plan, and (2) synchronizes them carefully.

A real case example will illustrate the complexity of the process lying behind business system innovations. A few years ago, engineers at Safe-Conduct,[15] a security equipment specialist, designed a 'cash-case' for transferring banknotes from retailers to banks, or from local bank agencies to head office, without having to rely on the usual armored vans and heavily armed security guards. The cash-carrying case, like something out of a James Bond movie, was equipped with a system capable of destroying all the banknotes inside instantaneously[16] if the lock was tampered with or forced open. The business case for the project anticipated that the device, if adopted, would dramatically reduce retailers' cash handling costs. Now the transfer could be carried out by a single unarmed person driving an unmarked car, a much cheaper solution than traditional security convoys. The success of the concept depended on the assumption that armed robbers would not attack the security guard carrying the case, because they would know that they could not open the case without the highly secure machine that only banks would own. The expected cost benefit was to be enhanced by a lower robbery insurance premium, for both the retailer and the security company. Safe-Conduct was also counting on additional administrative cost savings from a cash-counting feature in the system, and software for making automatic accounting entries for all cash deposits.

The system, which included several features beyond the cash-carrying case, required the involvement and cooperation of a number of partners besides Safe-Conduct, the case inventor:

- a company agreeing to design a banknote feeding system coupled with store check-out counters so clerks could insert cash safely into the carrying cases;
- security companies willing to take the risk of sending a single driver in an unmarked car to transfer cash in these safe cases;
- a banking equipment specialist, capable of engineering a secure and safe system for opening the cash cases at the receiving end;
- insurance companies willing to lower their premiums to retailers and security companies adopting the system;
- plus, of course, retailers and banks agreeing to equip their sites with the system at a significant investment cost.

After multiple negotiations, Safe-Conduct managed to convince two equipment companies to develop dedicated cash handling machines, one for retailers and one for banks, compatible with the cash-carrying case design. The physical part of the system was ready but complex process issues rapidly emerged during the launch process, namely:

- banks would not invest in the receiving equipment without a guarantee that a large enough number of retailers would adopt the system;
- retailers would not invest in the cash depositing equipment and in the carry cases without a guarantee that their banks were ready to handle the cases;
- insurance companies would not reduce their premiums unless statistics showed a significant reduction in the number of attacks on security guards;
- security companies would not modify their practices unless forced to do so by a high and growing number of retailers adopting the system, and the like.

Safe-Conduct found it was not equipped to handle such a complex launch process and reluctantly abandoned the system, which was ultimately taken over and simplified by a larger and better financed company. Clearly, the relatively small, engineering-oriented company lacked the high-level leaders required to build a consortium of interested parties, muster government and police support, and overcome the many obstacles that hindered the implementation of the system.

## Deploy Corporate Strategy Task Forces to Come Up with a New Model

Business model or business system innovations generally need to involve cross-functional and cross-departmental task forces for both the analytical and implementation parts. The sensitivity of the strategic and implementation issues covered by these task forces justifies a high degree of top management involvement. This is why such endeavors are often initiated and steered by the corporate strategy function, when it exists, or by a subset of the top leadership team, acting as project steering group.

## Spread a Culture of Openness to Challenge and Partnership

The development and introduction of a new business model or business system requires a great deal of openness across the board, from top management to functional and operational units. Openness is needed to challenge the current status quo, business practices and industry assumptions, and to accept the need to sacrifice 'sacred cows' in an attempt to rethink the industry or the way to compete. Openness is also required to accept outsourcing some activities hitherto conducted internally, and to partner with external organizations, relinquishing some degree of control and inventing new modes of working together.

## Give the Task to 'Broad-Bandwidth' and Cooperative Builders

The business remodeling process requires the intervention of managers capable of imagination, breadth of vision and a cooperation mindset. They need *imagination* to create alternative ways to deliver value to stakeholders and detect opportunities behind the arcane business system of their industry and the value chain of their business. They need *breadth of vision* to grasp the big picture, i.e. to see the forest and not just the trees, and to sense what kind of system they have to put in place to meet market needs more fully and economically. Finally, they need a *cooperation mindset* and a talent for getting things done with and through partners, while preserving the company's interests throughout the negotiation and implementation phases.

So, these 'broad-bandwidth' managers – as introduced in Chapter 3 – need to combine strong analytical *and* implementation capabilities across functional and organizational lines. This type of skill and attitude profile is rare. Although it can be developed further, it often needs to be proactively sought at the hiring stage.

## Developing a New/Improved Customer Solution

To move from products to 'solutions,' management needs to focus on its customers' unmet or latent needs and devise ways to satisfy them, even if this involves going outside and finding partners to complement the company's offering.

Logitech's entry into the digital pen market provides a good example of an innovative solution to electronic handwriting recognition. Because the technology – licensed from its partner, Anoto, in Sweden – is based on a proprietary paper matrix, Logitech found itself compelled to enlist stationery suppliers in its undertaking. Without the paper, its pen would not work. Similarly, the company had to approach an external software specialist, MyScript Notes®, to add handwriting recognition to its offering. Paper, pen and software are now all part of the Logitech io™ solution.[17] And the company is now trying to develop 'enterprise solutions' for its pen with the help of forms and solution software specialists.

Many of the requirements for the creation of a totally new business system apply equally well to the development of an incremental customer solution, which is a more limited variant of that strategy.[18] But choosing a solution approach has an additional specific characteristic: It requires management to focus thoroughly on its customer or user, if different.

## *Launch a Process to Capture the Customers' Experience*

Conceiving a satisfying customer solution or system starts with the development and implementation of an approach to target and understand the elusive concept of 'customer experience.' This implies understanding what that experience actually means, how it can be measured, what contributes to it, and how to develop and test offerings that will provide customers with an unbeatable and repeatable experience. Companies like Logitech and Intuit, the personal financial software specialist, and particularly Harley-Davidson, the iconic motorcycle company, have developed research approaches to discover how their customers experience their products, objectively, subjectively and emotionally. All these approaches share the same simple principles, namely:

To understand your customers' experience:

(1) Go, meet and live with your customers – and your 'non-customers' – wherever they are, and particularly whenever and wherever they use your product and those of your competitors.
(2) Once with your customers and your competitors' customers, look at how they live, how they use the product, how they feel about it, what they miss that would make their experience richer.

Harley-Davidson is probably unique in the world in at least two aspects of providing innovative solutions to its customers:

(1) It allows – and even encourages – its customers to design their own motorcycle from a myriad of combinations of parts and accessories. No two Harley bikes will ever look identical.
(2) It offers its customers a wide range of customized services that go well beyond traditional maintenance and repair. For example, it has a special section on its website for women, and dealers hold 'Garage Parties' – women-only events offering fun, basic information for those wishing to embark on the Harley experience, including advice on technical issues and the best clothes to wear for biking. It also organizes riding schools, riding events, owners' rallies and overseas trips.

This ability to sense exactly what its customers will like is built on decades of intimacy with its riders. Through the 'HOG' (Harley Owners' Group) organization, Harley-Davidson managers are particularly well equipped to mix with their customers during rallies that, each year, gather thousands of bikers in most parts of the world. Harley managers are expected to attend at least two customer events per year, whatever their function in the organization. These events allow them to dress like bikers and mix with customers in a relaxed atmosphere. In this way, they can fully understand, and even feel through their senses, how their customers live their 'riding life' and experience their 'journey into the brand.' This type of insight far exceeds what other companies learn about their customers through traditional market research.

### Organize and Steer Managed Intelligence Networks

Companies wishing to compete through a strategy of innovative solutions need to build a permanent way to collect and interpret customer intelligence. Customer, consumer or end-user insights must be collected by everyone in the organization, not just by marketing and sales functions. Traditional marketing research mechanisms have limitations: They cannot detect early signs of changes in customer preferences or identify unmet or – even worse – latent needs. To be effective, they need to be complemented by company-wide, experiential customer sensing approaches. Companies that do not have the innate and deeply ingrained customer-oriented culture of Harley-Davidson should proactively recruit volunteers within their organization to find new trends and capture customer insights. One way is to set up managed intelligence networks, organized around a particular customer segment, a product application or even a customer concern.[19] Marketing will then be tasked with the set-up, delivery, debrief and application of these networks' findings.

### Promote a Culture of Customer Intimacy and Empathy

A customer-centric culture, as described in Chapter 3, is important for all types of innovation but particularly so for the development of fully satisfying customer solutions. Indeed, developing innovative solutions requires a high degree of customer or consumer intimacy and empathy, which can only be acquired through a systematic and widespread market immersion. Marketing literature is full of advice on[20] and examples of how to build that kind of culture. But the critical element remains the personal attitude and commitment of company leaders, as exemplified by Harley-Davidson's management team.

Richard Teerlink, Harley-Davidson's former chairman and CEO, seemed to be a living personification of that culture. Invited several years ago by IMD to address the faculty, he surprised everyone by arriving in the school's boardroom dressed like one of his customers/bikers in a black leather jacket and pants and black cowboy boots. He apologized for his rather unconventional business attire, saying that he had just been hanging around with customers at the local Lausanne HOG chapter and had not had the time to go back to his hotel to change. Mixing with customers on every possible occasion, he stressed, was expected from every manager at Harley-Davidson, a rule that his successor maintained. When the example comes from the top, even the most conservative managers hear the message.

### Implement through Pragmatic, Flexible Organizers

A focus on solutions will be successful if the project team includes a number of pragmatic and flexible organizers. One might argue that this profile is necessary for the implementation part of most product and service development projects, which is true. However, developing an innovative solution requires a touch of pragmatism to make all the elements of the solution work together. It also demands a lot of flexibility to cope with the complexity of working with partners that one does not control.

## ACTIVATING SPECIFIC CHANGE LEVERS TO SUPPORT YOUR STRATEGY

The necessary conditions for the successful implementation of an innovation strategy rarely pre-exist, at least in a fully developed form. As a consequence, after choosing the innovation thrust(s) that you will focus on, it is important to reflect on what each requires in terms of specific process, organizational mechanism, culture and people profile. This is best done at the top management team level, and it can be very instructive.

As they went through this type of self-analysis, the senior managers of a global building materials company discovered why they had rarely been successful in branching out of their traditional strategy of incremental product and process innovations. Although the company had set the ambitious goal of searching for and pursuing more radical innovations in terms of customer-oriented systems/solutions, it had never reached this objective.

Disappointing results were largely due to the original company culture, which stressed operational excellence and predictability and discouraged risk taking. The management team recognized that it had not established the proper processes or set up adequate organizational mechanisms to steer and coach its high-risk projects. The company conducted all innovation projects in the same traditional way, under the scrutiny of the same type of leaders, and within the same rules and performance measures. Becoming aware of the underlying reasons for the company's past failures, management established a special, parallel track for running high-risk, disruptive innovations, alongside its incremental ones. This new track was appointed to a top management committee, which is now working on the design of a new process and is empowered to make all new project leadership appointments.

Besides reviewing the way in which you treat the four different innovation thrusts described above, in terms of process, structure, culture and people, it is interesting to think of the various levers that you can activate to induce and stimulate change. Change priorities will always be company-specific, yet some change levers can be particularly effective if begun early to support a chosen thrust. So, if you decide to focus particularly on one of the innovation thrusts described in this chapter, here is some advice on how you can stimulate change.

### Demand Shorter Lead Times to Boost Your Ability to Produce New/Improved Products, Processes or Service Offerings

There are many ways for innovation leaders to shake up a complacent organization and gain a sustainable advantage on the new product or service front. The issue is rarely a lack of good ideas on what to do to take the lead over competitors – most companies have more ideas than they can handle. The challenge is in choosing and implementing these ideas effectively, in terms of optimizing time, costs and resources. The objective of any change in this area is, therefore, to move forward on two levels in parallel by: (1) improving effectiveness (doing the right things), and (2) gaining in efficiency (doing things right).

One of the most interesting stimuli for achieving this dual objective is to launch a *radical* lead-time reduction drive for the development of new products or services. Starting an exercise to drastically reduce (i.e. by an order of magnitude) time-to-market or – even better – time-to-profit is a formidable way of breaking down the entire product or service creation process into all its components and making its deficiencies visible. As all product development practitioners know, *time-to-market* is conditioned by several factors:

- the quality, precision and clarity of the new product or service brief;
- the quality and empowerment level of the cross-functional development team;
- the early involvement of suppliers and early prototyping practices;
- the quality of the process and reduction in the number of change loops;
- the content and quality of communications within the team, with functional departments and with top management;
- and many more factors that become transparent when a diagnostic is conducted.

*Time-to-profit* is influenced by all the factors above, plus:

- the intrinsic quality of the customer value proposition behind the new product or service, which guarantees early customer adoption; and
- the quality and smoothness of the launch, and the speed with which the new product or service is deployed in various markets.

All of these factors, once identified and prioritized, can lead to specific and concrete improvement drives that will enhance your product or service creation process.

### Encourage a Systematic Opportunity Search to Enhance Your Chances of Developing Totally New Product or Service Categories

If you decide to embark on a radical innovation thrust to create entirely new product or service categories, you need to focus all your efforts, at least initially, on the search and validation of opportunities. The role of management is twofold:

- First, it is to define the market territory to be explored, as Philips has done by staking out consumer healthcare as one of the priority domains in which it wants to develop.
- Second, it is to select those managers who will be entrusted with the mission to scout for great new product, service or business ideas.

An opportunity search, by its very nature, is much broader in scope and more open-ended than a traditional market research effort. The concepts discovered should be the precursors of future mainstream products. For this to happen, they should leverage long-term market trends and hit the market at the right time.

This type of open-ended search may be difficult to initiate if your company has been very focused only on the 'core business' and managers may not be motivated to search for new opportunities. Looking to create a new category 'beyond the core' may be seen as a dilution of efforts when so many resources are already needed to defend or grow the core. Plans to revolutionize your offering with a breakthrough may also be resisted by more conservative managers, worried about cannibalization threats or failure.

As a management team, you may want to lower the risk of internal opposition by limiting the search team to a few dedicated managers, for example in your new business development function. A more constructive approach encourages every manager to be a 'hunter,' giving them a specific objective to search for and using a rigorous process to evaluate the opportunities identified.

## Promote 'System Thinking' to Prepare for the Development of a Totally New Business Model or Business System

The main enemy of any business (re)modeling initiative is the parochial perspective of middle managers, emotionally and intellectually holed up in their functional silos, and steeped in the current status quo of their business. This is why business process reengineering faces so much resistance and sometimes outright opposition from operational departments.

To break such resistance, you will need to develop your manager's capability to see patterns and think in systemic terms. *Pattern recognition* is needed to recognize opportunities in the evolution of markets and the convergence of industries. *System thinking* is needed for managers to understand how the pieces of a business model fit together, or what the various entities contribute to a common process. It is particularly critical to make managers aware of the root causes of vicious circles and, conversely, to enable them to discern the triggers of elusive virtuous spirals. Pattern recognition and system thinking are not innate skills; as a consequence, they are not equally distributed among managers. They clearly deserve to feature prominently in the strategy module of management development programs.[21]

## Enforce Market Immersion to Steer the Development of New/Improved Customer Solutions or Customer Systems

Attempts to move from products and services to solutions will fail unless they are rooted with an in-depth understanding of the customer's world, not just his/her needs. Genuine customer-centric cultures allowing this degree of intimacy are rare. This is why the first and perhaps most important effort, before attempting to devise solutions, is a broad-based market immersion exercise, involving several functions.

Market immersions are different from the opportunity searches mentioned for the creation of a totally new product category, because they focus on – and limit themselves to – a defined customer group. Routine customer visits by salespeople or technical service staff, although important for collecting customer reactions, do not qualify because they seldom lead to captured insight and foresight. Market immersion is a process by which small teams of managers – cross-functional teams bring richer perspectives – visit leading customers without any agenda other than listening, probing and speculating with them. The objective is to bring home not just the customer's voice but the customer's latent needs, frustrations, feelings and dreams. Such immersion will not happen unless you and your top management team, emulating Harley-Davidson:

(1) show the way by practicing the discipline yourselves;
(2) establish appropriate metrics to track the immersion activities of your staff;
(3) build incentives to encourage that behavior; and
(4) set up mechanisms and organize events to share and exploit the type of learning and discoveries generated.

To complement market immersions, marketing consultants have developed a number of tools to capture the customer experience and turn it into innovative solutions.[22]

The next four chapters will illustrate, with real company examples, the type of leadership profile most suited to carrying out and implementing each of the four innovation thrusts described in this chapter. We will propose that a specific leadership style corresponds to each thrust.

## ENDNOTES

1. Excerpt from 'The Art and Discipline of Innovation' by InnovationPoint, http://www.1000ventures.com/business_guide/innovation_strategic_byip.html accessed 22 November 2007.
2. This list of parameters to be aligned borrows from Jay R. Galbraith's Star Model™, except that for the purposes of this exercise, Galbraith's fourth parameter – rewards – has been replaced by culture. A description of Galbraith's model is available on his website http://www.jaygalbraith.com/star.html.

3. For seminal books on product development, refer to:

   - Wheelwright, S.C. and Clark, K.B. (1992). *Revolutionizing Product Development: Quantum Leaps in Speed, Efficiency and Quality.* New York, The Free Press.
   - Rosenau Jr., M.D. (1996). *The PDMA Handbook of New Product Development.* New York, John Wiley & Sons, Inc.

   For a seminal book on benchmarking, refer to:

   - Dimancescu, D. and Dwenger, K. (1996). *World-Class New Product Development: Benchmarking Best Practices of Agile Manufacturers.* New York, AMACOM.

4. Ketteringham, J. and Nayak, P.R. (1990). *Breakthroughs.* Boston, Harvard Business School Press.
   Diebold, J. (1990). *The Innovators: The Discoveries, Inventions and Breakthroughs of our Time.* New York, Penguin Group.

5. Ketteringham, J. and Nayak, P.R. (1990). '3M's Little Yellow Note Pads: "Never Mind. I'll Do it Myself."' *Breakthroughs.* Boston, Harvard Business School Press, pp. 50–73.

6. Refer to the history of the serendipitous invention of aspartame on http://www.swankin-turner.com/hist.html.

7. Deschamps, J.-P. and Nayak, P.R. (1995). 'Devising a Bold Game Plan: Canon's Copier Breakthrough.' *Product Juggernauts: How Companies Mobilize to Generate a Stream of Market Winners.* Boston, Harvard Business School Press, pp. 113–127.

8. Zook, C. (2004). *Beyond the Core.* Boston, Harvard Business School Press.

9. Ryans, A. and Pahwa, A. (2005). 'Ryanair: Defying Gravity.' IMD Case No. IMD-3-1633.

10. Kumar, N. and Rogers, B. (2000). 'easyJet: The Web's Favorite Airline.' IMD Case No. IMD-3-0873.

11. Kim, W.C. and Mauborgne, R. (1997). 'Value Innovation: The Strategic Logic of High Growth.' *Harvard Business Review*, January–February: 103–112.

12. C.K. Prahalad and Venkatram Ramaswamy have carried the concept of 'experience innovation' even further in their article 'The New Frontier of Experience Innovation,' *MIT Sloan Management Review*, Summer 2003: 12–18. They advocate that individual customers should be allowed 'to actively co-construct their own consumption experiences, through personalized interaction, thereby co-creating unique value for themselves.'

13. I personally recommend recognizing seven sub-processes in product creation: business intelligence; technology intelligence; technology resource development; idea management; product and technology strategy and planning; program management (which includes both product development and launch/deployment); and product life-cycle management. For details, refer to Deschamps, J.-P. and Nayak, P.R. (1995). 'Implementing a World-class Process: From R&D to Product, the Toshiba Way.' *Product Juggernauts: How Companies Mobilize to Generate a Stream of Market Winners.* Boston, Harvard Business School Press, pp. 175–213.

14. Markides, C. and Charitou, C.D. (2004). 'Competing with Dual Business Models: A Contingency Approach.' *Academy of Management Executive* **18**(3).

15. Disguised name.

16. An explosive sprayed indelible ink and acid on the notes inside, making them useless.

17. Deschamps, J.-P. and Pahwa, A. (2003). 'Logitech: Getting the io™ Digital Pen to Market.' IMD Case No. IMD-5-0662.

18. The main differences between the two thrusts can be found in the level of ambitiousness of the undertaking (a business system is more far-reaching and complex to set up) and the nature of the driver (a solution strategy is generally driven by a specific manufacturer's desire to enhance his offering, whereas a business system tends to be developed by a coalition of partners).

19. For more information on 'managed intelligence networks,' refer to Deschamps, J.-P. (2001). 'From Information and Knowledge to Innovation.' *Competing with Information.* Ed. D.A. Marchand. Chichester, John Wiley & Sons, Ltd, pp. 127–145.

20. Classic examples of recommended approaches for discovering customers' experience are presented in:

    • Gouillart, F.J. and Sturdivant, F.D. (1994). 'Spend a Day in the Life of Your Customers.' *Harvard Business Review*, January–February: 116–125.
    • Shapiro, B.P., Rangan, V.K. and Sviokla, J.J. (1992). 'Staple Yourself to an Order.' *Harvard Business Review*, July–August: 113–122.
    • Barwise, P. and Meehan, S. (2004). *Simply Better: Winning and Keeping Customers by Delivering What Matters Most.* Boston, Harvard Business School Press, pp. 61–87.

21. For a simple and effective way to learn and communicate to managers what system thinking entails, refer to Senge, P., Roberts, C. and Smith, B.J. (1994). *The Fifth Discipline Fieldbook: Strategies and Tools for Building a Learning Organization.* New York, Doubleday/Currency.

22. Ulwick, A.W. (2002). 'BEST PRACTICE – Turn Customer Input into Innovation.' *Harvard Business Review*, January: 5–11.

# LEADING THE DEVELOPMENT OF NEW/IMPROVED PRODUCTS OR SERVICES REQUIRED: TEAM SPORTS COACHES TO FOSTER INNOVATION DISCIPLINE

*I believe in rules. Sure I do. If there weren't any rules, how could you break them?*

*Late Leo Durocher, famous American baseball coach*

*The most important quality I look for in a player is accountability. You've got to be accountable for who you are. It's too easy to blame things on someone else.*

*Lenny Wilkens, famous American basketball coach*[1]

A recent book, *Blue Ocean Strategy*, strongly advises against competing in what it calls 'red oceans,' along with the crowd of 'incrementalists.' Focusing on new/improved products or services in your traditional markets, argue its authors, will only bring you marginal benefits. Instead, they recommend 'creating uncontested market space and making the competition irrelevant' by introducing new rules of the game in your industry – what they call a 'blue ocean strategy.'[2]

This point of view has the merit of inducing managers to think creatively about their environment and to carve out their own market by inventing new ways to compete. But taking this precept too literally would mean stopping or reorienting 80% or more of all R&D efforts worldwide, which is obviously unrealistic. Indeed, all companies make a living from selling established products and services in current markets, and they all depend on how well these products and services do against competitors. Reinventing a new market space is highly desirable, particularly when a company finds itself stuck in a competitive stalemate. But opportunities to completely change the rules of the game are scarce. And besides, agile competitors are quick to invade attractive new market territories, once discovered. So, even for the 'blue ocean strategy' adopters, success ultimately hinges on gaining and keeping a competitive edge. And this means playing a more effective game of incremental product or service innovation.

In every industry, some companies seem to play the incremental innovation game quite successfully. They launch streams of market winners and grow in market share and profits, while others struggle behind. The losers always seem to be taken by surprise by their competitors' innovations. Yet others appear to do well for a while, then somehow lose their touch, as if they can no longer get their act together, and fall behind.

Many factors contribute to uneven levels of product development performance, for sure. But one comes top in most cases, i.e. the quality (or lack of it) of the leadership required for this type of incremental new product or service innovation. Winning companies have, in most cases, managed to build up a strong cadre of innovation leaders over time to supervise their process and build a supportive culture. Losing or struggling organizations have not; or if they have done at one time, they seem unable to sustain this type of leadership over the years.

This chapter will focus on these particular innovation leaders – the incrementalists. They manage to get everyone in the organization mobilized to compete and win in the unending battle for new products or services. They are the innovation backbones of their companies. We shall first propose a short profile of these leaders, based on their most commonly shared characteristics. Second, using the example of Medtronic's pacemaker business, we shall illustrate what they do, concretely, to make innovation happen in their organization. Third and finally, we shall review some of the limitations of these types of leaders, if they are left alone.

## INNOVATION LEADERS AS TOUGH TEAM SPORTS COACHES

### Incremental Product/Service Innovation is a Competitive Team Sport

Management scholars have always been attracted by the world of team sports, like basketball, football, hockey and others, because they offer a permanent crucible for leadership. Some studies on the behavior of teams of athletes have stressed the role of team leaders – the captains.[3] Others have tried to assess the characteristics of a good coach, one who makes his/her team stay on top more regularly than competing teams. Business leaders' interest in the wisdom of team sports coaches has reached a point where famous coaches have written their own books on leadership.[4] The best known among them are frequently asked to address groups of managers at corporate conferences. Academics, too, for example Professor Julian Birkinshaw of London Business School, have taken up the baton to extract leadership lessons from these great coaches.[5]

The metaphor of the 'leader as a team sports coach' applies undoubtedly to a number of business situations, but it is particularly apt for the product creation process. It fits with the way companies reliably come up with streams of incremental – new/ improved – products or services. The analogy between the two types of activities is strong on at least four factors:

• Product creation, like basketball, football or hockey, is foremost a team exercise. Teams, not just individuals, make the right decisions and win (or lose); their performance reflects both the intrinsic skills of their members and the quality and cohesion of their team play.

• Product creation, like team sports, is subject to a single performance measure, i.e. the score. What is the company's new product or service hit rate? Will the next new product or service be better than the competitors' offering? Will it make the company win in terms of market share and profits?

- Product creation, like team sports, is conducted with very tight restrictions on 'play time.' Most windows of opportunity for new products or services are narrow. Product cycle times are becoming increasingly shorter, and both organizational and decision speed turn into key competitive assets.
- Finally, in product creation, as in team sports, no one ever wins 'for good.' Competitive product and service battles never end. Each new product or service launch is like a new match in sports; it reopens the scoreboard and the company and the team have to prove, again, that they can do even better to win.

## The Three Priorities of the Innovation Leader/Team Sports Coach: Challenging, Setting Goals and Measuring

In product creation, as in sports, the classical roles of the leader/ coach are manifold. He/she has to:

- select a range of complementary players, and compose the best possible teams for each new challenge;
- attend to the development of individuals and build up team skills, while coaching the trainers;
- establish open communication channels at all times between the team members, and between the team and management;
- develop a strategy and process to win, and ensure that everyone understands it, adheres to it and applies it in action;
- stimulate and motivate the team before each challenge, and debrief it after every performance for lessons learned and improvements to be made.

However, in product creation as in sports, three priorities take particular importance because they determine a specific type of leadership: *Challenging, setting goals and measuring.*

- *Challenging* the functions and teams responsible for product creation is needed whenever top management perceives a decline in the competitiveness of its product lines, be it in terms of market coverage and share, customer satisfaction or product economics. One of the most effective ways to challenge a product team is to confront it with the performance of best-in-class competitors, whether on innovation, quality, lead times or costs. This is typically done through benchmarking.
- *Setting goals* is the privilege of top management. If it chooses lead-time reduction as the main change lever in product creation, then it will set a new demanding target for time-to-market or time-to-profit. Experience shows that, to be effective and force teams to rethink their process entirely, the new lead-time targets must be significantly below best current performance. But product creation is broader than lead times, and this is why goals can be set for other factors as well, such as product quality, performance and cost.
- *Measuring* results is usually the next priority for top management. Innovation leaders for incremental product or service improvements generally establish a pyramid of metrics. They balance different types of performance parameters: lagging indicators, in-process benchmarks and, most importantly, leading pointers that measure the rate of learning of the organization.

## The Leadership Style of the Innovation Leader/Team Sports Coach: Demanding but Supportive

Team sports coaches are advised to apply a number of traditional leadership principles, which apply equally well to the innovation leader, e.g.:

- *require excellence; do not expect perfection;*
- *understand your athletes (team members) before you can influence them;*

- *create trust and command respect;*
- *motivate and inspire.*[6]

Sports analysts have also observed four basic different leadership styles in the team sports coaches that they have analyzed,[7] namely:

- Two types of autocratic styles: the *telling* mode, which could be interpreted as meaning: 'Do what I am telling you to do, because it is the only way to win,' and the *selling* tone, which conveys a more open attitude, like: 'If you agree to do it this way, then you'll have a better chance to win.'
- Two types of democratic styles: the *sharing* approach, which is the equivalent of saying: 'Tell me what you think we should be doing to win,' and the *allowing* style, the most liberal of the four, which stands for: 'The objective is to win, now you find out how you want to do it!'

Conducting similar kinds of observations on sports leaders, academics have come up with a fairly similar list of coaching styles, such as the typology of Woods and McIlveen:[8]

- *Command style – direct instruction, coach dictates.*
- *Reciprocal style – athlete takes some responsibility for their own development, monitored by the coach.*
- *Problem solving style – athlete solves problems set by the coach.*
- *Guided discovery – athlete has freedom to explore various options.*

The 'team sports coach' leader can be equated to what famous management author Robert Tomasko[9] calls a 'warrior-leader,' because some team sports – think of football, basketball, soccer, rugby or ice hockey – are sometimes run like mini-wars. They bring into play a strong dose of aggressiveness, albeit controlled, and require absolute dedication to winning. Figure 7.1 summarizes what Tomasko sees as the positive traits and excesses of this type of leader.

All these styles are obviously representative of different personalities and are applicable to many kinds of leadership situations, not just sports. They definitely apply to the management of incremental innovation, i.e. to the new/improved products and services thrust covered in this chapter.

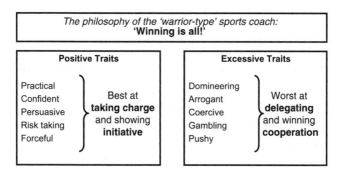

**Figure 7.1** The team sports coach as 'warrior-leader'
Reproduced with permission from Robert M. Tomasko.

Even though it is no longer part of the current management climate, the autocratic or command style has proponents in the product creation area, as the following case example illustrates. This style is much needed when the company has lost its sense of urgency, often after a period of excessively laissez-faire management, as experienced by Medtronic.

But the democratic style – be it of the problem solving or guided discovery type – is often judged preferable because it seems more acceptable in today's organizations. Note, though, that it requires a high degree of process maturity, and teams that combine a strong dose of intrinsic and extrinsic motivation. The democratic style is also better adapted to a world of growing complexity, as Julian Birkinshaw stresses:

> The more complex the world gets, the more simple the strategy has to be. Detailed planning simply doesn't work in very complex systems – look at the old command economies in the former Soviet bloc. When things are simple, and stable, you can map out your strategy to some extent from the centre. But as the world becomes more fast-moving, this becomes less tenable. What you need to do is lay down certain parameters, and then give people enormous freedom in figuring out what they need to do.[10]

In summary, and whatever their actual leadership style, innovation leaders/team sports coaches need to share two distinct traits: They should be *demanding* but *supportive*.

Being *demanding* means:

- Proposing (or imposing) stretch targets . . .
  - but making sure that these targets are not ridiculously unrealistic;
- Expecting staff always to perform at their very best . . .
  - but recognizing that people occasionally have lows and accepting it;
- Insisting that everyone respects mutually agreed rules, standards and processes . . .
  - but being open to changing those that prove ill-adapted;
- Demanding an absolute level of personal and team integrity . . .
  - but showing the same level of integrity in their own behavior.

Being *supportive* means:

- Providing their teams with the resources for the task at hand . . .
  - but being tough in asking for resource justifications and chasing waste;
- Remaining accessible for solving problems with the team . . .
  - but avoiding being drawn into a mode of constant interventions;
- Defending their teams against unfair management criticisms or undue pressure . . .
  - but facing reality and addressing issues of team underperformance;
- Rewarding individual and team performance and celebrating success . . .
  - but fighting arrogance and complacency by always raising the stakes.

The following case on Medtronic's Brady pacemakers business provides a good illustration of an innovation leader/team sports coach in action.

Mike Stevens is remembered by Medtronic's former CEO and chairman, Bill George, as the tough leader who restored the company's position in Brady pacemakers, its breadwinner, at a time when the company was slowly sliding downward. The purpose of this case is not to make a hero of Stevens – despite his qualities, some of his staff considered him controversial in many respects. Nor is it to claim that everything he did was perfect. It is, instead, to illustrate the power of a coherent set of leadership values and skills in the most difficult situations a leader can face. Indeed, Stevens had to:

(1) shake up a highly successful organization that did not see its impending decline; and
(2) change the habits of a creative but disorganized culture to restore a higher degree of discipline.

This case also shows how important it is for management to guide the sports coach leader and to compensate for some of his shortcomings.

## STRAIGHTENING OUT MEDTRONIC'S INNOVATION PROCESS[11]

### Even Historic Innovators Can Lose Their Touch

Medtronic Corporation's reputation as the world's leading medical technology company is undoubtedly linked to its pioneering role in developing and bringing the cardiac pacemaker into general use. Pacemaking, as a concept, was invented by a famous open-heart surgeon, Dr C. Walter Lillihei in the 1950s. But it was Earl Bakken and his partner Palmer Hermundslie, Medtronic's founders, who developed and engineered the first battery-operated, implantable pacemaker in 1960. Since then, this device has regulated millions of deficient hearts worldwide, saving or prolonging as many lives.

Bakken was not just an exceptionally talented engineer. He was also a source of great inspiration for his staff. Early on, he articulated a clear mission for his company – to restore and prolong human life – which is still very much respected today. He also introduced a strong set of values, like integrity, engineering excellence and dedication to the company's mission and to the patients, among others. To enable his employees to fulfill their mission, he fostered a climate of creativity and entrepreneurship that persisted long after he left. Scientists and engineers were provided with a large degree of freedom to pursue their own technological ideas, at their own rhythm, whether or not these projects addressed the expressed needs of the cardiologists for whom they were intended.

### Growing Sales and Profits but Losing Market Share

Medtronic, being the innovator, fully owned the small but fast-growing pacemaker market, as cardiologists rapidly adopted the device and implanted it in patients with heart defects. Throughout the 1960s, and at least part of the 1970s, the company grew and prospered, concentrating all its resources on the pacemaker. Working closely with leading cardiologists, its scientists and engineers developed a range of devices for hearts that beat too slowly (bradycardia – the biggest market segment) as well as those that beat too fast (tachycardia). Over the years, Medtronic's pacemakers got smaller, benefited from a much extended battery life, and incorporated a number of intelligent features. Pacemakers rapidly became the 'standard of care' for what were still life-threatening diseases.

Medtronic's success rapidly attracted a number of small and large competitors, who brought innovations of their own to this burgeoning market. As a natural consequence, the company's market share started to decrease. The decline accelerated rapidly in the 1970s, but Medtronic's management did not seem overly worried. Of course, the company was losing its absolute market dominance, but its top and bottom line growth remained strong. The continuous and rapid international growth of the market actually masked the company's steady loss of market share. Medtronic felt protected by its illustrious reputation with cardiologists and its economies of scale in R&D, manufacturing and marketing. In addition, the market for pacemakers proved to be relatively price-insensitive – after all who would quibble over a few thousand dollars for a device that could save lives? – a consideration that authorized regular price increases.

## Moving from Leader to Follower

Medtronic's steadily declining market share – from 70% in 1970 to 29% in 1986[12] – was not caused only by the entry of new competitors into the market. The company lost share also because it ran into major quality problems; for example an insufficient hermetic sealing system led to body fluids seeping into the device, causing battery malfunctions. Equally worrisome, Medtronic started losing its market reputation as an innovator, as its new products consistently lagged those of its competitors, who were often first with new features. The only exception was in 1986, when an independent-minded engineer, Ken Anderson, with the support of top management, developed a revolutionary 'patient rate-responsive' pacemaker, the Activitrax,[13] despite the initial lack of interest expressed by leading cardiologists and his R&D colleagues.

Bill George, who joined the company as president and COO in 1989, comments:

> We were still very much the leader in the pacemaker business . . . , but then we hit two major quality problems, and the company went into denial. One [occurred] in 1975; it was actually because the company did not innovate. A group of people left the company, took the innovation – it was a new long-life battery – and went to another company because Medtronic rejected it, and that almost sunk the company! So, there was a failure, and people were trying to hang on to what they had and becoming too conservative. We were clearly no longer the technology leader. We had become so conservative and so risk averse . . . and our products took so long – in those days it took 48 months to get a product out of our development labs![14]

Internal development problems were compounded by cuts in pacemaker R&D, as management diverted cash to fund external acquisitions, believing that the growth potential of its business had reached a plateau.

## Lacking Both a Sense of Urgency and Discipline

The combination of a proud innovative past and the set of deeply humanistic values promoted by Earl Bakken created a unique culture that attracted many top scientists and engineers, at least in the beginning. But when the company started to lose share and lag competitors in terms of bringing innovations to market, the frustration level grew. Some of the most innovative engineers left the company to create their own start-ups, while others went into denial mode.

Executives exposed to the Medtronic pacemaker case are quick to note worrisome elements in the cultural backdrop of the company. Indeed, many aspects of Medtronic's culture, which could originally have worked in favor of innovation, had probably turned negative. For example:

- The company had a proud past as an innovator and a culture of technological leadership, but was it now resting on its laurels and becoming complacent? Were engineers favoring their own ideas more than those of their customers?
- Medtronic's informal, benign and people-oriented culture had contributed to making it a great creative workplace, but was the lack of management pressure diminishing everyone's sense of urgency?
- Bakken and his successors had encouraged openness to new ideas and creativity in all parts of R&D, but had this freedom bred a lack of accountability and discipline? Was management providing enough guidance?

Bill George summarized this dilemma in his first book.[15] Is there an innate contradiction between a values-centered culture and peak performance?

> The company's long history of success had led to a soft underbelly that manifested itself in a lack of discipline. The company was extremely values-centered, but its internal norms of consensus decision making, conflict avoidance and lack of personal accountability all undermined the company's performance. For all its strengths, it was my impression that Medtronic's culture was too Minnesota Nice.[16] I realized that these aspects of Medtronic's culture had to

change if we were going to be an effective competitor and realize our vision of being the global leader in medical technology.

## Bringing in a Disciplined Change Leader: Mike Stevens

Medtronic's Pacing Business was led by a creative president, Bob Griffin, who supervised both the Brady pacing and the Tacchy arythmia management businesses, plus the internal battery and integrated circuits units that supplied both businesses. The Brady pacing business, by far the largest unit, was led by a strong, business-oriented president, Steve Mahle. He oversaw the Pulse Generator and Programming Systems (PGPS) division, responsible for developing the core of the pacemaker, and the Brady Leads division, which produced the leads connecting the pacemaker to the heart.

Conscious of the need to improve the innovation performance of their business, in 1987 Griffin and Mahle brought in Mike Stevens as head of the PGPS division. Stevens was not an internal candidate, neither was he totally external. He had been associated with Medtronic for many years as a supplier of microelectronic components, first with Motorola, then as an independent supplier financed by Medtronic. In this special position, he had observed how the company had progressively lost market share and its innovative touch. When he joined PGPS, Medtronic's market share was at its lowest level ever (29%).

### Focusing on Processes

Mike Stevens was a no-nonsense type of leader who knew, almost instinctively, what was wrong with the business:

> Though I didn't have a background in product development, I saw much of Medtronic's problems as Management 101. We had very strong functional roles. People were being measured by cost centers, and there was no accountability for the delay or failure of a new product. I felt the basic values and ethics of the company were still really strong. But what needed work were its processes. I felt if we

could get those straightened out, then we could bring the Brady business back to its past glory.[17]

Stevens started to focus on the innovation process in all its dimensions, and no aspect was overlooked during his tenure. Together with the functional management colleagues he mobilized behind him, and over almost a full decade, he carried out a comprehensive innovation process overhaul, including:

- a new product platform strategy and process;
- a discipline for managing technology off-line;
- a clear process for determining strategic project priorities;
- a tight product planning schedule;
- a new project path with clear gates and fully empowered project leaders.

All these process changes are well detailed in Clayton Christensen's case, which probably remains one of the most comprehensive stories ever written on an innovation process turnaround.

None of these changes was exceptional per se. They all reflected well-known best practices. What is perhaps unique in this example is the way changes were introduced. This is why it is so interesting to focus on Stevens' leadership style and explain why it can be equated to that of a tough sports coach.

### Introducing Discipline

Stevens knew that his first move, before addressing the process issue, would be to restore a sense of discipline in his organization. Christensen's case quotes him as saying:

> People ask us what the secret is, to make a development organization work effectively. I tell them there aren't any magic bullets that kill the problems. It's just discipline. You need to do what you say needs to be done. You need to be in it for the long haul. There are no quick fixes![18]

Bill George contrasted the personalities of Mike Stevens and Bob Griffin, the Pacing Business head, as follows:

> Bobby Griffin was smart enough to recognize that Mike Stevens was someone very different from himself. He was like Griffin's

opposite. Griffin was creative, always full of ideas . . . Stevens was disciplined. Griffin was human . . . Stevens was tough. Using the sports coach analogy, he was like these tough soccer coaches. They aren't nice guys! They keep telling you that you can do a lot better. They won't tolerate any absence from the training field. 'The next time you do that to me, you're gone! Because I just can't afford to have you as a member of the team.' You see? A tough sports coach, not a loving one![19]

For Stevens, restoring discipline within his PGPS organization meant three things: First *challenging* his managers, then *setting goals* for the organization and *measuring* . . . measuring everything.

## Challenging people on accountability and sense of urgency

The arrival of Mike Stevens shook up the organization because his management style was completely different from that of most Medtronic managers before him. Bill George calls his style 'closed loop management.' It starts with an absolute enforcement of commitments.

> Mike would tell you, say on a Wednesday, 'John, we're going to have a project review next Monday morning at 8 am. Here is your assignment – he was giving everyone an assignment – and I want you to report to me on this assignment by Friday 2 pm.' On Friday morning, he would get back to you to remind you of your 2 pm commitment. If, in the traditional Medtronic way, you said to him, 'Sorry, Mike, but I need a few more days,' he would go nuts and say, 'I will meet you in my office on Monday at 7 am and we will go over your results, because at 8 am we have our project review.' At that time, you knew that you would have to spend the whole weekend on the job with your team to meet his deadline. A lot of people thought that his attitude was mean, cruel, merciless, but it taught people that if you make a commitment, you'd better deliver. That's closed loop management! Note that he was very fair in his demands – he wouldn't ask you to do something he wouldn't do himself – he wasn't unfair, he was just tough![20]

Stevens knew instinctively that he would have to 'walk the talk' to be credible when demanding accountability, as Clayton Christensen explains:

Managers of the PGPS Division got a taste of Stevens' belief that commitments are sacred when, shortly after arriving at Medtronic, he held management to the project milestones they had agreed upon at the beginning of fiscal year 1988. Their incentive compensation was tied to these objectives, and 1988 was the first year in memory that management did not receive year-end bonuses that were tied to objectives.[21]

## Setting goals

Managers wishing to boost their innovation performance know that they have to work on three parameters simultaneously, which Japanese companies combine under the term QTC. In this acronym, Q stands for *quality* (both intrinsic product quality and innovation quality); T represents *time*, in other words short, predictable and reliable lead times; and C means lowest possible *costs*. Stevens and his team were no exception in picking these objectives and, as we shall see later, in measuring performance against them. But Stevens did not stop there; he established specific goals in a number of other, yet related, areas.

For example, Stevens seemed particularly obsessed by the goal of achieving 100% product reliability, both in terms of zero defects and delivery time. He was fully aware of the impact that unmanaged or undue risk taking could have, after sign-off, on the reliability of product launch schedules. He held the latter as an essential performance indicator. As a consequence, he was fierce in rejecting most changes in projects after the sign-off gate, where, in his opinion, strict launch commitments were made. He was also restrictive on the amount of risk he was willing to take with unproven technology, as Bill George explains:

> Up until a project was put on its track, you could be very creative. But once Stevens had approved the numbers and launched the train, then, he became very rigorous in his way to handle risk. His approach was to go over all the risks in the project, figure out and assess the risks that could screw the project so as to get them under control. Those he could not control, he would actually take them off the critical path. So, if you had a risk caused by a new technology that wasn't fully proven, he'd ask you to wait and work on it until the next project came along. So, you might be angry about

seeing your innovation fall off the project, but you knew there would be a new one a year from now. And that kept people going. Stevens was not going for breakthroughs, as Griffin was. He was not taking risk on quality, he was taking a risk in not getting the last innovation idea! He was a very, very good assessor of innovation risk. And customers loved him because he always delivered. When he said a product could be delivered in February, it came out in February, not March![22]

## Measuring everything

Stevens' philosophy was: 'You get what you measure!' And he used a series of metrics covering the whole QTC area. His particularity was to measure what he called FAPC, or fully allocated product costs – and this despite his managers arguing that they were being measured on costs they could not control. He justified it by stressing that FAPC forced his team to think in terms of volume, hence market share.

Another area of focus was quality, which he measured very thoroughly, as Bill George remembers:

He put in Six Sigma . . . But we are not talking about Jack Welch's Six Sigma. I am talking about real Six Sigma, you know, measuring parts per million, deviations per million. He wasn't just talking about it, he was doing it. There weren't any 'black belts' or any of that stuff. There was no show. He was genuinely concerned about quality: 'How many defective parts per million are you gonna have in your device? Because, you know, we can't take that risk! People will die, you know!'

## Getting Results

The culture and process changes, introduced by Mike Stevens and supported by top management, led to a dramatic improvement in performance in most areas, as shown in Table 7.1.

## Was Mike Stevens Really an Innovation Leader?

This question is frequently asked by executives who discuss the Medtronic case. The interrogation is understandable because there

**Table 7.1** Impact of the changes introduced in Medtronic's cardiac rhythm business (partly thanks to Mike Stevens)

| | |
|---|---|
| • Pacemaker market share | From 29% to 51% |
| • Reduction in costs | 30% |
| • Cardiac rhythm gross margin | From 65% to 80% |
| • Cardiac rhythm net profit on sales | From 18% to 30% |
| • Net cash outflow | $500 million |
| • Product development lead times | From 48 to 16 months |
| • Reduction in quality problems | 90% |
| • R&D expenditures (as percentage of sales) | From 7% to 10% |

Source: Reproduced with permission from Bill George.

is little in Mike Stevens' personality or leadership style that conjures up the vision of an innovation leader, in the more traditional sense of the term. On the face of it, most people would call Stevens a tough operational manager, period! In contrast – even Bill George recognizes it – we tend to describe as innovation leaders *only* those executives who are always open to new ideas, always intrigued by them, always willing to explore new paths, experiment with new technologies, take a risk and try out things. At Medtronic, both Bob Griffin, president of the Pacing Business and Glen Nelson, the vice chairman, were much better fits with the traditional image of innovation leaders.

Despite our prejudices, it is fair to call Mike Stevens an innovation leader on several grounds.

First, we should remember Professor Preston Bottger's definition of leaders, introduced in Chapter 1:

> Leaders do or cause to be done all that must be done and is now not being done to achieve what we say is important! They provide a sense of purpose, direction and focus. They build alignment and get commitment![23]

Based on this definition, Stevens was clearly a leader, and since all his efforts focused on a single objective, i.e. boosting Medtronic's innovation performance, we can safely state that he was a true innovation leader. And we could add that he was extremely successful at that, judging by the exceptional results he obtained for his company during his tenure.

Second, remembering the distinction we made in Chapter 2 between front-end and back-end innovation leaders, Stevens undoubtedly belongs to the second category. In fact, many of the innovation leaders active in the lower left-hand corner of the innovation thrust matrix in Chapter 6 (refer to Figure 6.1) are of the back-end type. The reason is straightforward: In an incremental innovation strategy focusing on new/improved products or service offerings, the focus of management is quite different from that in a strategy aiming at breakthroughs. What counted for Stevens, above all, was to boost the company's product innovation performance in order to compete on the basis of the most up-to-date, competitive and attractive pacemaker portfolio . . . and to be perfect in execution.

Third, innovation leaders have passion and, clearly, Stevens was passionate! He shared the same passion as his colleagues for the societal mission of his company, i.e. restoring health and prolonging life. But his way to fulfill the mission was to ensure that excellent and reliable products would get quickly out of the labs into the market. As Bill George explains:

> If Mike Stevens was so tough about protecting his launch schedule, it was not for the sake of simply meeting his target – it was because there were people out there dying because they would not get access to the technology on time. He would say: 'If a person's life is at risk, and you have a great innovation, but it is never perfect enough and it never gets into the stream of the FDA[24] [which is a very rigorous process], what good is it?'[25]

## LIMITS OF THE 'TEAM SPORTS COACH' LEADER

The same qualities that make 'team sports coach' leaders so effective are also their greatest limits. These innovation leaders are highly *focused* on winning, but winning in only one type of game, and even within that game, on one type of strategy. They succeed by developing and training teams to their image, and by encouraging them to reach excellence in turning the rules of the game to their advantage. These types of leaders cannot easily change strategies, they are even less able to learn new games, and they are generally totally impervious to the idea of changing the rules of the game or, even worse, of playing different games simultaneously. They are also intolerant of players who follow their own path and do not listen to their admonitions. And this of course limits their potential as innovation leaders. They cannot easily be deployed and play well in other corners of our innovation map.

## What Would Have Happened to Medtronic Under Mike Stevens?

Bill George, who became Medtronic's CEO in 1991, four years after Mike Stevens started his pacemaker turnaround campaign, is in a unique position to acknowledge Stevens' formidable contribution to the company. Thanks to him, indeed, Medtronic built solid business and financial foundations for its future growth. At the same time, says George, toward the end of the nineties, Stevens had somehow reached the upper limit of his career progression, first and foremost because that is what he wanted. He simply was unwilling to practice another game.

> Mike, who took early retirement in the late nineties for personal reasons, loved what he did, but he didn't want to be promoted. It's not like he was bypassed and didn't get a promotion, you know, he simply didn't want to be promoted. He wanted to keep his freedom to operate in his own way.[26]

When we discuss the Medtronic case with executives in class, after acknowledging the stunning results Stevens helped to achieve, I generally like to ask the participants two questions:

(1) 'How do you think Mike was perceived by his staff throughout his tenure? Who do you think liked him and who resented him most?' and

(2) 'What are the limits of his approach? What would happen over time if Medtronic only had access to leaders like Mike Stevens?'

The discussions that follow are usually very interesting, and they clearly indicate the need to combine complementary types of innovation leaders in order to sustain growth.

## Who Will Typically Appreciate or Resent a Leader like Mike Stevens?

Executives exposed to the Medtronic story are quick to guess what happened around Mike Stevens. Confronted with such a leader, most people individually feel stimulated, even though, in the case of Medtronic, a few probably felt bullied by some of Stevens' tough methods. This view is confirmed by Bill George and can be generalized to most types of innovation leaders in the 'sports team coach' category.

> Leaders like Mike are like basketball or soccer coaches – they create great loyalty. People will say, 'You know, at times I hate working for Mike but I know it's good for me! It's teaching me discipline and rigor, and he is very fair. If I perform, he'll reward me!'[27]

Most functions will also support such kinds of change programs, at least when results start becoming visible. This was the case at Medtronic:

- Marketing and sales were probably the greatest beneficiaries of the changes Stevens introduced. They were relieved to see a growing number of new products hitting the market, predictably according to plan. This undoubtedly facilitated their relationships with customers.
- Finance was, of course, happy to see growth in product margins and more effective use of engineering resources, as projects that were started would generally be brought to their term, avoiding the waste created in the past by stop-go policies.
- Development engineers had been frustrated by the overall ineffectiveness of their previous development process, and they resented the loss of their company's innovation leadership position. They now felt comforted to see their projects receiving adequate resources and hitting the market successfully.

- Business management obviously liked what it saw, i.e. an organization that had regained faith in itself, learned how to work together smoothly and time effectively, and delivered strong results in market share, profits and customer satisfaction.

Does this mean that everyone was happy with Mike Stevens? Well, not quite!

Some of the scientists, the most creative ones, felt frustrated to see their brilliant but untested ideas systematically rejected by Stevens because they were too risky. Through his insistence on launching projects with the regularity of Swiss trains, and on stacking four or five successive generations in parallel, Stevens committed all his R&D resources to the official product cycle plan. He left no slack in his system for unplanned innovations, for untested technologies or for risky exploratory ideas. In other words, Stevens' approach was ideal for continuing to turn out new variants of the same products, generation after generation, but not for branching out toward totally new product concepts or different applications of Medtronic's technologies.

Some of the most creative opinion leaders – cardiologists with brilliant but 'different' ideas – partly lost their privileged access to Medtronic's researchers. They could no longer tinker about with new untested product concepts, as they had done in the past, and hope that Medtronic would follow up, simply because Stevens' R&D staff was fully booked on current projects. This made them side with the company's unhappy scientists, and some of them were probably tempted to join smaller, more flexible competitors to develop their new ideas.

### The Shadowy Side: Limiting Growth and Exposing the Company

Under Mike Stevens alone, Medtronic's pacemaker business would most probably have prospered and maintained its leadership position for quite a while. However, two things could predictably have happened: Growth might have tapered and Medtronic might have been exposed to disruptive innovations.

Growth analysts note that attractive untapped opportunities generally lie at the periphery of current businesses, or at the interface between two business units. They therefore recommend that growth leaders should develop a broad, multifaceted curiosity. Focusing narrowly on your core market is critical, but up to a point. This is why we talked about the importance of promoting broad-bandwidth managers in Chapter 3. If left alone, would Stevens have allocated enough resources to defibrillators, a different type of implantable cardiac device, but one that used very similar technologies? And without top management insistence, would he have taken the risks needed to catch up with more advanced competitors and turn it into a fast-growing business?

But the greatest risk incurred by adopters of extremely focused strategies is blindness to disruptive technologies or disruptive innovations. As Clayton Christensen convincingly demonstrated,[28] companies steeped in a competitive game of never-ending performance improvements (and in the cost increases that go with it) are likely to miss opportunities for 'low-end disruptions.' New entrants are indeed often tempted to target customers who do not need – or cannot afford – the full performance valued by customers at the high end of the market. Medtronic avoided that risk – the introduction of low-cost pacemakers by competitors – because, as we show below, its Pacing Business president, Bob Griffin, was on the alert for such kinds of innovation. Griffin was indeed a different type of innovation leader from Stevens, and he had very complementary skills. This is why CEOs need to combine talents to innovate.

## Establishing a Parallel Path for Wild Ideas

Bob Griffin was always on the lookout for new ideas, always willing to listen to innovators and fund the development of wild concepts with his own slush funds. Whenever Mike Stevens turned down an idea because of its lack of demonstrated feasibility, Griffin was ready to step in and fund an exploratory project. This is what happened with the super-low-cost pacemaker story.

### Breaking the Rules, then Stealing Ideas with Pride

Stevens had established a rigorous plan to reduce the factory cost of his pacemakers, say from $1300 to $1000 and, within a few years, to $800. Like everything he did, the plan was ambitious but realistic in its incremental approach, and hence feasible. If he managed to bring down the cost of a product that represented 70% of the company's sales, from $1300 to $800, the benefit for the company would be terrific. But in his approach, Stevens never challenged some of Medtronic's sacred rules, e.g. that pacemakers needed special batteries, designed and produced in house; custom-made hybrid circuits; and an expensive, double hermetic sealing system. Griffin, by contrast, thought differently, as Bill George comments:

> Griffin wanted to free up people so that they would think differ-ently about things, like costs – that's the way Griffin thought – like going from a $1300 pacemaker to a $100 device, not to a $1000 one. This just drove Stevens nuts! That meant changing all the rules! Stevens wanted the rules, Griffin wanted to challenge the rules![29]

So, Griffin funded a small super-low-cost pacemaker project to explore these avenues. Of course, this low-end product could open up new markets in emerging countries. But this was not Griffin's main motivation. He wanted to challenge the status quo, knowing full well that, if successful, there would be interesting technological fallouts on Stevens' business.

Griffin's project team challenged all previously held assump-tions in the design of pacemakers, for example:

- Why use specially designed batteries? Couldn't Medtronic use watch batteries that were a lot cheaper and had proved their reliability?
- Why use custom chips as a source of intelligence, when stan-dard microprocessors could perform the same function?
- Why use a double hermetic sealing system when the watch industry had developed much simpler ones, even for water-proof diving watches? And the like.

Ultimately, the team built a working prototype, estimating its manufacturing cost at $250, against a goal of $100, but still a far cry from the $1000 targeted by Stevens' engineers. The device did not sell well, but that was not the point of the exercise.

As could be expected, Stevens found many deficiencies in Griffin's super-low-cost prototype. But he was no fool, and the experiment intrigued him enough to find out, discreetly, how Griffin's team had managed it . . . and to steal some ideas (like the principle of using standard microprocessors). He took these concepts, perfected them in his own rigorous way, and arrived at a $650 cost for a mainstream pacemaker, an extraordinary result.

### Combining Mr Creativity and Mr Discipline

At Medtronic, Bob Griffin was clearly Mr Creativity, a front-end innovation leader, and Mike Stevens, Mr Discipline, a back-end innovation leader. Table 7.2 presents how Bill George highlights the differences and complementary nature of these two types of leaders by summarizing their personal philosophies in a nutshell.

It is the combination of these two types of leaders that gave Medtronic an edge over its competitors. Without Griffin, the company would have missed many exciting growth opportunities. Without Stevens, it would perhaps have missed the market benefits of these innovations, simply through a lack of faultless execution.

It is interesting to note that Griffin was Stevens' indirect hierarchical boss (since Stevens actually reported to Mahle). This probably explains why the combination was so effective, albeit not without tension, as Bill George reports, stressing that 'they fought all the time!' Had Stevens been on top, would Griffin have been given the freedom – and the slush funds – that he needed to experiment with radical innovations?

My concluding remark to all senior executives is an exhortation: Look inside your organization to identify your Mr (or Ms) Discipline and your Mr (or Ms) Creativity! Do you have both types of innovation leaders? Are they positioned at the right level in the hierarchy to be effective? Do they work well together and respect each other? And how can you help them create momentum for growth *and* deliver?

**Table 7.2**　Contrasting the philosophies of Mr Discipline and Mr Creativity

| Mr Discipline (*Mike Stevens*) | Mr Creativity (*Bob Griffin*) |
| --- | --- |
| Innovation is a disciplined process | Innovation is a creative process |
| Commitments are sacred | Try something new |
| Schedule is king | New ideas dominate |
| Work within the rules | Break the rules |
| Success is mandatory | Learn from failures |
| Optimize inside the box | Think outside the box |
| Focus on proven technology | Focus on new inventions |
| Apply the first principles of engineering | Apply the first principles of science |
| Happiness comes from results | Happiness comes from breakthroughs |

*But for both:*
You get what you measure
The mission is paramount

Source: Reproduced with permission from Bill George.

Chapter 7 has covered the innovation leader/team sports coach, perfectly suited to steering and running incremental innovations in products and services. Chapter 8 will bring us to another type of innovation leader – the sponsor – who builds totally new product categories or service offerings, and thus creates new businesses through radical innovation.

## ENDNOTES

1. Source: http://www.ffbookmarks.com/coaching_quotes.htm.
2. Chan, K.W. and Mauborgne, R. (2005). *Blue Ocean Strategy: How to Create Uncontested Market Space and Make the Competition Irrelevant*. Boston, Harvard Business School Press.
3. Jowett, S. and Lavallee, D., eds. (2006). *Social Psychology in Sport*. Champaign, IL, Human Kinetics.

4. Wooden, J. and Jamison, S. (2005). *Wooden on Leadership*. New York, McGraw-Hill.

5. Birkinshaw, J. and Crainer, S. (2004). *Leadership the Sven-Goran Eriksson Way: How to Turn Your Team into Winners*. Chichester, Capstone Publishing/John Wiley & Sons, Ltd.

6. Refer to the Sports Coach website: http://www.brianmac.co.uk/.

7. Refer to the Sports Coach website: http://www.brianmac.co.uk/.

8. Woods, B. and McIlveen, R. (1998). *Applying Psychology to Sport*. London, Hodder & Stoughton cited on the Sports Coach website: http://www.brianmac.co.uk/.

9. Robert M. Tomasko has written the following books on leadership and organizational effectiveness:

   • *Downsizing: Reshaping the Corporation for the Future* (1987/1990). New York, Amacom Books.
   • *Rethinking the Corporation: The Architecture of Change* (1993/1995). New York, Amacom Books.
   • *Go for Growth: Five Paths to Profit and Success – Choose the Right One for You and Your Company* (1996). Hoboken, John Wiley & Sons, Inc.
   • *Bigger Isn't Always Better: The New Mindset for Real Business Growth* (2006). New York, Amacom Books.

10. 'Can Business Learn from Sport,' interview with Julian Birkinshaw, London Business School, in CEO Forum at http://www.ceoforum.com.au/article-detail.cfm?cid=8288.

11. This story is based on three sources of information: (1) the case study 'We've Got Rhythm! Medtronic Corporation's Cardiac Pacemaker Business,' authored by Professor Clayton M. Christensen in 1997, Harvard Business School Case No. 9-698-004; (2) Bill George, former CEO and board chairman of Medtronic, observed while he was discussing the above case with executives at IMD, then personally interviewed by the author in 2001 and 2007; and (3) Bill George's book *Authentic Leadership: Rediscovering the Secrets of Lasting Value* (2003), San Francisco, Jossey-Bass.

12. Christensen, C.M. (1997). 'We've Got Rhythm! Medtronic Corporation's Cardiac Pacemaker Business.' Harvard Business School Case No. 9-698-004, p. 4.

13. The Activitrax was equipped with sensors capable of detecting the level of activity of the patient, and electronic intelligence allowing the pacemaker to adapt its pulses to the patient's biological rhythms.

14. George, B. (2001). 'Leadership and Innovation.' Videotaped interview by J.-P. Deschamps, IMD, Lausanne, reproduced with permission.

15. George, B. (2003). *Authentic Leadership: Rediscovering the Secrets of Lasting Value*. San Francisco, Jossey-Bass, p. 76.

16. Based on the historic strength of Minnesota's residents of Scandinavian origin, Minnesota-based companies had the reputation of favoring consensus decision making, and its managers of being sometimes too 'nice' to their staff, to the detriment of company performance, hence the expression 'Minnesota Nice.'

17. Christensen, C.M. (1997). 'We've Got Rhythm! Medtronic Corporation's Cardiac Pacemaker Business,' Harvard Business School Case No. 9-698-004, p. 5.

18. Christensen, C.M. (1997). 'We've Got Rhythm! Medtronic Corporation's Cardiac Pacemaker Business,' Harvard Business School Case No. 9-698-004, p. 10.

19. Author's personal interview with Bill George on 28 June 2007, reproduced with permission.

20. Author's personal interview with Bill George on 28 June 2007, reproduced with permission.

21. Christensen, C.M. (1997). 'We've Got Rhythm! Medtronic Corporation's Cardiac Pacemaker Business,' Harvard Business School Case No. 9-698-004, p. 5.

22. Author's personal interview with Bill George on 28 June 2007, reproduced with permission.

23. Bottger, P. (2008). 'The Leadership Imperative.' *Leading in the Top Team: The CXO Challenge.* Ed. Preston Bottger. Cambridge, Cambridge University Press.

24. FDA: Federal Drug Administration, an organization that delivers authorizations to put medical devices on the market, based on the result of a series of clinical trials.

25. Author's personal interview with Bill George on 28 June 2007, reproduced with permission.

26. Author's personal interview with Bill George on 28 June 2007, reproduced with permission.

27. Author's personal interview with Bill George on 28 June 2007, reproduced with permission.

28. Christensen, C. and Raynor, M.E. (2003). *The Innovator's Solution: Creating and Sustaining Growth.* Boston, Harvard Business School Press.

29. Author's personal interview with Bill George on 28 June 2007, reproduced with permission.

# CHAPTER 8

# LEADING THE CREATION OF A TOTALLY NEW PRODUCT OR SERVICE CATEGORY REQUIRED: NO-NONSENSE SPONSORS TO STEER THE NEW VENTURE[1]

*Sponsor: A person or an organization that pays for or plans and carries out a project or activity.*
*No-nonsense: Serious, businesslike, a 'no-nonsense manager.'*
*Merriam-Webster online dictionary*

Large companies in mature markets – think of Nestlé, Kraft and Unilever in the food industry – are confronted with a growth dilemma. They feel mandated by financial investors to grow at a faster rate than their snail-paced market; yet, they know that their options are limited. Sound acquisitions are becoming increasingly hard to find and very expensive, and hence financially burdensome. Geographical market expansion, a traditional source of growth for multinationals, is nearing its limit as solvent markets are aggressively exploited. Growing existing categories in mature markets through incremental product improvement usually yields a marginal growth benefit; it reinforces market positions rather than expanding them significantly. And fighting for market share through marketing campaigns is often a costly game margin-wise.

A promising, but challenging, option is organic growth through category innovation, i.e. creating new business segments through totally new product concepts. However, few management teams seriously choose to go down that route. They know how difficult it is to invent totally new products or services that offer real value and cater to customers' unmet or even latent needs. But, when successful, growth through category innovation can be spectacular. Nestlé experienced this in the 1990s with its revolutionary Nespresso™ system, already mentioned in Chapter 2. Its success story is particularly impressive if one considers how stagnant the coffee bean market was throughout the previous decades.

As noted in Chapter 6, category breakthroughs generally occur in a top-down process. They are fueled by management's vision and its desire to bring the company into a completely new market space, beyond the scope of its current businesses. This is exactly what happened at Tetra Pak, the liquid food packaging giant. Its senior managers dreamed of capturing a big share of the food canning market through the introduction of the first retortable[2] carton package. Displacing the traditional metal food can was a way for the Swedish firm to build a totally new business, next to its milk and juice processing and carton packaging units.

## INNOVATION LEADERS AS NO-NONSENSE SPONSORS

### A Strategy with a Long and Uncertain Payback

No matter how they occur, category breakthroughs are scarce for two related reasons:

First, the creation of an entirely new product category is a very high risk strategy. Innovation analysts have underlined the consistently high rate of failure of new *products* in most industries – and we are not even talking here about new categories. Some studies claim that new product hit rates in the fast-moving consumer goods industry[3] reach only 20% on average. Marketing experts ascribe this low ratio to inadequate marketing research.[4] If so many new products fail when launched in existing markets, imagine the success rate of companies that venture beyond their known markets to create a totally new category! Such endeavors cannot be reliably guided by marketing research since the market, by definition, does not yet exist. This is why Chris Zook, author of *Beyond the Core*,[5] advocates proceeding through 'adjacent moves.' If you are going to develop a new category, he suggests, at least ensure that your new products share something with your existing line, for example the same distribution network. The Tetra Pak story that follows illustrates the merits of favoring adjacencies, i.e. of leveraging current assets and strengths in creating the new category. In this particular case, Tetra Pak planned to fully exploit its carton know-how and its network of converting plants.

Second, this type of breakthrough is singular because it generally comes about after a long and often erratic process, from initial product idea to successful launch in the market. As Figure 8.1 shows, Nestlé bought the patent that ultimately led to its Nespresso system in the seventies. After developing the system, the company tried to market it in the food-service market and then to offices, in both cases without much success. It was only in the early nineties that the new independent company created to market it – Nestlé Coffee Specialties – hit the jackpot with the household

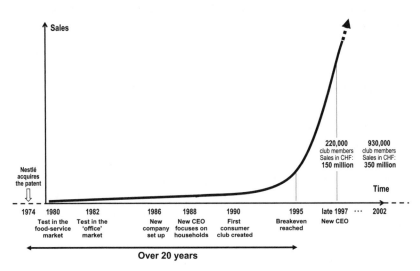

**Figure 8.1** Nespresso™ system timeline
Source: Reproduced with permission from Dominique Turpin, IMD.

market. Its managers adopted an original marketing concept: Selling the product directly to consumers through the 'Nespresso Club.' In total, it took Nestlé slightly more than 20 years to go from invention to breakeven.

But CEO Peter Brabeck could only rejoice that his management team persisted with the venture over so many years, given the exceptional results of this new business. Nespresso is, indeed, likely to hit its 2-billion-Swiss-franc sales objective – $1.61 billion – in 2009, instead of 2010 as originally planned. In comparison, the time line for Tetra Pak's revolutionary package appears much shorter. It took only eight years to bring Tetra Recart™ from the initial idea to the first commercial product hitting retail shelves. However, in 2007, 14 years after starting the venture, the company has yet to reach a positive return on its investment. But again, remembering the impact of its phenomenally successful Tetra Brik™ system, Tetra Pak's management is adopting a long-term return perspective. This patient attitude is of course easier to defend in a privately held company not subject to financial-market pressures.

The high risk level and lengthy process explain, in large part, why the internal development of a totally new product or service category, and the new business that goes with it, are relatively rare phenomena. Managers often lack the determination and patience to carry out highly uncertain projects over such long periods. They give up or, more frequently, don't even start.

## The Need for Sponsors

Category breakthroughs are so uncertain and take so long to materialize that they will only occur when extremely committed leaders initiate projects and steer them personally. In doing so, these senior executives are willing to take a significant career risk, given that many of these projects will ultimately fail. Why do some senior executives sponsor innovative but risky ventures? The answer is always a combination of three factors:

(1) a desire to grow faster than would be possible in their current market;

(2) an instinctive trust in the attractiveness of a given product or service concept; and

(3) a longing for innovation and a belief that such projects are unique opportunities to grow entrepreneurs and learn.

In most cases, these leaders act as supportive but pragmatic 'no-nonsense' sponsors.

In their new book, *Profit or Growth? Why You Don't Have to Choose*, Peter Lorange and Bala Chakravarthy, call these types of sponsors 'entrepreneurs–managers' and list four of their essential skills:

- They see the big picture and shape strategy.
- They communicate and market the value proposition.
- They manage stakeholders, gain support and mobilize resources.
- They assemble and motivate a team of experts.[6]

As we shall see in the Tetra Pak example, new venture sponsors meet all these listed requirements as they focus on three successive priorities: (1) *nurturing* the project they initiate; then (2) *challenging* the project team with progressive intensity to ensure that it reaches its objectives; and (3) *empowering* and *supervising* the young business management team resulting from the realization of the project.

### Nurturing

Nurturing is needed because no major venturing project can be created and survive without the strong and sustained backing of at least one innovation leader, but ideally several working together in a support chain. The role of these leaders, acting both as advocates and involved venture capitalists, is manifold. They need to:

(1) set reasonable management expectations for their new venture, particularly in terms of time–to–market and time–to–profit;

(2) get everyone – in management as well as in the team – to commit to realistic common objectives;

(3) provide access to resources that the team will need over the project time frame – cash, of course, but also manpower and expertise;

(4) release resources to the team against agreed and progressively scheduled deliverables;

(5) act as mentors to the team, helping it address and surmount the usual formation crises and all obstacles in its way throughout the project;

(6) encourage personal and team development and ensure team members learn fast from their unavoidable mistakes;

(7) behave collectively as their team's 'sword and shield':

- sword to slash through the corporate bureaucracy that could choke the new venture to death;
- shield to protect it against all good (and less good) reasons to kill it, particularly when the company is experiencing difficult times.

## Challenging

Challenging is desirable, provided the project steering group does it progressively to avoid early discouragements. It should ensure that the venture team:

(1) chooses the best technical and market options to minimize risk as much as possible and to maximize the appeal of the new concept in its target market;

(2) stays focused on meeting its fundamental objectives, despite unavoidable temptations to drift in new directions when the project faces difficulties on its original path;

(3) develops a sense of urgency and becomes passionate about going to market, despite the temptation for members to keep reworking and perfecting their offering as new opportunities arise.

## Empowering and Supervising

Empowering the emerging business management team and supervising the first steps of the new business, once created, is the ultimate priority of innovation leaders. This requires the ability to:

(1) withdraw progressively from day-to-day involvement in the venture and from controlling its key decisions; and

(2) take a supportive back seat as the venture team takes charge of its newly created business.

## Forming a 'Chain of Leadership'

As noted earlier, leadership is generally considered as an individual and highly personal talent, but for radical innovation to occur, leadership has to be collective. Because of their long development cycles, breakthrough projects are unlikely to be steered by a single leader from idea to market. Managers may have to change jobs, and besides, projects require different types of supervision and assistance over their life cycle. This is why we should be talking about mobilizing a *chain of leadership*, i.e. enlisting several and different types of innovation leaders/sponsors, working together or in succession, to support and steer new venture projects.

Chapter 3 indicated that innovation requires the combined involvement of three types of champions, each with a complementary role, i.e. technical, business and executive champions. The chain of leadership comprises these three types of champions, and it must remain uninterrupted. It must stay active for as long as it takes to bring the venture to success, despite the fact that managers change jobs regularly. As a consequence, leaders need to step in and out over time, each bringing a special type of expertise to the venture.

One of the primary tasks of that chain of leadership is to bring the prospective innovators to understand what will trigger the 'chain of adoption' for their new product.

Tetra Recart, Tetra Pak's revolutionary retortable carton package, illustrates the range of leadership talents that are needed to carry out a strategy of radical innovation. The case is particularly interesting because it covers the full 10-year story, from initial idea and technical project to market launch and creation of a new business unit. Over this time frame, a lot of managers were involved, either in the project team or in the steering group. Many joined, then left, called by other duties, and were replaced by new leaders with complementary talents. It is this combination of technical, business and executive champions, working together and in succession in an uninterrupted chain of leadership that ultimately made a breakthrough innovation possible.

## NEW BUSINESS CREATION AT TETRA PAK: REINVENTING THE FOOD CAN[7]

### Tetra Pak: A World Leader in Carton Packaging

Founded in 1951, Tetra Pak has rooted its growth over the past half-century on category innovation and fast and global commercial exploitation of its inventions. Tetra Pak, one of the world's largest and most successful packaging companies, was created specifically to exploit a breakthrough innovation of its Swedish founder, Ruben Rausing. The history of the company provides a compelling illustration of a vision-led innovation process.

Rausing, who was working in the packaging industry, was driven by a vision — that of transforming the antiquated bulk milk distribution system that prevailed in 1950s Europe by adapting it to the mass-retailing supermarkets that were emerging. For the first time, someone tried to optimize a package by creating value throughout the chain, from producers to users, via transporters and retailers.

Rausing's vision that a package should save more than it costs led him to search systematically for rational container shapes and efficient filling systems. This search led him, in turn, to invent the first tetrahedron carton package, now called *Tetra-Classic*™, and a few years later, the ubiquitous *Tetra-Brik*™. And it was this same vision and ambition to add value to his dairy customers, retailers and consumers that brought him, after a few years, to introduce the first aseptic filling systems and packages. This innovation created an entirely new product category: UHT[8] milk and juice, which retained most of the qualities of pasteurized product versions, yet offered a long shelf-life in ambient conditions. In a couple of decades, Tetra Pak aseptic filling machines and cartons became the world's most widely used packaging system for ambient liquid food. In 2006, Tetra Pak reached sales of over 120 billion packs, for a turnover of $10.3 billion. It employed 20 000 people in more than 165 countries, and counted 48 manufacturing plants and 19 R&D centers. Industry observers have recognized Tetra Pak's innovations as real breakthroughs because they radically changed the liquid food packaging industry and created an entirely new market.

In 1991, Tetra Pak acquired Alfa Laval, another Swedish engineering company, mainly to access its dairy and food processing equipment technology. This acquisition provided the company, now called Tetra Laval, with an opportunity to diversify into solid food packaging. Tetra Laval Food (TLF) was set up in 1993 as a separate business unit, next to Tetra Pak, to provide packaging and processing solutions for solid foods.

## Targeting the Canned Food Market (1993–1996)

TLF's CEO, Nils Björkman, and his chief technology officer (CTO), Stefan Andersson, were anxious to find packaging growth opportunities in solid foods. They had toyed for some time with the idea of developing a carton alternative to the ubiquitous metal food can. They saw it as a huge market with little innovation, and hence prone to be disrupted by new technologies. Andersson comments on their choice of target:

> Our internal appetite for organic growth was very high because we didn't really have any other option to grow. We could not make packaging acquisitions, given our very high market share, and the canned food market was the biggest possible target we could go after in terms of homogeneous volumes. Besides, it was a way of extending our core technologies around laminated boards, sealing, printing and other areas. It was a completely new area with no risk of cannibalization of our current business. So, the can market was on top of the new TLF management team's agenda.[9]

### Setting up a Project to Address the Challenge

To preserve food, Andersson believed, the company needed to shift away from its aseptic technology paradigm and pursue other approaches. Retorting carton-based packages seemed an intriguing option, but boiling a cardboard box for a couple of hours in pressurized steam at temperatures of 120°C to 130°C was a bold undertaking. Nevertheless, and with the full backing of his boss, in October 1993 Andersson started a small R&D project on carton retorting.

The project was entrusted to a team of two highly experienced and entrepreneurial engineers, and a small steering team was set up to guide and supervise the project. It was chaired by Björkman, TLF's CEO and executive champion, and included Andersson, who latter served as senior technical champion. He was to provide an unbroken line of supervision and advice throughout what became a long and complex program. Björkman remembers the primary focus of his initial steering team:

> The overall base for the project was the economic benefit of this new carton package and the possibility of tapping into a huge market – the whole food can market. But the members of the steering group were very technical at the beginning.
>
> There were a couple of different areas that we focused on. One was, of course, to make sure that we really managed to get the resources in Tetra Pak to continue the development of the packaging materials; because we were really dependent on the knowledge within Tetra Pak R&D of how to compose the packaging material. And we also had to make sure that we could produce this packaging material in the Tetra Pak packaging materials plants – because the whole idea was to leverage the converting structure within Tetra Pak and make it possible for us to get very competitive packaging materials in Tetra Laval Food.
>
> We had to make sure that we cracked all the technical difficulties that we had, and also of course, to ensure that the board of the Tetra Laval Group approved this project, which became, slowly but surely, the biggest development project within TLF.
>
> Did we get the full support that we wanted? It was never difficult to get the resources, but getting the initial buy-in wasn't easy because we were moving a packaging project from being always focused on aseptic processing into something that was new for Tetra Pak and for Tetra Laval Food, a retorted carton. And that, conceptually, was quite a big step for us to take because it opened up new markets but also new competitive challenges for carton packages.[10]

## Testing the Concept with Customers

As none of the project team members had a commercial background, Björkman played the role of senior business champion. He wanted to gauge the interest of some of the largest canning customers in Europe before committing significant time and money to the technology. So, very early on, members of both the project and steering teams started visiting large food canners. They explained their concept and presented handmade package prototypes. Members of Tetra Pak's group leadership team, including the head of Region-Europe, Bo Wirsén, took part in some of these exploratory visits. Two companies showed an early interest in the new concept: Family-owned Bonduelle in France – Europe's largest vegetable canner – and Nestlé. Rupert Gasser, a member of Nestlé's executive leadership group and a recognized innovation champion, became intrigued with the new technology.

Encouraged by the generally positive reactions of the canners they visited, TLF top managers agreed to fund the development of a transportable demonstration prototype of their system. This 'junior machine,' as it was called, was made with the help of a small entrepreneurial Italian machine manufacturer. It incorporated a batch retorting autoclave provided by a Swedish sterilization equipment specialist.

## Solving Technical Problems and Retorting Cartons

The first retorting tests that TLF's engineers undertook were disastrous, as water seeped into the color-printed package sample, which ended up white and contorted as if it had spent hours in a tumble dryer. The team had yet to understand the interface between packaging materials, printing ink and product during the retorting process. These problems brought the project to a definite low point. At that time, only four or five people believed that there was still something to salvage from the project, including the two originally assigned to the project and the key steering team members. What saved the day was the interest that Gasser and his staff at Nestlé had tentatively expressed. This prompted the TLF team to work intensely with Tetra Pak's R&D group to solve the materials development problem. They were helped in their task by their external board and by ink and retort supply-partners. This cooperation ultimately bore fruit and led to an impeccable retorted carton. The team, which had grown in size and competence, had progressively managed to develop the right kind of laminated material and control all the retort parameters.

Reflecting on this first phase of the venture, Andersson evokes the pioneering spirit that prevailed around this project:

> There was a good mixture of enthusiasm and also pragmatism and realism around the project in Tetra Laval Food, and I think that we maintained the balance between these two mindsets all the time . . . Keeping a very positive drive, but also being very realistic about the risks and the structure that we needed to put in the project, because at the beginning, you have to take a lot of decisions to reduce complexity. I still think that I tried to keep a good balance between the technical and commercial aspects, to integrate the two perspectives.[11]

## Restarting and Reorienting the Project (1997–2001)

In January 1996, Tetra Laval decided to refocus on its core business and closed its TLF division, selling off parts of its portfolio. For a few months, the project remained in limbo. Its members, now numbering 35 full-time people, wondered whether they would be needed in a new organization totally dedicated to liquid food packaging. As Björkman was appointed to head Tetra Pak-Europe, Andersson took over. He tried to maintain team morale and defend the purpose and focus of the project, which a number of senior managers in Tetra Pak were seriously questioning. Björkman pleaded with his CEO to give the project another year, highlighting Nestlé's interest, and obtained it.

### Ensuring Tetra Pak R&D Would Adopt the Project . . . Even Modified

The project, now looking for a home within Tetra Pak, ended up naturally in the corporate R&D center. But the head of that lab was reluctant to continue the project in its existing state with such a large group of people. He believed in the concept of the retortable carton, which he had helped develop, but thought there were flaws in the system TLF had conceived. So he decided to take the project back one stage in the process, to the 'pre-study' phase. He wanted the team to explore simpler alternatives than the concept embodied in the first machine platform. Andersson, who had been the project's first technical champion, bowed gracefully and accepted the challenge of his technical colleague:

> It was my objective to save the project! To get it forward, I wasn't going to argue on technical issues, because any person who comes in with a technical background is bound to bring a different perspective on the design or on risks. So, I took a very low profile, thinking that this was not the end of the world! As long as my colleagues adopted the project, I was not going to make it a matter of personal ego or prestige.[12]

### Making the Team and Steering Group Evolve

So the project team, now reduced to 10 people, rose again from its ashes, thus its name: Phoenix. A new project leader was appointed to take over as the previous one left Tetra Pak. Although he had been trained as an engineer, this new project leader had also been broadly exposed to the commercial side of the packaging business. The team was also reinforced with its first commercial member, Erik Lindroth, who joined on a part-time basis, before becoming full time in 1999. Lindroth, the first dedicated business champion on the team, launched a series of market research studies to test the acceptance of the new carton by consumers and retailers, with very encouraging results.

As Björkman was no longer available, given his new position within Tetra Pak, a new steering group was set up. It was chaired first by Andersson, who provided a vital link with the past, then by Bo Wirsén who, like Björkman, was a member of the group leadership team. After a turbulent period that almost killed it, the project had its second executive champion on board. Andersson remained in the steering group, again for continuity reasons. Other steering group members included the head of Tetra Pak's R&D unit – second senior technical champion – and the head of Tetra Pak-France. The latter, another business champion, was brought in to nurture the two most promising customer contacts developed thus far: Nestlé's pet food development center and Bonduelle's vegetable canning headquarters, both located in France. The steering group decided to meet every two to three months to revisit the commercial viability of the project and supervise its technical aspects.

When asked, years later, how he felt about leaving the project he had initiated and passing the chairmanship of the steering group to a top management colleague, Björkman commented:

> I never really thought that we would drop such a promising development project. What we had to do, though, was take a step back. And that's one of the reasons – it was not the only reason of course – why I stepped out of the project, because it was time to take a look at it with fresh eyes. When we had managed to sell it to the Tetra Pak organization, it was good to have a new team taking a look at it and checking whether the assumptions that we had made were the right ones . . . I think it's very important to have an evolvement over time. But it has to be an evolvement with continuity, hence the importance of having maintained Stefan Andersson as the red thread throughout. It's good to have new people coming in at different stages, as long as it's not too often. I strongly believe that you have to commit for quite a few years when you go into a project like this because, otherwise, you never really get stability in the different decisions.[13]

## Redesigning the System and Launching Commercial Field-Test Projects

The new Phoenix team was asked to reassess every aspect of the system, gathering fresh resources from within R&D to tackle the remaining issues. Within a year, and with the help of Tetra Pak's specialists on packaging materials, and good relationships with raw material suppliers, they had overcome all hurdles. After validating the technologies, the team assembled the components of the system into a single rig – a new mobile unit – and tested it.

Toward the end of 1996, encouraged by their earlier discussions, Tetra Pak's top management (represented by Wirsén) started a concrete common project with Nestlé (represented by Gasser). Its aim was to validate the retortable carton concept on real food products. After some internal debate, Nestlé chose to target its Friskies™ pet food business and to launch a field test in Italy. The pre-commercial agreement defined how intellectual property (IP) and all costs would be shared. It also determined the level of exclusivity granted to Nestlé for that particular application, and provided a time schedule for the field tests. Product trials could now start in Nestlé's French pet food R&D center.

By mid-1998, Bonduelle also expressed an interest in the Phoenix carton. The team was happy to bring a strong second potential customer on board because it proved the legitimacy of retortable cartons as a viable alternative to the can, even for its most traditional application – vegetables. It also reinforced Tetra Pak's motivation to keep funding the project, now that it had a second and different type of customer lined up for a new product category. So a new project was set up with Bonduelle, and several product varieties were tested before beans were chosen. Bonduelle proved to be extremely demanding on visual and taste quality. It required many adjustments to be made to the process and materials, which delayed the tests.

This second relationship taught management an important lesson: Each individual customer was bound to have its own requirements and processes. Tetra Pak would, therefore, have to conduct extensive retorting tests in each new product category, probably over a year or more, before meeting its customer's quality requirements. On the positive side, the Phoenix team members were seeing their knowledge and confidence level grow with each new product category, as they added new test results to their database.

### Reinforcing Project Organization and Visibility

In 1997, Tetra Pak's top management embarked on a major corporate drive to improve its innovation process. Wirsén, who had by now passed on to Björkman his function as head of Tetra Pak-Europe, led that effort in his position as steering group chairman. He was convinced that Tetra Pak should manage its key innovation projects more professionally. This meant appointing an experienced business leader to run each project under the supervision of a high-level, cross-functional steering group, chaired by one member of the global leadership team. Each project would also be subject to the company's new innovation process with a number of tollgates.

Having been involved in early customer discussions about the retortable carton concept and in the first pre-commercial agreement with Nestlé, Wirsén was keen to apply his new philosophy to Phoenix. Shortly thereafter, the head of Corporate R&D left the company, and hence his position in the steering group, but the newly appointed corporate CTO, Göran Harrysson, another member of top management, took up his place. With two members of the global leadership team on board, Phoenix was now placed firmly in top management's spotlight, at a time when staffing and investments were starting to become significant.

Wirsén strongly believed in Phoenix, and he was intent on quickly turning it into a true business endeavor. This, he felt, would require putting a senior business leader at its head. In 1999, he hired the managing director of Tetra Pak-Sweden, Joakim Rosengren, as part-time general manager for the project, which allowed the project manager to concentrate his efforts on technical development. The project team liked having a real businessman at its head and started building its own identity within R&D. Around this time Wirsén began toying with the idea of spinning off the project into a separate business unit.

Reflecting on all the changes that took place under his leadership, Wirsén comments:

> At the beginning, when we created it, the steering group was there really to help the project team take decisions of some importance. The team had a timetable to work to, and it had a budget to work to – and that budget stretched over five years, if I remember correctly. But outside the set framework, there were of course a lot of decisions that needed to be addressed, on the material side, on the machine side, on the supplier and customer side. We were helping the team come to decisions on all these points.

Later on in the project, we changed the role of the steering group to become more of a steering board. We had to leave what was then a fully fledged management team to take on its own agenda and to work with the operational decision-making themselves.

That happened when we got a Tetra Pak managing director, Joakim Rosengren, involved on a part-time basis to really take charge. And I wanted him to also start to prepare for this project to become its own company. That was in itself not easy because that had not been done before. And, of course, the big R&D organization had its doubts about the wisdom of doing that, and they argued that it was too early. But I wanted them to have, in essence, their own P&L accounts, so they would understand what resources they were spending. And I also wanted them to have a balance sheet because we were starting to get involved very much with suppliers in building up stocks of different parts of the machine. I think, in retrospect, that was a very important juncture for the project group, because all of a sudden they were not a 70-man band within a very big R&D organization, they were the Tetra Recart people – or rather, they were on their way to becoming the Tetra Recart team. There were still then known as the Phoenix team. But they had their own identity all of a sudden.[14]

Wirsén was also keen to increase the visibility of the project with top management and the company board.

When Joakim came on board, we started building a return map for the project and calculating a breakeven. We forecast spending hundreds of millions of Swedish kronor up to launch. I wasn't surprised by that investment, but I saw the importance of showing to all who were involved how much we were spending. I also wanted other members of our global leadership team to be aware of it. They were all supportive, and so was the family [Tetra Pak's owners/shareholders.][15]

## Turning a Project into a Business (2001 onward)

### Starting Real-life Field Tests and Preparing for Business

By January 2000, Tetra Pak had signed a field-test agreement with Nestlé's Friskies for a new line of premium dog food to be launched in Italy. By mid-2000, a similar agreement had been signed with Bonduelle, for a line of beans, by coincidence also in

Italy. The two field-test contracts reinforced management's confidence in the commercial viability of the Phoenix concept. It was now time to move from project mode to business mode.

The first step was to conceive a proprietary brand for the new product. 'Tetra Recart' (a contraction of **re**tortable **cart**on) was chosen by mid-2000 and the Phoenix team, which was still part of the R&D group, was renamed accordingly. The second step was to refine the breakeven and return calculations that Rosengren had initiated when he joined the team. Breakeven would now occur when an annual sales volume of one billion packs was reached. This volume would be possible by 2005, assuming four or five high-volume customers signed up.

### Setting up a New Company: Tetra Recart AB

Discussions about spinning off the project team into a new business unit intensified and management decided to set up Tetra Recart as a separate fully owned company by January 2001. Hiving off a large project team from the corporate R&D center and setting it up as a separate business unit was not an easy task, particularly since R&D had to keep involved in materials development for that project. This induced management to appoint Harrysson as the direct line supervisor of the new Tetra Recart unit. As CTO, Harrysson headed corporate R&D; he was therefore in a good position to strike a balance between the two organizations and keep them motivated to cooperate.

Wirsén, who had remained on the steering group as chairman, and his senior colleagues believed that the new unit should have a dedicated business manager. Rosengren having chosen another responsibility, a search started for a new managing director for Tetra Recart. The steering group pondered whether the new job should go to an outsider familiar with the food industry. But Tetra Pak had relatively little experience with hiring outsiders in senior positions. Besides, management wanted the new unit to fully leverage the company's technical, production and commercial capabilities and relationships. Wirsén chose Jan Juul Larsen, an experienced senior manager:

> In the end, I wanted a Tetra Pak-cultured person. I knew Jan Juul Larsen who reported to me as managing director of Tetra Pak-Taiwan. He had proven leadership qualities, was very focused, and showed an appetite for the challenge. We could always bring in outsiders with category knowledge under him.[16]

In May 2001, before Larsen had relocated in Lund to take over the new Tetra Recart organization, the Friskies field tests started in Italy. The new line gained rapid acceptance with retailers and consumers, and initial consumer tests showed that Tetra Recart beat the can on most key attributes.

## Developing the Tetra Recart Organization and Business

When Larsen took over in July 2001, his first concern was to build a professional business organization and establish an appropriate governance process.

> When I arrived, there were 50 people in Tetra Recart. The steering group was very engaged in operational decisions; they felt ownership! But you cannot run a business when all decisions move from one steering group meeting to the next one. We needed to gain our management freedom and start operating as a normal business unit. However, the project was getting very big so we needed to maintain a high degree of top management visibility and support. Tetra Recart AB was already set up as a legal unit, so I proposed creating an embryo for a completely independent business unit.[17]

Wirsén endorsed Larsen's proposal. The project steering group with its bimonthly operational meetings was dismantled. The new company, Tetra Recart AB, would have a board of four members, three of them members of Tetra Pak's group leadership team. Wirsén (now head of Region Asia-America) remained as chairman of the new board, which held quarterly meetings, and Harrysson remained as Larsen's direct line manager, helping him set up his own organization. The creation of a board at top management level was well accepted by everyone within Tetra Pak. It was also welcomed by the two field-test customers who saw it as yet another sign of Tetra Pak management's commitment. Larsen was given carte blanche to sign new contracts with customers.

Larsen was aware that he had to focus his team entirely on making a success of the two field tests and adding new customers to his backlog. Unfortunately, Nestlé, which in the meantime had bought Ralston Purina, changed its pet foods strategy. It dropped the project, despite the fact that its market test was very positive and the brand saw its market share increase regularly. This was a blow for the organization, but fortunately, there was a second field-test customer: Bonduelle.

While trying to solve his daily load of technical problems and maintaining his field-test customers happy, Larsen also had to try to build a professional organization. This, he felt, would require a mix of insiders with strong experience of Tetra Pak and outsiders, bringing in-depth knowledge of the food industry. His board gave him free rein to recruit from both sides. So the nucleus of an organization started to take shape.

Larsen was aware that top management, although fully supportive of the new business unit, would expect him to show results and to do so quickly. He saw four major challenges ahead:

- Choosing target customer segments: should Tetra Recart target multinational brand owners like Nestlé, which controlled the volume? Should it go after smaller regional canners like Bonduelle? Or should it favor 'non-canners,' or a combination of the three?
- Defining a product development strategy: given the likely entry of competitors into the market, when should Tetra Recart start filling up its product pipeline – developing new systems and package sizes – and what should be its portfolio development priorities?
- Choosing how to go to market: what market approach would guarantee that Tetra Recart keep control over its business while leveraging the strong Tetra Pak market organization? How much control should Tetra Recart keep over its marketing and sales organization?
- Reducing time-to-profit: what strategy and sales approach would accelerate the process by which customers made decisions, thus reducing the anticipated time to reach breakeven? How could Tetra Recart lower the risk for its customers and induce them to shift to the new system?

Toward the end of 2004, with several new customers lined up, Tetra Pak's global leadership team looked at its new Tetra Recart business with prudent optimism. The new company had enlisted an encouraging number of new customers, in Europe as well as America. The business was taking off and the focus was now on international growth. To reflect that change, the direct line responsibility moved, once again, within the Tetra Recart board, from Harrysson, the CTO, to Alex Anavi, the head of global marketing and business development. Over 11 years, Tetra Pak's leaders had turned vision into reality and a highly uncertain project into a business ready for strong commercial takeoff. They were about to realize their initial dream, i.e. to revolutionize the canning industry.

## Drawing the Lessons

When asked whether he had expected, upon starting the project, that it would take so long to bring his project to fruition, Björkman replies:

> No! I don't think that we had any idea that it would take this long. Our time span was more five to seven years at the time, when we really got into the project.[18]

On his side, reflecting on what was on his mind as chairman of the steering group throughout these many years, Bo Wirsén comments:

> I think that you have to decide for yourself which are those fundamentals that really convince you that the project has a very good chance of success. And I think, in my case, there were two aspects. The first one was the cost profile, i.e. to make sure that, on a stand-alone basis, Tetra Recart would be cost-competitive. The second one was that it would offer a lot of interesting attributes, from the consumer community point of view. These were two fundamental things that we checked on all the time. And sometimes to the irritation of the other project team members, because we spent quite a lot of time when we got together discussing these two fundamentals, particularly during the early development.
>
> It is so easy when you see one of these fundamentals disappearing out of focus to then introduce a lot of new variables that all of

a sudden become much more important. But to really go back to these two factors in this case and just drum them in and make everybody realize that nothing is going to change the board's mind on cost competitiveness. We can have ten interesting attributes, but we still have to stay on track for cost. I think that is something I learned that was very, very useful. And there were times I thought to myself, may be we can sort of compromise on this very aspect. But we never did![19]

## EVOLVING LEADERSHIP IMPERATIVES IN NEW BUSINESS CREATION

### Tetra Recart: A Real-Life Example of 'Chain of Leadership'

The Tetra Recart story illustrates the power of a collective chain of leadership. Despite some champions stepping in and out of the project at different times, the venture did not suffer from any discontinuity in leadership for more than 10 years. And one champion − Stefan Andersson − actually stayed involved throughout, maintaining the momentum of the project, particularly when an external corporate reorganization threatened its survival. As in a chain, the interweaving of different types of links − in this case, technical, business and executive champions with complementary talents − reinforces resistance to breakage.

Reflecting on what made the Tetra Recart chain of leadership apparently so effective, Andersson proposes a number of success factors:

> First, obviously, continuity is important, and you have to make sure that, even if people change positions in the company, they don't necessarily step out of the steering group.
>
> Second, the size of the steering group is also important. You have to keep it to a maximum of four or five people. Beyond that, the dynamics get completely different; people are there to represent an interest and they start sending substitutes to meetings. You really want everyone involved to feel a personal responsibility and passion for the project.

Third, the steering group members need to really, genuinely, put the interest of the project in front of any other personal agendas or organizational interests. They should also have a balanced focus between actually 'doing work' – adding value concretely to the team – and their steering mission, which means coaching and controlling.

Fourth, it is important to ensure that there are no big egos in the steering group, because they can become stumbling blocks, for example by leaving no space to the project leader and preventing team members from thriving and being proud of what they achieve. On our project, there was not any sort of competition between individuals. Everyone put the good of the project in the forefront.

Finally, you have to make sure that you organize team-building exercises and that you encourage good personal bonding between the members of the steering group and between them and the project team.[20]

The story of Nestlé's Nespresso, mentioned earlier in this chapter, presents a very similar chain of leadership pattern, both at the steering level and within the project, as well as in the early-stage business organization. And there are many other similar examples of long-cycle innovation projects. This is why it is interesting to go deeper and try to understand why a chain of leadership is required. How do leadership imperatives change over the duration of a new venture project, from initial idea to new business creation? What should be the focus of the different types of leaders in the various phases of the venture?

## The Different Phases in New Business Creation through Innovation

From a business leadership point of view, innovative new ventures like Tetra Pak's retortable carton package go through three broad phases as they move from initial idea to steady growth (refer to Figure 8.2):

- A phase of *invention and proof of concept* as the underlying technology and the new product are developed and validated. In this phase, leaders need to provide the initial vision, and they

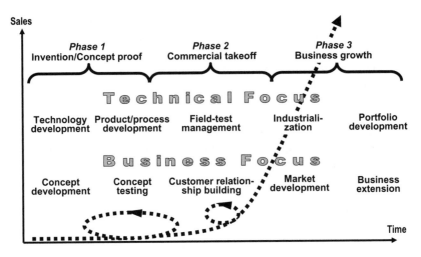

**Figure 8.2**   Phases in new business creation

encourage and support the team in its creative problem solving efforts.

- A phase of *commercial takeoff* as the team establishes its first commercial customer relationships. In this phase, leaders need to challenge and guide the team as it fine-tunes and tests its product, before confronting the business reality by going to market.
- A phase of *business growth* as the venture moves from project mode to business mode. In this last phase, leaders need to set up a fully functioning organization and build an infrastructure that will carry the business through its early growth phase and prepare it for its long-term development.

For Tetra Recart, the first phase lasted from the fall of 1993 – launch date of the initial technology development project – until 1997, when the system was validated. As often happens with technology development projects, this period was not without hiccups and loops. The most notable one was the rethink of the product architecture (by restarting the project at a pre-study stage) when TLF was folded into Tetra Pak's R&D department. The second phase lasted from the spring of 1997 until the spring of 2001, when the first Nestlé-Friskies packages were sold and Tetra Recart was set up as a special business unit under the leadership of Jan Juul Larsen. This second phase was not without changes

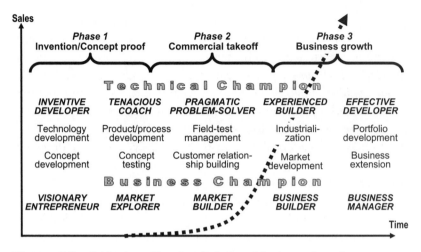

**Figure 8.3**    Desired profile of technical and business champions

and reworkings in response to field-test results, but they were less significant than during the first phase. From 2001, Tetra Recart was in its early growth phase with the addition of several new customers and the development of its product portfolio.

## The Changing Profile of Technical and Business Champions

As noted earlier, innovation requires the involvement and personal commitment of three types of champions. New business creation projects like Tetra Recart, which stretch over a long period, generally require a change in emphasis of these champions' contribution over time. This is particularly true for the senior technology and business champions, as Figure 8.3 shows.

### The Championing Imperative in Phase 1: Adaptive Persistence

In their first phase, innovative venture projects focus on demonstrating both the technical feasibility and the market attractiveness of the new product concept. They require from their technical and business champions a combination of practical inventiveness, visionary entrepreneurship, resourcefulness and willingness to explore and experiment. Some scholars[21] have coined the term 'adaptive persistence' to characterize an ability '*to overcome miscalculation and mistakes and take advantage of serendipitous events outside of one's field of vision.*' Persistence is desirable to overcome discouragement and try a new approach each time an explored avenue – be it a technical solution or target market – proves to be a dead-end. But leaders also have to be adaptive, not just doggedly persistent, to continually adjust their choices to the reality they discover, and thus to learn.

Stefan Andersson, the initial technical champion, demonstrated this skill amply as he doggedly supported the project despite its uncertainties. The same can be said of his boss, Nils Björkman, who played the dual roles of business and executive champion during this early phase. The arrival of a second senior technical champion – the head of Tetra Pak's central R&D department, to which the project was transferred – reinforced the technical leadership chain at a critical time. He was able to bring a fresh technical perspective to the project steering group by showing the limitations of the technical solutions that had been chosen. He then convinced his colleagues of the benefits of rethinking the product architecture. In retrospect, this decision delayed the project but it actually saved it, as the new technical platform proved more competitive than the previous one. It is to Andersson's credit that he recognized it and agreed to start afresh.

### The Championing Imperative in Phase 2: Pragmatic and Fast Learning

During Phase 1, the team's task is to prove that the technology works, at least in the lab, and that the product concept looks attractive to its target market, if only on first exposure to customers. Phase 2 is when the real challenge starts, i.e. when the project team confronts the reality of the market. This phase requires a lot of pragmatic learning and problem solving skills on the part of the technical team and its champion. It also requires an ability to establish solid customer relationships and to build a business case on the commercial side.

In the Tetra Recart example, Phase 2 witnessed the progressive reinforcement of the business leadership chain in three progressive steps: First, with the arrival of a commercially experienced project leader; second, with the entry on stage of a marketing resource, Eric Lindroth; and third, with the appointment of a senior business champion to direct the project, Joakim Rosengren. When questioned about the reasons for such late reinforcement of the business leadership side of the project, Tetra Pak's senior executives justify their approach on two grounds. On the one hand, they claim that Phase 1 was essentially focusing on technology development; the project remained too uncertain to induce customers to embrace it and start real tests. On the other hand, they stress the fact that Björkman – the executive champion – was able to enlist the help of several of his top management colleagues, including Wirsén – his future successor – for conducting preliminary customer visits.

### The Championing Imperative in Phase 3: Flexible Professionalism

The last phase starts when what was a R&D project, albeit a big one, is set up as a business unit of its own – whether inside the corporation as a new SBU, or spun off as a separate entity with its own governance system. The new business needs to build its proper functional organization, marshal resources and formulate plans to achieve its business objectives. The new venture and its leaders will then have to become more professional in establishing proper business processes. However, they must remain very flexible to adapt fast to unexpected customer demands or competitors' reactions.

In most cases, this transition requires a significant change in leadership at the business level. The entrepreneurial project leader may indeed lack experience in managing a fast-growing organization and in building an appropriate business infrastructure. Change may also be needed at the technical level as R&D resources and processes have to be put in place to support fast market growth. Tetra Pak recognized this necessary mutation in two ways: (1) by establishing its retortable carton project as a separate company – Tetra Recart AB – under the leadership of an experienced business leader, Jan Juul Larsen; and (2) by hiring an experienced technical manager to keep on developing its product portfolio.

## The Changing Role of Executive Champions

If the leadership profile and the emphasis of technical and business champions change in the course of a project, so does the role of the executive champion, the high level 'godfather' and conductor of the venture. Remember that we defined the executive champion as the sponsor and protector of an innovation project on the top management team or, in the words of Lewis Lehr, 3M's former CEO, as the person who *'follows the fellows who follow a dream.'*[22] The role of the champion is to represent and defend the project not only to the top management team but also to external stakeholders. These can be shareholders – Tetra Pak's owners always knew about and supported the Tetra Recart venture thanks to regular information provided to them by management – or financial analysts or institutions with vested interests in the company.

As already stressed, it takes guts to be an executive champion and risk your reputation by backing fledgling projects, given the fact that many ventures never make it to market. It exposes you to colleagues on the top management team, particularly those who play safe and never volunteer as innovation champions. Long after the facts, the latter may be tempted to hint treacherously at the lack of judgment of those who backed failed projects. Yet, executive champions play a vital contribution throughout the life of the venture and, as Figure 8.4 shows, their role changes with each phase.

### The Executive Champion in Phase 1: Nurturing Sponsor

During the first phase, the main task of the executive champion is to serve as the main sponsor of the project by legitimating it in

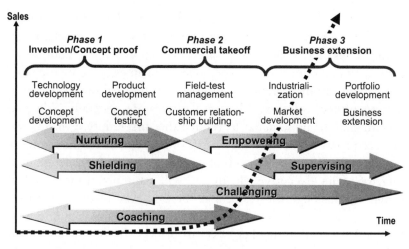

**Figure 8.4** The evolving role of the executive champion

the eyes of top management. The executive champion plays a role not unlike that of a hands-on venture capitalist or a film producer. He/she will:

(1) clarify and communicate his/her vision of the opportunity;
(2) sell the vision and the project to top management colleagues;
(3) secure resources, in terms of talent and cash;
(4) assemble the best possible team for the task at hand;
(5) target the most attractive and accessible markets; and
(6) help the team navigate around the first internal and external obstacles.

As already noted, the Phase 1 executive champion will also serve as the team's 'sword and shield.' Björkman, as CEO of Tetra Laval Food (TLF), was uniquely positioned to act as the executive champion of the new retortable carton venture. His contribution was more in terms of coaching than shielding because TLF was a relatively small organization, run independently of the larger Tetra Pak, and besides, his CEO status guaranteed a minimum of interference with the team from others.

Sponsoring and supporting a venture project does not mean giving a blank check to the project team. Early on, executive champions need to start challenging the team. Their first emphasis should be on risk management, forcing the team to clarify its assumptions and follow a professional approach to address all project uncertainties. In best-practice companies, executive champions typically make funding approval conditional on satisfactorily passing project tollgates. These milestones are generally linked to specific actions undertaken to reduce the uncertainty level. As the project progresses from technical development to business undertaking, the nature and level of the management challenge will increase. The executive champion will naturally want to bring others to challenge the team, and the best way to do so is to set up a high-level and cross-functional project steering group, which is what happened in the Tetra Recart project. In some cases – high risk projects involving the development and/or application of a completely new technology – the steering group may set up a special 'design review team.' This is generally a group of technical experts, from inside and outside, who are enlisted to act as a source of both advice and challenge to the team.

### The Executive Champion in Phase 2: Challenging Sponsor

As the project moves along to its second phase – commercial takeoff – the role of the executive champion will evolve. Coaching and shielding remain critical, at least in the early part of Phase 2, but challenging becomes more and more vigorous. As the level of management pressure on the team rises – generally for getting to market fast and showing results – so should the level of autonomy and empowerment granted to its leader. In the Tetra Recart case, it is the newly appointed executive champion, Bo Wirsén, who introduced this shift in emphasis as he brought in an experienced senior business leader, Joakim Rosengren, to lead the project. Progressively, as the project increasingly resembles a business undertaking, the proactive coaching role of the executive champion tends to become more subdued and turns into empowering and supervisory modes.

### The Executive Champion in Phase 3: Empowering and Supervising Sponsor

Phase 3 is generally marked by the venture's transition from the status of an R&D project to a business. The first role of the executive champion is to determine the right time for such a transformation. Timing is often conditioned by several factors:

(1) In some cases, maintaining a very large project team within the R&D department becomes unwieldy. R&D managers may object to having to keep housing and funding a large team with its own identity (and late additions from other departments) past the technology and product development stages.

(2) But timing can also be determined by the business outlook – is the team about to move into commercial operations? – and by the availability of a business leader whom management trusts.

The existence of a corporate incubator, within or with close relations to R&D, may facilitate the transition from project to business. Projects will typically move from R&D to the incubator, if it exists, at the end of Phase 1, after passing the go/no-go point. In the incubator, they will be encouraged to develop their autonomy and business sense. The move from incubator to separate business unit can then be organized more smoothly, when all the business and leadership conditions are met.

As the structure and identity of the venture changes, so does the role of the executive champion, i.e. from coaching to empowering, and finally to supervising. In the Tetra Recart case, this transition occurred when a new senior business leader was hired to run the new unit, Jan Juul Larsen. It was Wirsén who turned the steering group he was chairing into a supervisory board of Tetra Recart AB, the new company created to run the new business. This was more than a cosmetic designation change; it meant that day-to-day issues would be handled by the management team of the new business and no longer by the steering group. The Tetra Recart board was to become a regular corporate board, albeit more like the board of a start-up – on standby for requests for help and guidance – than that of an established company.

## The Importance of Venture Steering Groups or Boards

The desirable leadership profile of technical, business and executive champions changes so much in the course of a venture, from idea to market, that one can only wonder how the same individuals could ever handle all the phases in sequence. Keeping the same team of champions throughout, irrespective of the fact that it would require long commitments on their part, might lead to a sub-optimization of talents. Indeed, some champions may feel more comfortable performing certain roles than others. Changing leaders at each phase, as in a relay race, to bring the most adequate profiles when they are needed, may not be ideal either. This will most probably bring about a loss of continuity in leadership as knowledge and experience may be wasted in the phasing in/ phasing out process. A solution for maintaining a certain level of consistency in the leadership of the new venture is to enlist several champions and ensure that, if some have to leave, their tenure overlaps to some extent.

The best mechanism to achieve this type of continuity is the venture steering group or board. Just as a corporate supervisory board is able to provide multi-disciplinary governance and guidance to a company's management on a continuous basis, despite occasional director movements, so can a venture steering group. The choice of steering group members and the way their entry to and departure from the group is managed is, therefore, a critical success factor in managing a new business venture. Of all the lessons one can derive from the Tetra Recart story, this is probably the most important. The steering group is the privileged place where technical, business and executive champions gather and bring their complementary leadership talents to turn an innovation vision into business reality.

As Figure 8.5 shows, the nature and focus of venture steering groups need to evolve together with the project.

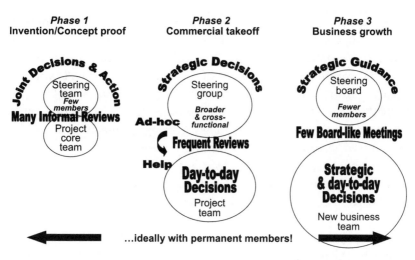

**Figure 8.5**   The evolving role of steering groups over the life of a venture project

During Phase 1 – invention and proof of concept – the number of project team members will generally be limited, and likewise for the steering team. But despite its small number, the steering team can be expected to get very involved in day-to-day project activities and decisions that will orient the venture, technically or commercially. Tetra Pak's Andersson refers to this hands-on functioning of the steering team at an early stage as a 'doing role,' as opposed to the 'advising, coaching and controlling' roles that it will subsequently play in later phases. Having a small and very active steering team allows it to work rather informally, addressing issues as they arise, not according to a formal review calendar.

As the project enters Phase 2 – commercial takeoff – the project team will generally need to be beefed up substantially. So will the steering group, if only to get commercially oriented leaders to support the process of building up customer relationships. A bigger and cross-functional steering group will, of necessity, operate more formally than the smaller, hands-on steering team of the first phase. It will hold frequent reviews, but they will be scheduled around important project milestones, and its focus will be on strategic decisions, more than on day-to-day project operations. The 'doing role' of the steering group will diminish – limited to ad hoc calls for help by the project team – and its 'advising, coaching and controlling role' will come to the fore.

The nature and functioning of the steering group will typically change significantly as the venture enters Phase 3 – business growth – and the project team becomes the nucleus of a new business management team. The steering group will typically become a 'steering board,' adopting a supervisory role over the management team. Strategic decisions will generally be passed on to the management team, under the overall guidance of the steering board. There will often be fewer reviews and they will focus on business progress. In many ways, even if the new business is not spun off as a separate entity, its steering board will operate like a board of directors.

In summary, senior executives should give their full attention to the way they steer long-cycle innovation projects. This means understanding how to make the governance of their venture projects evolve from Phase 1 to Phase 3, and make sure that the right leaders are involved at the right time, while maintaining a maximum of continuity in the process.

Ultimately, senior executives should perceive that participating in project steering teams, steering groups and steering boards is as important as sitting on the board of subsidiary companies. Participating in innovation steering mechanisms is a critical task to which *all* top and senior managers should commit as part of their innovation leadership mission. The benefits to be derived from such commitment are fourfold:

(1) shared accountability, which reduces the burden felt by individual executive champions confronted with critical go/no-go decisions;
(2) collective leadership, which improves the quality of risk assessments and business decisions;
(3) continuous open communications within the top management team and with stakeholders, since everyone will be somehow involved in critical projects;

(4) continuity in leadership, despite unavoidable changes in steering group membership.

The next chapter will also deal with radical innovations, but this time focusing on new business models or systems, together with partners. As we shall see, this type of thrust requires another completely different breed of innovation leaders.

## ENDNOTES

1. This chapter is adapted from a previous article by the author: 'A Chain of Leadership for New Business Creation,' published in *Die Unternehmung – Swiss Journal of Business Research and Practice,* April 2005: 335–352.
2. Retorting is the technology currently used to sterilize food products in a container, be it a metal can, glass jar or plastic pouch. It consists of heating the food in a sealed container for a couple of hours under pressure in a sort of steam boiler called a retorting tunnel (or vessel).
3. Crawford, M.C. (1977). 'Marketing Research and the New Product Failure Rate.' *Journal of Marketing* **41**(2): 51–61.
   Cooper, R.G. (1979). 'The Dimensions of Industrial New Product Success and Failure.' *Journal of Marketing* **43**(3)(Summer): 93–103.
4. Among other studies, refer to the report published by Tim Eales (January 2007) 'New Product Success in Europe.' Bracknell, Information Resources Inc.
5. Zook, C. (2004). *Beyond the Core: Expand Your Market without Abandoning Your Roots.* Boston, Harvard Business School Press.
6. Chakravarthy, B. and Lorange, P. (2007). *Profit or Growth? Why You Don't Have to Choose.* Harlow, Wharton School Publishing, pp. 90–95.
7. Deschamps, J.-P. and Pahwa, A. (2004). 'New Business Creation at Tetra Pak: Reinventing the Food Can.' IMD Case No. IMD-3-1448.
8. UHT refers to an Ultra High Temperature conservation process.
9. Author's videotaped interview with Stefan Andersson in 2005, reproduced with permission.
10. Author's videotaped interview with Nils Björkman and Bo Wirsén in 2005, reproduced with permission.
11. Author's videotaped interview with Stefan Andesson in 2005, reproduced with permission.
12. Author's videotaped interview with Stefan Andesson in 2005, reproduced with permission.
13. Author's videotaped interview with Nils Björkman and Bo Wirsén in 2005, reproduced with permission.
14. Author's videotaped interview with Nils Björkman and Bo Wirsén in 2005, reproduced with permission.

15. Author's videotaped interview with Nils Björkman and Bo Wirsén in 2005, reproduced with permission.
16. Author's videotaped interview with Nils Björkman and Bo Wirsén in 2005, reproduced with permission.
17. Videotaped intervention of Jan Juul Larsen in an open program at IMD in 2004, reproduced with permission.
18. Author's videotaped interview with Nils Björkman and Bo Wirsén in 2005, reproduced with permission.
19. Author's videotaped interview with Nils Björkman and Bo Wirsén in 2005, reproduced with permission.
20. Author's videotaped interview with Stefan Andersson in 2005, reproduced with permission.
21. Lilly, G.A., Redington, D.B. and Tiemann, T.K. (1999). 'Can We Teach Adaptive Persistence?' presented at the Ninth Annual Business/Economics Teaching Conference, sponsored by DePaul University and Elmhurst College, Chicago, April 1999.
22. Lehr, L.W. (1979). 'Stimulating Technological Innovation: The Role of Top Management.' *Research Management*, November: 23–25.

# CHAPTER 9

# LEADING THE CREATION OF A TOTALLY NEW BUSINESS SYSTEM OR MODEL REQUIRED: PRAGMATIC ARCHITECTS TO PUT ALL SYSTEM ELEMENTS IN PLACE

*Always design a thing by considering it in its next larger context – a chair in a room, a room in a house, a house in an environment, an environment in a city plan.*[1]

*Eliel Saarinen, a legendary architect*

In its generic definition, a 'business system' describes how a set of players cooperate (and sometimes compete) along an industry supply chain – suppliers, manufacturers/converters or service providers, 'complementors' and distributors. They usually pool resources to deliver a set of products and/or services to customers or consumers. Similarly, a 'business model' reflects how a company structures its operations and that of its suppliers and outsourcing partners to go to market, and how it intends to price its products or services and make a profit from its operations.

In Chapter 6, I proposed combining these two terms to describe special types of radical innovations that usually combine products and services. These innovations have a 'system' component, in the sense that they result from an ad hoc alliance between several partners along the value chain of their industry, each delivering a part of the final system. But often they also include an original business model element. This is the definition which will be used and illustrated in this chapter, and I will refer to the resulting offering as a 'system.'

The task of conceiving, developing and implementing a totally new business system or business model is, arguably, one of the most complex undertakings in innovation; particularly when success depends on the contribution of external partners. It is also an area where time-to-success and time-to-profit are very long. Customer adoption always tends to be slower than anticipated, and most innovators need to be patient before getting their money back. If and when success occurs, it often comes after a decade or more of effort, not a few years. We tend to admire the market success of an 'e-tailer,' like Amazon.com, but frequently forget the time it took the company to break even, and the dozens of resounding failures that marked the early developments of e-commerce. And when it comes, success remains elusive and fragile. Technological or environmental changes and competitive pressures generally require frequent reappraisals of the validity of the assumptions on which the system or model has been built. Even iconic business model innovators like Michael Dell come under fire when the robustness of their success formula starts eroding.

Uncertainty and the long time it can take to achieve success are inherent in all types of radical innovations, for sure. Indeed, as illustrated in Chapter 8, most attempts at creating a totally new product or service category – when they don't lead to outright failure – are characterized by a very long takeoff time. But the conception, development and implementation of a totally new business system or model introduces yet another major element of uncertainty, i.e. the need to partner with other companies to bring critical system components to market and make the new model work.

The story of the supposedly safe cash transfer box, described in Chapter 6, illustrates this type of complexity. Despite unique product characteristics and potentially attractive benefits for all actors in the value chain – retailers, security companies, insurance companies and bankers – the visionary inventors of this safe cash-case had no way to go to market alone. The success of their system hinged on the contribution of several stakeholders, i.e. on their willingness to take risks and provide, without any guarantee, a critical system component (complementary equipment) or element (lower insurance premiums). How to convince and motivate these partners that it was in their interest to take the risk of developing and bringing to market their part of the system? If one of the elements is missing or comes late, then the system cannot deliver its supposed value to customers, and the innovation fails to take root.

To avoid this risk, new business system or model innovators often aim to remain in full control of their final system or model. They try to establish a customer-supplier relationship with their system complementors. But even if they do, they ultimately always depend on their partners' willingness to cooperate and on their capabilities. In all cases, these types of innovation succeed only if they lead to a 'win-win' proposition for each partner in the chain. And they become sustainable only if the initiator of the new business model or system is willing to reappraise the partnership formula as market and competitive conditions change, and thus to make the original win-win proposition evolve.

## INNOVATION LEADERS AS VISIONARY BUT PRAGMATIC ARCHITECTS

The leadership qualities required to bring forth an innovative business system or business model are threefold:

- Innovation leaders need *imagination* to envisage the benefits and added value, to both customers and the company, of a radically new way to satisfy an unmet or latent need, or to perform a particularly burdensome chore. I characterize this type of imagination – visualizing what *could be* instead of what *is*, and the conditions for making this happen – as a talent for *visioning*.
- Innovation leaders need *persuasion* to share their vision with external partners and complementors, and to preserve their

original system integrity in their partnership discussions. I characterize this type of persuasion – combined with an ability to sense what is in it for everyone in the common project and to build win-win proposals – as a talent for *partnering*.

• Innovation leaders need *pragmatism* to understand what it will take to make the new business system or model work, to steer the project in the right direction and properly sequence all implementation steps. I characterize the ability to see concretely how the various system or model components need to fit together, and to organize smooth implementation, as a talent for *master planning*.

Imagination, persuasion and pragmatism in building a totally new business system or model – particularly one that requires a coalition of motivated partners – are qualities one might attribute to a *visionary but pragmatic architect*.

## Building a Vision Simultaneously on Several Fronts

Visionary architects, like Richard Buckminster Fuller who built the famous 'Biosphere' (American pavilion at the Montreal Expo 1967),[2] innovate by leaving aside contemporary notions of form and function to reinvent entirely new ones. They are generally driven by a search for functional efficiency and economy of means.

Radical business system or business model innovators – like visionary architects – think out of the box and dream big. They invent solutions to problems that most people are not aware of having or have not yet experienced, at least consciously. And they imagine ways to deliver value by organizing a new business system around their offering, enlisting and lining up suppliers and partners in a unique business model configuration. Southwest Airlines' Herb Kelleher in the US or Ryanair's Michael O'Leary in Europe dared to rethink the way flights are priced. Michael Dell was bold enough to think that computers could be ordered remotely, by phone or through the web, making retail outlets less relevant (at least up to a point). Amazon's Jeff Bezos presumed that people would enjoy browsing through and ordering from the widest possible choice of books, records and other goods on his user-friendly website. And Michael Ramsay and Jim Barton at TiVo, as I explain later in this chapter, dreamed of changing the way people plan, receive and use television entertainment. Like visionary architects, these innovation leaders went beyond offering a new product or service. They dared to propose a new business system or model that would dramatically improve their customers' experience.

Business system or business model innovators, like architects, think in terms of space and time. Their visioning talent takes several forms:

First, they somehow build an instinctive mental picture of how they could revolutionize a currently unsatisfactory customer experience with a totally new and attractive system combining products and services. They envision their potential offering, at least in its most basic form, as a radical alternative to what exists today. They can imagine and even visualize how it will work, once available, and what features it should have to capture their customers' 'wow!' Of course, the concept will evolve over time, but this first vision is generally compelling enough to get suppliers, partners and complementors intrigued and willing to explore cooperation opportunities.

Second, they seem to share an uncanny ability to see concretely how to get to where they want to be. They clearly see the missing pieces that are needed to complement their own capabilities and offering, and the most likely partners to help make it happen. They imagine how the pieces should fit together for a smooth product and service delivery.

Finally, they build a vision of how they might evolve their concept over time, imagining how they might add enhancements and features to broaden the appeal of their system, thus preempting competitors. They want their concept to satisfy current needs, but also to be robust and flexible enough to cater to their customers' evolving needs.

### Partnering to Complement or Enhance their Offering

Radical business system or business model innovations are infrequent because they are difficult and complex to set up. Indeed, they generally require a coalition of partners to unite to deliver a given product or service, often a complex one. The setting up of travel assistance contracts by insurance companies, mentioned in Chapter 6, illustrates the variety of partners/service providers who need to be enlisted to offer door-to-door risk and assistance coverage to travelers, e.g. emergency medical service providers; international car repair organizations; emergency logistics specialists; financial and payment organizations; travel specialists and so forth.

There is generally a lead partner – the main architect of the system – who has to plan and launch the new concept by selecting the most appropriate companies to complement or enhance his offering. The difficulty of setting up such business systems or models – aligning all partners behind the same vision and ensuring a collective win-win proposition – also acts as the lead partner's protection. There is, indeed, a premium given to first movers since, having a wider choice of partners, they can enlist the best ones.

Partnering is a complex process which demands a range of unusual talents on the part of the 'architect':

- openness to the external world and talent at networking;
- ability to communicate a vision and inspire others;
- capacity to inspire trust;
- ability to understand the negotiation positions of all partners;
- willingness to compromise (but not too much) to arrive at a win-win outcome;
- leadership to mobilize partners on an execution plan, and so forth.

Many partnerships fail not only because of a lack of business logic but also because the leaders who initiate them have poor partnering qualities. This is why these qualities are essential for all innovations that involve external parties.

## Master-Planning for Perfect Execution

Visionary architects cannot stay at the level of grand designs and mock-ups. They have to turn dreams into reality and execute their project, and this requires master-planning, i.e. the systematic sketching and phasing of all the requirements and moves that will lead a project all the way from the big picture to the smallest details. The more complex the business system and the higher the number of partners to be mobilized, the more difficult will be its execution, and hence the more important will be the planning phase. Granted, not all developments can be planned ahead of time; nevertheless business system or business model architects are bound to be good at execution.

The example of TiVo — US pioneer of easy-to-use digital video recorders (DVRs) and DVR-enabled television services — illustrates the concept of a business system and/or business model innovation, and the type of leadership that it entails. Most Americans know TiVo, which recently joined the list of America's most significant and highly valued customer innovations in the field of entertainment.

Despite its remarkable popular success with its customers — most of them having become unconditional TiVo devotees — the company remains a controversial conversation topic among business and financial analysts. While TiVo's management reaffirms its belief that it will, one day, reach critical scale and conquer the market thanks to its unique product and service concept, some observers predict the impending demise of the company.

The purpose of this chapter is certainly not to enter into such a debate. As exemplified by other business system/model innovators, like Dell, which need to struggle to keep their success formula competitive, few business system/model innovations are totally future-proof. The TiVo story is interesting, not because of its future outlook but because it highlights the role of a special type of innovation leader, i.e. the visionary yet pragmatic architect, in this case Mike Ramsay, TiVo's founder. And it illustrates the importance of the three talents that make these business system/model innovations possible: *visioning, partnering and master planning.*

## TIVO: A BUSINESS SYSTEM/MODEL INNOVATION[3]

### What is TiVo?

TiVo Inc. is a Silicon Valley firm, created in 1997, which, like Amazon, has received considerable acclaim in the US for pioneering a completely new type of business in the digital media world. It provides a good example of a company built around both a business system and a business model innovation. Its offering illustrates what the term 'system' means – a combination of hardware, software and services.

If you asked TiVo customers – Americans who own a TiVo DVR and subscribe to the TiVo service – what TiVo means to them, you would get the same type of answer: 'It is a totally new way to watch television.' Indeed, TiVo is changing its customers' TV experience and, because of that, it has become an American 'cult product,' to the point that it has entered the popular TV vocabulary – 'Come home tonight, I have TiVo-ed your favorite show!'

### Customer Features and Benefits

Basically, through digital video recording (DVR) technology, TiVo replaces the old VCR in allowing customers to watch the TV shows they want, when they want through its time-shifting functionality. But it dramatically extends the VCR's basic functionality through various digitally enabled, easy-to-use hardware and software features, such as:

- a very long recording time (up to 180 hours in standard definition);
- very user-friendly controls on a simple remote;
- pause and rewind features with instant replays even in high definition (HD);

- fast-forward feature to accelerate replays (hence skip unwanted commercials);
- intelligent search feature for HD movies and sports;
- movie recording in standard or high definition;
- possibility to download movies from the Internet;
- access to music and photo libraries with the remote control;
- possibility to set TV recording from any computer when away from home;
- possibility to send favorite recordings to a Windows PC, using TiVo ToGo™;
- and more.

But the company goes much further than offering an excellent DVR line. What enthralls its customers is the unique range of services that come with a TiVo subscription, notably:

- the possibility to receive, via a phone, satellite or cable connection, regularly updated TV programs and to choose what to watch or record through an 'Electronic Program Guide' (EPG) with easy-to-use menus on screen;
- the possibility for customers, through TiVo's 'season pass,' to have TiVo automatically record their favorite shows all season long, irrespective of schedule changes, as well as to skip reruns if desired;
- the possibility to activate the 'thumbs up' and 'thumbs down' buttons on their remote, to express their preferences and indicate the types of shows, movies, actors or directors that TiVo will record automatically;
- the possibility to express preferences for and receive certain types of advertising; and so forth.

### Network Features and Benefits

Even though it was conceived as a way to take control away from the networks and put it in the hands of the customer, TiVo, unlike its competitor ReplayTV®, was designed and promoted in such a manner as to avoid clashing with the networks and advertisers. Going beyond a non-aggression pact, TiVo is convinced that it has a contribution to make to the media and advertising world.

In that spirit, the company has developed a range of services for networks and advertisers, for example by including its Showcase™ and StopIIWatch™ services (described in more detail later in the chapter).

## Seizing a Market Opportunity

### Toying with and Refining a Vision

The founders of TiVo – Mike Ramsay and Jim Barton – were no starry-eyed apprentice entrepreneurs. Both had worked for many years at Silicon Graphics Inc. (SGI) in Sunnyvale, California, a manufacturer of high-performance computing solutions specializing in imaging technology and video applications. While Barton was more of a scientist than Ramsay, both had strong operational experience and both were intrigued by the enormous potential they saw in using computing technology for consumer and media applications, as Ramsay notes:

> When I left SGI, I didn't have the TiVo idea in mind, but I knew that if I were to do something, it would be in the consumer space and the media space because of the interest this sector was bound to create . . . Jim had been out of SGI for a year and he had actually been trying to start his own company. His experience was working with Time Warner Cable on a powered video-on-demand project. He had been the lead architect on this and developed a strong interest in that kind of technology. We had known each other for a very long time – probably 15 years – but we got together almost by accident for a lunch meeting. We started chatting and we had a free-flowing discussion about what could be done and what new ideas were floating around. We got together several times and developed some ideas around, not actually DVRs, but home media servers . . . You know, having a central media hub in the home and, from that, networking from your television to other media.[4]

After many exploratory discussions, Ramsay and Barton developed a number of ideas on how to build a home media center business, which, they thought, could form the basis of a company. The DVR was part of it because it was a concrete first step in establishing their vision. But the two dreamers were already thinking about accessing the web and the range of services that could be derived from it.

### Winning Financial Support and Setting up TiVo Inc.

Believing they had a cool concept to build upon, Ramsay and Barton started approaching Silicon Valley venture capitalists (VCs) to exchange ideas with them. But they rapidly discovered that their vision did not fit well into the classical venture capital model. Their idea was simply too complex, the implementation time too long, and the investment required to build a consumer business too large. 'Nine times out of ten we got a pretty bland response,' confessed Ramsay.

But a few, probably more visionary, entrepreneurs – Stewart Alsop of New Enterprise Associates (NEA) and Geoff Yang of Redpoint Ventures – were sufficiently intrigued by Ramsay and Barton's vision to agree to provide funding to create a company. So, in 1997, TiVo Inc. was set up in Sunnyvale (CA). Mark Perry of NEA and a founding board member of TiVo remembers:

> Mike [Ramsay] understood the opportunity to take the technology that had been developed principally for business-related activities and get it to the lower price-point and the usability necessary for the consumer around the concept of a home network. He had some innovative ideas on what to bring to the consumer. The TiVo DVR was just one node of their original diagram. It was clear the company needed to focus on one part as it would be impossible to have the resources and the funding to do the whole vision.[5]

Randy Komisar, who built his reputation helping entrepreneurs create and run new technology-based businesses,[6] recalls his first encounter with Ramsay before joining TiVo's board in 1998:

> Mike was not a 'newbie.' He was an extremely seasoned operator and did not need the same input as many first-time entrepreneurs. But he had never done a start-up before, so he did need guidance and counsel for things like phasing, partnering, financing and building strong ecosystems that are particular to start-ups. He had all the skills in the world but no first-hand start-up experience . . . I liked them both right away – Mike is incredibly charismatic. His Scottish

origins give him a mellow edge. He exudes confidence and seems like a good partner, someone who listens well . . .'[7]

## Formulating Corporate Values

Interestingly, while they were developing their concept, Ramsay and Barton gave a lot of thoughts to the kind of company they wanted to build. Jim Barton remembers:

> Originally, we drew up on butcher paper three concepts that were more corporate concepts than product concepts. We wanted to start a company with the idea of doing something interesting and creating interesting products. But we had a concept on how the company would operate and what the company would be like. We were fixated on not doing certain things, especially since we came from large companies and saw a lot of big companies not operate well, and we wanted to make this one run well. One of the main principles was to create balance and not be a typical start-up where people work insane hours and divorces happen because the start-up becomes their life. We wanted to create a balance; build the most effective environment; respect the individual; promote a culture of high integrity. This was the genesis of our ethics statement, our code of conduct . . .[8]

TiVo's code of conduct − a 15-page document that each employee received and endorsed − rapidly became a centerpiece around which employees united. It remains almost unchanged today, even though Ramsay has passed the baton on to a new CEO. Very early on, the two founders defined the set of corporate values they would promote, which Ramsay summarizes as follows:

> Number one, we wanted a company that was comfortable and capable of working with third parties in a very collaborative way . . .
> Number two, we were going to make sure that we were never going to reinvent the wheel. We would only put effort into things that truly added value. And for things that didn't necessarily add value, we would find the best people and work with them.
> Number three, we were going to be a technology company with high standards . . . We were going to hire the best people that we could find and pay them competitively, even though we might

be resource constrained. Our high priority for investment would be in people – the top people we could attract to the company.

And there was also another aspect around how we would treat each other and work with each other. For example, we set out to say that we were going to overcommunicate every step of the way. Every employee would be involved in decisions and we wouldn't make major decisions without knowing exactly what was going on.[9]

This emphasis on open communication was taken very seriously, including in the way space was organized, as Barton emphasizes:

This building is arranged on both floors in a circle. We organized and designed the space so people would interact. We have common open spaces and we have arranged our offices in a circular pattern so that people have to walk through common areas and interaction happens. We architected it so people had to run into people.

### Building a High-Power Team

Loyal to their principle of hiring the best talent available, Ramsay and Barton started looking for and attracting the heads of their key functions. They were helped in some cases by their VC investors who provided the contacts. The climate that pervaded the whole Silicon Valley ecosystem in the late 1990s helped them also, as many corporate executives were attracted by the huge upside of technology start-ups. Ramsay describes his hiring spree as follows:

On the technology side, we hired a great VP of engineering; Jim was going to be the chief technology officer; and we then hired three or four key people that we knew were just the best that we could get, and so we got the engineering team going.

But we knew we had to find some additional kinds of people that we were not familiar with. One person joined us who came out of the media industry. We also knew that we needed a lot of capital. And so early on, I hired a CFO who came out of the investment banking world and had a huge amount of experience in raising capital.

We then realized that we needed somebody in business development who was really strong. And we found an incredibly talented individual who came out of a legal firm in San Francisco and had specialized in mergers and acquisitions. He came on board to really manage our deals with partners.

We also hired somebody in the information technology area who knew how to set up a service structure. We hired a marketing VP as well, who had a lot of experience in consumer marketing.

We had this broad cross-section of people and we were all in a mix together – doing it all together. And that created a very different dynamic than a bunch of engineers sitting around, thinking about a product. You can imagine, with extremely bright people in all of these areas, how stimulating and rewarding it could be to create something which was more than a product – it was a real business!

Ramsay's recruiting philosophy was heavily centered on the person, as opposed to the job. He was interested more in talents, energy and leadership than experience in a given function. In fact, his personal experience had taught him to mistrust people who were too focused on a specific industry – experts who could get too entrenched in their view of the world – as they might be too inflexible for a start-up.

## Establishing the Business Model and Enlisting the First Partners

The business plan that Ramsay and Barton presented to their initial financial investors built on the idea of a home media server connected to both a source of television broadcasting – cable, satellite or over the air – and broadband internet. It consisted of a set of hardware and software that gave an integrated consumer experience.

This initial hardware focus was challenged by the VCs, as Randy Komisar remembers:

We had a big debate. They wanted to go into the hardware business. This was the model they presented me with and I disagreed. I viewed it as more of a software business. The hardware would be the vehicle for the services, and the true monetization would be from selling continuous services to the customer.[10]

These early discussions helped the founders refine their business model. They realized that they needed to go to market in a year to 18 months and that their initial concept had too broad a scope to be implemented in that time frame. They narrowed it down, looking at the technology available and decided that they would design a DVR with unique, user-friendly software features, as Barton stresses:

> We thought the product should work for the common person and meet the 'mother test,' i.e. if my mother can't use it, then we are building the wrong thing. As a technologist, the greatest expression of what I can do is to create something that everyone can use. It takes more engineering and effort to make something simple!

The DVR, they thought, would be made unique and valuable through its ability to communicate with broadcasters and the programming service derived from it. The sets would be developed and designed by TiVo; they would feature the TiVo software and would be TiVo-branded. The company would focus its business model on selling services, as Ramsay notes:

> We wanted to sell the hardware at a very low cost, if we could, and then have people buy a monthly service fee. We would provide them with data, information and a direct customer relationship that would enable them to get the best entertainment that they possibly could. The hardware was relatively generic, but the software had a unique technology component . . . it simply didn't exist in the consumer electronics industry. Therefore, it would give us a competitive advantage. I think that by and large VC firms understood that and realized that − if nothing else − the company was going to build an asset base of intellectual property that could be leveraged in the future, as part of the business model . . . We are not a consumer electronics company, we are a media company providing home entertainment services, and yes, it requires a hardware platform. The value that we provide is the software and the service that we offer.[11]

Right from the start, Ramsay knew that TiVo's lack of resources and its focus on services would require the enrollment of partners, starting with the outsourcing of DVR manufacturing and distribution. But he was clear in his mind on the need for TiVo to keep control of the entire process. Ramsay comments:

Our ability to get to market was based on our own efforts and not on a critical dependency on some third party. So we built those servers, we built a service back-end, we did our own customer support, we had our own billing. We put the effort into creating a broad-based infrastructure that we could manage on our own. You don't want to sit around, putting in money, waiting for partners to do their part, whatever it is. As a company, we felt very strongly about it, and no matter what happened, we had to be in charge of our destiny. We had to have the final decision on when the product went out. And we had to have full control over the schedule and the resources that we needed in order to get the product out. But we also knew that we would not be able to launch this on our own – the most effective way to do it was to launch it with third parties to create a bigger and broader market or create more upside for us over faster growth . . .[12]

The first two partners we went for were DIRECTV[13] and Philips. The idea with Philips was that they would be a high profile brand that would be able to resell TiVos through retail. And we just literally handed them a design. We said, 'This is a TiVo, put your name on it, go build it, make a profit on the product, and we won't charge you a license fee as long as people buy the product and sign up for the service.' We did the same with Sony very shortly thereafter. We never considered that we would make money on the hardware ever . . . We needed to have that control and yet leverage the assets that partners could bring.

We also started a dialogue with DIRECTV, trying to convince them that they should take the TiVo technology and embed it into their service and make this an integrated DIRECTV offering. It took about a year or more to convince them that this was a good idea. As for Philips, we literally designed the whole thing, built it and handed it to them on a plate, saying 'Look, why don't you incorporate this into your service!' It became a big success but we really had to drive it on our own.

To entice its consumer electronics partners to promote the sets aggressively, TiVo subsidized them on a per set basis, at least in the first few years. Thanks to this policy, TiVo-enabled DVRs rapidly obtained strong distribution coverage, first through Best Buy and Circuit City, then through Sears' channels. DVR buyers[14] were offered the TiVo service on a subscription basis, for either a monthly or annual fee or, alternatively, for a lump sum payment valid for the lifetime of their DVR.[15]

## Gaining Customer Loyalty and Changing TV
## Viewing Habits

Sales picked up rather slowly, at least initially, as the system introduced a significant technology change over the VCR, which
customers had to understand and appreciate. Clearly, the company
needed to make an effort on consumer education, which it did
through advertising campaigns and demos on the TiVo.com
website.

Once customers were hooked and bought a TiVo-enabled
black box and subscription service, they still had to set up the
DVR and learn how to make the system work with the help of
TiVo.com. But once it worked, customers raved about TiVo as
they discovered how it changed their TV viewing experience.
Word-of-mouth started buzzing louder as the media reflected
viewers' enthusiasm and spread the TiVo revolution. The company
was still not making money but its investors were confident that
the business model would work.

## Partnering with the Media to Overcome
## Their Resistance

Not everyone was enthusiastic about the success of TiVo. Customers quickly learned how to regain their programming independence, and time-shifting allowed them to fast-forward ads
when replaying shows that their TiVo box had recorded. Clearly,
this independence and the ad-fast-forward feature did not appeal
to advertisers, or to the media – the broadcasters – who lived and
prospered through advertising. Mike Ramsay explains:

> Network psychology is to have a line in the sand mentality. If you
> are on one side of the line, you're their friend. If you're on the
> other side of the line, you're their enemy. Advertising the ability
> to skip commercials is on the other side of the line. We designed
> the technology so that it didn't infuriate the networks.[16]

Ramsay was quick to understand that the success of his company
would not be possible if TiVo went directly against the interests

of broadcasters and advertisers, who control the TV world. So, he adopted a conciliatory approach.

> Early on, we went to broadcasters; we went to advertisers; we described this idea to them. And generally we were kicked out of their office – they were incensed by the notion that we would touch their programming. Because, first, you could skip ads, and that was not very popular with the advertisers. We discovered that fast-forwarding through commercials was OK, but automatically skipping commercials was not OK. One of our rivals, ReplayTV, actually implemented an automatic skipping of commercials and got sued by the industry, and it lost!
>
> Second, we were destroying the notion of prime time – we were allowing viewers to select the programming they watched; we were really stepping on what was the fundamental component of their business. And their first reaction was unbelievably negative and very threatening.
>
> We didn't just want to be a Silicon Valley technology company. We truly wanted to be a mix of technology and entertainment. And we were going to set up the company that way. So, we hired a senior executive who came out of the media industry – he had actually been at CNN. And we put him in charge of developing relationships with the media industry, meeting all these people – and getting kicked out of their office. So this guy was losing friends thick and fast. But at the end of the day, despite the fact that we were not very popular, these companies had smart people working for them. And it didn't take long for them to realize that we were aware of the issues they were facing, and that we were willing to work with them to transform those issues into opportunities. It convinced them that we were not a Napster, a fly-by-night, screw-the-media-industry kind of company. We are a company of mature people who understand the television industry, are aware of their issues and want to collaborate with them.[17]

TiVo managers understood that they could build a business faster by partnering than by trying to do everything on their own. The big opportunity was not just on the side of the product but also on the media side, as the company was developing a fundamentally new way of distributing television programming. It is in this spirit of collaboration, not confrontation, that TiVo launched a series of initiatives to add value to its media and advertising partners.

Collaborating with Nielsen Media Research, TiVo launched a platform for collecting and analyzing audience viewing statistics, thus helping broadcasters fine tune their programs. The information that TiVo provided focused on customers' viewing habits, i.e. channels most frequently watched, programs most frequently recorded, ads most frequently skipped or watched, etc. Those data – TiVo claimed – were more reliable than traditional viewer panel methods and contributed to the media accepting the new technology.

Its StopIIWatch™ service provided second-by-second program and commercial ratings for both live and time-shifted viewing, data increasingly in demand by advertisers and agencies.

Going further in the direction of advertisers, TiVo introduced its Showcase program. The idea was that consumers would not skip ads that interested them, particularly if they were presented in an attractive, humorous and informative way. Under this program, TiVo automatically placed ads and short films of brand advertisers on the hard drive of customers who had expressed an interest in a particular domain.

All these initiatives brought TiVo additional revenues, which, although modest, were welcome for a company that was still burning cash faster than it was collecting it. It also passed a positive message to its partners, as former president, Martin Yudkovitz, comments:

> TiVo has already changed the way people watch TV. We think it can also dramatically alter the way advertisers deliver their message and programmers determine their programming . . .[18]
> TiVo has gone from being pure evil to being a curiosity, to being a little bit of a darling in the ad industry.[19]

## Evolving the TiVo Business Model

As the number of TiVo subscribers expanded and the reputation of the company grew exponentially, two kinds of pressures weighed heavily on management's shoulders: financial pressures and competitive threats.

### Changing TiVo's Business Model to Cut Losses

Ramsay's strategy, like that of Amazon's Jeff Bezos, had been to raise as much capital as possible to reach economies of scale. TiVo had invested heavily in marketing and product development; it was artificially supporting DVR sales – in this case by subsidizing its branded DVR manufacturing and distribution partners – all of this to grab as much market as fast as possible. This approach weighed heavily on the company's profit and loss account at a time – from 2001 onwards – when the market turned rough. The subscriber base was 500 000, far off the targeted 5 million. The current base was not sustainable and growth appeared to be falling off. The financial community was wondering how much time it would take for TiVo to show a profit. In 2002, the company's losses from operations reached $150 million on sales of only $19 million.[20] A large part of these losses were due to the company's subsidy scheme, as Ramsay explains:

> When the bubble burst and everything sort of fell apart, we had to re-evaluate our company's business model, simply to reduce burn rate. And it was a tricky time for the company because we still had Philips and Sony who were reselling the product, and DIRECTV was just getting going; they were all competing and we were subsidizing all of that. So the first decision we made was to no longer subsidize the product because it was just too expensive on cash and we had to dramatically lower our burn rate.[21]

Faced with this change in policy, Philips and Sony – TiVo's two major retail distributors – reacted by dropping their TiVo business. The company found itself with only one reseller – DIRECTV, the satellite broadcaster – and no retail presence. Confronted with this situation, management had no choice but to build its own sales force and to sell TiVo-branded sets to retail chains on its own. Best Buy and Circuit City were approached and agreed to resume selling TiVo sets, this time under the TiVo brand. Jim Barton remembers this troubled period:

> We pulled through by being honest with ourselves; we had to do something or the company would be gone. We were committed to TiVo. No one was interested in getting bought out and going to bigger companies. We saw we needed to change the subsidy

model because it was too much money out the door and it was not worth it. We decided that, if needed, we would fill a semi up with TiVo sets and sell them on the street. There was a lot of fear – fear of going alone – we had never done it before, we had to figure it out and have the courage to keep going. When you start operating on your new paradigm, then things come out of the woodwork. For us, that was when Best Buy said they would distribute us and suddenly we were in 4,000 storefronts and we did not have to pay any subsidies.[22]

To boost revenues, management decided to increase the price of both the sets and subscription services. The company also started to license its technology, for a fee, to other DVR manufacturers, like Pioneer, Toshiba and Humax.

Reflecting on this turbulent period, Randy Komisar comments on Ramsay's ability to react and adapt his business model to the reality of the market:

Mike knows when to take a step away and reconstitute himself. He took a brief sabbatical in order to regroup and come back energized. He displayed management brilliance in keeping together his team during this time and transforming what the business needed to do to survive. His new approach was focused more on sustainability. Mike is an incredible leader. He is charismatic and people who work for him like him and want to do great things for him. They are vested in him and he has vested himself in them as well. Mike is also very pragmatic, with a bottom-up style and a focus on execution. I view the team that he has put together as a bunch of thoroughbred horses, high powered and champing at the bit for success.[23]

## Facing Competition and Looking for New Partners

TiVo found, over time, that its satellite broadcasting partner – DIRECTV – was accounting for an increasing share of its business. With TiVo, DIRECTV was able to retain its best subscribers, increase revenue from each consumer and steal subscribers from its cable competitors. It rapidly saw how this technology could help it grow. DIRECTV was critical to TiVo, and not just for customer acquisition. It handled all the billing, which would have been a big cost for TiVo. This is why it had become part of the business model, despite the fact that TiVo was getting better margins – and its independence – from its retail sales.

But as its TiVo-enabled business grew large, DIRECTV decided to broaden its base of DVRs, taking on a second supplier of DVRs – through Microsoft and its UltimateTV product – and launching its own programming subscription package. Worse, DIRECTV's new owner, News Corporation, had announced its intention to provide DVR service free of charge to its subscribers. It also wanted to replace TiVo's sets and DVR services with those of NDS, a company it owned that offered competing sets and services on News Corp's BSkyB satellite system. This was a major threat to TiVo's customer base.

Ramsay accepted the new competition, which came from within its biggest and best partner, quite philosophically. Fortunately, TiVo was approached by Comcast, one of the largest US cable operators, which was worried that it was losing subscribers to DIRECTV in large part because of the TiVo service. It wanted to offer TiVo as a competitive premium service. The arrival of Comcast was a welcome addition to TiVo's partner list. Ramsay summarized his views on competition as follows:

> At this time [in 2005], there were over two million subscribers to TiVo with DIRECTV. And these customers are especially happy with the service. So, that is a big chunk of DIRECTV's population. And they have got to figure out how to manage that. Not only might they lose these customers, but it will cost them a lot of money to do that. DIRECTV is moving to a different platform? They have an alternative? Well, we acknowledge that and we shall compete with that. They did that before with Microsoft; we competed with Microsoft and we actually beat Microsoft. So, who knows where all that is going to go! Things like that are catalysts for us to do a deal with Comcast and we will do a lot of other deals in order to maximize our distribution. And these deals will come and go – that is the nature of our business. I think you have got to be prepared to deal with major media companies. If, for whatever reason, they don't work with you any more, you have to move and go to the next partner. And you have got to be agile enough and open enough to do that. That is what we are; that is the way we look at it in the company![24]

## Passing the Baton to a New CEO

In 2004, Mike Ramsay went to the board, saying it was time to bring on new leadership. While Jim Barton would stay with the company as CTO, Ramsay had decided to step down from his chairman and CEO position and hand over to Tom Rogers, his vice-chairman. He explained his move as follows:

> My contribution to the company was around the vision and building the team – so very much the start-up part, the experimentation, trying to develop a new market, building relationships, seeing what works and what doesn't.
>
> Just about two years ago [i.e. in 2002], I started to think about where the company was going and concluded that there were probably different qualities that the company needed now than the ones I was bringing. They centered on financial performance, growth and future relationships. That meant moving from being an early stage pioneering company to an established corporation with a predictable business model, predictable growth rates, something that the investment community could really value and, as a result, bring more value for shareholders.
>
> And that was my thinking in deciding that I would step aside. We would bring in somebody new. We ultimately ended up with Tom Rogers who, I think, embodies a lot of those qualities. He is about as good as you can get in terms of relationships and deals with the media industry, and is comfortable operating in that sphere. He has lots of experience running companies and achieving financial results with those companies. He is generally a more big-company kind of person, whereas I am more of a start-up kind of person. So if the theory works, I can pass the baton to him and he can take the company to the next level.[25]

Randy Komisar deeply appreciates Ramsay's humility:

> Mike has incredible emotional intelligence to be able to understand when the company will be best served by other leadership. He has been remarkably agile and was able to build core relationships, but was aware that he cannot build the next set of relationships that TiVo needs in order to scale. Tom Rogers will be able to do that as he has those contacts and he is focused on that strategic goal. Mike will always be a big part of TiVo, its culture and its legacy.[26]

## LESSONS FROM THE TIVO STORY

### An Example of Innovation in Business System and Business Model

TiVo is a business–system innovation on two grounds:

First, what it offers its customers can be qualified as an innovative 'system.' It is a system because it combines in the same offering, and for the first time, a new piece of hardware (a DVR), a new type of software (a proprietary and user-friendly show selection and programming system) and a subscription service for show selection on demand and automatic programming.

Second, when it was set up, it created a new type of 'business system' in the media industry, involving a network of independent partners which, together with TiVo, contributed to providing customers with a seamless TV experience. The actors in the business system include:

- TiVo itself, as the system integrator and main customer contact point;
- consumer electronics (CE) suppliers that produce the TiVo-enabled DVRs;
- multi-service operators (MSOs) – e.g. satellite, cable and phone;
- TV networks and advertisers that provide special ads for consumers;
- research agencies that use TiVo data to monitor customer viewing habits.

TiVo is also an example of business model innovation on two grounds:

First, the company pioneered an entirely new way to go to market as it established different parallel distribution channels (CE partners and licensees, satellite and cable operators, plus its own distribution).

Second, the company's economic model is unique, since it combines different streams of complementary revenues:

- margins on the sale of its own TiVo DVR hardware (limited);
- license fees from CE companies for the use of TiVo's DVR design (limited);

- subscription fees from customers (the biggest revenue source);
- fees from advertising research firms for access to TiVo data (limited).

Like Amazon, TiVo's economic business model is highly dependent on its ability to rapidly achieve volume, and thus scale economies, i.e. on the speed at which it can enlist a large number of customers. So, like Amazon in the beginning, TiVo is not yet profitable. The company is highly dependent on its network partners (particularly the MSOs) for reaching that volume. As a consequence, strategic partnering is at the heart of TiVo's business model.

## What Can We Learn from Mike Ramsay about This Type of Innovation?

### Starting with a Set of Inspiring and Mutually Consistent Visions

TiVo is rooted on a strong fundamental (first-level) vision of its founders. Both Mike Ramsay and Jim Barton dreamed of bringing digital imaging capabilities into consumer homes and providing customers with a home platform for digital entertainment. But their overarching vision gave birth to three types of complementary and internally consistent (second-level) visions:

(1) A practical vision about the kind of unique customer value they wanted to deliver through their business concept. Ramsay emphatically proclaims the philosophy on which the company is based:

> Everyone, no matter how busy, deserves to enjoy the home entertainment of their choosing, at their convenience. People have lots of interests. TiVo lets you go out and live your life AND pursue those interests because it connects you to entertainment, to the content you care about, when you want it.[27]

(2) A vision about the kind of company and business environment they wanted to create to fulfill their dream. This is akin to formulating what some authors[28] call a 'core ideology,' i.e. a set of values and beliefs. The 'code of conduct' that Ramsay

and Barton formulated created the context of their business model. It is still applied in the company today and is shared by all employees. Its key principles had a strong influence on most management decisions over the years.

(3) A vision of the economic model they wanted to build for their business. For Ramsay, that meant enlisting the biggest number of customers as fast as possible and getting revenues primarily from the service side (subscription fees). This meant, in turn, that TiVo would subsidize the hardware side (DVR suppliers), at least at the start, and fully leverage the market presence of its network partners (e.g. DIRECTV).

## Bringing the Vision down to Earth in a Pragmatic Fashion

Ramsay and Barton's fundamental vision – building the 'digital living room' – went far beyond providing people with a DVR and a smart programming subscription service. But building a 'digital hub' in people's home looked years away, whereas the possibility of having customers buy a user-friendly DVR and subscribe to a TV programming service looked immediately feasible. This is why TiVo started with a DVR strategy, considering the DVR as the first step in the realization of a full home-entertainment network system.

Proponents of business model innovations must be pragmatic and should not hope that great revolutionary steps are achievable in one go. Being pragmatic means focusing on an immediately actionable part of the grand vision, even if it covers only a fraction of the initial concept. Ramsay was in favor of a step-by-step approach, moving progressively toward the grand scheme he and Barton dreamed of implementing.

## Defining a Clear Partnering Philosophy from the Start, and Sticking to It

Not all business model innovations require the involvement of external partners, but most business system innovations do.

For TiVo, partnering was an essential part of its business model, and Ramsay's philosophy in this regard was built on two principles, both directly derived from the company's code of conduct:

First, in all cases, TiVo wanted to maintain full control over its brand and product offering, even if the latter built on the contribution of external partners (like the CE manufacturers selling TiVo-enabled DVRs). This guiding philosophy was a way for TiVo to ensure that it was perceived as the ultimate provider of a fully satisfying customer solution.

Second, TiVo was also committed to building 'win-win' agreements, the only way to make partnerships sustainable over the long term. This rule was clearly brought to the fore when the TV networks that live through advertising revenues started objecting to the fact that TiVo's DVRs allowed customers to skip ads by fast-forwarding when replaying recorded content. TiVo's competitor – ReplayTV – confronted the networks head-on by loudly advertising this feature of its DVRs. TiVo, by contrast, refrained from doing so, to avoid antagonizing its partners. Confronting the networks would be suicidal in TiVo's kind of business, Ramsay believed. But the company went beyond this neutral attitude by developing the Showcase system, which allowed the networks to broadcast entertaining or informational ads that customers signed up to receive. In other words, TiVo found a way to satisfy the fraction of its customers allergic to unwanted ads while meeting the needs of its advertising-dependent network partners. This is a good illustration of its win-win partnering philosophy.

TiVo investor and board director Mark Perry praises TiVo's management for having maintained equilibrium and setting realistic expectations for its partners, while running itself when some partnerships dissolved:

> Mike's idea, from the beginning, was to set things up in a non-adversarial way, to protect property rights and content but have respect for his partners. He saw that the right approach was to respect them, not to confront them![29]

## Adapting the Business Model to Industry Circumstances and Partner Changes

The TiVo story is one of constant reassessment and adaptation of its strategy – a critical success factor in the volatile media world where partners come and go. The pragmatism that served the founders well when they focused on an actionable element of their vision – a DVR and service package – proved vital as they gained experience, as Mark Perry comments:

> Jeff Bezos probably had more comfort in what Amazon needed to do to reach a large scale. His vision has never changed; it has always been, from day one, to build an incredibly large online retail channel. For Mike, the vision and business model has had to adapt. It has not been the same since day one. There was a time when the business model did not work. The subsidizations being requested by other companies were unaffordable. To confront the business model and make changes, that was probably the hardest time for Mike. Not that they made mistakes, but because they had to change. It was like changing the engine on the car while it was running.[30]

## Focusing on Execution

Great visions are no guarantee of success; execution is what matters. The TiVo story illustrates the importance of having assembled a top notch team from the start – Bill Fischer would probably call it a 'virtuoso team'[31] – for faultless implementation of Ramsay and Barton's vision. Despite the novelty of their technology, architecture, software and design, TiVo's DVRs worked fine, as expected, from day one. Similarly, TiVo's subscription service was implemented without serious glitches, as the tone of consumer reactions on various TiVo-related chat sites testifies. Randy Komisar attributes this strong execution capability to Ramsay:

> When compared to CEOs of other innovative startup companies, Mike exhibits a level of sophistication that most don't. His strength is less about vision and more about execution and leadership.

### Knowing When to Pass the Baton

Chapter 8 introduced the 'chain of leadership' concept whereby a series of leaders with complementary skills follow in each other's steps seamlessly and bring a particular project or business to its next development stage. That concept is valid for all kinds of projects and business undertakings, including of course long cycle time business system and business model innovations. Authentic innovation leaders avoid the temptation of going on ego trips and sticking to their job beyond their level of competence. This is clearly what Mike Ramsay did when he stepped down from his position and handed over to a new CEO, whom he admired for his highly complementary skills. Mark Perry comments on that unusual character:

> I view the following three dimensions as necessary for the leadership of a start-up and the qualities we look for in a CEO: (1) someone who is innovative, sees it, anticipates it and has a passion for it; (2) someone who can get it done and execute it; (3) someone who can build and scale the organization beyond his own ability. We usually see people who can do the first and maybe the second element. Usually the VCs work with the founding CEO for the first two stages, and then we find another CEO to come in to complete the last phase. It can be a challenge for the entrepreneur to step out and let someone else lead. Mike brought the third level with him, which was one of the reasons I was so personally excited to back TiVo.[32]

### Concluding

Management books often fall into the trap of drawing hasty conclusions from their analysis and directly linking market and financial success to the management behavior they have observed and want to highlight as a model. This is by no means my intention, for two reasons. First, in the world of innovation, success is more the exception than the rule. It depends on many factors beyond the quality of leadership of the management team. And second, because TiVo has reached neither the market penetration that its founders were justified to hope for nor the financial performance that its investors expect. The company is still trying to reach the scale that will make it profitable.

Nevertheless, this story illustrates very well the characteristics of a certain type of innovation leader, which I compared to those of a visionary but pragmatic architect. And even if TiVo's market and financial performance, as expressed in pure number terms, are below the objectives of its management and investors, it is a company that has brought a significant innovation to market, as Randy Komisar notes:

> TiVo's biggest innovation is forever having changed the broadcast system. This is Mike's legacy, although claiming the spoils of this success has been difficult. The way people watch TV and this category, which is new, will never be the same again.[33]

## ENDNOTES

1. Quote from famous Finnish architect Eliel Saarinen (1873–1950) source: http://www.saidwhat.co.uk/quotes/favourite/eliel_saarinen.
2. Refer to: http://biosphere.ec.gc.ca/The_Sphere/A_Futuristic_Architecture-WS85D4C846-1_En.htm.
3. This story is based on the following sources:
   - TiVo's website: http://www.tivo.com;
   - Wathieu, L. (2000). 'TiVo.' Harvard Business School Case No. 9-501-038;
   - Wathieu, L. and Zoglio, M. (2002). 'TiVo in 2002: Consumer Behavior.' Harvard Business School Case No. 9-502-062;
   - Yoffie, D., Yin, P.-L. and Darwall, C. (2003). 'Strategic Inflection: TiVo in 2003.' Harvard Business School California Research Center Case No. 9-704-425;
   - Shastry, Umashanker under the direction of Madhav, T.P. (2004). 'TiVo: Pioneering the Interactive Television.' ICFAI Business School Case Development Centre Case No. 504-048-1, Hyderabad (India);
   - Gayatri, D. under the direction of Madhav, T.P. (2004). 'DVRs and Advertising Industry: Opportunity and a Threat?' ICFAI Business School Case Development Centre Case No. 504-106-1, Hyderabad (India);
   - Datamonitor report of 22 March 2005;
   - Personal interviews, conducted on 13 September 2005 by Michèle Barnett Berg, IMD, with:
     - Randy Komisar, founding director of TiVo and board member;
     - Mark Perry, of NEA Partners and TiVo board member;

- Personal interviews, conducted on 14 September 2005 by Michèle Barnett Berg, IMD, with:
  - Brodie Keast, former vice president of TiVo and general manager – consumer division;
  - Jim Barton, cofounder of TiVo and CTO;
- Author's personal interview, on 1 September 2005, with Michael Ramsay, cofounder of TiVo, former CEO and member of the board.

4. Author's personal interview with Michael Ramsay on 1 September 2005, reproduced with permission.
5. Personal interview with Mark Perry by Michèle Barnett Berg, IMD, on 13 September 2005, reproduced with permission.
6. After founding and running several companies and becoming a founding director of TiVo, Randy Komisar joined Kleiner, Perkins, Caufield and Byers, Silicon Valley's star VC firm.
7. Personal interview with Randy Komisar by Michèle Barnett Berg, IMD, on 13 September 2005.
8. Personal interview with Jim Barton by Michèle Barnett Berg, IMD, on 14 September 2005, reproduced with permission.
9. Author's personal interview with Michael Ramsay on 1 September 2005, reproduced with permission.
10. Personal interview with Randy Komisar by Michèle Barnett Berg, IMD, on 13 September 2005, reproduced with permission.
11. Author's personal interview with Michael Ramsay on 1 September 2005, reproduced with permission.
12. Author's personal interview with Michael Ramsay on 1 September 2005.
13. DIRECTV is a large satellite communication broadcaster in the US.
14. The set was priced at $499 for a model with 14 hours capacity and $999 for a model of up to 30 hours.
15. The charge amounted to $9.95 per month, $99 per year or $199 for the lifetime of the unit. Source: 'TiVo,' by Luc Wathieu (2000). Harvard Business School case No. 9-501-038, p. 3.
16. Comment reported in 'Boom Box,' by Michael Lewis, *New York Times*, 13 August 2000; cited in 'TiVo,' by Luc Wathieu (2000). Harvard Business School Case No. 9-501-038, p. 7.
17. Author's personal interview with Michael Ramsay on 1 September 2005, reproduced with permission.
18. Comment reported by John McIlory in 'TiVo Plans to Sell Info on Ads Skipped' on http://www.pvruk.co.uk on 2 June 2003, cited in 'DVRs and Advertising Industry: Opportunity and a Threat?' by D. Gayatri under the direction of T.P. Madhav (2004). ICFAI Business School Case Development Centre Case No. 504-106-1, Hyderabad (India).
19. Comment reported by Jack Myers in 'Advertisers Rethinking Attitude towards DVR' on http://www.jackmyers.com on 5 February 2004, cited in 'DVRs and Advertising Industry: Opportunity and a Threat?' by D. Gayatri under the direction of T.P. Madhav (2004). ICFAI Business School Case Development Centre Case No. 504-106-1, Hyderabad (India).

20. Yoffie, D., Yin, P.-L. and Darwall, C. (2003). 'Strategic Inflection: TiVo in 2003,' Harvard Business School California Research Center Case No. 9-704-425, Exhibit 6.
21. Author's personal interview with Michael Ramsay on 1 September 2005, reproduced with permission.
22. Personal interview with Jim Barton by Michèle Barnett Berg, IMD, on 14 September 2005.
23. Personal interview with Randy Komisar by Michèle Barnett Berg, IMD, on 13 September 2005, reproduced with permission.
24. Author's personal interview with Michael Ramsay on 1 September 2005, reproduced with permission.
25. Author's personal interview with Michael Ramsay on 1 September 2005, reproduced with permission.
26. Personal interview with Randy Komisar by Michèle Barnett Berg, IMD, on 13 September 2005, reproduced with permission.
27. Source: The TiVo story: http://www.tivo.com.
28. Collins, J.C. and Porras, J.I. (1994). *Built to Last: Successful Habits of Visionary Companies.* New York, HarperBusiness.
29. Personal interview with Mark Perry by Michèle Barnett Berg, IMD, on 13 September 2005, reproduced with permission.
30. Personal interview with Mark Perry by Michèle Barnett Berg, IMD, on 13 September 2005, reproduced with permission.
31. Boynton, A. and Fischer, B. (2005). *Virtuoso Teams: Lessons from Great Teams that Changed Their World.* Harlow, FT Prentice Hall.
32. Personal interview with Mark Perry by Michèle Barnett Berg, IMD, on 13 September 2005, reproduced with permission.
33. Personal interview with Randy Komisar by Michèle Barnett Berg, IMD, on 13 September 2005, reproduced with permission.

# CHAPTER 10

# LEADING THE DEVELOPMENT OF NEW/IMPROVED CUSTOMER SOLUTIONS REQUIRED: CONDUCTORS TO DELIVER AN ENHANCED CUSTOMER EXPERIENCE

*We have launched a new theme 'Break away and excite.' It means that our new concepts will have to be strongly differentiating, breaking away from our competitors . . .*

*A nice product is OK; an experience is much better because that is closer to the heart of consumers. But to develop that, you have to work together with other companies . . .*[1]

*Ad Veenhof, former President of Philips DAP division*

Marketers in a variety of companies and industry sectors increasingly talk about their new focus on providing comprehensive 'solutions' for their customers. Enriching traditional 'black-box' products or services, they claim, helps meet customers' needs more fully. Solutions add extra value to customers – and to the company that supplies them, of course. Indeed, good customer solutions, if and when they meet a market need, help increase turnover, gain a differentiating competitive advantage and build customer loyalty.

Two different types of strategies focus on customer solutions:

The first strategy – the most classic – consists of adding a 'customization' element to a general product or service offering. This happens routinely in the information systems industry through system customization and consulting services. In other industries, like performance chemicals, managers also talk about solutions, but they proceed differently. They send application or sales engineers to analyze their customers' specific requirements and recommend the most suitable formulas. Then, downstream, application engineers or tech-service specialists help ensure that customers make optimum use of the problem-solving compounds they have bought. This type of customization strategy certainly falls under the general customer solutions heading, but it does not include a generic innovation element. As a consequence, it will *not* be the focus of our upcoming discussion.

The second type of customer solution strategy consists of designing and proposing innovatively 'enriched' products or services as part of the company's product strategy. Its objective is to meet a larger proportion of customers' needs, and hence to enhance their experience and win their loyalty. This type of solution strategy is very different from the 'solution through customization' strategy mentioned above, because it is the result of an authentic innovation process, and it affects the company's normal product line or part of it. It always starts from a deep desire to understand generic customer problems and needs and address them more comprehensively. Searches for solutions are generally initiated and directed by management as part of a strategy of differentiation through innovation.

Some companies implement this strategy entirely on their own, adding value for customers by combining several products from their own organizational units into a single offering. For example, as part of its 'platformization' strategy, Intel offers complex chipsets with rich functionalities to its mobile telecommunications customers, and fully integrated system motherboards to PC manufacturers. Although these are legitimate and often innovative solutions, we shall not focus on them in our discussion either. They are less complex – and hence require less of leaders – than the solutions that result from several distinct companies pooling their forces to enrich a particular product offering, which is the main focus of this chapter.

Philips' Cool Skin™ electric shaver illustrates the type of innovative solutions that result from a specific cooperation agreement between different companies. Philips is the world's leading manufacturer of rotary electric shavers, sold worldwide under the Philishave™ brand (Norelco™ in the US). The company sees its business being challenged by waves of innovation launched by its main 'wet shave' competitor, Gillette. The battle is being fought on shaving closeness, but since both blade and electric razor systems provide similar shaving performance, it is increasingly focusing on image and customer experience. Whereas mature customers often choose electric shavers for their convenience, young shavers are attracted by the 'contemporary male' image projected by the advertising messages for blade razors. Some users also prefer the wet-shave experience that blade razors offer, as electric shavers can occasionally irritate sensitive young skins.

To offset what it perceived as a handicap, both in image and shaving experience, Philips designed its Cool Skin™ line. This concept, which has now become an important part of Philips' shaver offering, includes a dispenser of NIVEA FOR *MEN*™ lotion and can be used under the shower. It is this type of cooperative innovation with a partner – in this case German cosmetics giant Beiersdorf – that we want to discuss, because it is typical of a new wave of open-source innovations and requires a particular type of leadership.

## INNOVATION LEADERS AS ORCHESTRA CONDUCTORS

The conception and development of winning customer solutions, particularly those requiring the involvement of external partners, does not happen spontaneously. They are made possible by the personal commitment and dedication of leaders, who (1) interpret customers' unmet needs creatively; (2) orchestrate a response, by enlisting the cooperation of a complementary partner; and (3) smoothly integrate the partner's contribution into their company's offering to create a comprehensive solution together. Interpreting, orchestrating and integrating are three skills that great orchestra conductors tend to have.

## Interpreting Customers' Unmet Needs

When a company decides to go from selling products to conceiving enriched solutions, it is generally because it perceives a broader ill-met or unmet customer need that no one is addressing. This happens in a variety of cases:

- *Case 1*: Some products, if sold individually, only partly fill the needs of those customers who want to deal with 'one-stop' suppliers. So-called tier-one automotive component manufacturers provide a good illustration of this particular situation. For example, original equipment manufacturers (OEM) in the car industry generally expect ready-to-assemble solutions from their suppliers of plastic-molded dashboards. These solutions typically integrate the control instruments and wire harnesses of tier-two suppliers. So, these tier-one suppliers no longer sell only the plastic panels that they produce; they assemble and supply completely finished dashboards, ready for final assembly.
- *Case 2*: Some products lack functionalities, features or benefits – both objective and subjective – that would significantly enhance their usage and make customers prefer them over other products. Solutions are then designed to fill the gap. This is the case with Philips' conventional electric shaver line. It was perceived as providing a lower level of 'shaving freshness' than competing blade razors, creating an opportunity that the Cool Skin™ line aimed to exploit.
- *Case 3*: Other products may be intrinsically good, but prove difficult to use, dispense or implement on their own. Solutions are therefore found by conceiving dispensing or implementation devices. In the pharmaceutical industry, such devices can be convenient drug delivery systems, for example easy-to-use insulin injection pens or asthma drug inhalers.
- *Case 4*: Yet other products may be excellent and have many features, but prove to be difficult to clean, service or simply

dispose of. The solution is to set up additional service organizations that provide such functions, thus relieving customers
of some of these basic chores. A number of industrial firms
providing hazardous materials or large and complex equipment
requiring thorough on-site servicing have followed this
route.

Identifying and interpreting customer needs requires a high degree
of customer intimacy. The challenge starts with (1) understanding
how various types of customers prioritize their own needs; and
(2) identifying common missing elements. The questions to ask
are threefold:

- What are the broad common needs of our customers that no
  one seems to be fully addressing?
- Are these customers looking for a comprehensive solution to
  their problems or needs, and what could that solution consist
  of?
- How much would these customers be ready to pay for a satisfying solution to their problems or needs?

This last question is important, as it allows the company to assess
how customers will perceive the value of various alternative solutions. Interpreting these various elements correctly is no mean
task. They will determine the architecture of the solution and its
price, and hence the company's chances of achieving market
success and profitability.

## Orchestrating an Innovative Solution

Merriam-Webster's online dictionary defines 'orchestrating' as
'arranging or combining so as to achieve a desired or maximum
effect.' This is exactly what is necessary when a company wants
to conceive a solution to its customers' problems that requires the
involvement of a contributing partner.

Prior to orchestrating an innovative solution, management
needs to identify and address the organizational and operational
issues that are bound to appear as it challenges the definition and
boundaries of its current businesses. For the management team of
Philips' electric shaver business unit, this meant understanding the

implications of two things: (1) enlarging the mission of the division from providing electrical appliances to selling cosmetic-enhanced 'experiences,' and (2) entering the field of marketing and distributing 'consumables,' as opposed to 'durables.' Management also needs to sell its solution concept to the third party whose contribution is required and encourage it to join forces in order to arrive at an optimal solution.

The orchestration itself consists in defining, codifying and harmonizing the specific contribution and remuneration of the various parties involved in delivering the targeted customer solution. When working with external partners, this orchestration generally requires a mix of rigor and diplomacy. In the Philips electric shaver example, orchestrating the solution involved:

- Selecting the best cosmetic partner to work on the project – in this case Beiersdorf – based on brand reputation, competences, perceived willingness to partner and flexibility.
- Convincing the selected partner to join forces with Philips and to contribute to the solution, on the merit of the proposed concept and attractive market growth and profitability estimates for the finished solution.
- Agreeing on a fair economic model for sharing the costs and profits of the joint product, and ironing out all possible contentious issues regarding the evolution of the model over time to sustain a 'win-win' formula.

## Integrating All Inputs into a Smooth Solution

Once a partnership has been established, the most difficult part starts, i.e. How to make it work in practice and align different design teams, sometimes located far apart, to work smoothly together.

In some instances, and Philips' Cool Skin™ shaver is one of them, one of the partners – in this case Philips – acts as the lead partner and overall project leader. The contributing partner – Beiersdorf – is only expected to (1) develop its part of the project, i.e. the lotion itself and the feeding mechanism according to agreed specifications; and (2) provide adequate distribution coverage for the refills. In other cases, as we shall see in the Senseo™ story, the two parts of the system – the coffee machine and the coffee 'pods' that it uses – are developed separately by each of the partners through coordinated projects. The two partners share the full responsibility for the venture.

Partnering skills are essential to implement the solution smoothly across organizational boundaries and disciplines and, over time, to launch a succession of enhancements in response to customers' feedback.

# SENSEO: AN INNOVATIVE CUSTOMER SOLUTION[2]

## What is Senseo?

Senseo™ is an innovative single-serve coffee brewing system developed and marketed jointly by two Dutch giants:

- Sara Lee Douwe Egberts (SLDE), one of the world's leading coffee roasters belonging to the Sara Lee Corporation; and
- Philips Domestic Appliances and Personal Care (DAP), one of the world's leaders in small domestic appliances.

The system is presently sold in eight European countries, as well as in the US, Canada, Australia, China and Japan.

The Senseo system consists of two elements:

- An appliance, produced by Philips DAP and equipped with a unique low-pressure coffee extraction system. It can deliver, consistently, one or two freshly brewed cups of coffee with a smooth frothy layer.
- Coffee bags or 'pods' for individual cup servings, produced by SLDE and sold in various package sizes and coffee choices (basic coffee types, coffee blends and gourmet varieties). Later additions to the range included mug-sized servings for cappuccino and coffee-choco beverages and even espressos.

The system is marketed and sold under the Senseo umbrella brand, but the machines also bear the Philips name and the pods carry the name of SLDE's regional or local coffee brands next to the Senseo label.

The Senseo story is exceptional in at least two aspects:

First, this innovative coffee system became an amazing market success shortly after its launch, with customers adopting the system enthusiastically. Only three years after its 2001 introduction in the Netherlands, Senseo had already entered 5 million households, in just five European countries. It provided coffee drinkers with an individual solution that was both considerably tastier and more convenient than traditional filter coffee – or drip coffee – systems, while remaining affordable. For the trade, it created a new profitable category in the coffee market, smartly positioned between cheaper filter coffee machines and the more expensive espresso machines or systems like Nespresso.

Second, Senseo is the result of an unusual partnership between two companies that could be compared to an 'economic marriage.' The two Dutch partners pooled their resources to develop and market the system together. They agreed to share equally both the intellectual property rights of the system and the ownership of the brand, without tying themselves into a formal joint venture contract. According to their agreement, SLDE would remunerate Philips on the volume of consumables – number of pods sold – that its machines generate. Making money on coffee rather than on machines – both partners believed – would allow them to price the appliance very low so as to accelerate market penetration.

## SLDE – Searching for Growth Opportunities in Coffee

### A Coffee Heavyweight

Over the past three decades, Chicago-based Sara Lee Corporation has grown through multiple US and European acquisitions in foods and other consumer goods. Among these acquisitions were two Dutch coffee, tea and grocery companies: Van Nelle and Douwe Egberts. They formed the core of Sara Lee Douwe Egberts (SLDE), which was in charge of the company's worldwide coffee and tea, as well as its household and body care activities.

In 2003, SLDE employed 26 000 people and generated sales of € 4.7 billion. Its coffee and tea division generated its € 2.7 million sales mostly in Europe and the US, with tea accounting for less than 10% of turnover. The company was strongly positioned in both the out-of-home coffee business – nearly half of sales – and the retail business. It was the third coffee producer in the world with a 10% market share, just behind Kraft (13%) and Nestlé (12%). Kraft and Nestlé offered soluble coffee under the Maxwell House™ and Nescafé™ brands, respectively, and Kraft also sold roasted coffee under a number of brands. SLDE sold only premium roasted coffee under a number of regional (Douwe Egberts™) and national brands.

In Europe, the division was strong in the retail markets of Benelux, Denmark, Hungary, France, Spain and, to a certain extent, in the smaller UK market, which was mostly an instant coffee market. SLDE was present in neither the € 3 billion German market nor the € 1.5 billion Italian market. In the out-of-home market, which accounted for 22% of the overall European coffee category, SLDE distributed its Cafitesse™ liquid coffee for refilling coffee machines. It was second to Kraft with sales of € 400 million.

In the US, SLDE sold mostly coffee for the out-of-home market. Its Superior™ brand had generated $750 million sales in 2003 and was the market leader by far, with a 32% share by value.

SLDE hoped to grow its coffee business profitably through a simultaneous emphasis on global branding, marketing and innovation. Innovation was directed toward developing and commercializing higher value products that would meet changing consumer needs in terms of convenience and individualism. Senseo and its in-home coffee machine was one of them.

## The Vision behind Senseo: A Perfect Cup of Coffee ... Every Time

In 1994, faced with very low margins and declining volumes in its mature European coffee market because coffee was less and less appealing to young consumers, SLDE management decided to react. The beverages management team started generating ideas that would rejuvenate the company's coffee business. Among all the proposed ideas, four were developed. One emerged as the most attractive, that of a single-serve system that would prepare the 'ideal cup of coffee,' the premium cup, called Senseo Crema, which Vincent Janssen,[3] general manager of Douwe Egberts Netherlands, personally championed.

The Senseo idea capitalized on a number of significant changes in European society, namely:

- the decline in average household size (from 3.5 family members in 1960 to 2.2 in 2000), and a corresponding growth in single-person households;
- the growing number of working women in the population, accelerating a trend toward individualized and more convenient products;
- the growing demand for 'gourmet' and 'indulgence' products in most food and beverage categories;
- the rapid growth of expensive espresso machines, to the detriment of traditional filter appliances.

For SLDE, packing premium coffee in single-serve pods – something that was relatively new at the time – was also a way to differentiate its products and generate fatter margins, on a per-pound basis, than selling bags of roasted coffee.

Convinced that its idea would be better implemented if it partnered with a coffee machine specialist, in 1997 SLDE approached its Dutch neighbor – Philips. But the company's Domestic Appliances and Personal Care division (DAP) was in the midst of similar discussions with the management of Nestlé, which was toying with a closely related idea for Nespresso. Because of what it perceived as a conflict of interest, Philips DAP turned down SLDE's offer. SLDE could have turned to the French SEB Group, owner of Rowenta™ and Krups™, two leading coffee and espresso machine brands. But SEB was also very much engaged with Nestlé's Nespresso, this time on espresso machines. So, SLDE management decided to go ahead on its own and develop what became the Senseo coffee system, with the help of a Dutch contract design firm, a Dutch engineering firm and an outsourcing manufacturing partner.

## Philips DAP – Seeking to Rejuvenate its Mature Coffee Maker Line

### *A Domestic Appliances Giant Looking for Partners*

Philips DAP was the world's second largest producer of small domestic appliances. It marketed its products under its Philips brand and competed with the French SEB Group and its multiple brands – T-Fal™, Krups™, Rowenta™, Moulinex™ and Seb™. In 2003 its sales amounted to € 2.2 billion and it had 8200 employees. Philips DAP operated in four business units: shaving and beauty; oral healthcare; home environment care, and food and beverage, which included the coffee machines business.

Philips DAP was the European market leader in the € 1 billion coffee machines market, but relatively small in the € 500 million US market. The division was a very strong producer of filter coffee machines. But, by the early 1990s, the category was commoditizing rapidly. China was entering the market, leveraging its large scale, low-cost manufacturing infrastructure against which Philips could not compete. So Philips' margins on coffee makers remained slim. The company had entered the fast-growing espresso machine market rather late, and it had experienced major quality problems with its first outsourcing partner. It had then started working with a Swiss espresso machine specialist and supplier of major OEM brands, but its position in this high-ticket market remained limited. The company was therefore seriously interested in developing new segments to its business, and innovation was the chosen way to go.

Led by Paul Bromberg,[4] Philips DAP's beverage marketers shared SLDE's belief that the market was moving toward 'cup-by-cup' systems. They had developed a small two-cup coffee maker, the 'Duo,' but it had been held back by the wide acceptance of the Melitta™ coffee filter standard. The idea of developing its own system, based on the individual 'pod' concept, was unrealistic given its lack of a captive coffee producer. So, Philips DAP looked for a coffee partner to enter the coffee system business with it. Philips DAP's CEO, Ad Veenhof, encouraged entrepreneurial initiatives and thus supported Bromberg's move.

### Working on an Aborted Project for Nespresso before Returning to SLDE

An opportunity arose in 1994, when Philips DAP's Swiss espresso machine supplier asked it to cooperate on a product extension roadmap for Nespresso, which was being successfully rolled out into the market. As a first step, the plan included a lower priced, affordable line of Nespresso machines. Its second step covered a premium line of cup-by-cup coffee machines aimed at displacing conventional drip filters. Paul Bromberg accepted the offer and started work on the first project. The new system – code-named 'Goldpresso' – was to be positioned somewhere between a Nespresso machine and a filter coffee machine. However, in 1998, Nestlé suddenly decided to drop the Goldpresso project on which Philips DAP had worked because it was becoming too close to the original Nespresso proposition, and the company feared it would merely cannibalize its existing system.

Philips DAP and Nestlé then started working jointly on the 'premium filter proposition.' However, shortly thereafter, partnership negotiations between the two companies ended in a deadlock over disagreements on core principles. Indeed, throughout its relationship with Nestlé, Philips DAP was convinced that it would be in everyone's interest in the industry to establish a common standard for single-serve coffee machines and pods, as Melitta had done for filter papers. It had even brought SLDE to participate in a joint meeting with Nestlé for that purpose. But the Swiss giant was not interested and decided to keep its proprietary standard. Philips DAP was also pushing the idea of a real, i.e. equal, partnership but Nestlé was opposed to the idea of tying up too strongly with a machine manufacturer. As a consequence, Philips DAP found itself without a partner.

So, despite having turned down SLDE's cooperation offer a year earlier, Bromberg and his boss – Ton van der Laan, head of Philips DAP's kitchen appliances business – went back to the coffee company and proposed working on its Senseo system. After two weeks during which Janssen and his executive team studied the pros and the cons of partnering with Philips DAP, they finally accepted the offer. Bromberg remembers SLDE's hesitation:

> SLDE had a low pressure coffee extraction system and a machine, using local design and engineering consultants. They were targeting a very low sales price for the machine in order to speed up market adoption, and hence sales of coffee pods. They were unable to find an 'A' brand manufacturer to produce it, so they were planning to outsource production in China. When we came back to them, they first didn't know whether they could trust us because of our past close relationship with Nestlé! This is why they hesitated for two weeks. Then they said to us, 'We are halfway through the project; we don't want to start from scratch again! Either you accept to join us where we are, or we continue on our own.' We started with a NDA [non-disclosure agreement], and a month later we signed a letter of intent.[5]

Bromberg freed one of his senior product managers to work half time on the project and lead the Philips DAP team that was going to work with SLDE on the new development project.

### Looking at SLDE as a Partner

For Bromberg, working with Nestlé – as Philips DAP had hoped to do – had a number of advantages: A considerable competence in coffee processing and manufacturing, as well as a truly global presence and a strong brand portfolio. But working with SLDE also had its benefits. Its familiar Dutch culture and physical proximity were reassuring, and its flexibility and entrepreneurial spirit – the company was much smaller and nimbler than Nestlé – was expected to lead to faster decisions.

The technological concept on which the Senseo Crema machine was based was innovative. Most espresso machines operated under high pressure (10 bar) to extract the full coffee flavor and produce the frothy foam layer – the famous 'crema' so dear to coffee and espresso lovers. By contrast, SLDE's prototype worked under a low pressure of one bar, yet managed to produce the desired crema. A low pressure machine – Philips DAP knew – required a significantly less sophisticated manufacturing solution and would be much cheaper to produce.

Nevertheless, the SLDE machine developed by the consultants would have to be completely reengineered for mass production and quality. But that did not frighten Philips DAP's engineers, given their company's extensive machine development and manufacturing capabilities. Philips DAP's senior managers felt comfortable that, ultimately, after some further development, SLDE's new brewing system could be turned into a low-cost machine that would still deliver a premium cup of coffee. They also believed that by combining their strengths, both in branding and distribution, the two partners had a unique opportunity to be first in the market with a winning solution.

## Sharing a Common Vision

SLDE and Philips had surveyed the coffee market – first separately then together – and collected consumer insights to guide their research and development efforts. They found a number of significant trends that reinforced their belief that single-cup coffee systems could become a big market opportunity:

- Customers were less interested in a full pot of coffee and more interested in saving time.
- Increasingly sophisticated coffee drinkers demanded quality along with convenience.
- Gourmet coffeehouse chains had raised consumers' expectations for a good cup of coffee.
- 'Coffee lovers' typically considered at-home coffee to be less satisfying than coffeehouse coffee.[6]

These findings helped the two partners define their common vision for Senseo:

To provide consumers with a solution that is:

- Individualized – tailored to individual consumption moments and tastes;
- Better tasting – offering better quality, variety and more enjoyment; and
- More convenient – requiring less time and handling.[7]

Adriaan Nühn, who became the head of SLDE's coffee and tea division and the chairman of SLDE,[8] summarized the essence of the Senseo project as follows:

> The idea was really to go for the individual cup of coffee as opposed to the big pot of filter coffee. Basically satisfy those who want their own cup, strength and flavor.[9]

Both partners pledged to develop Senseo and market it jointly as the new global standard for single-serve coffee.

This initial vision was later summarized in three words – '*taste, variety, convenience*' – which became the heart of their business philosophy. Believing that these three vision elements needed to be communicated convincingly to consumers, the two partners defined the three foci of their marketing strategy: '*see, try, buy.*' This, they believed, could be implemented through (1) a massive advertising campaign of the new system, to create awareness – *see*; (2) systematic in-store demonstrations – *try*; and (3) locating and merchandising coffee pods and coffee machines next to each other in retail stores – *buy*.

As part of their shared vision, the companies recognized that both companies were experts and leaders in their own fields and that they needed each other to come up with an innovation such as Senseo. As we shall see later, this was more easily said than put into practice.

## Engaging Both Companies in a Balanced Partnership

After signing the non-disclosure agreement and the letter of intent, the two companies worked on a partnership contract. The headlines of the contract were successfully negotiated in two or three months, but agreeing on the details took a lot longer.

Nevertheless, and despite a change in management within SLDE – Vincent Janssen passed on the role of championing Senseo to Frank van Oers[10] and Frank Reefman – the two companies remained loyal to their original vision.

Nühn later compared the partnership SLDE had signed with Philips DAP to an alliance and almost to a marriage. It was neither a joint venture nor a conventional procurement contract. As it was a partnership and not a traditional supplier contract, both parties had an incentive to achieve a fair deal. The idea was to motivate each partner enough to ensure a continuous relationship. The contract was highly unusual on several counts:

(1) It determined that both companies would go to market together, but if one of the two companies was not prepared to enter a particular market, the other was free to find another partner and go with it.
(2) It gave the two companies joint ownership of the intellectual property rights for the coffee extraction technology and the entire system, even though SLDE had originally developed the basic system.
(3) It also made the two partners equal co-owners of the common brand – Senseo – with Philips DAP owning the brand on the machine side and SLDE owning it on the coffee side.
(4) It specified that Philips would be paid a fixed amount for each pod sold under the Senseo brand, in order to ensure that Philips DAP could make money despite a very low price for its machine.
(5) It set a fixed minimum advertising budget and apportioned it between the two partners calculated on their respective expected revenue streams. Based on the assumption that over the anticipated five-year ownership of a Senseo machine, a typical consumer's investment in coffee pods would be four times more than the cost of the machine itself, it was decided that SLDE would support the largest part of the launch marketing expenses.

The price of the machine was one of the contentious points that were discussed at many meetings. SLDE had started with a demand that the retail price of the machine be specified in the contract.

It had set a price that Philips DAP thought unrealistic – it did not leave Philips DAP much freedom to generate a manufacturing profit – and inconsistent with a positioning on premium quality. Nühn justified his company's position as follows:

> The main idea was to penetrate markets as fast as possible by selling the machine at a very low price. Philips is not making money with the machines. Thus, they get a royalty on the pods. The more machines they sell, the more pods we sell and we are both happy. Plus, they have no incentive to partner with another coffee manufacturer. Of course, going forward, we hope they start making some money on the machines as well.[11]

Philips DAP managed to get its position accepted, i.e. the machine price would be left out of the contract but would be negotiated at various intervals. Nühn did not want to disclose the exact amount of Philips' fee per pod, but agreed that, although it was relatively small per bag, it was very significant overall because of high volumes.

> Let's not forget that we make most of the initial investment when we enter a new country. For Philips, the Senseo machine is another coffee machine in their range. We have to launch the brand. Anyway, a small amount on a huge number of pods is still a lot of money.[12]

To make the partnership work and ensure regular communication between them at all management levels, the two partners established a number of management and coordination mechanisms, both formal and informal. The two chairmen met monthly in a joint steering committee, and cross-functional steering teams in the R&D, marketing and supply chain areas met every two weeks. This management infrastructure enabled flexibility and took into account the different objectives and cultures of the two companies without sacrificing the effectiveness of the venture.

## Designing the Product Together

In total, the Senseo system required more than six years in research and development before it was ready for market launch. The internal working of the machine alone, where the coffee extraction occurred, took two years to finalize. A senior marketing and sales manager at SLDE recalled:

> We had to delay the launch twice because the machine was not working properly. It was a revolutionary system, especially the low-pressure extraction technology that enables us to make foam without using the same 10-bar pressure as an espresso machine. Not having the cost associated with the 10-bar technology is a key competitive advantage for us.[13]

SLDE patented the brewing chamber[14] and shared the patent with Philips. The pods were not patented because the concept already existed in the market.[15] In less than a minute, the Senseo machine was able to consistently deliver one or two freshly brewed cups of gourmet coffee with a unique smooth frothy layer. The frothy layer, which so far had only been achieved with espresso machines, was one of Senseo's key features. It protected the taste of the coffee, locking in the aroma and giving a velvety texture.

In terms of positioning, the Senseo product matched the ideal profile determined by consumer research. The majority of users perceived Senseo as round, pleasant, elegant and happy. This was in sharp contrast with espresso coffee, which was perceived more as arrogant, strong and energetic. For SLDE, the following characteristics were the trademarks of Senseo:

- A different quality of coffee than espresso.
  *'With an espresso maker, you extract all flavors, both the good and the bad ones like bitterness. Senseo is rounder, less aggressive.'*
- The foam layer.
  *'We are the only ones who can make foam without using high-pressure technology.'*
- The new positioning, more like a sexy drink product than just coffee.
- The revolutionary design – modern and with a blue machine color.
- A low price machine to speed up market penetration.
- Initially, four varieties of pods: regular, dark roast, mild roast and decaf (later complemented with blend and gourmet varieties).

Philips chose the blue color – a strong shift from conventional coffee machines, which were usually black or white – after market research suggested that this color would have the most impact with customers. SLDE considered it with skepticism. A senior SLDE manager explained:

> We were reluctant at first. Why blue for a coffee machine? At the end of the day, it made a huge difference because it singled out our machine on the shelves.[16]

## Achieving Faster Market Penetration than DVDs

### Rolling Out Senseo in Europe

The Senseo machine, initially manufactured in China, was launched in the Netherlands in February 2001. It was an immediate success, with appliance and pod sales exceeding the most optimistic expectations by a factor of two. These unexpected results accelerated the roll-out of the system in Belgium, France, Germany and Denmark over a period of two and half years. Henk de Jong, who replaced Paul Bromberg as business manager of the Philips beverages business in October 2001, led this successful roll-out on the Philips side. Given the limited patent protection that Senseo enjoyed, a fast roll-out was essential to claim market leadership. In 2005, Adriaan Nühn shared his enthusiasm and that of his SLDE colleagues:

> We have sold 5 million machines in three years, faster than Playstation™. Our vision is: The coffee world will go to single serve![17]

The original Dutch guilder price for the Senseo machine in the Netherlands – it was launched a few months before the shift to the euro – was NLG 129, which corresponded to €59. This was roughly the cost price of the machine and included a welcome pack of coffee pods worth €14. Within a few months, an exceptionally high demand and limited supply allowed the companies to increase the machine price to €69. Traditional filter coffee machines were priced at €27 to €31. Basic espresso machines began at €113 with high-end versions retailing at up to €900.

In June 2005 – four and half years after launch – Senseo had sold 10 million machines and close to 8 billion pods. The future outlook was bright as the companies started to seriously attack the huge US market. The pattern in the market share growth was nearly the same for each of the successive roll-outs. The starting point correlated strongly with the original market shares of Philips and SLDE in the country, but then it followed the same rapid slope. Both companies envisioned a 20% to 30% market share in in-home coffee machines within each country entered.

## Changing Customer Habits

For a senior marketing and sales manager at SLDE, Senseo was more than just a successful coffee product. They had created a new category in the coffee market. He explained:

> Senseo is used in addition to classic filter machines, not to replace them; 94% of our sales are additional. Most owners keep their drip coffee machines when they have a lot of coffee to make and use Senseo occasionally.[18]

When introduced to the Senseo concept, 35% of the general public said they would buy the product. This figure rose to 45% once they had actually tasted Senseo coffee. Early adopters were praising the product, with a satisfaction rate above 90%. Thanks to their 'seeing + trying = buying' strategy, and positive word of mouth, benefit awareness reached 70% six months after the launch in each country.

## Building Manufacturing Capacity

After experiencing problems with its Chinese manufacturer, Philips moved production to Poland before opening a second manufacturing site, in China again, but this time in its own domestic appliance plant. Philips now had the capacity to produce 2 to 3 million machines a year in two plants, a volume beyond which it would be difficult to improve economies of scale.

The unexpected high demand had created some pod manufacturing challenges too. SLDE had to quadruple its pod production capacity in less than three years, which meant completely rebalancing its coffee production mix. In January 2004, more than half of the Utrecht plant was dedicated to Senseo pods. SLDE was also using cutting-edge technology. In order to protect its market, it had negotiated exclusive contracts with two equipment manufacturers. The result was two high-speed pod-manufacturing machines. The first one could make 1000 pods a minute and the second one was a combination of four machines, each with a capacity of 300 pods per minute and thus a total output of more than 1000 pods. It was a key competitive advantage, since other machines on the market could only make 300 pods per minute.

### Reaping the Rewards but Continuing to Invest

Product margin was three times greater than that for traditional roast and ground coffee. By 2004, the Senseo business was already profitable for SLDE and the return on invested capital was in line with that of other beverage businesses, even with continued roll-out investment.

Philips, however, did not become profitable immediately, particularly as the success of Senseo significantly reduced its sales of conventional filter coffee makers. The huge pod volume growth that Senseo experienced brought Philips' profitability back to normal levels, since the company received a fixed income for each pod sold in compensation for its low margin on the machines. The company could also hope to turn its manufacturing operations into a profitable business. It could take advantage of experience curve effects and introduce new machine generations with lower-cost designs. The second-generation machine that it launched in September 2002 with two additional colors – black and white – was actually of higher quality and cheaper than the first one. This, combined with a € 10 price increase (from € 59 to € 69), somewhat improved Philips' machine economics.

However, this fast build-up came at a cost. One of the critical tasks was the setting up of a joint consumer hot line. Both companies agreed that they could not let consumers hang around while each partner referred to the other to solve a particular problem.

Marketing spend was up 36% for SLDE in 2003, driven primarily by the continued roll-out of Senseo.

## Facing Competition

As with any successful innovation, however, competitors were stepping up their R&D efforts to catch up. A number of companies were indeed preparing to offer pods that could work in Senseo machines, and some developed their own coffee systems.

### Pod Manufacturers Make Inroads

Unlike the design of the brew chamber, which was patent protected, the pods were the Achilles' heel of the Senseo concept. The best protection against future entrants, management felt, was to lock in all available capacity of the third-party high-capacity pod machine manufacturer. However, competitors were quick to realize that there was still an opportunity to enter the market utilizing the 300 pods-per-minute machines.

In France and Germany the market leader, Kraft, was offering pods that were compatible with the Senseo machines. Although the giant company was smart enough not to state it directly, customers were invited to check online whether they could use Kraft pods in their coffee machines. Private labels, which already held 30% of the segment in Germany, had sometimes been less subtle, and SLDE had been quick to take them to court. The judicial battle that followed left the issue unresolved, which convinced management that legal means alone would not suffice to protect their business, they would have to roll-out Senseo faster. Nühn remained confident, though:

> We have to accept competition will increase on the pods. Our system is semi-closed; you can put in other pods. But we are so strongly branded that the consumers are in principle very loyal, and have the emotional feeling that they get the best results with Senseo.[19]

Another unpleasant surprise was that, despite their cost disadvantage of not having access to high-speed pod machines, private labels were still able to compete on price with SLDE. A senior SLDE manager commented:

> We made a small mistake here. They came in and bought 10 machines at 200 pods per minute and still have a low cost structure.[20]

He admitted, however, that this growing competition over the pods had forced them to review their marketing mix:

> We only make money on the pods, so we had to change the advertising mix. At first, we advertised the machines more than the pods. Now we are focusing on the coffee brand to link it back to the mother brand. We have built a strong Senseo brand; let's make sure that consumers associate it with SLDE.[21]

## Appliance Competitors Respond with their Own Systems

Other manufacturers were preparing to introduce competitive low-pressure systems as well. In February 2004, Kraft announced its intention to launch Tassimo™ in France, an in-home coffee machine that used its popular coffee brand there. Kraft had also partnered with the Italian espresso machine maker, Saeco, to offer a proprietary on-demand home coffee system. The machine was distributed in France by Braun and was able to make a frothy cappuccino at the press of a button, without using the traditional steam rod. In the US, Procter & Gamble – in cooperation with Black & Decker – and Salton were also working on single-serve coffee systems of their own. And, boosted by the success of its Nespresso espresso system, Nestlé was also expected to enter the single-serve, plain coffee system segment of the market.

SLDE and Philips acknowledged the threat but thought they were prepared to tackle it. The Tassimo™ machine, which used a higher pressure than Senseo, was perceived as significantly more expensive. Besides, based on qualitative comparative studies made in North America, the two Senseo partners learned that consumers preferred the Senseo system to competitors' entries. They particularly liked the frothy layer and Senseo's consistently great taste.

## Testing the Partnership: The Philips Machine Profitability Dilemma

Philips' managers were not too worried about competitors under-cutting their machine on price; they felt unbeatable on cost. But they were concerned about the threat of 'pirate suppliers' entering the pod market, because Philips' profitability totally depended on its pod income. The company was convinced it needed to start making money on machines as well to reduce its dependency on pods, but how?

Increasing the retail price of the current machine was out of the question, now that competitors were emerging. Opportunities for reducing machine costs through economies of scale would be limited at the very high current volumes. The solution would probably lie in redesigning the machine to achieve a further cost reduction, but Bromberg was aware of the constraints:

> Reengineering the machine for a lower cost would require chang-ing its basic design. But we don't want to change the design too much now that it is fully recognized in the market. Consumers are now familiar with that new category. It looks like neither a filter machine nor an espresso machine. Can we afford to introduce a totally new design without confusing consumers?[22]

Another option was to introduce new higher-margin products but, again, Bromberg saw the limits of that strategy:

> As long as we are the only ones in the market, we do not want to compete against ourselves. Maybe, we need only one machine! We will expand our range only if the trade or competitors force us to do so. But we should not fall into the trap of offering a product for every price-point.[23]

Nevertheless, Philips was toying with the idea of introducing a new premium machine to complement its basic model, hopefully with an attractive margin. But what kind of machine should it be and what kind of feature would induce consumers to trade up, say, to a price point of € 99? Would design and finish alone do it? Consumers had suggested one option: Offer the possibility of adjusting the volume of water to obtain, at will, a stronger or weaker coffee. But, would this not go against the basic vision of

Senseo's partners, which was to offer a perfect cup of coffee and adjust coffee strength by buying different varieties – mild, regular or strong?

With Senseo, SLDE and Philips had changed the way consumers experience coffee drinking at home – forever. They now had to continue working together to protect and expand their business while ensuring their partnership remained a win-win proposition.

## BUILDING AND LEADING AN INNOVATION-FOCUSED PARTNERSHIP

The Senseo story provides a rich lesson of collective innovation leadership. Aspects of this type of leadership have already been alluded to in Chapters 8 and 9, notably the critical importance of:

(1) Starting with a compelling customer-oriented vision. In the Senseo case, the vision centered on designing and delivering a comprehensive 'coffee solution' that provided consumers with a unique experience in terms of taste, variety and convenience. That vision was equally shared by the two partners.
(2) Recognizing the benefits of partnering around an innovative concept. In the Senseo case, the partnership went much beyond traditional supply relationships, as the partners developed and marketed the innovation together, sharing risks, costs and profits.
(3) Accepting that significant innovations require the simultaneous and successive involvement of different types of leaders, working over time in a smooth chain of leadership. In the Senseo case, that chain of leadership straddled the two organizations and, in 2007, was still uninterrupted.

Great innovation stories are rarely attributable to a single leader, they generally require a collective leadership effort. In the Senseo case, several 'conductors' from the two partners agreed to align their organizations behind the same chosen score to play music together. They were willing to share a common approach in (1) interpreting consumers' unmet needs; (2) orchestrating a common 'well-tempered' response; and (3) integrating their operations to present a common front to the market.

The most interesting aspect of the Senseo story from an innovation leadership angle is, perhaps, the way the two companies handled their partnership.

## Agreeing to Partner to Deliver an Innovative Customer Solution

Senseo's success is directly linked to the unique type of partnership that the two companies created. Early on, their respective management recognized that:

(1) Alone, they could not have developed and marketed a system optimized to such an extent (in terms of affordability and consumer experience).
(2) Only a flexible and balanced partnership, ensuring equal status and a fair allocation of both investments and profits, would be sustainable over time.

### *Partnering to Capitalize on Each Other's Strengths*

SLDE could have been tempted to stick with its original 'go-it-alone' strategy, producing and marketing the entire system with an outsourced machine from China. Alternatively, it could have adopted the Nespresso approach, i.e. keeping all intellectual property rights and maintaining full control over its system, then licensing several coffee machine manufacturers like Philips. But the company was not in a strong enough position to proceed alone. Unlike Nestlé, which had strong patent protection on both its coffee extraction system and its aluminum capsules, SLDE lacked protection on pod design and manufacturing. It was therefore in a weaker position vis-à-vis competitors, and vulnerable to attacks by suppliers of private label pods. It could only win through speed – preempting competitors – and through continuous innovation.

The strengths of Philips, both as a quality yet low-cost manufacturer and as a strong 'A-brand' owner in domestic appliances, improved SLDE's position significantly. It largely contributed to achieving rapid market penetration, establishing the Senseo brand on the market and gaining customer loyalty, thus reducing the impact of attacks by other pod suppliers and private labels.

Conversely, and since it did not have a coffee business, Philips would never have been able to launch a coffee system on its own. It would have had to fight for the rights to produce the machines of other proprietary coffee systems like Nespresso or Kraft's Tassimo™, while trying to maintain its filter coffee machine business alive. SLDE brought its impressive coffee manufacturing and marketing knowledge and resources, plus its well-established coffee brands and distribution coverage.

## Establishing a Flexible and Balanced Partnership

The two partners fully recognized the complementary nature of their respective contributions, and this is why, despite having started first and designed the core of its system, SLDE agreed to share the opportunity with Philips. In the same spirit, they devised the formula whereby Philips would make money on pod sales to compensate for a machine price that was set purposely low to encourage early customer adoption. Paul Bromberg recognizes that SLDE management made very significant financial concessions to keep Philips DAP motivated. Such kinds of partnership can be sustained only if the two parties view it as a win–win proposition.

## Evolving the Partnership

### From Contractual to Working Relationships

The original partnership contract played an important role in the pre-launch phase, as it established the principles that would govern the cooperation between the two companies. It was also important in the first couple of years as the two partners were still in the process of getting to know each other, and new people came on board on both sides. Kristine Klaassen, who, in June 2005, managed the Senseo business from SLDE's side, commented on the evolution of the contractual relationships between the two partners.

When you aren't quite sure that you understand each other's strategic thinking or direction and what drives each other's business, then it's very good to have a fixed paper that you can go back to to help you sort out issues. That was the first phase and the contract supported us to make sure that we'd go as quickly as possible given the differences between our two huge corporations.

Now, we've been in the market for quite a few years; a lot of people are involved in the business. We have a lot of different relationships at different levels, and therefore we are better able to discuss and align outside of the contract if it makes business sense for both parties. That's the flexibility and the strength of our 'marriage.' Over time, you get to know each other a lot better. You also trust each other in a whole new perspective than you did in those first two years.[24]

The contract was reasonably detailed but, of course, its signatories could not be expected to predict the future and the way the market would develop, so they left out a number of issues that proved important later on. Klaassen commented:

We also need to become more flexible now because the market has changed versus what we thought four or five years ago when we drafted the first contract, and there are certain things that we didn't take into consideration. So we can choose between two different approaches. We could have ten lawyers on each side, making addendums to the contract each time we have a new idea and make a new iteration, keeping a lot of people occupied. Alternatively – and this is what we have chosen – we can sit down as business partners and just look at the business opportunities and come to some conclusions, find solutions in our very competitive environment.[25]

### Building Working Relationships at All Levels

As the two partners moved from project mode to business mode, they had to build a range of formal and informal relationships across all functions and geographic organizations, as Rens de Haan, who took over the management of Philips' DAP's Senseo business, explains:

All the disciplines within our companies work together in various teams. We want to have close cooperation at all levels. At the highest level, we have so-called international steering committee meetings every other month, where we discuss all kinds of topics as they occur, be it on pricing, packaging, promotion and so forth. The bosses of our country organizations work closely together. So do the sales and marketing managers. On every level, throughout the organization, we have been able to establish links. So that if you want to visit a retailer, you go together. It's a marriage between the coffee and the appliance.[26]

Difficulties arose each time newcomers joined either of the two teams. Unaware of the history of the relationship, they were tempted to model their behavior on contractual terms and to reopen operational issues that had already been addressed. Leaders of the two teams then had to spend much time explaining and re-explaining the vision and the mode of operation between the two companies.

Klaassen explains what these relationships entail in terms of personal discipline on a day-to-day basis:

> We are very dependent on personal relationships and, as we have seen over time, building those relationships takes time. We need to understand how the individual works, not just how the other company works. We have to make decisions based on our understanding of what the other person needs and wants, and on whether that person has got the necessary approvals within his/her company. Rens [de Haan] and I are counterparts and we run the international daily Senseo sales business. We steer the international teams – the marketing teams, the innovation teams, the roll-out teams, the operational teams. Our managers need to develop their own relationships for the decisions they have to make at their level. One thing that guides us is what we can do – together with our direct reporting managers – to ensure that we don't lose sight of our end objective.[27]

## Adapting Each Other's Leadership Style to the Realities of a Marriage

### Building Trust

Building a trusting relationship was not an easy thing to do, as Paul Bromberg recognizes:

In the beginning, SLDE didn't know how much they could trust Philips. This played an important role during the contract negotiations. We indicated that we could not make enough money under the conditions of the initial letter of intent. We did not have an agreement on an 'open book' basis, so they needed to take our word for it. If we had abused that trust, it would have broken up our partnership later on.

On another point, in the beginning SLDE felt that they knew about machine design. From our side, we were challenging their brewing specifications. We felt we could bring the machine price down by changing certain elements of their specification. I guess that we all had to learn to respect each other's areas of expertise and authority![28]

Yet, ultimately, it is mutual trust – a feeling that they were mutually dependent on each other – that kept the relationship working over time.

## Learning to Work Together Despite Major Cultural Differences

The two Dutch multinational companies have completely different organizational cultures. Philips DAP is much more centralized than SLDE. It has more structure and relies on processes to a greater extent than its consensus-based partner. This translates into very different ways to go to market, as de Haan at Philips stresses:

> Once we make a decision centrally, we can be a little more forceful with our local organizations in the countries and say to them, 'OK, this is how we are going to do that!' SLDE, on its side, has to do a lot more selling of its story to its own country organizations.[29]

Adriaan Nühn acknowledged the difference, noting the pros and the cons of the two contrasting approaches:

> The management style at Philips is centralized and ours is decentralized. Centralization is good for advertising and speed of development. Once a decision is taken, all countries apply it. However, when forecasts are wrong, they can miss some sales whereas we are quicker to adapt locally.

These differences in culture and management style added complexity to the relationship between the two partners, requiring a good deal of flexibility from all. At one stage, the leaders organized a joint two-day workshop with their teams, under the guidance of a culture consultant. It was designed to identify what in the culture of each company put the other team members off. This workshop resulted in a shared recognition that the team members' motivations were very similar, despite differences in organizational culture. Nevertheless, in a number of cases, some team members were removed from the venture because they could not deal with each other. And on several occasions, some people who had been involved in the early contractual relationships had to learn to let go, as some of the supposedly 'non-negotiable' elements had to be renegotiated. So, as could be expected, there were ups and downs in the relationship between the two companies, as in any marriage.

## Keeping the Vision Alive

The marriage held steady and was still going strong in 2007 because, despite many temptations to become embroiled in conflicts over operational details or annoyed by differences in organizational culture, both management teams strived to keep the partnership alive. Paul Bromberg explains what kept the cohesion of the teams together:

> For partnering, there is one leadership skill that is essential: The ability to step back to the common vision on which the partnership is based. We came from different cultures; we each had a different focus. At times, you can get frustrated by each other's way of discussing problems and making decisions. Yet you have to keep the common vision as a guidepost and use its guiding principles to take away roadblocks that are essentially cultural.[30]

Overall, and that is one of the main lessons of the Senseo story, Adriaan Nühn deemed the partnership was not only a success but also a key driver in Senseo's development. He insisted on attributing this success to the partnership with Philips:

We would not have succeeded without them. We may have the R&D capacity to build good machines, but they brought their power and expertise in the appliance market. At first thought, we did not think it would work: We had to succeed simultaneously in two different channels, go global in local markets and manage a loose partnership.[31]

The Senseo story, once again, illustrates innovation leaders in action. Paul Bromberg at Philips DAP and Vincent Janssen at SLDE championed a common project from the very beginning. Together, and with their successors in each company, they interpreted customers' and consumers' unmet needs, orchestrated an original partnership to address these needs and integrated their contribution to develop a balanced solution.

# ENDNOTES

1. Extract from a videotaped interview with Ad Veenhof, former president of Philips DAP Division (Domestic Appliances and Personal Care Division), conducted in Appeldoorn (Holland) on 3 April 2003.
2. This story is based on the following sources:

   - Senseo's website: http://www.senseo.com.
   - Extracts from the IMD case: 'Senseo: Establishing a New Standard in the Home Coffee Market,' by Henri Bourgeois with the help of Atul Pahwa, under the supervision of John Walsh and the author (2004) IMD Case No. IMD-5-0674.
   - Personal interviews, conducted by John Walsh and Henry Bourgeois in April 2004, with:
     ○ Adriaan Nühn, at the time chairman of the board of Sara Lee Douwe Egberts (SLDE)
     ○ Christian van Besien, at the time regional vice president of SLDE.
   - Author's personal interviews, on 3 June 2004 and 19 October 2007, with Paul Bromberg, at the time vice president strategy and business development of Philips DAP.
   - Videotaped interview, conducted at IMD on 28 June 2005 by John Walsh and the author, with:
     ○ Rens de Haan, vice president and Senseo business manager, Philips DAP
     ○ Kristine Klaassen, vice president and Senseo business manager, SLDE.

3. In 2007, Vincent Janssen was executive vice president and CEO, Sara Lee International – Household & Body Care.
4. In 2007, Paul Bromberg was senior vice president and general manager of Senior Living and Business Development at Philips Lifeline in the US.

5. Author's personal interview, in August 2004, with Paul Bromberg, at the time vice president strategy and business development of Philips DAP, reproduced with permission.

6. 'Senseo, Partnership in Innovation Leads to a Sensational Cup of Coffee.' InSite Publication, (Sara Lee intranet), 26 April 2004.

7. Walsh, J., Deschamps, J.-P., Bourgeois, H. and Pahwa, A. (2004). 'Senseo: Establishing a New Standard in the Home Coffee Market,' IMD Case No. IMD-5-0674.

8. In 2007, Adriaan Nühn was the chairman of Sara Lee International.

9. Walsh, J., Deschamps, J.-P., Bourgeois, H. and Pahwa, A. (2004). 'Senseo: Establishing a New Standard in the Home Coffee Market,' IMD Case No. IMD-5-0674, reproduced with permission.

10. In 2007, Frank van Oers was executive vice president and CEO, Sara Lee International – Coffee & Tea.

11. Walsh, J., Deschamps, J.-P., Bourgeois, H. and Pahwa, A. (2004). 'Senseo: Establishing a New Standard in the Home Coffee Market,' IMD Case No. IMD-5-0674, reproduced with permission.

12. Walsh, J., Deschamps, J.-P., Bourgeois, H. and Pahwa, A. (2004). 'Senseo: Establishing a New Standard in the Home Coffee Market,' IMD Case No. IMD-5-0674.

13. Walsh, J., Deschamps, J.-P., Bourgeois, H. and Pahwa, A. (2004). 'Senseo: Establishing a New Standard in the Home Coffee Market,' IMD Case No. IMD-5-0674.

14. According to Philips company information, 'The Senseo system was a mixed design. It had a pump and a pressure chamber, like traditional espresso makers, but the pressure was much lower (just above one bar instead of 10 bars). The low-pressure brewing system infused the water with more coffee than conventional percolators. It used servings (or pods) and the brewing process was fixed for time, temperature and pressure. Operation was automated and therefore coffee quality was constant, always fresh and easy-to-use. At low pressure, no cream could be expected, but there was an attractive frothy coffee layer. The taste of the coffee is always the same and no 'old' coffee had to be thrown away. The taste is somewhere between normal filter coffee and espresso.'

15. An Italian coffee and espresso specialist – illycaffè – had pioneered the concept of packing coffee in pods for use in espresso machines.

16. Walsh, J., Deschamps, J.-P., Bourgeois, H. and Pahwa, A. (2004). 'Senseo: Establishing a New Standard in the Home Coffee Market,' IMD Case No. IMD-5-0674.

17. Walsh, J., Deschamps, J.-P., Bourgeois, H. and Pahwa, A. (2004). 'Senseo: Establishing a New Standard in the Home Coffee Market,' IMD Case No. IMD-5-0674, reproduced with permission.

18. Walsh, J., Deschamps, J.-P., Bourgeois, H. and Pahwa, A. (2004). 'Senseo: Establishing a New Standard in the Home Coffee Market,' IMD Case No. IMD-5-0674.

19. Walsh, J., Deschamps, J.-P., Bourgeois, H. and Pahwa, A. (2004). 'Senseo: Establishing a New Standard in the Home Coffee Market,' IMD Case No. IMD-5-0674, reproduced with permission.

20. Walsh, J., Deschamps, J.-P., Bourgeois, H. and Pahwa, A. (2004). 'Senseo: Establishing a New Standard in the Home Coffee Market,' IMD Case No. IMD-5-0674.

21. Walsh, J., Deschamps, J.-P., Bourgeois, H. and Pahwa, A. (2004). 'Senseo: Establishing a New Standard in the Home Coffee Market,' IMD Case No. IMD-5-0674.

22. Walsh, J., Deschamps, J.-P., Bourgeois, H. and Pahwa, A. (2004). 'Senseo: Establishing a New Standard in the Home Coffee Market,' IMD Case No. IMD-5-0674.

23. Walsh, J., Deschamps, J.-P., Bourgeois, H. and Pahwa, A. (2004). 'Senseo: Establishing a New Standard in the Home Coffee Market,' IMD Case No. IMD-5-0674.

24. Videotaped interview, conducted at IMD on 28 June 2005 by John Walsh and the author, with:
    • Rens de Haan, vice president and Senseo business manager, Philips DAP;
    • Kristine Klaassen, vice president and Senseo business manager, SLDE.

25. Videotaped interview, conducted at IMD on 28 June 2005 by John Walsh and the author, with:
    • Rens de Haan, vice president and Senseo business manager, Philips DAP;
    • Kristine Klaassen, vice president and Senseo business manager, SLDE.

26. Videotaped interview, conducted at IMD on 28 June 2005 by John Walsh and the author, with:
    • Rens de Haan, vice president and Senseo business manager, Philips DAP, reproduced with permission;
    • Kristine Klaassen, vice president and Senseo business manager, SLDE.

27. Videotaped interview, conducted at IMD on 28 June 2005 by John Walsh and the author, with:
    • Rens de Haan, vice president and Senseo business manager, Philips DAP;
    • Kristine Klaassen, vice president and Senseo business manager, SLDE.

28. Author's personal interview, in August 2004 and October 2007, with Paul Bromberg, at the time vice president strategy and business development of Philips DAP, reproduced with permission.

29. Videotaped interview, conducted at IMD on 28 June 2005 by John Walsh and the author, with:
    • Rens de Haan, vice president and Senseo business manager, Philips DAP, reproduced with permission;
    • Kristine Klaassen, vice president and Senseo business manager, SLDE.

30. Author's personal interview, in August 2004 and October 2007, with Paul Bromberg, at the time vice president strategy and business development of Philips DAP, reproduced with permission.

31. Walsh, J., Deschamps, J.-P., Bourgeois, H. and Pahwa, A. (2004). 'Senseo: Establishing a New Standard in the Home Coffee Market,' IMD Case No. IMD-5-0674, reproduced with permission.

# PART III

# DEVELOPING A CADRE OF INNOVATION LEADERS

# CHAPTER 11

# BUILDING AN INNOVATION LEADERSHIP ENVIRONMENT: THE LOGITECH CASE[1]

*Even though we might soon be a one-billion-dollar company, I still look at Logitech as being a small company, made up of business units, each of them having to survive in this world. Each of them acts or should act like a start-up. In a start-up, the reason to be is only to innovate; so, for us, innovation — and I would even extrapolate for many companies nowadays — is the way to survive.*
Daniel Borel, (2002) Cofounder and former Board Chairman

Since Daniel Borel made this comment, Logitech passed the $1 billion mark in sales in fiscal year 2003, and it reached $2.1 billion in 2007. It expects to reach the $3 billion mark well before 2010 . . . and still the company features the dynamism, innovativeness and agility of a large, disciplined start-up. Investors have recognized the continuing performance of this NASDAQ-quoted company by rallying behind its stock, which has appreciated phenomenally over the past decade. They remained confident in it even during the difficult period after the dot-com bubble burst. With a discipline for consistent product innovation in digital peripherals, the company has opened up a number of new product categories. It has received several industry accolades and has realized considerable success with word-of-mouth advertising.

At the end of calendar 2007, Logitech saw a major top management change. Daniel Borel, its cofounder and board chairman, passed the baton to Guerrino De Luca, who had been CEO since

1998. Jerry Quindlen, a veteran from the Eastman Kodak Company, became Logitech's new CEO. He joined the company in 2005 as senior vice president of worldwide sales and marketing. This management change is unlikely to alter the company's unique characteristic – Logitech's ability to grow through innovation in a very competitive environment does indeed seem sustainable. This is essentially because it builds upon a deep-rooted innovation leadership culture. This chapter will try to describe the multiple facets of such an innovation-enabling environment.

## LOGITECH: ORDINARY OR EXTRAORDINARY COMPANY?

The few companies around us that seem able to sustain innovation year in, year out deserve to be looked at carefully because they can teach us a lot about innovation leadership. Logitech is one of them. The company is particularly interesting because its outstanding results do not seem to come from a unique set of skills or resources.

- Logitech's top managers are certainly charismatic, but they do not belong to the small clique of 'prima donnas' who seem to continuously search for and attract media attention.
- Logitech does not benefit from a unique mastery of specific technologies. It has very competent engineers, definitely, but they are probably not that different from those in many other high-quality electronic companies.
- Logitech does not pretend to create 'cult-like' products through its spectacular design. Yet, it has excellent products and designers, and its recent MX Air Mouse has been requested by the Museum of Modern Art in New York City for an exhibit.
- Logitech does not come up with spectacular marketing campaigns that everyone remembers. It is a smart and cost-effective product marketer, but its marketing and advertising budgets are rather modest.

We could go on, highlighting the fact that Logitech is, indeed, an excellent company, but by no means truly exceptional in any particular area. In fact, both management and staff come across as rather low key and modest. They know that, in their volatile industry, their stream of market successes can be interrupted at any time. They never take anything about their success for granted.

What *is* exceptional in Logitech is that the company seems to be innovating *better*, *faster* and *more consistently* than most others in its industry. Besides, its execution is generally faultless, leading to continuing market success. This is largely due to the combined action of a broad and distributed pool of innovation leaders, and a big team of talented and motivated people, who work hard and fast in unison across the world and functions. They all constantly try to serve their markets better and reinvent themselves. The company's leaders seem to have integrated, in their collective behavior, the essence of sustained innovation, i.e. that unusual mix of:

- creativity and discipline;
- culture and process;
- top-down and bottom-up approaches –

in short, everything that this book is about. And *this* is probably unique!

At Logitech, innovation leadership is not limited to the top management team. It seems to pervade multiple layers of the organization, down to the operating levels. Through its values, attitudes, policies and processes, management has created an environment in which innovation leaders can develop and grow. This is undoubtedly the company's best weapon for sustaining innovation over time.

## A Start-up that Succeeded

Logitech started as a small Swiss-based software development company in 1981. It grew to become a well-known global specialist of peripheral devices that people use in order to work, play and communicate via their computers, game consoles, TVs or mobile digital devices.

In its early days Logitech installed a manufacturing facility with a capacity to produce 25 000 mice, even though the worldwide market was far below this capacity. But its founders sensed the full potential of the market, as Daniel Borel stresses:

> We were a small group of people with a great dream. From the beginning, we dreamt of a day when Logitech would be established in the world market with a recognized name, providing fun and innovative products.

Logitech's vision was to be the interface between technology and people, and the mouse was intended to be the tip of the iceberg of this vision. The idea was to make the personal computer *personal*. That meant utilizing the optimal combination of design, technology and manufacturing processes to introduce appealing, user-friendly and affordable products in the market. From the beginning, Borel insisted on the personal and almost emotional character of the company's products, contrasting this with the cold, technical image of the computers they served.

Logitech's growth was linked with the development of the computer mouse. Its origins lay in the original equipment manufacturer (OEM) sector, which remains an important part of its business. To its OEM customers, who include most of the world's largest PC manufacturers, Logitech stands for high volume, low cost, and quality in design and manufacturing. Its strengths lie in its responsiveness to changes in technology or market conditions, and in its efficient worldwide distribution.

However, over the years, the company has built a strong presence in the retail sector as consumers enhance their digital systems with more fully featured interface devices. Logitech has, indeed, dramatically broadened its product offering with a range of mice and track balls, keyboards, webcams, audio speakers, gaming accessories, universal remote controls and the like. These products add functionality and cordless freedom to desktops and laptops. They also cater to new applications such as gaming, audio, multimedia and visual communication on the Internet, home entertainment control, streaming music and home video self-monitoring – Logitech's latest acquisitions.

The company enjoys strong brand recognition in retail outlets all over the world, as well as on several web-based retail sites. Its objective is to provide the market with best-of-category in a broadening array of products. To do this, Logitech supplements its internal engineering and manufacturing strength with additional products and technologies through strategic acquisitions and industry partnerships.

Logitech barely survived tough times between 1993 and 1995. Fierce competition from Asian imports, falling prices in the computer industry and a high cost structure forced the company to restructure. Manufacturing was consolidated in China, management was reshuffled, and the company moved from being a functional organization to one built around business units. After two quarters in the red, Logitech resurfaced.

## A Matrix Organization with a Difference

The company operates under a matrix structure. Sales & marketing is divided into four zones: EMEA (Europe, Middle East and Africa), Americas, Asia-Pacific (excluding Japan) and Japan. It also operates one worldwide products group made up of several business units: control devices, internet communications, audio, gaming, streaming media and remote controls.

Business units are led by a general manager who reports to the executive vice president of products. In most cases, the business unit includes a head of marketing as well as a head of engineering. Business units consist of a number of product units, focusing either on the OEM or retail sales channels. Some of them, as exemplified by the retail pointing devices unit, which focuses on mice sold in retail channels under the Logitech brand, can be very large. But unlike business units, product units are not led by a single person. A team consisting of an engineering head and a product-marketing head, *working in partnership*, run them jointly. As one manager explained:

> By forming these pairs, we made sure that we would remain a strong, engineering-driven company while not losing touch with the market. Business ownership is shared by both functions. At the

end, they have to come to the business unit head and show a roadmap that is agreeable to both!

Making this 'management duo' work as a team is one of the personal tasks of the business unit head, as a business unit senior vice president stresses:

> How do we make the cooperation between marketing and engineering work? Well, sometimes we don't! It requires a tight synchronization! But at the end of the day, they must come to an agreement.

This pairing of marketing and engineering extends to the operating level. Product managers from marketing regularly team up with project leaders from engineering. Both share responsibility for a given project while reporting to different bosses.

Besides the usual corporate functions, such as human resources, management information systems, finance and legal affairs, Logitech has established a corporate business development function. Reporting directly to the executive vice president of the Products Group, the senior vice president strategy has two roles pertaining to growth and innovation. He has to:

(1) help implement the business development initiatives launched or approved by Logitech's executive team; and
(2) be a source of stimulation, ideas and challenge to help business units find promising new business opportunities and potential partners to grow and expand in their markets and beyond.

## Manifestations of Logitech's Innovation Leadership

Financial analysts generally focus on a company's performance track record against industry benchmarks, and on the extent to which management meets *their* expectations, quarter after quarter. When a company disappoints the market, which means that its results fall below the analysts' own estimates, then its stock takes a beating and analysts immediately start speculating about the company's assumed vulnerabilities. They talk about glitches in its strategy, botched product launches or missed opportunities. Despite an impressive growth track record, Logitech has not escaped this type of scrutiny. So goes the stock market!

The problem with financial analysts is that their analyses focus almost exclusively on financials. They rarely go deeply into the quality of a management team or the dynamics of a company's culture. As a consequence, they provide few insights into the future ability of the company to keep performing. No one, of course, can predict with certainty the outlook of the company in such a volatile and competitive environment. However, one thing is obvious to the careful innovation observer – Logitech has created an innovation leadership environment that will probably endure, despite management changes or industry convulsions. The company should therefore be capable of reinventing itself, even if it disappoints financial analysts at times.

Logitech's favorable innovation leadership environment results from the combined effect of a number of *innovation-stimulating drivers, an innovation-enhancing culture and values,* and *a pragmatic and effective innovation process,* which are briefly described in this chapter. In short, an innovation leadership environment works like a complex system made up of a number of complementary elements that reinforce each other.

## LOGITECH'S INNOVATION-STIMULATING DRIVERS

It is always difficult to identify the real drivers of innovation in a company. Some of them are purely intrinsic, like management's vision, attitudes, policies and processes. Others are extrinsic and reflect the particular competitive dynamics of the market. Logitech's innovation drivers are a combination of these two categories. They include:

- a compelling vision that evolved together with the company;
- a strong, non-complacent push for growth;
- a relentless focus on well-designed new products;
- openness to external technologies and ideas;
- an obsession with costs.

## A Compelling Vision that Evolved Together with the Company

Logitech's original claim to fame was its ability to carve a market space for its brand next to the powerful PC manufacturers. Mice were standard peripherals with every PC sold for over a decade. As an internal vision document states:

> Beginning in late 1985, the mouse, beyond its role as a pure product, helped to define the first vision for Logitech – i.e. the icon of the interface between technology and people – an icon which continues to express the company's mission today.[2]

Logitech's determination to reshape the computing environment to enhance the user experience led the company to create products with emotion and color, capturing the theme of 'user-friendly innovation' as its official motto. So, 10 years later, the company redefined its vision and mission as follows:

> Vision: A humanized computer in the hands of every individual;
> Mission: To provide every computer user with the very best computer senses.[3]

From its early days when he envisioned Logitech having 'fun and innovative products,' Borel felt that providing employees with such a vision gave them something to aspire to. So, as the company entered the new millennium, Logitech's vision and mission evolved once again:

> Vision: The interface that links people and information will transform the way they work, learn, communicate and play.
> Mission: Logitech brings to markets tools that enrich the interface between people and information.[4]

Within Logitech, innovation goes beyond the realm of product development. It also extends to systems and processes within the organization, as a product unit engineering director notes:

> Innovation is not just in product development. We try to be innovative in how we implement our systems so that they can grow and scale up.

## A Strong, Non-complacent Push for Growth

Most product unit managers work under strong top management pressure for continuous product renewal and growth. Pressure from the stock market – the tyranny of the quarterly performance outlook – is felt throughout, but accepted. Competition is an especially strong driver of managers' energy, as a business unit vice president stresses:

> We have a great competitor in Microsoft. Microsoft is a wonderful brand, credible! They do great things. We challenge each other very nicely. We may do a new product and get them going. They may create a new product and they get us going. It is not that we are obsessed with Microsoft at all, but it creates points of energy. A periodic infusion of energy is the best way I can say it.

## A Relentless Focus on Well-designed New Products

Logitech continuously renews and expands its product lines with new introductions. With an average market life cycle of between 12 and 18 months for its products, Logitech generates more than 50% of its annual revenues from new products. To deliver consistently on such a demanding product launch schedule, the company places strong emphasis on design. The marketing director of a product unit comments:

> We don't talk about design anymore . . . it is a given! Logitech needs to create products that have emotion in their shape or color. The PC is now a mainstream consumer market. We have moved from boring beige to more exciting colors.

The company also keeps a watchful eye on burgeoning industry trends. Realizing that the industry ecosystem is shaped by a multitude of players, Logitech works closely with other companies to improve the overall user experience. In the words of a product marketing director:

> We watch players who influence the hardware and software infrastructure. Microsoft introduced significant improvements into

managing digital media in its software. When we look at the media evolution, we can leverage some of these trends that are cool, useful and fashionable. We then ask ourselves, 'What can I make the user discover that is hidden in the operating system today? How can I take it and bring it visually into my product and market?'

## Openness to External Technologies and Ideas

The company has always been open to both internal and external sources for new product innovations. Despite its deep engineering-based roots, Logitech has learned not to rely solely on its own technological resources. Even its engineers recognize that the important thing is not where the technology is sourced, but what ultimately delivers greatest value to the customer. So, every engineer within Logitech is encouraged to keep abreast of external technology developments and sources in his/her area of knowledge. They are helped in this by the continuous scanning done by the vice president for new business development and his staff in areas adjacent to the company's technology portfolio.

But the most effective incentive for not reinventing the wheel probably comes from an acute pressure for short lead times, equally shared by the marketing and product development staff. Keeping the fast new product development rhythm imposed by the market is so demanding that any temptation to redesign a module that already exists commercially is quickly dispelled.

## An Obsession with Costs

The most striking aspect of Logitech's innovation philosophy is perhaps its obsession with developing very affordable, yet quality products. Marrying innovation and costs is one of the key challenges of Guerrino De Luca, its former CEO and now chairman, who believes the company is not yet where it should be. Logitech needs low costs to reach its ambitiously low, targeted retail price points (95% of its products retail for less than $99 and most of them for under $49). But it also needs low costs to make its expensive items affordable.

Such a focus on costs actually helps make technology sourcing more attractive, as the vice president of business development explains:

> Innovation is linked to costs! We have been drilled so much by the OEM market to try to analyze, reduce and factor in the ultimate cost that this forces you to agree that the time to get there is a cost as well; so it is an incentive to use outside technologies to save time and thus costs. We had an even higher focus on costs than the Taiwanese! A lot of engineers don't like that, but it is a challenge. Ultimately, they can see it as rewarding. Today, we have a consumer brand valued by the market with the inherent cost structure of an OEM supplier!

But even when it sources technology outside, Logitech finds new ways to work on it and optimize it in terms of performance and/ or features, so as to adapt it for mass production and cost reduction. Its business development vice president explains:

> Given our strong OEM background, we cannot buy, retag and sell low-cost stuff. We are forced to think about buying technology, then bringing it inside and working on it.

## LOGITECH'S INNOVATION-ENHANCING CULTURE AND VALUES

Logitech's corporate culture and values deserve to be singled out as one of the company's most potent innovation enablers. Corporate values are strongly felt at Logitech, despite the fact that many of them are more tacit or implicit than formally expressed. Nevertheless, managers frequently refer to them in their discussions, and it is easy for the outside observer to come up with an informal list of what makes the company tick:

- a sense of passion, dedication and commitment, from top to bottom;
- a global mindset;
- a willingness to empower and trust people based on openness and sharing;
- a willingness to take risks and accept failures;

- a preference for an informal, hands-on management style;
- a focus on realism and rigor in execution;
- an acceptance of constructive confrontation;
- a quest for 24-hour efficiency;
- healthy humility and restraint with regard to success.

One of the product units – retail pointing devices – has reiterated its guiding principles in the following set of values:

- Innovate anytime, anywhere, on anything (not only products).
- One global culture (that encompasses the best of each site culture):
  - Fight 'not invented here.'
- Transparency and visibility (plans, issues, design, decisions . . .) because of geographical dispersion.
- Partnership and mutual respect (rather than internal customer vs. supplier):
  - Challenging is encouraged.
- Strong project management practices:
  - Risk management – proper use of post-completion reports.
- Spirit and acknowledgment of contribution:
  - Focus energy on tasks that add value to the company.
- Process orientation:
  - Flawless execution; attention to detail;
  - Issues translate into process improvements and training.
- Efficiency:
  - Judicious use of available IT tools: Lotus notes, e-mail, telephone, netmeeting;
  - Meetings have an agenda, preparation and minutes; laptops are encouraged in meeting rooms to get information and speed action items.
  - Documentation of proceedings, decisions, action items.
- Humility (success is never final . . .).

The unit head ensures that its functional managers transmit these values to its teams.

It is not difficult to notice that conforming to these values is essential in order to thrive within the company, as an engineering vice president explicitly states:

> Logitech regroups people who share the values and accept to learn. People who come from larger companies or believe that they have a lot of experience may have a hard time embracing our values. We make sure that we have the right people on the bus . . . generally young people, at a stage in their careers where they are very malleable. We look for people's ability to jell, to team up, to see the big picture. People are not paid by the hour, but are paid for results and contribution. There are no 9 to 5 jobs at Logitech.

## A Sense of Passion, Dedication and Commitment, from Top to Bottom

When Borel was looking to hand over the reins of the company to a new CEO in 1998, he too pointed to the importance of the cultural fit between the existing organization and the person he would ultimately choose. It was important to him that his successor should have strong global experience, be a charismatic leader, have known business success and failure, and most importantly be passionate. He explains:

> I felt that I would want my child – Logitech – to be happy and successful, and I wanted to get a replacement for myself who was passionate!

The CEO he selected, Guerrino De Luca, had been Apple's executive vice president for worldwide marketing. He brought with him the experience of a company that Logitech had long admired for its passion to create exciting new products with revolutionary designs. But he had also learned, through new product failures, to remain humble. The duo – the chairman and his CEO – shared the same passion but expressed it differently, as a regional sales and marketing vice president comments:

> The key to the success of Logitech over the last years has been the power and energy that Daniel and Guerrino can create together. Guerrino is an excellent businessman, excellent marketer. He is a tough guy when things are not working well, and he can be very

demanding. He is brilliant on the operating side. Then you take Daniel who is more of an entrepreneur and a visionary, a little bit more of a dreamer, excellent for PR. He is a very charismatic person. The team is a very good team. They work well together.

One of the attributes of successful organizations is their attention and dedication to their core business, as Logitech realized during the crisis it faced in the early 1990s. It had temporarily lost sight of its bread and butter product – the mouse – as it turned to other products. An engineering vice president elaborates:

Dedication is key. You need people living, breathing, dreaming these products all the time. The worst thing we did, 10 years ago, was having the mature business almost die. The new business is so much more 'sexy' than the core business – you need to keep attention on the core business.

Financial incentives are obviously a strong driver at Logitech – the stock boom of the late 1990s made a significant number of millionaires among the 'old-timers' with stock options – but they are never the main driver. What fires employees with enthusiasm is the job content. The fact that they see the fruits of their labor in products sold worldwide is one of the most tangible positive attributes of working there, as the same engineering vice president reflects:

Some engineers doing the soldering have a million in their bank account! And those people still continue working! They haven't changed anything in their life . . . they just continue to have this passion for their job.

## A Global Mindset

Logitech prides itself on its truly global culture, taking the best of each of the cultures of its various locations: Swiss engineering rigor and sense of perfection; US marketing and innovation finesse; Irish design excellence; Taiwanese pragmatic engineering talent and Chinese cost-consciousness. Interestingly, in each location, the company is perceived as a local manufacturer. Top management makes sure that local managers staff each operation. Yet, staff exchanges across labs and offices are frequent.

Besides facilitating inter-office cooperation, this global mindset provides a 'reality check' on competition and removes any tendency to be complacent, as a Swiss project leader noted after a three-year posting in Taiwan:

> Being in Taiwan gives you a strong sense of rivalry. The competition is just behind you. Copycat products generally appear six months after you launch an innovation. You have that in the US as well! The dangerous place is Switzerland because you do not see competition. It removes your sense of urgency. If Logitech had remained Swiss, it would have gone bust years ago!

## A Willingness to Empower and Trust People Based on Openness and Sharing

From its time as a start-up, Logitech has retained a strong culture of encouraging personal initiatives and empowering its managers. In the technical area, this means giving project responsibilities to young engineers fairly early in their careers, but with coaching assistance. In all cases, it means encouraging staff to ask for help in case of problems. A regional sales and marketing vice president comments:

> As a manager at Logitech, if you have an issue, if you have a problem, you typically go to your boss or other managers and ask for advice on how to resolve it. At another Swiss multinational company I worked for, if you had a problem, you tried your best to hide it because if anyone else found out about it they'd use it to stab you in the back.

In the markets, empowerment means letting executives run their business without too much interference, as a regional sales and marketing vice president confirms:

> Take our General Manager–France. He's like an entrepreneur. He's got a team of 12 people, he's got a lot of pressure on him, but he runs Logitech France as if it were his own company. And I think it's hard to work in a more centralized organization after you are used to that concept. If you empower people, it's certainly a motivating factor. Our philosophy is to find the right people in the local markets and empower them. A long time ago, we realized that you couldn't fully understand and manage it from a distance.

## A Willingness to Take Risks and Accept Failure

Taking risks is not only tolerated but also encouraged, and that suggests an acceptance of failure. Logitech products tend to be near-perfect technically and functionally, but some have fizzled out on the market. Borel is the first to recognize that the Logitech museum, at the Swiss headquarters, contains a number of great products that did not make it. Many of these products, like the world's first digital camera, were simply introduced too early. Borel's belief that you should not punish failure – failure is part of the game – is seconded by an engineering director:

> There is a 'no-blame' culture at Logitech, although it depends on the size of the mistake and how many times you repeat it. I have made a certain number of serious mistakes in the company in the almost 14 years I have been there – one where I should have been in much trouble. But my boss dismissed it saying 'You know, you have several successes, so that is good.'

## A Preference for an Informal, Hands-on Management Style

To the visiting outsider, Logitech managers – from Borel and De Luca down to the more junior operating level – share common traits:

(1) A strong sense of congeniality and informality. People deal across hierarchical levels on a first-name basis and dress casually.
(2) A pragmatic, hands-on management style. This style is described vividly by the business unit head of control devices:

> I am a fairly involved executive. I am involved in product updates, and through these updates, the questions that I ask and the discussions we end up in are critical to people feeling what is important to me; it helps reinforce some of the priorities and values I want to convey. And secondly, it helps people feel a better sense that management cares, understands, appreciates and is sensitive to what the challenges are.

## A Focus on Realism and Rigor in Execution

Through its past experience as an OEM supplier and its financial crisis in the early 1990s, Logitech learned the hard way the importance of rigor in execution, the nitty-gritty part of innovation. Borel himself recognizes that some of the biggest flops the company experienced in the past – for example, Logitech's 'Photoman,' the first digital camera on the market – were caused by a lack of realism. In the case of the first digital camera, the technology turned out to be expensive, making the product too special, hence with a limited market potential.

A senior manager sums up the need for such implementation rigor, given the size of his business unit and the kinds of volumes he is dealing with on an annual basis:

> If I have a problem, a major issue – if I need to recall 500 000 mice – I'm dead!

## An Acceptance of Constructive Confrontation

Logitech managers are expected to speak their mind, and challenging each other is accepted, as a young program manager explains:

> There are tons of conflicts but we have to solve them. I often disagree with my boss. If the conflict is irrational, based on gut feel, then you are in trouble. But, in most cases, the conflicts are about facts, not people.

Senior managers make a point of living by the tacit rule, as one of them stresses:

> We are probably about as democratic as a company can get. If people question my decisions, I'll sit down – I won't throw them out of my office – and I'll talk to them, no matter who it is, and if the person comes back to me with some good valid points, then I'll change my mind.

But some managers see things a bit differently and fear that the culture is becoming too tolerant. When asked whether managers challenged each other as peers, i.e. across business or product units, a senior technologist declared:

> We are a very gentle company . . . too much sometimes! We are very friendly with each other. Sometimes, we are not challenging enough. Many times I complained that we are too gentle. So, Guerrino is pushing to have the business units working more and more together. He forces them to challenge each other on how we can differentiate ourselves from our competitors.

## A Quest for 24-hour Efficiency

Time, not just cost-efficiency, is a real concern at Logitech, and the company is an eager adopter of new information and communication technologies. Engineering and manufacturing databases are centralized and accessible by all engineers, no matter where they are located worldwide. E-mail and web-based messenger services are used extensively, and the people in the company are avid users of the company's latest innovations.

More surprisingly, perhaps, the company promotes absolute transparency to ensure that everyone is working with the same information. Many documents – even the more strategic ones – are available online to all people potentially concerned. And some managers go so far as to encourage people to work on e-mail during meetings, recognizing that not all issues are relevant to all attendees.

The location of Logitech's engineering offices and plants in all corners of the world helps make optimal use of a 24-hour day, as a senior technologist explains:

> When I have a problem one evening, I can explain it by e-mail to my colleagues in California. They will work on it while I'm asleep, then possibly pass it on to our colleagues in China or Taiwan to work on. When I get back to the office the next morning, more often than not, I find an answer to my questions.

## Healthy Humility and Restraint with Regard to Success

Borel, De Luca and their senior managers know full well that Logitech's success, in terms of market and financial performance, is never assured. They realize innately that a single big failure in the product introduction pipeline or a momentary drying up of product creativity will knock the company off its pedestal. This is why they promote a sense of humility, as a business unit vice president stresses:

> Unless you are paranoid, you will sit back, be comfortable and rest on your successes and say, 'I know what is happening out there.' We listen, we are humble when it comes to competition, and part of that humbleness comes from experience. Logitech has had its share of cycles, good and bad, and that reinforces that this success could all vanish tomorrow!

When asked what worries him the most, De Luca conveys the same message:

> My worry? We talk a lot about success; that worries me! We shouldn't become complacent. If you know how to analyze your failures, you learn so much! The degree of leadership and determination to change things should increase with the amount of success. It is difficult to change when things are going well. The idea that 'it worked before' is prevalent. You have to shake the organization to make people change.
>
> There are three types of companies when it comes to managing through crises:
>
> - The bad companies: They fail when the crisis arrives;
> - The good companies: They react well to the crisis;
> - The great companies – and they are few: They work ahead of the crisis to avoid it.[5]

In that spirit, when presented with the list of innovation drivers and values listed above, De Luca reacts with genuine humility:

> The description of Logitech that you seem to be giving is definitely what we would like to be. If it works – sometimes – this is what we are, but not always![6]

## In Conclusion: A Family or a Community?

To the casual visitor, Logitech may conjure up the image of a vibrant 'family,' and managers with long service in the company often refer to the 'family atmosphere' inherited from its early period. As with most families, there are occasional tensions between members, but somehow, there seems to be a kind of common bond that unites them. As the company is reaching a significant size, De Luca prefers to talk about a 'community' rather than a 'family':

> If family spirit means knowing everyone in the organization and being familiar with everyone, then I believe that we have passed that stage. We have grown too big for that. But for me, family spirit means that everyone within the organization believes in the same things, sharing the same vision and values. If everyone lives by these values and is aligned behind them, then they are part of your family. It is a community rather than a family in the traditional sense of the term.[7]

## LOGITECH'S PRAGMATIC AND EFFECTIVE INNOVATION PROCESS

### Market- and Competition-oriented Strategy and Planning

Given its dynamic industry environment and demanding investors, Logitech feels the need to be on top of its sales forecasts and budgets on a regular basis. Three-day operational meetings are held every quarter with the full top management team (the CEO and all of his vice presidents). Their main focus is to review quarterly business unit results and plans and discuss product and technology roadmaps. In parallel, budgets are redone each quarter based on prevailing market conditions. For example, projects are reprioritized if there is more or less money than originally budgeted. Products, markets, sales and competition take up the majority of these meetings.

In addition, every January a more restricted group of top managers meets for a strategic planning retreat off-site. During that retreat, participants typically review a three-year roadmap of each business unit, new business ventures and the upcoming annual budget. Time is also spent discussing the core competences of the company, its vision, mission and values.

## Company-wide Market, Competitor and Customer Intelligence

Logitech has two marketing functions which provide insights into the market. The regional sales and marketing organizations are in day-to-day contact with customers and retailers, and thus indirectly with competitors. Their focus is clearly on selling, not creating, new products. Nevertheless, they provide invaluable insights into market developments, channel strategies, competitors' perceived tactical moves, and customer reactions, albeit within a rather short time horizon.

The product marketing organizations within each business and product unit are responsible for integrating all market inputs, developing product strategies and roadmaps, and specifying the new products to be developed.

Engineering departments are also deeply involved in discussions on market trends and customer preferences, as well as in decisions on product design and features. At Logitech, senior engineering heads are expected to be 'market-savvy' and to think about more than just their function. The company culture requires that everyone wear a broad corporate hat. At the end of the day, their bonus is structured not just on engineering metrics but also on how well their unit performs and how well Logitech performs.

Logitech's senior management recognizes that the company is far from having developed a good grasp of the motivations and unarticulated needs of its customers, as one of its business unit vice presidents comments:

> I would honestly say, and maybe this is part of our humbleness, that we are not yet a very good customer company today. We can get a lot better. We can raise the bar in lots of different areas. How close are we to the customer? We don't know as much as we think! Talking about that, challenging that, forces us to raise the bar, dig deeper, do things to get closer. I think one of our big challenges is to find out why someone buys a cordless mouse versus a cordless desktop with mouse included? What is their behavior? What is their decision process? Where do we go from here? We are not going for the early adopters anymore.

## Increasingly Structured Idea Generation and Concept Development

Logitech's top management has traditionally given its business units a great deal of freedom in developing ideas into concepts and turning concepts into commercially viable products. Historically, the company did not try to enforce a common, stereotyped process across the business units. The degree of formalization varied greatly from unit to unit. Some product unit heads were perceived as relatively structured, and they used systematic approaches and tools for generating and screening ideas. Others were perceived more as 'mavericks,' relying much more on gut feel or intuition. But as the company prepares for its next phase of growth, it has undertaken to implement more uniform, structured methods, which are becoming accepted because they are leading to successful product introductions.

## Simple but Disciplined Product Creation and Development

Logitech has implemented a simple but rigorous process company-wide to steer its product creation projects, which typically last from 6 (for product extensions) to 18 months (for totally new concepts). This process leaves the project teams a lot of day-to-day freedom, but it requires them to prepare for, and pass, four tough management reviews, or 'toll gates,' before commercial launch. These gates are passed in the course of animated meetings attended by the business and product unit heads, as well as senior engineering and marketing managers.

The first one is called *Gate 0* or *Project Authorization Gate*. This first review gives a group within Logitech the license to work on the project. The debates involved at this level include whether the new product concept is interesting and promising enough, and whether the company should spend money on it.

The most important gate is the next one, *Gate 1* or *Go Gate*. Here, the team is supposed to articulate the full product concept convincingly to management, and to present prototypes that validate its technical feasibility. The team is also asked to present the key elements of its business case, including market and sales volume estimates, detailed price and cost assumptions and the resulting margins after deduction of expected marketing and distribution costs. Finally, the team is expected to commit to the broad project deliverables in terms of development cost, schedule and performance. A key 'deliverable' is the product 'availability date' – the date when shipments to retailers can start. Each element of the plan is scrutinized, and not many proposals make it through the *Go Gate* at the first attempt. Management gets involved in the details, probes financial, operational and marketing aspects of the plan, and asks as many questions as it needs to feel comfortable with the project. Management's tough stance is intended to minimize potential issues down the road, silence the strongest critics and appeal to the most discerning customers once the product is launched in the market.

The next gate, *Gate 2*, is held well before mass production. All plans are carefully scrutinized once again before committing to suppliers and building millions of dollars of inventory. For totally new products, a final market check is conducted prior to this decision point.

A final gate, *Gate X*, is a review of the entire customer experience with the product. A product cannot go into mass production if it does not meet Logitech's standards for what a customer should experience with the product.

In between these gates, the overall project responsibility lies in the hands of the program manager, reflecting a decentralized management style. Each week, project leaders for specific modules of the overall project report on the status of their individual modules to the program manager, and an entry into a Notes® database ensures speedy project status updates within the rest of the organization. An engineering program manager comments:

> At Logitech, a program manager does not have to do detailed reporting on a project unless there is a problem. He/she is the only person who ultimately makes the decision of what to communicate to management. There is a lot of trust from management. But, of course, project leaders are coached at the beginning, either by their functional manager or by their program manager.

The program manager summarizes the status of his team's progress through a system of green, yellow or red flags posted on the project tracking system. If, during the course of the project, a problem or delay occurs, a 'yellow flag' is raised, triggering notifications to all involved. The project manager is still responsible for tackling the problem. But if it gets out of control, a 'red flag' alerts senior management. The business unit head is the only person empowered to alter the project schedule and reset the product availability date.

## Extensive Use of External Design and Manufacturing Supply Sources

Logitech has kept its own manufacturing centralized in a large plant in Shuzhu in China. But more than 50% of the company's manufacturing – in terms of cost – is outsourced in several different locations. De Luca explains:

> We have two types of outsourcing partners:
>
> • Contract manufacturers: We specify and design the product and hand the whole manufacturing process over to our partners who produce, test, assemble and package the products for us, and provide the logistics.
> • Original design manufacturers (ODMs): We define the product description and specification, and they go and design it for us, then they build it for us.
>
> There is a single leadership for worldwide operations, but we have lots of distributed operations. So, at this stage, we don't need to split totally – and probably won't need to do so for three or four more years. The benefits of synergy in operations still prevail over the disadvantages of increased complexity.[8]

## Increasingly Prudent Product Launch Decisions

In the past, the decision of whether or not to launch a new product was sometimes based on pragmatic gut feel, intuition and first impressions, as a business unit engineering vice president explains:

The user may react to a product design – it may be a conscious or an unconscious reaction – but the fact that we have dealt with such questions for over 25 years makes us see what the user feels but will not express. Sometimes, when the mouse is too big or some functions are not well positioned, the user is not going to say it because he cannot compare one device to another. He will buy it, use it and get used to it. But at the end of the day, by having the experience of the full range, you can predict what the user is going to say and what he is going to feel but not going to be able to express.

Increasingly, to support this intuitive approach of predicting the success (or failure) of a new product, Logitech conducts usability testing through focus groups. Users are carefully monitored and videotaped while doing various activities, from taking the sealed package and opening it to getting accustomed to using the product. Logitech immediately begins to recognize patterns, as the same engineering vice president notes:

You need no more than 10 users to get very good feedback – 80% of what you need to know you can get from 10 users picked from among random buyers.

The company is aware that over 50% of revenues in the year ahead typically come from products that have not been manufactured yet, and people realize how critical the product launch process is to the company. The engineering vice president emphasizes the challenge:

We bet the whole company on an annual basis. If the product platform does not work, we are going to have a 12-month negative cycle.

## 'On the Ball' Sales and Marketing

Once the products have been engineered and manufactured, it is time for sales and marketing to do their magic and translate the engineered new concept into revenues and satisfied customers. Products, however, do not sell themselves and it takes a great deal of salesmanship to get them on store shelves, as a regional sales and marketing vice president explains:

> We have excellent products, but there are a lot of beautiful products that do not sell. If you want to succeed in a company like ours, you have to be a super salesman. You need to have a very strong customer focus. You need to be able to generate revenue for the company. But you also need to be a general manager.

Logitech benefits from a strong brand franchise, slowly built through clever word-of-mouth, selective advertising, striking packaging design and aggressive merchandizing. Yet, there are limitations to what the brand can do, as the same sales and marketing executive stresses:

> In a relatively complicated consumer electronics environment where people don't always understand what they are buying, I believe you tend to put more faith in brands. A brand has to bring value. But in this day and age, you cannot overcharge based on brand. If you are competitively priced, if the value proposition you are offering is just as good as a Taiwanese product, then our brand might bring us to a 15% to 20% premium, but you've got limits on that.

## Proactive, Opportunity-focused New Business Development

The business development group is responsible for scoping out potential partnerships and acquisitions outside the current business areas of the three existing business units. It considers external proposals (both solicited and not) and directs potentially interesting opportunities to the appropriate individuals within the organization. The group does not look for new technologies as such, but for new business opportunities. Scanning the horizon for disruptive technologies is left to the individual business units, which are aided in the process by a senior technologist acting as an advisor to the process. The business development vice president comments:

> Early on in the process, we realized that some of the company's assets and strengths were a very strong brand and access to channels, plus an ability to define what people might buy. One way to leverage this is not necessarily to reinvent all products and product lines, but to accept proposals from the outside world.

When they receive a proposal that meets the necessary criteria, they put a team of people together from different business units: product marketing, operations, and engineering, and work aggressively on turning the opportunity into something tangible.

The io™ digital pen was a typical outcome of this process. Anoto, a Swedish high-tech company, had commercialized its core technology within the mobile phone market. Logitech's business development team steered Anoto into the PC environment, created a product strategy around it, and successfully sold the concept to both Anoto's and Logitech's executive management.

To be accepted into the organization, new ventures brought to the table have to be reasonably close to existing areas of business to benefit from potential synergies in technology, operations, and sales and marketing.

## LOGITECH'S FUTURE CHALLENGES

### Specific Management Concerns

When asked about the main challenges he sees for the future, De Luca mentions three concerns:

> My first challenge? The invisible barriers, or the issue of scalability of our processes. Each company sets a certain way of working at a certain stage in its life. How far can that way of working – the processes – be extended as the company grows? Example: We have a product launch machine. Our process of launch until recently was defined for 10 to 15 new products per year. If you launch 60 to 100 new products a year (as we are doing routinely now), your process may reach its limit, beyond which it will not be scalable and the number of risks you take becomes intolerable. So, which of our processes are not scalable, and what can we inject, in terms of change, before a crisis comes around?
>
> My second challenge? Marrying innovation and costs. Developing meaningful innovations and driving costs down are inextricably linked, and yet the two are not put on the same level. We hold 'patent dinners' to reward our innovators. But we have not yet established 'cost dinners' to honor those who have shaved costs from our products. We need to develop an absolute obsession on costs

in a creative way and reward people for it. We are moving into higher price points (for example top-end speakers marketed under our Logitech brand in the $300 to $400 range), but that does not mean that we want to push our entire line up. What is happening, simply, is that we are stretching our product line to the top, offering higher points for selling up, but we do not want to lose track of the entry-point product (we have a mouse that retails at $9). This is why we need to maintain our cost leadership.

My third challenge? Entering new categories that we are creating (as with the Harmony remote or the Squeezebox network music player). There are multiple marketing needs – customer insights, building awareness, creating demand, educating people about the benefits of the solution. Our marketing teams need to be creative about how to address these challenges cost effectively.

Entering a category that exists (like audio equipment) we know how to do. The problem is when you create a new category, such as is the case with our newly acquired Squeezebox. I tell my people: 'Look at Palm, when they created the PDA category; copy what they did.' We have good marketers, but I am afraid that they are 'classic marketers,' they look at it in a traditional way. Their first approach is to say, 'This is the budget we need.' Their solution to the problem is to spend $10 million on it. My reaction is, 'Go back to the drawing board and come back with another approach.' I tell them, 'This is a new challenge! Create some buzz, interest and curiosity in the market, and make sure to satisfy the early adopters. Don't disappoint them if you want them to promote the product by word-of-mouth advertising.'[9]

## The Perennial Questions of a Fast-growing High-tech Start-up

More generally, beyond these specific management concerns, Logitech confronts the classical challenges of fast-growing high-tech start-ups. Since the company established itself as the leader in digital peripherals at the turn of the century, its senior managers have always wondered how far, where and how they can continue to grow, and whether they can keep growing without losing some of their original start-up qualities. A number of questions remain on their minds:

- Can we keep meeting the market's expectations quarter by quarter? What will happen if our markets saturate? How do we find new growth opportunities in a maturing market?
- How can we continue to rejuvenate, redefine and reinvent our core businesses? Can we constantly top the last successful product? What unarticulated customer needs (if any) should we go after?
- How will we continue to find new businesses that can leverage our core design, manufacturing and branding strengths, and that will fit with our comfort zone in terms of price points, volumes and channels?
- Will we be able to leverage our key technical, operational and marketing strengths to enter new markets that may be further away from our familiar digital peripheral world, for example in the mobile and home entertainment areas?
- Will our current organizational culture and leadership resources bring us to the next stage in our growth? How do we expand without losing our start-up mentality?
- How can we maintain our innovative informal culture and keep growing at the same time? Will our current organization be able to cope with more complexity, in terms of countries, channels, segments and products?
- What new leadership talents are required to steer the company in all these promising new directions? What should top management do, specifically, to define, detect and groom such talent?

These challenges are formidable. However, given its strong innovation leadership environment, Logitech may be more prepared to handle them than many of its bigger or smaller competitors.

## ENDNOTES

1. This chapter is adapted from the case 'Innovation Leadership at Logitech' by Atul Pahwa under the supervision of the author (2003) IMD Case No. IMD-3-1337. Unless otherwise specified, all the management quotes cited in this chapter are extracted from that case.

2. 'Logitech's Vision/Mission over the Years,' undated internal company document.
3. 'Logitech's Vision/Mission over the Years,' undated internal company document.
4. 'Logitech's Vision/Mission over the Years,' undated internal company document.
5. Author's personal interview, on 27 June 2003, with Guerrino De Luca, Logitech's president and CEO, updated in November 2007, reproduced with permission.
6. Author's personal interview, on 27 June 2003, with Guerrino De Luca, Logitech's president and CEO, updated in November 2007, reproduced with permission.
7. Author's personal interview, on 27 June 2003, with Guerrino De Luca, Logitech's president and CEO, updated in November 2007, reproduced with permission.
8. Author's personal interview, on 27 June 2003, with Guerrino De Luca, Logitech's president and CEO, updated in November 2007, reproduced with permission.
9. Author's personal interview, on 27 June 2003, with Guerrino De Luca, Logitech's president and CEO, updated in November 2007, reproduced with permission.

# CHAPTER 12

# ATTRACTING, DEVELOPING AND KEEPING INNOVATION LEADERS

*Those leadership competencies that you see developing have to be coached, corrected, and you need to give people with the right talent and the right profile step-by-step challenges that fit those profiles, or lead those profiles to develop. People have a lot of latent capabilities. It is a matter of challenging them in those capabilities to develop them.*[1]

Ad Huijser, former CEO of Philips Research

Having read all the chapters of this book so far, you may be tempted to compare the innovation leadership environment that they describe with the realities in your company. You can probably point to a number of talented and motivated individuals who make up your current and potential innovation leadership pool. Some may be creative types; others may be reliable, execution-oriented leaders. But you may question whether they truly belong to the innovation leader category and whether your company has enough of them to make a difference.

Indeed, for innovation – as for many other important corporate challenges – isolated leaders are unlikely to be effective. You need to reach a minimum critical mass to influence the rest of the organization. And you may wonder how to proceed to build a cadre of energized innovation leaders in your organization. These fundamental questions are, unfortunately, the most difficult to answer and there is no ready-made model to help you in these critical tasks. This domain remains relatively unexplored and warrants new research and tool development activities. I shall nevertheless try to address these questions with some of the lessons from this book.

## ASSESSING YOUR INNOVATION LEADERSHIP RESOURCES

### Have You Identified Your Innovation Leaders?

It is generally quite easy to determine who the innovation leaders are in a company. Ask middle or senior managers to point out some of their colleagues, subordinates or bosses whose management behavior – they intuitively feel – fits the description, at least in the way they imagine the role. Indeed, innovation leaders tend to have personalities that others easily associate with innovation. Of the six attributes of innovation leaders proposed in Chapter 2, three are easily noticeable by everyone:

- Their acceptance of uncertainty, risks and failures, which translates into a willingness to experiment.
- Their almost infectious passion for innovation, which often leads to deep personal involvement in innovation projects.
- Their innate ability – one could even call it 'magnetic' – to attract innovators into their teams. People are attracted by their kind.

These three attributes are often the insignia of those managers characterized as 'front-end' innovation leaders.

The other three attributes in the list – a mix of creativity and discipline; openness to external technologies; and willingness to stop, not just start, projects – are generally less frequently noticed, at least at middle management level. They tend to be associated with the behavior of senior and top managers.

Authentic innovation leaders, particularly if they are in top management, are often the subject of stories that highlight their unique character. Surprisingly, anecdotes of how these leaders influenced others continue to circulate even after the leaders in question have left their company or retired. I was able to witness this in the course of a business school program with senior executives from a variety of multinational companies. After introducing the innovation leadership concept and asking the participants to describe a person whom they believed fitted the bill, a senior manager from Nestlé proposed his former boss, Rupert Gasser, a former executive vice president of the company, now retired.[2]

Gasser is well known within Nestlé for having led one of the company's most important and successful strategic business groups – coffee and beverages, milk and food services – and, in this position, having sponsored the highly successful Nespresso™ business. He also headed Nestlé's corporate technical, manufacturing and R&D activities worldwide, being de facto and simultaneously the company's chief manufacturing, technology and innovation officer. However, that manager was not referring to his official functions, but to his behavior as an innovation leader. The two anecdotes he recalled are worth sharing here, because they do more to characterize an innovation leader than many long academic discourses.

The manager in question was trying to solve a complex problem in a chocolate manufacturing plant. He came up with a solution and went to Gasser to present his idea. Upon hearing his solution, Gasser apparently said, 'I don't think that your idea will work; I tried it years ago and it didn't work out. But, I am willing to have you try it . . . and I am even willing to give you some money to try it, because unless you find out by yourself that it won't work, you will be so enthused with your solution that you won't try anything else.' The manager tried and discovered, just as Gasser had warned, that his idea did not work. This – he confessed – taught him a big lesson on the value of always envisaging alternative solutions.

The second story concerns a female manager who had come up with a risky project about which she felt very strongly, but which she had to sell to Gasser. Fearing the notoriously tough challenging that was the mark of her boss, she prepared herself for all kinds of objections. After hearing her present her project, Gasser apparently told her, 'Go ahead with your project. I see your eyes are shining, which means that you are passionate about it. So, you will succeed thanks to your passion!'

Prominent innovation leaders of the caliber and status of Gasser are, obviously, easy to notice. Others can be spotted just by looking around, asking colleagues and listening to stories. Yet others may remain more discreet. They will be detected only by combing through the company's project track records and cross-checking the names behind successful innovation projects.

Whichever way they are identified, if these leaders constitute a precious resource, one wonders why so few companies ask their HR talent managers to build a list of innovation leaders and keep track of them. It is, indeed, reasonable to believe that if innovation rates high on the corporate agenda, then CEOs should be aware of their pool of innovation leaders, i.e. they should find out:

- the number and type of innovation leaders that have been identified (front-end vs. back-end leaders);
- any changes in their number – whether it is increasing or decreasing (in which case this should ring alarm bells);
- their seniority and the level in the organization at which they are operating (top management vs. second or third management levels);
- their distribution across business units and functions (e.g. between marketing and R&D) in order to identify gaps.

## Do Your Leadership Resources Match Your Strategy?

Besides formally identifying their innovation leaders, CEOs should investigate whether they have the *right kind*. This means checking that they have the appropriate leaders for their innovation strategy.

Chapter 6 introduced a simple model for characterizing an innovation strategy. It defined four generic innovation thrusts, based on their objective, scope, intensity and boundaries:

- the development of *new/improved* products or services;
- the creation of a *totally new* product or service category;
- the creation of a *totally new* business system or model; and
- the development of *new/improved* customer solutions.

Management should clearly define which of these thrusts the company wants to pursue as a priority, overall or – if different – for each of its business units. This is important because, as highlighted in Chapter 6, each thrust requires a specific enabling *process*, a different structural *mechanism*, particular *cultural traits*, and a distinctive *staff profile*. And each thrust will respond specifically to a different *change lever*.

Chapters 7 to 10 emphasized the particular leadership focus required to implement each of these four thrusts and the metaphoric vignettes that characterize their leaders – team sports coach; no-nonsense sponsor; pragmatic architect and orchestra conductor. These priorities and styles are summarized in Figure 12.1.

At this stage, a word of warning is necessary. Although it is based on the behavior patterns of actual innovation leaders, a characterization of this nature can – quite justifiably – be perceived as somewhat arbitrary and oversimplified. One could argue that all these leadership styles are relevant and important for innovation at various times, irrespective of the thrust chosen. There are indeed a number of overlaps in focus across these four thrusts, as underlined in Figure 12.2.

So, one could argue that true innovation leaders should possess all the qualities mentioned in this book, and that they should

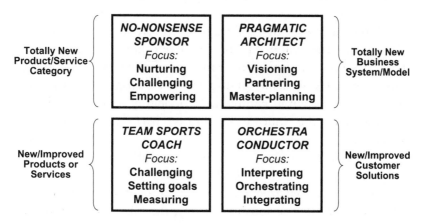

**Figure 12.1** Specific leadership style and focus for each innovation thrust

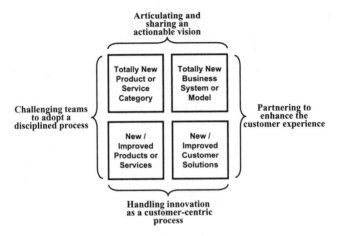

**Figure 12.2** The common leadership imperatives of innovation thrusts

combine in the same person all the leadership styles attributed to each thrust. However, this may not be realistic. As in other management areas, individual innovation leaders have their own strengths and weaknesses; they will be most effective when they are deployed on innovation thrusts that largely leverage their qualities and leadership style. It is therefore up to the CEO to ensure that his/her top management team includes the innovation leadership styles that are needed to support the company's innovation strategy.

Companies with the ambition to embark on a multi-faceted innovation thrust will need a broad range of innovation leadership styles. It is thus interesting to review the personalities and intuitive leadership styles available among the top management team and map them, as shown in Figure 12.3, to identify resources and gaps, and therefore the innovation thrusts that can or cannot be launched.

Broader-based leaders may exhibit a combination of styles that will make them suitable to lead different types of thrusts. Others may be more specialized and should be deployed only on the thrusts that fit their personality. Finally, the CEO may realize that some innovation thrusts might be jeopardized if there is no leader with a suitable style. Of course, the broader the company's inno-

What is the profile of our current innovation leaders?

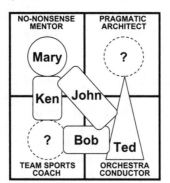

Are we lacking certain profiles given our innovation strategy?

**Figure 12.3**    Mapping innovation resources according to leadership styles

vation leadership pool, the greater its competitive advantage, since this will allow it to pursue a broad range of innovation thrusts in parallel.

Based on these considerations, management should ask the following questions:

- What particular leadership focus and style is required to lead each of the innovation thrusts we have chosen?
- Do we have the leaders who match these profiles within our organization and can they be put in charge of these thrusts?
- If we do not have appropriate leadership resources, can we develop or acquire them reasonably fast?
- If we cannot access these resources in the foreseeable future, should we change our innovation strategy?

## SELECTING AND HIRING INNOVATION LEADERS

Senior innovation leaders tend to promote or hire managers who share the same values as they do, and who will continue to promote the innovation agenda in their company. When they talk about the criteria they use to select, hire and promote future innovation leaders, four words come up again and again: *Passion, mission, vision* and *performance*. Steve Jobs at Apple summarizes it convincingly when he says:

> Ultimately, the results should lead you to the people. As a matter of fact, that's how I find great people. I look at great results and I find out who was responsible for them.
>
> However, sometimes young people haven't had the opportunity yet to be in a position of influence to create such results. So, here you must evaluate potential. It's certainly more difficult, but the primary attributes of potential are intelligence and the ability to learn quickly. Much of it is also drive and passion – hard work makes up for a lot.[3]

## Detecting Passion

Since passion is one of the common denominators of innovation leaders, it is not surprising that they aim to attract, select and hire passionate candidates. Logitech's leaders are no exception, as Daniel Borel emphasizes:

> We make a living, we exist, and we survive because of innovation. So, if someone does not share that passion, at every level, he/she should not join Logitech.[4]

When asked what they look for in a candidate, apart from basic intelligence and technical fit for the position, Logitech managers reply that they look for a sense of passion, emotion and connection with the product. A business unit vice president explains:

> I would like someone to give me a sense of love of products, not necessarily from Logitech. Someone who is passionate about the product is also going to be passionate about the user.[5]

Several other senior managers echo the same sentiments, suggesting that one can generally spot a candidate's enthusiasm at the job interview. One reason for Logitech's success, according to them, is that people believe in what the organization stands for and in the products that they are selling. But of course, that passion is expressed differently by different functions. Engineers are passionate about technologies and products; marketing and sales people about beating competitors.

Another innovation leader and former Nokia president Pekka Ala-Pietilä explains the importance of attitudes – not just talent – in his company's staff selection process:

> I don't believe that we can influence anyone's attitudes. We can only detect people who share what we see as critical attitudes for Nokia. We are not saying that our attitudes are right or wrong, but they are important for us, and we have to preserve and further cultivate them. And therefore, in our recruitment process, in promoting people, we pay special attention to that part of the personality. So you have to be professionally top, but that is not enough; that is a prerequisite. You have the attitude side, as well. You have to have this element of passion.[6]

Ala-Pietilä explains how he detects passion in the people who would like to work with Nokia, or in Nokia:

> If they want to learn, if they are curious, if they see that they can change the world, if they see in front of them that change is an opportunity, not a threat – a disruptive element is something which we can leverage, something which would be a springboard for us to do things better and differently – then we have people who have the passion, the passion to change the world, the passion to make things better, the passion always to strive for better results and always excel.[7]

Steve Jobs has a personal way to detect passion in job interviews, as he explains:

> Many times in an interview, I will purposely upset someone: I'll criticize their prior work. I'll do my homework, find out what they worked on and say, 'God, that really turned out to be a bomb. That really turned out to be a bozo product. Why did you work on that?' . . .
>
> What I look for is someone to come right back and say, 'You're dead wrong and this is why.' I want to see what people are like under pressure. I want to see if they just fold or if they have firm conviction, belief and pride in what they did. . . . If your company is a meritocracy of ideas, with passionate people, you have a company with a lot of arguments. If people can't stand up and argue well under pressure they may not do well in such an environment.[8]

## Demanding Devotion to the Company's Mission and Vision

Passion per se, despite being a great source of managerial energy, is not sufficient. It has to be embedded in a sense of purpose and channeled toward common objectives. And this is where the notion of mission fits in. Innovation leaders try to detect in job candidates an affinity with the company's declared mission and vision, which often reflects a deep interest in the company's products or services and in its customers.

Medtronic's founder, Earl Bakken, built his company on a strong sense of mission that former chairman and CEO Bill George continued to exalt and promote. He placed the company's mission at the heart of his leadership development efforts. He explains:

> The common denominator was that people were passionate about the mission. Even the chief information officer was passionate about the mission. Even the CFO – he used to get so excited . . . he would go out and see procedures and come back and say: 'Did you see what I saw?' I think people who had no passion, who were just purely process-oriented and had no passion for the patients, the doctors, the actual process of the company, did not fare very well in that culture. The mission – to restore people to full life and health – was the driving force. So when I interviewed people to come into the company in key roles, if I sensed they didn't have a passion for the mission, we didn't hire them.[9]

A strong understanding of and dedication to the company's mission is a guarantee that the new hire, particularly if he/she is a senior manager, will pull in the right direction. But companies express their mission very differently, of course. For a company in life-saving or health-restoring medical devices like Medtronic, the mission is easy to communicate. For Logitech, the mission reflects the company's sense of identity and builds on its *raison d'être*, as Daniel Borel stresses:

> We have a very strong vision and mission of who we are and what we do. . . . So, as we evolve, we have to hire new people who have new skills in new areas, and those people need to be trained in the same way. We can never repeat enough the 'who we are' to make it alive. . . .

So this is why it is so important to have a shared vision. When we say: 'We are going to be the interface company . . . We are going to allow the world to communicate, to digitally reach other people communicating, entertaining, getting information,' then you get from your organization, from everywhere, ideas, new ideas, which help you stay ahead.[10]

Adhering to the company's mission and vision is essential to become an innovation leader, but it is not sufficient. When he was at the helm of Medtronic, Bill George asked for more. He expected his new managers to have a vision of their own. He explains how he tested candidates' visioning ability:

Certainly, you could look at what they had done; you could listen to them talk; you could ask them what are their dreams, what are their hopes, what would they like to do, how they see the business evolve. And that would come through in those kinds of questions, whether they had vision. It wouldn't be about a specific vision – it is more the capacity to have a vision of where you want to take the company.

Of course, I am talking here about business . . . the people who ran the businesses. I am not talking about two or three levels below that; I am not talking about an engineering manager; not all engineering managers would have that level of vision. But the people who ran a business – say a hundred million dollar business or a billion dollar business – would have that kind of vision.[11]

## Setting High Performance Standards

Companies like Apple or Logitech, which are led by genuine innovation leaders, tend to look for innovation leadership skills in most of the managers they want to hire, and they set high personal standards both by their own behavior and their demands. Guerrino de Luca at Logitech is not shy about his expectations:

I need people that can think intelligently and learn fast. This means people who are not content with the obvious answer. People who are challengers! People who – because they have not done it before – bring elements of creativity and discipline. If I have to choose between two people for an important mission: Someone who has done it before and someone who has not done it before but is on his way up, then I choose the second one. We need hungry people who have something to prove . . . who take risks.[12]

Concerned about the danger of an excessively inbred culture – a risk faced by start-ups that have built their own culture and grown rapidly – De Luca does not think twice about looking for and bringing in very senior managers from outside the company. He justifies a policy that was relatively new at Logitech, which traditionally tended to hire mostly at the entry level:

> In the USA, over the course of 12 months, we have replaced 10% of our staff. We have hired to upgrade our capabilities. We are not simply adding people at the entry level like young engineers out of university. Some people in the executive committee were hired from outside. The heads of two out of three business units came from outside. I challenge those who advocate hiring only people at the entry level, because this assumes that we know it all. You have also to hire some people that have seen something else, and you have to be tolerant enough to accept them.[13]

Autonomy and speed in decision making and taking action are characteristics that Logitech expects from its leaders, as a regional sales and marketing vice president illustrates:

> We have people who are driven, self-motivated. I would rather have a 'Smart Alec,' fast-moving guy who irritates me on occasion, who I have to hold back, than a guy who's fast asleep, who I have to kick in the backside to get going. Experience is that the guy who's running fast has the intelligence that I am looking for. You can always hold him back and put him in the right direction. If you've got somebody that doesn't move fast, he's never going to move fast.[14]

At Medtronic also, innovation leaders are expected to be achievers, as Bill George stresses:

> [The people who ran a business had to have] the vision to see what needed to be done and a commitment to get it done. I think everyone had to have a commitment to perform – it is a performance-oriented culture, not a research-oriented culture! . . . So you needed that combination; it is an unusual combination of qualities: Passion, vision and performance![15]

## DEVELOPING INNOVATION LEADERS

As announced in Chapter 1, we shall avoid the classic academic traps of discussing whether leadership is an innate or developed talent, and whether you hire on attitudes and train for skills or vice versa, because the answer to the two questions is, obviously: Both; it depends on the individual.

The nurturing and development of innovation-oriented leaders is not very different from the way senior executives hone the leadership skills of their managers. In his best-seller *True North*, based on 125 interviews of top leaders conducted and written with Peter Sims, Bill George summarizes the key principles of an authentic leadership development philosophy:

- 'Mutual Respect: The Basis for Empowerment
  - Treating others as equals.
  - Being a good listener.
  - Learning from people.
  - Sharing life stories.
- Empowering People to Lead
  - Showing up.
  - Engaging people.
  - Helping teammates.
  - Challenging leaders.
  - Stretching people.
  - Aligning everyone around a mission.'[16]

All these principles obviously apply to the development of innovation leaders as well.

Moving from philosophy to best practices, in a 2007 survey on leadership development, conducted by a team of reporters under the direction of Geoff Colvin,[17] *Fortune* identified nine practices that best-in-class companies seem to share. They:

- invest time and money;
- identify promising leaders early;
- choose assignments strategically;
- develop leaders within their current jobs;

- are passionate about feedback and support;
- develop teams, not just individuals;
- exert leadership through inspiration;
- encourage leaders to be active in their communities;
- make leadership development part of the culture.

Most of these general leadership development practices are relevant for the development of innovation leaders, of course. Concretely, though, senior innovation leaders seem to rely on three complementary approaches:

- promoting an open yet challenging environment;
- giving innovation responsibilities to people early on;
- coaching aspiring innovation leaders.

## Promoting an Open yet Challenging Environment

It is probably safe to predict that innovation leaders will naturally develop and grow faster in an environment populated with other innovation leaders – like attracts like. This means that, in common with plain innovators, they need an environment characterized by a strong innovation culture to blossom.

An important element of any innovation culture, as stressed in the Logitech case featured in Chapter 11, is complete transparency and openness: Transparency on the strategic objectives being pursued and openness on information dissemination. Steve Jobs is an advocate of these two principles:

> You must offer them the ability to make larger decisions and to be part of the core company. That involvement is what drives much of this fun.
>
> For example, you want people to make key company decisions without you even knowing it. They'd better have access to most of the company's information, so you'd better have an open communication policy so that people can know just about everything, otherwise they will make important decisions without the right information.[18]

But leadership talents will not fully develop if they are not stretched and aligned with demanding performance goals. Here again, Steve

Jobs believes in the virtue of honing leadership skills by demanding the almost impossible, as he openly states:

> Part of the CEO's job is to cajole and beg and plead and threaten, at times – to do whatever is necessary to get people to see things in a bigger and more profound way than they have and to do better work than they thought they could do.
>
> When they do their best and you don't think it's enough, you tell them straight: 'This isn't good enough. I know you can do better. You need to do better. Now go do better.[19]

Guerrino De Luca is an adept of this philosophy, although his style would probably be perceived as less brutal than Steve Jobs's.

> I believe in the theory of pushing great people to the extreme. This is what I learned from Steve Jobs at Apple. He used to say: 'You drive a great person crazy and he will do things that no one ever thought possible!' You have no idea what people can do under pressure! When you put that kind of pressure on them, then they listen and say, 'We have to do better!' And then, they want to prove to you that they can do it.[20]

## Giving Innovation Responsibilities to People Early On

When asked about the best way to develop the next generation of innovation leaders, senior executives in innovative companies often stress the importance of testing the leadership skills of their young managers by giving them a concrete experience early on in their career. Medtronic's Bill George and his chief innovation officer – Glen Nelson – were strong proponents of this approach, as George remarks:

> I think the best development path is putting people on the right road, saying, 'Would you take over a venture – let's see how you do it . . . Put together a little team of 12 people, and let's see how it comes out . . . Would you take over this new business and run it? Start this business from scratch and see if you can create something there!' That is the real test.
>
> We used to take a lot of young MBAs and put them into these kinds of roles. Some did well, and some didn't do well. The

analytical ones didn't do so well, but the ones who were really innovative and creative would do quite well.

I used to say, 'It is better to have a record of seven wins and three losses than it is to have one and zero.' You don't want someone who has one success and is afraid to have a failure.

And then, we would give them succeeding levels of challenge – the young engineers, the young scientists who came into the company – to see if they could take that on. Give them a chance, a small budget – a small risk, you know – but see how it came out. And we took the creative ones and gave them more and more responsibility, bigger and bigger projects, more and more challenge.[21]

Daniel Borel at Logitech recommends a similar approach:

What is nice in a small company – I call it small; maybe it isn't small any more, but I still look at it this way – is the fact that no one is limited by anything. The sky is the limit. So, people who are creative, people who are actually taking risk and accepting challenges, who are successful in the company, can keep going up and up. So, I think that the sorting process is a very natural one: To grow the stars who are going to help us tomorrow, leading a new business or developing a business big time. And I think that this is really what is visible in the company. It doesn't mean that everyone must be like that; actually only a few of them are – and they are actually growing and going to the next level.

Basically, I think that it is only through empowerment and the ability to make mistakes that people will eventually develop, grow and be successful.[22]

## Coaching Aspiring Innovation Leaders

In technical environments, coaching is accepted as a way of developing a cadre of future R&D leaders. At Logitech, as part of the induction process, each engineer typically spends an hour or two with every functional manager within the engineering team, not just his/her own manager. This allows newcomers to understand what the issues, technologies and work processes are across the organization. It also encourages a culture of cross-collaboration between various product groups, promotes a family atmosphere and reduces tensions between product groups. An engineering program manager comments:

One of the key influencers is personal coaching. The engineering family coaches you. What we have is a strong learning process – it's not a process, it's more about information sharing. Part of the culture is transmitted in this one-to-one, or in small team sessions. It is a very informal learning, through coaching and observing.[23]

This type of coaching is widespread in most R&D organizations, as Ad Huijser from Philips stresses:

Coaching is a personal aspect. We have a very flat organization. This implies that the young researchers are very near the top of the research pyramid. And so, coaching is pretty simple – you always have senior people close by. And of course, as you manage your research organization – and for development it is identical – the leadership team knows what is going on on the floor. And through this, you influence leadership skills – in both directions, by the way – because today's researchers have a different starting point and mindset than the management that has, say, 20 years of experience.

Our leaders do it on the basis of their experience, and I think that, in a company like Philips with long experience in innovation, you have a kind of de facto feel for innovation leadership capabilities and how to deal with them. Of course, there is a dynamic, so you see changes over time. We look to business capabilities much more than ever before, and we see that in the selection of our managers.[24]

In technical environments, coaching is particularly important as it allows management to sense the direction aspiring leaders want to go, as Bill George explains:

We clearly gave our scientists and engineers coaching, and I think it is a question of what direction someone wanted to go . . . At a certain point in time, we would sit down with someone, and it was almost like a fork in the road, and you would say, 'Do you want to go in the direction of management, or do you want to go in the direction of pure science, pure innovation? Do you want to be an innovation leader, but with a lot of managerial responsibilities?' And many of them didn't want this – they didn't want the budgetary responsibilities, the financial responsibilities. They wanted just to be creative. And that is fine, you know![25]

## RETAINING INNOVATION LEADERS

Innovation leaders are so precious – and in some companies they are so rare – that the question of how to motivate and retain them is of prime importance. This is particularly true in highly technical areas, like in Philips Research, as Ad Huijser confirms:

> The mobility of people today is much higher than 20 years ago, in Europe and worldwide. As an example, here at the Philips Research labs in Eindhoven, of our new hires – roughly 150 per year – 40% come from abroad, whereas 20 years ago maybe 4% came from abroad. So, we have seen that mobility – going to work where there is nice work – has increased tremendously. So, retention is a challenge because people move easily.[26]

Whenever one talks about motivating and retaining high performance leaders, the issue of financial compensation soon comes up. It would be foolish to dismiss it as irrelevant, particularly in environments like Silicon Valley and for start-ups and fast-growing technology-based companies. But, somewhat surprisingly, innovation leaders who head companies stress two important motivating factors beyond financial compensation and the desire to get rich: Work and success.

### A Spirit of Challenge and Fun

Innovation leaders tend to love the work they do and the challenges they have to overcome to help their teams succeed, as Steve Jobs states:

> I think that, ultimately, it's the work that motivates people. I sometimes wish it were me, but it's not. It's the work. My job is to make sure the work is as good as it should be and to get people to stretch beyond their best. . . . In the end, it's the environment you create, the co-workers and the work that binds.[27]

Huijser emphasizes the same point, i.e. the importance of working on cool projects, on leading-edge technologies with and for people you admire:

> People move particularly to the areas or the places where the excitement is. I believe that, certainly in the technical domain, people

want to work at the leading edge. You want to be with the winners. So, what you have to do is stay leading . . . at the leading edge. If you fall behind, the first thing you will see is that the good people, the best people, move out. Of course we have bonuses, we have stock option plans and so forth, but for me, the best motivators are two things: One is the challenge of the work; and the second is the leadership – the fact that people want to work for you.[28]

There are probably many reasons for this emphasis on work satisfaction. First, innovation leaders tend to display a higher level of passion than other types of leaders for whatever they do, and they typically choose to work on innovation-related issues and projects – there is always an element of excitement and fun in innovation, whatever the industry. Second, innovation leads to tangible results – like promising new technologies and new product or service launches – and innovation leaders like the pride that goes with introducing something new that customers will 'like to buy and love to use,' as Logitech's Daniel Borel puts it. Third, innovation leaders love success.

## Success – Loving to Win

Borel probably expresses the opinion of many CEOs when he recognizes that success breeds success. Innovation leaders are attracted by opportunities and successful companies offer more opportunities than struggling ones:

At the end of the day, if you are a successful company, you attract people and they stay with you. If you come up with innovative products that people talk about, they will stay with you. Internally, you need to create this pride that belonging to our company is good. And you can see other companies which were very creative and attracted a lot of people. Suddenly, the formula changes, the market judges them differently, and they lose their attractiveness and their people. So I think success is the key![29]

# INNOVATION LEADERSHIP IN A NUTSHELL

To conclude our journey, we ought to leave the floor to the innovation leaders that we have used as a red thread throughout this book. Surprisingly, they express the same message with a slightly different emphasis but very similar words:

## Daniel Borel, Cofounder and Former Chairman of Logitech

> Innovation leadership?
> It is looking at things with the eyes of the customers . . . It is tolerating mistakes, accepting failure; learning from that – quickly; you don't have time to make a mistake twice, but don't crucify the mistake, otherwise you kill innovation . . . It is being passionate about what you are doing . . . It is being realistic, because there is no innovation if there is no execution which leads to products that allow you to make money.
> It is not only these many attributes, but also the way you play with them . . . The talent of an innovation leader is to ensure that all these ingredients are together, and to navigate that fine line to make it hold . . . And finally, it is the team! The innovation leader has to be a team leader, no doubt![30]

## Ad Huijser, Former CEO of Philips Research

> Innovation leadership?
> Risk taking . . . But I think it is more . . . People who show their organization that they have a vision of the future . . . that they, by hook or by crook, will make happen. And they walk the talk, they know how to motivate their people; they can make people enthusiastic to follow them . . . That is, I think, what innovation leadership is all about.[31]

## Bill George, Former Chairman and CEO of Medtronic

> Innovation leadership?
> Passion and inspiration; engagement; hands-on, being involved with the process itself; being curious; being open to new learning – it is a continuous learning process and when one stops learning, innovation ceases. And so, it is that mix of qualities that says, 'Let's find a better way to do things!' We have to continually learn how to do it better, we have to be curious, we have to be passionate about getting it done, we have to have a vision about what it could be,

not what it is. And then a commitment to perform, because that is the end.[32]

## Pekka Ala-Pietilä, Former President of Nokia

Innovation leadership?
It is passion; it is learning; it is humility in front of the mistakes and errors, understanding that they are necessary elements to learn faster than the others . . . And it is the target-setting . . . yes, stretched targets![33]

# ENDNOTES

1. Huijser, A. (2001). 'Leadership and Innovation.' Videotaped interview by J.-P. Deschamps, IMD, Lausanne, reproduced with permission.
2. In 2007, Rupert Gasser was vice-chairman of the board of directors of Syngenta, a chemical company, president of Nestec SA and a member of the scientific advisory board of Alcon Laboratories Inc.
3. Jager, R.D. and Ortiz, R. (1997). *In the Company of Giants: Candid Conversations with the Visionaries of the Digital World.* New York, McGraw-Hill, p. 14.
4. Borel, D. (2001). 'Leadership and Innovation.' Videotaped interview by J.-P. Deschamps, IMD, Lausanne, updated and edited by Daniel Borel in November 2007.
5. Pahwa, A. under the supervision of Deschamps, J.-P. (2003). 'Innovation Leadership at Logitech.' IMD Case No. IMD-3-1337.
6. Ala-Pietilä, P. (2001). 'Leadership and Innovation.' Videotaped interview by J.-P. Deschamps, IMD, Lausanne, reproduced with permission.
7. Ala-Pietilä, P. (2001). 'Leadership and Innovation.' Videotaped interview by J.-P. Deschamps, IMD, Lausanne, reproduced with permission.
8. Jager, R.D. and Ortiz, R. (1997). *In the Company of Giants: Candid Conversations with the Visionaries of the Digital World.* New York, McGraw-Hill, p. 15.
9. George, B. (2001). 'Leadership and Innovation.' Videotaped interview by J.-P. Deschamps, IMD, Lausanne, reproduced with permission.
10. Borel, D. (2001). 'Leadership and Innovation.' Videotaped interview by J.-P. Deschamps, IMD, Lausanne, updated and edited by Daniel Borel in November 2007.
11. George, B. (2001). 'Leadership and Innovation.' Videotaped interview by J.-P. Deschamps, IMD, Lausanne, reproduced with permission.
12. Author's personal interview, on 27 June 2003, with Guerrino De Luca, Logitech's president and CEO, reproduced with permission.
13. Author's personal interview, on 27 June 2003, with Guerrino De Luca, Logitech's president and CEO, reproduced with permission.
14. Pahwa, A. under the supervision of Deschamps, J.-P. (2003) 'Innovation Leadership at Logitech,' IMD Case No. IMD-3-1337.

15. George, B. (2001). 'Leadership and Innovation.' Videotaped interview by J.-P. Deschamps, IMD, Lausanne, reproduced with permission.

16. George, B. with Sims, P. (2007). *True North: Discover Your Authentic Leadership.* San Francisco, Jossey-Bass, pp. 174–184.

17. Colvin, G. (2007). 'Leader Machines.' *Fortune Europe Edition,* 1 October 2007, **156**(6): 60–67.

18. Jager, R.D. and Ortiz, R. (1997). *In the Company of Giants: Candid Conversations with the Visionaries of the Digital World.* New York, McGraw-Hill, p. 20.

19. Jager, R.D. and Ortiz, R. (1997). *In the Company of Giants: Candid Conversations with the Visionaries of the Digital World.* New York, McGraw-Hill, p. 20.

20. Author's personal interview, on 27 June 2003, with Guerrino De Luca, Logitech's president and CEO, reproduced with permission.

21. George, B. (2001). 'Leadership and Innovation.' Videotaped interview by J.-P. Deschamps, IMD, Lausanne, reproduced with permission.

22. Borel, D. (2001). 'Leadership and Innovation.' Videotaped interview by J.-P. Deschamps, IMD, Lausanne, updated and edited by Daniel Borel in November 2007.

23. Pahwa, A. under the supervision of Deschamps, J.-P. (2003). 'Innovation Leadership at Logitech.' IMD Case No. IMD-3-1337.

24. Huijser, A. (2001). 'Leadership and Innovation.' Videotaped interview by J.-P. Deschamps, IMD, Lausanne, reproduced with permission.

25. George, B. (2001). 'Leadership and Innovation.' Videotaped interview by J.-P. Deschamps, IMD, Lausanne, reproduced with permission.

26. Huijser, A. (2001). 'Leadership and Innovation.' Videotaped interview by J.-P. Deschamps, IMD, Lausanne, reproduced with permission.

27. Jager, R.D. and Ortiz, R. (1997). *In the Company of Giants: Candid Conversations with the Visionaries of the Digital World.* New York, McGraw-Hill, pp. 19, 20.

28. Huijser, A. (2001). 'Leadership and Innovation.' Videotaped interview by J.-P. Deschamps, IMD, Lausanne, reproduced with permission.

29. Borel, D. (2001). 'Leadership and Innovation.' Videotaped interview by J.-P. Deschamps, IMD, Lausanne, updated and edited by Daniel Borel in November 2007.

30. Borel, D. (2001). 'Leadership and Innovation.' Videotaped interview by J.-P. Deschamps, IMD, Lausanne, updated and edited by Daniel Borel in November 2007.

31. Huijser, A. (2001). 'Leadership and Innovation.' Videotaped interview by J.-P. Deschamps, IMD, Lausanne, reproduced with permission.

32. George, B. (2001). 'Leadership and Innovation.' Videotaped interview by J.-P. Deschamps, IMD, Lausanne, reproduced with permission.

33. Ala-Pietilä, P. (2001). 'Leadership and Innovation.' Videotaped interview by J.-P. Deschamps, IMD, Lausanne, reproduced with permission.

# INNOVATION IN LEADERSHIP AND ORGANIZATIONAL CULTURE MODELS

## INNOVATION IS IMPLICIT IN KEY LEADERSHIP MODELS

Although innovation has seldom been treated explicitly as a specific component of leadership in the management literature, it is indeed fully compatible with some of the most widely accepted definitions and models as illustrated below.

### John Kotter

Even though the topic of innovation leadership does not appear formally in John Kotter's observation of 'what leaders really do,' it is implicitly part of his description of successful change efforts:

> In the most successful change efforts, people move through eight complicated stages in which they (1) create a sense of urgency, (2) put together a strong enough team to direct the process, (3) create an appropriate vision, (4) communicate that new vision broadly, (5) empower employees to act on the vision, (6) produce sufficient short-term results to give their efforts credibility and to disempower the cynics, (7) build momentum and use that momentum to tackle the tougher change problems, and (8) anchor the new behavior in organizational culture.[1]

Kotter equates business leadership with the ability to initiate and steer change efforts and this includes changes in the area of innovation. Indeed, most innovation drive efforts go through the same generic phases listed above. This supports the opinion that true leaders should be able to steer and sustain innovation if this becomes the No. 1 company priority.

## Jim Collins

Similarly, Jim Collins' observations of what makes 'good' companies become 'great' contains a number of principles that could have been written specifically for innovation. One of the six concepts in his framework – Level 5 leadership – deals with the profile of true leaders:

> The good-to-great leaders [. . . are] self-effacing, quiet, reserved, even shy – these leaders are a paradoxical blend of personal humility and professional will . . .[2]

Chapter 2 shows that the concept of humility, which conditions the capacity to learn from failures, is an intrinsic descriptor of innovation leaders. Collins' five other observations of what leaders of great companies seem to be doing also intuitively support an innovation attitude:

> First Who . . . Then What. We expected that good-to-great leaders would begin by setting a new vision and strategy. We found instead that they first got the right people on the bus, the wrong people off the bus, and the right people in the right seats – and then figured out where to drive it . . .[3]

This principle is at the heart of what we define as 'bottom-up' innovation (Chapter 3). Establishing a new vision and strategy, on the other hand, is typically a critical step in top-down innovation (Chapter 4).

> Confront the Brutal Facts (Yet Never Lose Faith) . . . You must maintain an unwavering faith that you can and will prevail in the end, regardless of the difficulties, and at the same time have the discipline to confront the most brutal facts of your current reality, whatever they might be . . .[4]

Breakthrough stories, such as how Tetra Pak reinvented the food can (Chapter 8), highlight the extent to which this type of innovation usually requires much more time to succeed than most managers anticipate at the start. This, in turn, calls for a high degree of persistence on the part of the management team, combined with a good dose of realism and self-challenge.

> The Hedgehog Concept... To go from good to great requires transcending the curse of competence ... If you cannot be the best in the world at your core business, then your core business absolutely cannot form the basis of a great company ...[5]

Chapter 7 illustrates how companies need continuously to reinvent their core business through innovation and what type of leader it takes to do so.

> A Culture of Discipline.... When you have disciplined people, you don't need hierarchy. When you have disciplined thought, you don't need bureaucracy. When you have disciplined action, you don't need excessive controls ...[6]

Innovation is a combination of creativity and discipline. Creativity is embedded in the innovation culture of the company and discipline comes from a strong process orientation, but, as is discussed in Chapters 3 and 4, these are not univocal relationships. There is a culture of discipline in innovation in the same way as there is process for creativity.

> Technology Accelerators. Good-to-great companies think differently about the role of technology. They never use technology as the primary means of igniting a transformation. Yet, paradoxically, they are pioneers in the application of carefully selected technologies ...[7]

This statement describes one of the key leadership roles of the chief technology officer (CTO): Making or helping management make fundamental technology choices and managing the technology portfolio. This is why the CTO, whose leadership tasks are described in Chapter 5, can be considered as one of the typical role models for innovation leadership, at least for technically-oriented leaders.

## INNOVATION IS AN INTRINSIC PART OF ORGANIZATIONAL CULTURE MODELS

### Dan Denison

The widely used Denison model[8] correlates the financial perform-ance of an organization with the profile of its organizational culture and the corresponding leadership focus of its executives. It characterizes organizations along two axes: Their instinctive focus – internal vs. external – and their dynamics – stable vs. flexible. These two axes determine four quadrants which represent different critical traits of culture and leadership – Mission, Adaptability, Involvement and Consistency – each trait being divided into three different sub-elements or 'indices' (refer to Figure A.1 below).

By measuring an organization or an individual leader on these 12 indexes through the use of a survey questionnaire, Denison

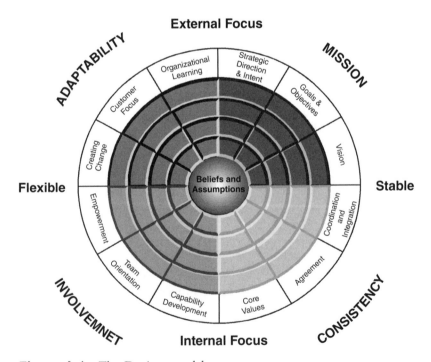

**Figure A.1** The Denison model
Source: Reproduced with permission from Dan Denison.

obtains an overall organizational culture and leadership profile, which can then be compared with other companies in the same or other industries. Organizations with a high and balanced score across all four traits, argues Denison on the basis of his data points, are much more likely to feature high performance in terms of growth and profits. A high score on external focus, he claims, tends to be a good predictor of growth. A strong internal focus, by contrast, is a good predictor of operating performance.

The innovation effectiveness of an organization is likely to be strongly influenced by the factors listed in all four quadrants. Indeed, a top score on 'external focus' will probably reflect a high degree of attention to markets, customers and competitors, an essential innovation prerequisite. A high score on 'internal focus,' by contrast, may signal that the organization is anxious to build up superb capabilities across its value chain, an imperative for being able to bring an innovation to market. Similarly, a high score on 'flexibility' is likely to indicate a talent for spotting innovation opportunities, while a top mark on 'stability' will correlate with a focus on delivering on those opportunities. In fact, each quadrant in the Denison model has implications for the kind of leadership that sustains innovation.

The *Mission* trait and its three indices – Vision, Goals and Objectives, and Strategic Direction and Intent – measure the extent to which the organization works under a clear sense of direction or purpose. According to the Denison model, leaders provide a clear answer to the question: 'Do we know where we are going?' This trait, as discussed in Chapter 2, is shared by most innovation leaders. It is also an essential driver of top-down innovation, as Chapter 4 highlights.

The *Consistency* trait and its three indices – Core Values, Agreement and Coordination and Integration – measure the effectiveness of internal systems, structures and processes of the organization. Leaders – argues Denison – ensure that people sense that their system creates leverage, hence enables them to meet their goals and accomplish the organization's vision and mission. Innovation, as discussed in Chapter 2, blossoms when creativity goes hand in hand with discipline and this Consistency trait is an essential element of innovation discipline. Back-end innovation leaders, who are described in Chapter 2, pay a lot of attention to Consistency.

The *Involvement* trait and its three indices – Empowerment, Team Orientation and Capability Development – measure the sense of commitment, ownership and responsibility of the organization. High-performance businesses have leaders who are constantly checking that their people are aligned and engaged. Innovation leaders, and particularly those who are trying to promote bottom-up innovation, as discussed in Chapter 3, cultivate in their staff a strong sense of involvement in innovation-related activities.

The *Adaptability* trait and its three indices – Creating Change, Customer Focus and Organizational Learning – measure, probably even more than all other indices, the ability of the organization to challenge the status quo, satisfy customers' needs and learn from its mistakes, three fundamental character traits of innovative organizations.

## ENDNOTES

1. Kotter, J.P. (1999). *What Leaders Really Do*. Cambridge, Harvard Business Review Book, p. 7.
2. Collins, J. (2001). *Good to Great: Why Some Companies Make the Leap . . . and Others Don't*. London, Random House Business Books, pp. 12–14.
3. Collins, J. (2001). *Good to Great: Why Some Companies Make the Leap . . . and Others Don't*. London, Random House Business Books, pp. 12–14.
4. Collins, J. (2001). *Good to Great: Why Some Companies Make the Leap . . . and Others Don't*. London, Random House Business Books, pp. 12–14.
5. Collins, J. (2001). *Good to Great: Why Some Companies Make the Leap . . . and Others Don't*. London, Random House Business Books, pp. 12–14.
6. Collins, J. (2001). *Good to Great: Why Some Companies Make the Leap . . . and Others Don't*. London, Random House Business Books, pp. 12–14.
7. Collins, J. (2001). *Good to Great: Why Some Companies Make the Leap . . . and Others Don't*. London, Random House Business Books, pp. 12–14.
8. Refer to Dan Denison's forthcoming book *Culture Strategies: Creating Competitive Advantage by Building Effective Organizational Cultures*, and to the website www. denisonculture.com for a detailed description of the model and its application for assessing the organizational culture and leadership profile of a company.

# GUIDELINES FOR USING THE IDEO VIDEO FOR 'IDEA MANAGEMENT' TRAINING

## POSITIONING THE VIDEO

The IDEO video can be used by companies for internal staff training and in executive education to convey important messages regarding *not just the process* of idea management — from business intelligence to concept development — *but also its cultural aspects*, i.e. the kind of attitudes that encourage a customer-centric, structured idea generation process.

It will be important to position the video carefully in the minds of the participants. This means highlighting its objectives and key success factors.

### Overall Approach and Timing

The minimum time recommended, to avoid having to rush through the discussion after viewing the video, is *between 1½ and 2 hours*, broken down as follows:

- Introducing and positioning the video:      10 minutes
- Watching the video:                         20 minutes
- Discussing the people, culture and          20 to 30 minutes
  leadership aspects:

- Discussing the process and identifying the   30 to 40 minutes
  process steps:
- Reflecting upon and summarizing the        10 to 20 minutes.
  lessons learned:

## Introducing and Positioning the Video

The instructor may want to make the following points before
showing the video:

- The video shows how a team of Californian industrial designers go about completely rethinking and redesigning a well-
  established product, the supermarket shopping cart.
- Although the emphasis of the video (and of IDEO) is on
  design, the proposed approach is, of course, valid for all types
  of innovation projects.
- However, the demo illustrates only the idea/concept phase of
  an innovation project, *not* the full project, because it ends with
  a concept prototype, not with a final product.
- Even though the exercise seems somewhat artificial,
  because of the extreme time constraint imposed by the TV
  program, it shows what a dedicated team can do in one
  week.
- Besides illustrating an approach, the video highlights some of
  the softer cultural and leadership aspects of innovation, which
  are worth discussing as well.

So, before showing the video, the instructor will ask the participants to pay attention to four aspects in the video:

- The *people* featured in the exercise: What strikes you about
  them? What about their characteristics, style, behavior?
- The *culture* of the place: What kind of workplace environment
  does IDEO offer? What kind of values does the culture
  convey?
- The *leaders* featured in the video: The project leader and the
  big boss, David Kelley. What kind of leaders are they? What
  strikes you about their style?

- The *process* followed: What steps are they following – both the ones that are clearly identified in the video and the ones that can be inferred from some of the statements made.

To highlight these four points, the instructor, who should have installed four flip chart stands or white boards around the screen ahead of time, will write one of the four topics, as a heading, on each of the four flip charts. These flip charts will be used to capture the participants' observations on each of these topics after they have seen the video.

## DISCUSSING THE PEOPLE, CULTURE AND LEADERSHIP ASPECTS

Having shown the video, the instructor has two options:

- Start a discussion with the whole group immediately, soliciting participants' spontaneous impressions and capturing and marking them down on the flip charts as they come; or alternatively
- Start with 5 to 10 minutes in small 'buzz groups' (chats in groups of two or three while participants stay in their place), before letting a spokesperson for each buzz group share their impressions, which will, again, be captured on the flip charts.

The buzz group option is recommended when the instructor feels that some participants would hesitate to speak up in a plenary session for fear of not being able to express themselves because of language problems or simply shyness.

### Discussing the People Side

Observations about the people involved in the IDEO shopping cart exercise will typically include some of the following qualifying adjectives. The instructor should not hesitate to call on participants if the list of adjectives provided spontaneously is incomplete, i.e. if it does not cover, at least, the following points:

- *Diverse*. In terms of gender (a key point to stress); age; educational background; culture. The instructor will undoubtedly want to emphasize the importance of diversity for innovation in every company, with the added possibility of building on functional diversity, an element that is absent from IDEO, since all the participants in the videotaped exercise are professional designers.
- *Creative*. Diversity certainly helps encourage creativity, but other factors play a role, like the kind of profile of the people that the company hires.
- *Young*. Mature participants will probably notice that the people in the video are young – they all seem to be in their twenties or thirties with the exception of one or two middle-aged members. This point, if/when made, should be picked up by the instructor to question whether age is a determining factor in creativity and innovation. He/she will have to acknowledge that younger people tend to be less inhibited and may come up with wilder ideas than older people, but this is not an absolute rule. More mature participants will contribute equally, albeit differently, hence the importance of diversity, i.e. assembling a balanced team of younger (fresher) and older (more experienced) people.
- *Playful* or fun loving. This is clearly highlighted in some of the scenes in the video and by the comments of the CEO, David Kelley.
- *Effective as team players*. This comment may trigger another question from the instructor: What are the character traits of good team players? (Respectful of others; disciplined; task-oriented; open; etc.)
- *Energetic and enthusiastic*. This particular remark will, typically, allow the instructor to refer to the company's organizational culture and the leader's attitude as key determinants of a team's energy and enthusiasm.
- *Outspoken*. This last quality may give the instructor a nice transition to the next topic, i.e. discussing IDEO's organizational culture as seen in the video.

## Discussing the Culture Side

The instructor will have warned the audience that the video has been shot in California, a part of the world where people are particularly relaxed and informal. It also features a 'design house,' i.e. a type of professional firm that usually attracts artistic and rather original – not to say maverick – people, hence IDEO's special culture. It will be important, however, to *let the participants reflect on whether the cultural aspects featured in the film are* exclusively 'Californian' by nature or whether some of them could well be *compatible with their company culture.*

The typical cultural characteristics of the IDEO environment, as picked up by the audience, are the following:

* a healthy disrespect for status and hierarchy;
* a combination of creativity and discipline;
* a bias for going out to the external world, rather than staying at one's desk;
* respect for individual freedom (asking for forgiveness rather than permission);
* being encouraged to speak one's mind and, even, disagree with the boss;
* strong task-orientation and respect for commitments and deadlines.

On each point, the instructor should ask: How does this aspect favor innovation? What message does it convey? What behavior does it encourage?

## Discussing the Leadership Side

The main leadership trait that participants will notice in the *project leader* for IDEO's shopping cart is that he is *'good with people'* (a statement made by the TV director in the video). This aspect may lead to interesting discussions with the participants who might be more inclined to select a project leader essentially on the basis of his/her competencies.

The instructor should try to elicit what is meant by 'good with people!' The following comments ought to come up from the ensuing discussion:

- Ability to motivate people, so that they focus all their energy on the project.
- Ability to maintain a high level of group discipline, particularly regarding timing.
- Ability to ban internal criticisms, yet build a spirit of constructive challenges.
- Ability to refocus the work toward the initial objective in case of deviation.
- Ability to make the distinction between – and combine – having fun and working hard.

A review of the leadership traits and style of the *business leader*, David Kelley, is likely to point to the following characteristics or adjectives:

- Demanding in terms of attitudes and results, yet fun to work with.
- Focused on and a believer in the 'process.'
- Open to challenge or contradiction.
- Respectful of his employees' freedom to express their own personal style.
- Involved in supporting the team, but not interfering in the day-to-day project work.
- Accessible and present for guidance at key moments in the project.
- Trusting the competence of his team and proud of them.

To conclude the discussion, the instructor should stress the high degree of compatibility and mutual reinforcement that typically exists in innovative companies between leadership, organizational culture and people. Consciously or not, the innovation leader is creating a cultural and physical environment for innovation that, in turn, is likely to attract and motivate the kind of people that the firm needs in order to innovate. The three elements are mutually reinforcing.

The discussion will, obviously, tend to compare the IDEO environment with the one existing in the participants' company and it will be the role of the instructor to highlight the similarities rather than the differences, which may vary from unit to unit.

## Discussing the Process and Identifying the Process Steps

The purpose of that discussion is twofold:

(1) Review and characterize, one by one, the *generic steps* in an idea management and concept development exercise, and understand their purpose, nature and the logic of their sequence.

(2) Make people see the process, from a helicopter viewpoint, as a series of *alternating divergent and convergent steps* – divergent when they focus on information collection and idea generation; convergent when they deal with synthesis, focus and choices.

To achieve this objective, the instructor will ask the participants to reflect on the video and *list the steps that they have identified, from the very beginning onwards.* The difficulty lies in the fact that the video is very explicit on some of the steps, less so on others, particularly at the beginning of the process. For example, step 1 – setting up the project team and defining objectives and constraints – is not stated explicitly anywhere in the video, but it should be elicited by the instructor as being implicit. Step 2, by contrast – selecting boundary conditions for the project and using them as idea screening criteria – can be inferred from some later comments in the video. The instructor will make sure that each of the 15 steps listed below is duly identified and characterized, even those omitted by the participants.

**Table B.1**    IDEO's Idea Management Process

| | |
|---|---|
| 1. | Appoint team and team leader and define clear objectives (outcome) and constraints (time limitations) for the ideation exercise. |
| 2. | Define clear criteria ('nesting' ability; cost limit; buildable in one week; etc.) to be used to screen ideas. |
| 3. | Gather general background data and search for a broad range of information on the industry. |
| 4. | Derive working hypotheses about the key problem areas to be addressed throughout the value chain (theft; child safety; etc.). |
| 5. | Go into the field to understand requirements from all actors in the value chain and validate/invalidate hypotheses re key problem areas. |
| 6. | Share field results, live, within the group (with visual aids to convey the way customers/users experience the problem areas). |
| 7. | Brainstorm (the 'deep dive') to generate as many ideas as possible to address the key problems identified/validated in the fieldwork. |
| 8. | Screen ideas collectively (through voting with 'Post-its') to eliminate those ideas that do not meet the criteria defined upfront. |
| 9. | Decide on the key themes to be selected for refocusing the idea enrichment exercise (theft; child safety; convenience; check-out). |
| 10. | Split the initial group into four 'theme sub-groups,' and ask them to come up with a prototype illustrating each of their themes. |
| 11. | Have the four teams present their prototypes incorporating the best idea elements selected under each theme. |
| 12. | Bring the group together and ask them to select the best elements of each 'theme prototype' to incorporate into the final concept. |
| 13. | Build a 'concept prototype' incorporating the elements selected from each 'theme prototype.' |
| 14. | Present the 'concept prototype' to management with a focus on explaining its benefits and get feedback. |
| 15. | Bring the 'concept prototype' to real customers and users to check their initial reaction and derive selling arguments from their reactions. |

Divergent process

Convergent process

It is unlikely that the participants will, spontaneously, notice a succession of divergent and convergent patterns in the 15 steps above. The instructor will have to stress this, for example through the use of arrows as in the chart.

## Reflecting Upon and Summarizing the Lessons Learned

The IDEO session should not end without asking the participants to reflect for a few minutes, individually or in buzz groups, on the lessons they have learned and to share with the group their impression regarding the transferability of those lessons to their company.

# FACTORS AFFECTING THE INNOVATION CLIMATE OF A COMPANY

## MANAGEMENT ATTITUDES

Management attitudes – conscious or unconscious, real or perceived – have a very strong influence on a company's innovation climate. Some of these attitudes will stimulate innovation by unleashing people's energy and creativity, while others will stifle or discourage employees from taking initiatives. Innovation leaders should therefore find out how their staff perceive the signals they get from management and take corrective action whenever needed.

Experience shows that the following attitudes have a strong impact on innovation, positively or negatively:

### Interest in Innovation

Do employees feel that management has a genuine interest in – and in fact demands – innovation, in both words and deeds? Or do they feel that management only pays lip service to innovation in its public statements, without really caring?

## Trust

Do employees feel that management really trusts its staff and their capabilities to achieve their objectives? Or do they feel that management tends to underestimate its own staff capabilities and/or motivation?

## Tolerance of Risks and Failures

Do employees feel that management leads by example, by accepting risk itself and for staff and tolerating a normal proportion of failures in projects and ventures? Or do they feel that management is often tempted to crucify mistakes and their originators?

## Learning from Failure

Do employees feel that management is interested in post mortem project analyses and encourages a systematic dissemination of lessons learned? Or do they feel that management is indifferent or would rather bury failures, particularly the painful ones?

## Payback Horizon

Do employees feel that management has a long-term vision for the company and judges individual proposals on their contribution to that vision? Or do they feel that management is only interested in actions and projects that have a very short-term impact?

## Tolerance of Mavericks

Do employees feel that management is open to hiring, deploying and supporting original thinkers who want to change the status quo? Or do they feel that management is intolerant of these kinds of people and the disturbances that they may create?

## Autonomy and Respect for the Hierarchy

Do employees feel that management wants staff to communicate horizontally to get things done, without necessarily passing through hierarchical levels? Or do they feel that management enforces strict respect for the company's vertical hierarchy?

## Norms and Rules

Do employees feel that management wants to give staff autonomy, allowing them to act responsibly in a way that will benefit the company? Or do they feel that management wants to legislate and regulate everything by enforcing stringent norms and rules?

## Tolerance of Uncertainty

Do employees feel that management accepts experimentation as a necessary condition of innovation? Or do they feel that management always demands endless justifications and validations of attractive new ideas before giving the go-ahead?

## Expectations on Results

Do employees feel that management is really demanding in terms of internal growth rate and that it sets stretch targets to itself and all units? Or do they feel that management is rather conservative in terms of its expectations?

## Expectations on People

Do employees feel that management is genuinely interested in the personal development of staff, not just for corporate benefits but also for their own sake? Or do they feel that management is only interested in the way people can contribute to the company?

### Coaching and Support

Do employees feel that management is prepared to actively coach, support and shield innovators and teams to help them meet their objectives? Or do they feel that management remains aloof in its ivory tower?

## MANAGEMENT POLICIES

Management attitudes and corporate values are often expressed concretely in the form of company policies – explicit or implicit – that affect the way people in an organization behave and take initiatives. Being management-made, these policies tend to be easier to modify than executive attitudes, if they are found to be dysfunctional in the way they affect the innovation climate.

Among the many possible policy domains, the following have been proven to have a strong impact on innovation, positively or negatively:

### Recognition and Rewards for Innovators

Is it company policy to expressly recognize and reward innovators and successful projects at all levels, and is that policy applied proactively and fairly? Or is innovation considered part of everyone's job, thus not rewarded specifically?

### Career Ladders and Paths for Innovators

Is it company policy to provide a dual career ladder for innovators, particularly in R&D (a managerial path and a scientific one)? Or are all staff members treated in a similar way with only one possible progression: Up through management responsibilities?

### Innovation Tracking

Is it company policy to keep track and measure innovation over time, in terms of both input and output? Or is innovation considered as essentially unpredictable, hence not trackable or not worth measuring?

## Attitude to Partnerships and Alliances

Is it company policy to encourage cooperation on innovation with external partners whenever possible, and is it applied systematically? Or does the company generally discourage partnerships and alliances for all kinds of reasons?

## R&D and Technology Investment Level

Is it company policy to invest in R&D above industry averages and to maintain R&D investment levels even during downturns? Or is the company trying to reduce its R&D investments and make them fluctuate with its market and financial results?

## R&D and Technology Focus

Is it company policy to earmark part of its R&D budget for cooperation with external technology suppliers and/or partners? Or are R&D investments entirely devoted to internal projects, almost exclusively for supporting current businesses?

## Innovation Resources

Is it company policy to earmark part of its R&D budget for unallocated support to new high-risk/high-impact projects, possibly leading to significant innovation and new business creation? Or are innovators constantly fighting to get access to risk money?

## Centralization/Decentralization

Is it company policy to decentralize decision making on innovation projects, so that it is as close as possible to field operations, and to fully empower local teams and project leaders? Or does management maintain full control centrally over all or most innovation projects?

## Cross-Functional Work Groups

Is it company policy to appoint cross-functional work groups of all kinds (task forces, venture teams, etc.) and rely on them each time a major innovation issue arises? Or does management basically rely on functional chains of command to address problems?

## Championing Teams

Is it company policy to formally appoint teams of champions (technical, business *and* executive champions) from day one and rely on them to run innovation projects? Or does management encourage and reward mostly individual initiatives?

## Outsiders' Involvement

Is it company policy to open its innovation mechanisms (e.g. advisory councils, idea generation exercises) to competent outsiders (experts, customers, suppliers) and associate them with its processes? Or does the company maintain a closed internal process?

## Removing Red Tape

Is it company policy (or management practice) to shield its innovation project teams from some of the usual red tape constraints faced by the operating organization? Or do the innovation project teams have to live by and submit to all the company's rules?

# MANAGEMENT PROCESSES

Processes tend to reflect a company's management culture and its policies. Some of these processes will also influence the innovation climate – positively or negatively – hence the importance of reviewing them critically to develop any that are missing and to change those judged to be dysfunctional.

## Market/Customer Intelligence

Has management taken initiatives to broaden and deepen the company's connection to its markets and ensured that every manager, including in R&D, maintains regular customer contacts? Or does market intelligence remain the preserve of marketing and sales?

## Innovation Vision and Strategy

Has management defined an explicit innovation vision and strategy, identifying in which specific areas innovation is desired? Or has management left the field of innovation uncharted, without defining what it expects from innovation?

## Planning Focus

Does management handle business reviews and planning meetings as a privileged forum for discussing innovative ideas and detecting new opportunities? Or are business reviews and planning meetings essentially perceived as a 'performance numbers' game?

## Idea Generation

Has management set up a simple and accessible central process and mechanism for generating and collecting innovation ideas, wherever they may come from? Or does management leave its staff to handle ideas in their own organization as they see fit?

## Idea Management

Has management established a transparent and objective process for acknowledging, evaluating, ranking and selecting innovation ideas? Or is the current idea management process haphazard and obscure in the eyes of idea submitters?

## Idea Funding and Programming

Is there a process in place for funding and programming innovative ideas generated outside the normal product planning cycle? Or is the funding and programming of such ideas ad hoc and dependent on the goodwill of managers or the availability of resources?

## Championing

Is it possible for idea submitters to volunteer to implement their ideas in practice, even if it leads to them abandoning their current functions? Or is the implementation of ideas generally entrusted to established organizational units?

## Planning Style

Is the planning process action-oriented, i.e. does it lead to clear targets, responsibilities and milestones? Or is it very analytical and meticulous, with all kinds of justifications to be provided for each initiative?

## Project Management

Has management established a clear and integrated cross-functional process for getting from new ideas to market, and are project leaders fully empowered to run it? Or are new ideas subjected to the traditional functional relay race together with other initiatives?

## Project Review

Does the project review process provide for an integrated cross-functional project appraisal and ensure that decisions are taken rapidly? Or is the review of projects subject to the whims of the various functional hierarchies?

## Project Learning

Has management established a systematic process to capture the learnings of each project – successful or not – and to disseminate them? Or are project debriefings handled only on an ad hoc basis?

## Communications

Is the flow of communications intense, informal and multidirectional, i.e. vertical both ways and horizontal across functions and units? Or are communications constrained by hierarchical lines?

# INDEX

*Index compiled by Terry Halliday*